Variation in German

# Variation in German

## A critical approach to German sociolinguistics

**Stephen Barbour**
*University of Surrey*

**and Patrick Stevenson**
*University of Southampton*

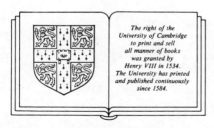

The right of the
University of Cambridge
to print and sell
all manner of books
was granted by
Henry VIII in 1534.
The University has printed
and published continuously
since 1584.

Cambridge University Press
Cambridge
New York   Port Chester
Melbourne   Sydney

Published by the Press Syndicate of the University of Cambridge
The Pitt Building, Trumpington Street, Cambridge CB2 1RP
40 West 20th Street, New York, NY 10011, USA
10 Stamford Road, Oakleigh, Melbourne 3166, Australia

© Cambridge University Press 1990

First published 1990

Printed in Great Britain at the University Press, Cambridge

*British Library cataloguing in publication data*

Barbour, Stephen
Variation in German: a critical introduction
to German sociolinguistics.
1. German language. Sociolinguistic aspects
I. Title II. Stevenson, Patrick
438

*Library of Congress cataloguing in publication data*

Barbour, Stephen.
Variation in German: a critical introduction to German
sociolinguistics / Stephen Barbour and Patrick Stevenson.
    p.      cm.
Bibliography.
Includes index.
ISBN 0–521–35397–1 – ISBN 0–521–35704–7 (pbk.)
1. German language – Variation.  2. German language – Social
aspects.  3. Sociolinguistics.  I. Stevenson, Patrick.  II. Title.
PF3074.7.B37  1990
306.4′4′0943 – dc20  89–9810 CIP

ISBN 0 521 35397 1 hard covers
ISBN 0 521 35704 7 paperback

VN

# Contents

Contents

# Contents

Contents

viii

# Contents

# Figures

# Maps

# Tables

# Acknowledgements

Without the help, advice and encouragement of many colleagues and friends, this book would probably never have been written. All are thanked most warmly, although space allows us to mention only a few by name.

Peter Trudgill, Norbert Dittmar, Martin Durrell and Reinhard Bichsel read large parts of the drafts, and offered much helpful comment and criticism. Peter Schlobinski provided information, motivation and hospitality on many occasions; his enthusiasm for his native Berlin was an inspiration to us and we hope it will be to other German linguists. Amongst our immediate colleagues we are particularly grateful to Anne Judge, Margaret Rogers, Olga Lalor, Clare Mar-Molinero and Bill McCann: their help and advice at various stages was indispensable. At CUP, Penny Carter, Judith Ayling, Marion Smith and Ginny Catmur guided us patiently through the editorial process.

Chris Moss was a partner in much of the discussion of the project, and almost became a co-author; his influence can be seen in many places, Chapter 3 bearing his imprint most clearly.

Finally, we would like to record our gratitude to the library of the Institut für Deutsche Sprache, Mannheim; to the Institut für Deutsche Sprache, 'Deutscher Sprachatlas', of the University of Marburg for making available its unique collection of primary and secondary literature; and to the Deutscher Akademischer Austauschdienst and the Universities of Surrey and Southampton for making it financially possible to work at these institutions in Germany.

# 1 Introduction

## 1.1 What is German and who speaks it?

### 1.1.1 Problems of definition

A major part of the study of language is the pursuit of serious answers to apparently trivial questions. If an adequate answer to these questions were as straightforward as might seem to be the case at first glance, the questions would indeed be trivial and the study of language would have no claim to being taken seriously as an academic discipline. However, many other areas of study, including not least the physical sciences, are also concerned with deceptively simple problems. For example, why does water flowing out of a bath swirl clockwise in the northern hemisphere and anti-clockwise in the southern hemisphere? Whether or not the study of linguistic variation can justifiably be considered a 'science', in the narrow English sense, it is certainly a complex and multi-faceted topic and it will be the task of this book to demonstrate this and the relevance of such a study both as an academic undertaking and as a basis for informing public discussion. After all, what aspect of human activity does every woman (or man) in the street have views on, if not language? Our attention will focus specifically on German but the questions raised may be of relevance to the study of any language.

This takes us back to the questions in the heading of this section. It is tempting to answer both simultaneously by saying that 'German is the language used in the German-speaking countries': most people would readily identify these countries as the Federal Republic of Germany (FRG), the German Democratic Republic (GDR), Austria, Switzerland and Liechtenstein, and would therefore understand this statement to mean that German is the native language of the inhabitants of these five states. The only serious objection would seem to be that only some Swiss are German-speakers, while others are 'native-speakers' of French, Italian or Romansh; this is easily resolved by referring to 'German-speaking Switzerland'.

However, there are other problems with this simple answer. Most importantly, a little reflection should be enough to allow us to realize that the definition is 'circular' and therefore not a definition at all. It is as illuminating as saying that 'red is the colour of red-coloured flowers': it may well be true but it still does not tell us what German is. Secondly, it may well be felt to be too exclusive a statement: for example, there are hundreds of thousands of people living outside the five 'German-speaking countries' who believe that the language they habitually use (or at least use under certain circumstances) is German. Various estimates of the number of German-speakers worldwide range from 100 to 120 million, and according to one source 92 million of these are spread across no fewer than sixteen European states (Löffler 1985: 62–3). Even allowing for the fact that self-declared language use (as given, for instance, in census returns) is a notoriously unreliable measure, the figures are too great for us to deny the existence in many countries of substantial populations who speak what they take to be German. And if the language they speak is not German, what is it?

A third problem, that is related to this last point, is that this temptingly neat answer suggests a uniformity in the language which no one with even limited exposure to it would accept. In fact, it is probably true that, unlike artificial languages such as Esperanto or COBOL, no natural languages are monolithic, i.e. free from variation. There are two aspects to this problem: one is to do with the external relationship between German and other languages, or deciding 'where German stops', and we shall consider this more closely in 1.1.3 below; the other aspect concerns the type and range of variation within German. It is a common experience for many foreign students of German to arrive for the first time in a 'German-speaking country' and discover to their horror that the language they encounter bears little resemblance to the German they learned at school or even at a higher level. More advanced students may well be aware of a temporal dimension to variation in German and might be prepared to accept that the following five texts are all in some sense German:

*The Gospel according to St Luke: Chapter 2, verses 4–6*

*1963:* Da wanderte auch Joseph von Galiläa, aus der Stadt Nazareth, nach Judäa in die Stadt der Familie Davids, nach Bethlehem. Denn er gehörte zur Familie und zum Stamme Davids. Und er ließ sich in die Listen des Kaisers mit Maria zusammen, seiner Verlobten, eintragen. Maria aber war schwanger. Als sie in Bethlehem waren, kam die Zeit für sie, zu gebären.

*1739:* Da machte sich aber Joseph auf, von Galiläa, aus der stadt Nazareth, in Judäa, in die stadt Davids, die Bethlehem heisset, weil er aus dem hause und familie Davids war, auf daß er sich aufschreiben liesse mit seiner braut Maria, die empfangen hatte. Und als sie daselbst waren, kam die zeit, daß sie gebähren solte.

*1522 (Luther's Bible):* Da macht sich auff, auch Joseph von Gallilea, aus der stadt Nazareth, ynn das Judisch land, zur stad Dauid, die da heyst Bethlehem, darumb, das er von dem hauße und geschlecht Dauid war, auff das er sich schetzen ließe mit Maria seynem vertraweten weybe, die gieng schwanger. Vnnd es begab sich, ynn dem sie daselbst waren, kam die zeyt das sie geperen sollte.

*1343:* Abir Jōsēph gīnc ouch ūf von Galilēa von der stat Nazarēth in Judēam in di stat Dāvidis, di geheizen ist Bēthlehēm, darumme daz her was von dem hūse und von dem gesinde Dāvīdis, ūf daz her vorjehe mit Marīen ime vortrůwit zů einer hůsvrowin swangir. Und geschēn ist, dō so dā wāren, dō sint irfullit ire tage, daz si gebēre.

*Early ninth century:* Fuor thō Ioseph fon Galileu fon thero burgi thiu hiez Nazareth in Iudeno lant inti in Dauides burg, thiu uuas ginemnit Bethleem, bithiu uuanta her uuas fon huse inti fon hiuuiske Dauides, thaz her giiahi saman mit mariun imo gimahaltero gimahhun sō scaffaneru. Thō sie thar uuarun, vvurðun taga gifulte, thaz siu bari.

(all texts taken from Von Polenz 1978)

*Modern English (New English Bible) version:* And so Joseph went up to Judaea from the town of Nazareth in Galilee, to register at the city of David, called Bethlehem, because he was of the house of David by descent; and with him went Mary who was betrothed to him. She was expecting a child, and while they were there the time came for her baby to be born.

However, few are prepared for the extent of variation they inevitably confront in contemporary German, especially in the spoken language. Variation may be associated with locality but may also be determined by other factors such as the relative formality of the situation or the perceived social relationship between the speakers. While English-speakers are familiar with these types of variation in their own language, the extent of variation and the degree of potential differences in German are considerably greater than in English.

### 1.1.2 The scope of variation in German

Consider the following short texts.

1(a)  Das Flugzeug wurde von einer mit einer Pistole bewaffneten Frau entführt und zur Kursänderung gezwungen.

  (from a report in the *Frankfurter Allgemeine Zeitung*)

1(b)  Eine Frau, die mit einer Pistole bewaffnet war, hat das Flugzeug entführt und es gezwungen, seinen Kurs zu ändern.

  *Gloss:* The plane was hijacked by a woman armed with a pistol and forced to change direction.

2(a)  Da bei dem Wolfe Verknappungen auf dem Ernährungssektor vor-herrschend waren, beschloß er, bei der Großmutter der Rotkäppchen unter Vorlage falscher Papiere vorsprachig zu werden.

  (from the *Zeitschrift für Strafvollzug*, reprinted in Eggerer and Rötzer 1978)

2(b)  Da der Wolf großen Hunger hatte, beschloß er, sich zu verkleiden und die Großmutter der Rotkäppchen zu besuchen.

*Gloss:* As the wolf was hungry, he decided to disguise himself and visit Red Riding Hood's grandmother.

3(a)  Gnädige Frau, ich hab de Pferde derweile angeschirrt. A Jorgel und 's Karlchen hat d'r Herr Kandedate schon in a Wagen gesetzt. Kommt's gar schlimm, da fahr m'r los.     (from Gerhard Hauptmann's play *Die Weber*)

3(b)  Gnädige Frau, ich habe die Pferde inzwischen angeschirrt. Der Herr Kandidat hat Jorgel und Karlchen schon in den Wagen gesetzt. Wenn es schlimm wird, dann fahren wir los.

*Gloss:* Madam, I've harnessed the horses. The tutor has put Jorgel and Karlchen into the coach. If things turn nasty, we'll get going.

4(a)  Das Antörnen der Teenies ist für unser Land eine echt coole Sache. Auch wird jeder ne geile Azubistelle raffen können, nur nicht immer dort, wo seine Alten rumhängen. Ein so aufgemotztes und aufgepowertes Land muß es checken, diesen Brasel zu schnallen.

4(b)  Unser Staat braucht die zupackende Mitarbeit der jungen Generation. In diesem Jahr werden alle Jugendlichen, die ausbildungswillig und ausbildungsfähig sind, eine Lehrstelle erhalten können. Allerdings wird nicht jeder – das sage ich schon seit Monaten – seinen Wunschberuf erlernen und nicht jeder dort in die Lehre gehen können, wo er wöchte, wo er wohnt. Ein hochentwickeltes Industrieland wie die Bundesrepublik muß es möglich machen, diese schwierige Aufgabe zu lösen.

*Gloss:* Our country needs the young generation to get stuck into work. This year all young people who are able and willing to work will be able to get a training place. Admittedly not everyone will be able to train for the job of their choice or to train where they want to, where they live. A highly developed industrial nation like the Federal Republic must make it possible to solve this difficult task.

(Version (b) is from a speech by Helmut Kohl (Chancellor of the Federal Republic) and both versions were printed in *Der Sprachdienst* 1/2, 1984.

5(a)  Der Bundeskanzler hat im Spionage-Skandal einen erschreckenden Mangel an Urteilskraft gezeigt.

5(b)  Der Kohl ist vielleicht auf'n Arsch gefallen wegen den Spionen!

*Gloss:* The Federal Chancellor showed an awful lack of judgement in the spy scandal.

6(a)  Darf ich Sie bitten, das Fenster zuzumachen?

6(b)  Mensch, mach doch mal endlich das Fenster zu!

*Gloss:* (Please) close the window.

7(a)  Der im Kanton Zürich immatrikulierte Autocar verweigerte dem Velofahrer den Vortritt und drängte ihn über das Strassenbord hinaus.

(from Haas 1982)

4

7(b)  Der im Kanton Zürich angemeldete Bus verweigerte dem Radfahrer die Vorfahrt und drängte ihn über den Straßenrand hinaus.

> *Gloss:* The bus, which was registered in the canton of Zurich, failed to give the right of way to the cyclist and forced him off the road.

Versions (a) and (b) in each case are two ways of saying the same thing, but that is not the whole story. The primary information content may be more or less the same in each version but there is another level of information contained in each of these short texts, which has less to do with the message denoted by the meaning of the words than with the message implied by the form of the words or the structure of the text. For example, both 1(a) and 1(b) are statements giving the information that a woman, armed with a pistol, hijacked a plane and forced it to change course. However, the use in (a) of the passive (*wurde . . . entführt und . . . gezwungen*), the participial phrase (*eine mit einer Pistole bewaffnete Frau*) instead of a relative clause, and the prepositional phrase (*zur Kursänderung*) instead of an '**accusative**† and infinitive' construction strongly suggest that this is taken from a formal, written text. That is to say, these **syntactic** features are characteristic of a particular **register** (marked in terms of formality) and text-type. Similarly, both syntactic and **lexical** features mark 2(a) as an example of a particular technical register (or *Fachsprache*), in this case a parody of 'legalese'. 2(b), on the other hand, has no such 'markers' and is more typical of the narrative style appropriate to a fairy tale.

3(a) is an attempt by a nineteenth-century dramatist to represent the **dialect** speech of a Silesian servant. Regardless of how accurate this representation is of a particular dialect, the important point for the writer is to use speech as a signal or emblem of the speaker's social status. This is reinforced by the contrast with the standard German spoken by characters of higher status, and the standardized version 3(b) shows what would be lost if this linguistic distinction were not made. More subtly, this enables the writer to make his characters reveal aspects of themselves by varying their speech, such as when the factory owner's wife reverts in a moment of panic from her (acquired) standard to her (original) dialect. This unconscious shifting from one variety to another according to changes in the immediate context is a common phenomenon and was evidently recognized as such long before linguists turned their attention to it. What we did not know previously was exactly what kind of linguistic changes were involved in style- or **code-shifting** nor exactly how changes in the extralinguistic context resulted in these temporary changes in language use.

---

† **Bold** type indicates an entry in the Glossary.

Examples 4, 5 and 6 are similar to each other in that the various versions contain features that imply something about the relationship between speaker and addressee. Like 2(a), 4(a) could be described as an example of a particular technical register although this term tends to be confined to varieties associated with specific professions or occupations (including therefore not only law, medicine, engineering etc. but also, for example, sport or needlework). Youth speech (*Jugendsprache*) as in 4(a) is one kind of **jargon** (*Sondersprache*): these varieties differ from technical registers in that their function is not to enable precise discussion of technical topics but to signal membership of a closed social group (although of course technical registers can be abused in this way). A further difference is that jargon is much more prone to rapid change, partly in order to make it difficult for 'outsiders' to acquire the code. While the job of a technical register is to enable optimal, accurate communication between the initiated, so that a high degree of standardization is essential, the purpose of jargon is at least as much to block communication with outsiders as to promote it with insiders. Thus it is quite likely that many German-speakers over the age of 25 would fail to understand texts such as 4(a).

No such communication problem is posed by 5(b) but again the choice of linguistic forms made by the speaker indicates a certain kind of relationship with the addressee, while this is less true of 5(a). However, the more 'marked' version in this example, 5(b), does not contain features specific to or typical of any technical register, dialect or jargon. Even more clearly than in example 1, the (b) version is obviously a spoken text and the (a) version probably a written text. But there is more involved here than simply a difference of formality, as was the case in 1. The use of the definite article before a proper noun (*Der Kohl*), the idiomatic expression (*auf den Arsch fallen*, 'to get egg on your face, make a mess of something'), and the **dative** rather than the **genitive** after the preposition *wegen* are features of a particular kind of spoken German, that is usually referred to as *Umgangssprache* and that we shall call here '**colloquial speech**' (see Chapter 5).

The difference between 6(a) and 6(b) is largely a question of formality, as in example 1, but in this case both versions belong to the same text-type: they are both spoken utterances. A further difference between examples 1 and 6, however, is that the stylistic distinction between 6(a) and 6(b) does not seem to be adequately captured by the labels 'formal' and 'informal'. The main linguistic differences are that 6(a) has the syntactic structure of a question while 6(b) has that of a command, and that (a) uses the formal *Sie* pronoun, (b) the familiar *du*. The sociolinguistic contrast lies in the implications of other aspects of these utterances.

For example, (a) is not simply a 'relatively formal request to close the window', such as someone might make to any person with whom they are on 'Sie terms', whether they know each other or not. A perfectly normal utterance under such circumstances might be:

6(c)  Machen Sie bitte das Fenster zu?
      Would you shut the window please?

6(a) in fact is a kind of 'double question' or two questions compressed into one, just as the English sentence

6(d)  I wonder if I might ask you to close the window?

is in effect saying two things:

(i)   May I make a request?
(ii)  Would you please close the window?

The point of this rather intricate analysis is to show that the difference between 6(a) and 6(c) is not merely a matter of 'degree of formality'. The real difference lies in the likely relationship between speaker and addressee. The use of *Sie* makes it clear that this relationship is 'formal' in both instances. However, while the speaker of (c) might well be acquainted with his or her addressee, the 'politeness formula' of the double question in (a) suggests that the two are not acquainted: if they were, it might well sound either ironic or humorous. What then of 6(b)? Again, the use of *du* indicates a familiar relationship but, again, more 'neutral' versions are available, e.g.:

6(e)  Kannst du das Fenster mal zumachen?
      Could you shut the window?

By prefacing the command/request with 'Mensch' (Hey!) and reinforcing it with the particles 'doch mal endlich' the speaker is clearly expressing impatience. That is to say, the difference between 6(b) and 6(e) is not one of formality but of tone or tenor. Therefore, to explain the sociolinguistic differences between 6(a) and (b), we need to refer not only to degree of formality but also to speaker–addressee relationship and to tone.

Finally, both versions of example 7 can be described as **standard** German and yet there are obvious lexical differences between them: the speaker/writer of 7(a) would be unlikely to produce 7(b) regardless of the external circumstances, and vice versa. The difference lies in the fact that 7(a) is in Swiss standard German while 7(b) is in (North) German standard German. Just as there are a few but well established and codified features of American English that differ from standard British English (again, mainly lexical – sidewalk vs. pavement; orthographic – color vs. colour; or **semantic** – rubber = condom vs. rubber = eraser), so there are regional varieties of standard German. Both English and German are, then, 'pluricentric languages' (Kloss 1978: 66–7; see also Clyne 1984: Ch. 1).

The examples we have discussed here are not intended to represent a comprehensive account of all forms of variation within German (for a fuller discussion, see Durrell 1990). However, they should be sufficient to give some impression of the nature, range and complexity of variation in the language. The discussion has also served to introduce some of the key notions that we shall refer to throughout the rest of the book, although we are going to concentrate only on social and regional variation, the aspects which are of central concern to sociolinguistics.

### 1.1.3 Fuzzy and discrete language boundaries

Clearly, our intuitive answer to the deceptively simple questions 'What is German and who speaks it' was unsatisfactory and we have not yet offered a more appropriate one. Another way of tackling this might be to consider the rather different question posed above: 'Where does German stop?' This is not an issue that is confined to German but is indeed relevant to all languages that are in some way related to and/or in contact with other languages. We shall refer to it here as the question of linguistic discreteness.

To the casual English-speaking observer, it often appears that the limits of English are quite clear: if other people speak English we can understand them, though there are sometimes certain comprehension problems; conversely, if we cannot understand them they are not speaking English, they are speaking a foreign language, which is in some ill defined sense absolutely different from English. Assuming for the moment that English is indeed as separate or 'discrete' from other languages as it is often held to be, it should still be stressed that this clear discreteness is not at all typical of the languages of the world. It is a characteristic of some languages (Japanese, for instance, provides a much better example than English), but a majority of the world's languages have clear similarities to other languages, which are obvious to the native speakers, and even have quite indefinite or 'fuzzy' boundaries from other languages. In other words, there are language '**varieties**' (see Hudson 1980: Ch. 2; the German terms most commonly used are *Varietät* or *Existenzform*) which cannot be unambiguously assigned to either one of two related languages.

Examples of varying and complex distinctions between languages can be found in most parts of the world. In India, for instance, some pairs of languages, such as Hindi and Tamil, are quite clearly distinct; other pairs of languages, for example Hindi and Punjabi, though distinct, nevertheless show strong similarities; while other pairs such as Hindi and Urdu are so similar that, in many types of conversation (though not in some), speakers of each language can understand speakers of the other with little trouble. Not only are the distinctions between Indian languages of very different kinds, there are also cases where it is difficult to decide to which of two related languages certain varieties should be assigned; certain dialects, for instance, cannot be said unequivocally to be dialects of either Hindi or Bengali (cf. Linguistic Minorities Project 1985; for a good summary of the linguistic situation in India, see Sutton 1984).

However, even the linguistic limits of English are not as clear cut as is often assumed. A speaker of English who is sufficiently willing and imaginative can understand some simple sentences in Dutch without having learnt the language, and while English-based **creoles** are generally considered by linguists to be fully-fledged languages, there is usually at least some degree of mutual comprehensibility with English. However, it is fair to say that this indistinctiveness at the 'edges' of English is not something of which the majority of English-speakers are aware. What actually escapes most speakers of English is that, while the limits of a language are to a certain extent fixed by purely linguistic criteria, whether or not two varieties are considered separate languages is often partly determined by whether or not the speakers of these two varieties wish them to be considered the same language. Their willingness to consider them the same language can be influenced by a host of factors to do with the relationship between the groups of speakers in question, such as whether or not they share a religion or a common sense of national, tribal or cultural identity. For example Hindi and Urdu, linguistically very close, may be considered separate languages since their speakers are separated by an important religious divide, being Hindus and Muslims respectively, while the various dialects of Arabic, linguistically very diverse, are usually considered a single language, since most of their speakers are linked by important religious and cultural affinities. In contrast Maltese, linguistically close to Libyan Arabic, is not generally considered to be Arabic because of the religious and cultural divide between Christian Maltese-speakers and Muslim Arabic-speakers. It should not be surprising then that a considerable portion of sociolinguistic study is devoted to the complex interplay between language and social, cultural, and political factors, and to the way in which these factors influence what we imagine to be linguistic judgements (see, for instance, Haugen 1972a).

Non-specialists not only underestimate the relevance of social and political factors to language, they may also overestimate it. While English-speakers in North America, where English is the major language of two nation-states, may be aware that national boundaries do not necessarily coincide with or determine language boundaries, English-speakers in Britain may be tempted to forget that languages and states are not coextensive (see Fasold 1984: Ch. 1). This temptation can also affect speakers of other languages in Europe, where languages often seem to be coterminous with states and where the names of nations, peoples and languages are often similar (Spanish is spoken by Spaniards in Spain, Italian by Italians in Italy, Danish by Danes in Denmark, and so on). However, we need only glance at other continents to see that the nation defined by or coterminous with the use of a single language is relatively rare (Japan being again an exceptional case), and while many European states seem to be coterminous with languages, the correspondence is hardly ever total. Apart from very small states like San Marino and Liechtenstein, the only European states without indigenous linguistic minorities are Iceland and Portugal (see Haarmann 1975: 42–66, 116–19).

The notion that languages are clearly distinct from each other can arise from the fact that, compared to many languages, English does have relatively clear limits, but it can also arise from the cultural insularity of English-speaking communities. The notion that states are coterminous with linguistic units arises from the fact that in the medieval or early modern period certain powerful and influential Western European states, notably France and Britain, were formed from relatively homogeneous linguistic groupings. This was a two-way process in that these states, once established, then pursued policies of extending linguistic homogeneity within their borders, the French state being particularly active in this respect (see Coulmas 1985: 30–1).

The rise to prominence of these states was accompanied, and indeed arguably aided, by the development in them of representative political institutions, which involved in government, at least as electors if nothing more, a far greater section of the community than had been involved in the feudal and absolutist states which preceded them, and which persisted elsewhere in Europe. Such representative institutions are much easier to operate if members of parliaments, and indeed also the electors, share a single language, and this political development was in its turn aided by the more or less monolingual character of these Western states; the representative political institutions then furthered the consolidation of these political units. The power and prestige particularly of France and Britain, and the spread of the ideals of representative parliamentary institutions, fostered the ideal of monolingual nation-states, established on an explicitly linguistic basis, throughout Europe, including in the German-speaking area. In fact one could say that the common language was one of the few features shared by all the various parts of the German Empire founded in 1871, and when the multi-ethnic Austro-Hungarian Empire and neighbouring territories in Eastern Europe were divided up at the end of the First World War this division was carried out on explicitly linguistic principles (for further details see Inglehart and Woodward 1972: 358).

Compared with the sociolinguistic pattern in many parts of the world, the sociolinguistic pattern in German-speaking Europe is not too dissimilar to that in Britain, but there are important differences. In one sense the German-speaking area represents less complexity: there are no very large German-speaking areas outside Europe, and so it would be more feasible to create a state including virtually all German-speakers than to create a state uniting all English-speakers, and indeed this was an element in the aggressive expansionist policy of the German fascists. However, in almost every other respect the German-speaking area is more complex. In the first place the boundaries of the German language are less clear than those of English. Most German-speakers are aware that their language is highly diverse; to a greater extent than English-speakers they are confronted with language varieties that are grouped under the same name as their own (*Deutsch*) but which they may find virtually incomprehensible. For instance, many rural varieties of German may be little understood by German-speakers from other regions. Speakers of standard English can encounter this problem with some traditional British dialects, but it is much less common than in the German-speaking area. Admittedly, speakers of standard English can also fail to understand English-based creoles, but the problem here is rather different (and is not shared by German-speakers) in that the creoles are associated with distinct ethnic groups.

Now, we have already remarked that the discreteness of English is partly illusory, since as well as being similar to the English-based creoles, it has clear affinities with some other languages, such as Dutch. In the case of German, the great diversity within the language contrasts with very strong similarities indeed between some related languages and at least some varieties of German. Anyone who is familiar with dialect in north Germany, and who knows some Dutch, cannot fail to be struck by strong similarities; rural Dutch dialects near the German border and rural German dialects near the Dutch border enjoy a high degree of mutual intelligibility (see Lockwood 1976: 188–9). Awareness of the considerable similarity between Dutch and German is quite widespread among German-speakers, and has even led to the (in our opinion erroneous) view that Dutch is a German dialect.[1] Particularly in north Germany, where

---

[1] This view is even supported, if sometimes only implicitly, by many German linguists but is robustly and convincingly rebutted by the Belgian Jan Goossens: see especially Goossens (1976).

there are strong historical links with Scandinavia, and where also local dialects often show strong resemblances to English, there is quite widespread awareness of similarities between German and the other **Germanic languages**, that is English and the Scandinavian languages. On the other hand, **Luxembourgish** and **Swiss German**, in their different ways, can be seen in some senses as varieties of German, in some senses as independent languages; both present very considerable comprehension problems to German-speakers from areas distant from Luxembourg or Switzerland.

In a case where the boundaries of a language are somewhat uncertain, the language can nevertheless have a clear separate identity as the language of an ethnic, national or cultural group whose other defining characteristics are clear. For example, Polish is not clearly distinct from the neighbouring Ukrainian, Czech and Slovak, but its identity is nevertheless clarified by its association with a distinct Polish nationality defined by other characteristics, for example by religion, where tradition-ally a strongly Catholic Poland has asserted its identity in opposition to a Protestant Prussia and an Orthodox Russia. German, however, is not associated with a strong national identity defined by anything other than language; there is little apart from the language which links, say, Protestant Hamburg, with its traditionally strong ties with the Baltic, Scandinavia and other parts of Northern Europe, to Catholic Vienna, looking traditionally to the Danube, the Mediterranean, the Balkans and eastern Europe.

German, then, is a highly diverse language, with, in a real sense, rather indefinite boundaries, and yet there is, in the eyes of millions of speakers, an entity called the German language (*die deutsche Sprache*). Why should this be so? This cannot be because it is the language of a clearly defined ethnic group; German-speakers are not united by religion or by any other obvious cultural characteristic which is not shared by other European populations. There are cases where inhabitants of a linguistically and culturally diverse area are considered to speak a single language at least in part because they form a unified nation-state; this is to a limited extent true of Britain and France. It is, however, scarcely true of the German-speaking area. Before 1871 the area was seriously politically fragmented (see 2.2), and even after 1871 major German-speaking areas, notably in Switzerland and in the Austro-Hungarian Empire, were not united with the German Reich. Since 1949 there have been no fewer than four European states – the two German republics, Austria and Liechtenstein – with an almost entirely German-speaking population; a fifth, Luxem-bourg, where almost all speak a variety that is either a German dialect or a closely related language (depending on one's point of view) and where virtually all have high passive competence in German; and a sixth, Switzerland, where the largest single linguistic group speaks German (albeit of a very different kind from that spoken in the other countries) (Löffler 1985: 65–6).

Why, then, is the speech of this highly diverse area considered to be a single, German, language? Part of the answer is, of course, that the various forms of German are not totally dissimilar to each other; although in some cases mutual comprehensibility may be low, nevertheless the various forms of German are obviously related to each other, in some sense of the term. Conversely, other speech forms within the German-speaking area, such as Sorbian in the GDR and Hungarian and Croatian in Austria which have little or no obvious relationship to German, are not considered by anyone to be German. However, as we have already seen, German does show an obvious relationship to Dutch and even to English and Scandinavian languages, and yet no coherent case can be made for describing these as German. A further complicating factor here is that one speech form within the German-speaking area, while obviously related to standard German, is nevertheless usually considered to be a minority language and not a German dialect: this is North Frisian. It should also be mentioned that some consider the **Low German** dialects of north Germany, clearly related to standard German, to be a minority language rather than a group of German dialects, but this is not a common position among linguists (see Sanders 1982: 30–5).

So while relatedness is an important criterion in linking many varieties together as forms of German it is in a sense too 'permissive': it allows us to draw together varieties which may have a very low degree of mutual intelligibility (e.g. Swiss German dialects and Westfalian (Ger. *Westfälisch*): see Map 3.4) but also permits the inclusion of varieties that we would not wish to call German. This last sentence reveals the fact that the drawing of language boundaries is to some extent arbitrary. For example, the Low Saxon dialects of the north-east Netherlands and the north-west of the Federal Republic may be linguistically very similar but their speakers would consider themselves to be speakers of a Dutch and a German dialect respectively. Why then should we not simply modify our criteria and say that 'German is the label applied to those linguistically related (Germanic) varieties which are spoken within the political boundaries of the Federal Republic, the GDR, German-speaking Switzerland, Austria and Liechtenstein'? The reason is that this would now be too restrictive, and it excludes those varieties spoken in other countries such as France or Italy.

A more promising solution might be that proposed by Kloss (see Kloss 1978; also Goossens 1977, Löffler 1980). This takes the notion of relatedness as the primary criterion but restricts it by reference to a superordinate variety, in this case standard German (the definition of 'standard' poses its own problems but we shall return to this in Chapter 5). Kloss' term for this relationship between standard and non-standard varieties of a language is ***Überdachung*** and this 'overarching' or umbrella effect of the standard can extend beyond national boundaries. Where standard German is the 'authority' to which speakers of a given variety appeal, the variety concerned is considered to be a form of German. So, for example, both Westfalian and the Rhineland dialect spoken in eastern Belgium are *überdacht* (overarched) by standard German, while the linguistically close Limbourgish is overarched by standard Dutch (for a similar explanation using different terminology, see Chambers and Trudgill 1980: 11). Whether or not we include under the label 'German' varieties that exist outside the shelter of standard German, such as those spoken in Alsace-Lorraine, the USA or Australia, depends not on the objective criteria of relatedness and overarching but on the strength of the 'language loyalty' felt by their speakers (see 8.2.1).

### 1.1.4 Conclusion

We have now come a long way from our initial superficial response to the questions 'What is German and who speaks it?' and by the end of section 1.1.3 we were approaching a more satisfactory answer. The object of this exercise, however, was not to devise a cast-iron definition of 'German' as there cannot be a single 'right' answer to such questions. The point rather was to demonstrate the complexity of such issues and to outline some ways in which to tackle them. It should now be clear that any attempt to resolve questions of linguistic identity must take a wide range of factors into account, not only linguistic but also historical, political, cultural and psychological.

## 1.2 Languages in society

### 1.2.1 Language contact and language change

Two further sociolinguistic questions now pose themselves: (i) what are the linguistic consequences of close contact between two languages? and (ii) what rôle does language play in the social lives of communities, or even states, where two languages are in use? A glance at a map of Europe will show why German lends itself particularly well to the study of such questions. By virtue of the geographical location of the German-speaking countries in central Europe, German comes into contact not only with many different languages but with several different language 'families': in the north, with other Germanic languages (North Frisian, Dutch, the Scandinavian languages and English); in the west and south, with **Romance** languages (French, Italian and Romansh; plus Romanian in the east); in the east, with Hungarian and with **Slavonic** languages (Slovene, Serbo-Croatian, Czech, Polish, Russian). Furthermore, as a result of changing political boundaries on the one hand and immigration and the influx of refugees and displaced exiles on the other, German comes into contact with some of these languages (and more besides) within the German-speaking area (e.g. Castilian Spanish, Portuguese, Greek, Turkish in the Federal Republic; Sorbian in the GDR; Slovene, Hungarian and Serbo-Croatian in Austria). As we pointed out in 1.1.3 above, it is often the case that language boundaries (*Sprachgrenzen*) do not coincide with state boundaries (*Staatsgrenzen*), so that contact with other languages on the margin of the German-speaking area often takes place not at the state frontier but on the territory of neighbouring states.

Given this remarkable geographical situation of the German-speaking countries, it should not be surprising if we find similarities between German and other languages. This is most strikingly the case with the other Germanic languages and is one of the factors that give rise to the problems of determining 'discreteness'. However, a distinction is conventionally made between similarities which are due to contact between (the speakers of) one language and another, and those which are due to the fact that two languages share what can be termed a 'common ancestry', although this distinction is not always easy to maintain in practice (see Bynon 1977: 253–6). 'Contact linguistics', as the name suggests, is concerned primarily with the former and seeks to account for such similarities in terms of the degree and type of contact between languages and their speakers. For example, the prevalence of (American) English words in contemporary German in the Federal Republic can be attributed largely to the growing economic and political dominance of the USA since the Second World War, which led to the emergence of English as the international language of science and technology and of popular culture, to some extent even in the Soviet bloc.

However, other similarities between English and German cannot be explained in this way. Innovations and **neologisms**, such as *Software*, *cool* or *Image*, are easily identified as such and even less obvious '**loan formations**' like *Gehirnwäsche* (literal translation of 'brainwashing') can be shown to be clearly the result of relatively recent contact. On the other hand, systematic resemblances in the basic vocabulary and in **morphological** structure are generally due not to contact between two distinct languages but rather to the fact that these two languages probably had a common origin. This applies not only to German and English, nor even just to the whole set of Germanic languages. Germanic, Romance and Slavonic languages all belong to the 'family' of languages known as **Indo-European**, which probably formed a group of closely related dialects about five to six thousand years ago, and although structural resemblances between Germanic and non-Germanic Indo-European languages are relatively difficult to detect, there are still in fact some important common features.

The study of such evolutionary developments is the realm of 'historical linguistics', which is concerned with establishing internal structural causes for language change. Our main concern here, on the other hand, is to examine the rôle of external, non-linguistic factors in the interplay between languages in contact. This is not to say that we can afford to ignore the historical context (part of Chapter 2 is devoted to this) but rather that sociolinguistic explanation of language change should take account of both the social, political and cultural aspects of that context, as well as the internal dynamics of a language, with the emphasis on the former.

### 1.2.2 Multilingual speech communities

Let us now return then to the question of the coexistence of two or more languages in one community. In section 1.1.3 we identified language varieties, both within and outside the German-speaking countries, that we wished to group together as forms of German, and suggested criteria for doing so. What we did not fully take into account at that stage is the fact that in its contact with other languages German enjoys a very different status in different countries. A first crude distinction is between those countries (Federal Republic, GDR, Austria, Switzerland and Liechtenstein) where German is the first language of the majority of the population and those (such as Belgium, Denmark and France) where it is used by a small indigenous minority. However, a close examination of the situation in individual countries soon reveals that this simple majority vs. minority distinction is inadequate. For example, German is the only official language in the Federal Republic, the GDR, Austria and Liechtenstein but in Switzerland it is just one of three official languages. Furthermore, there is a constitutional distinction in Switzerland between these three (German, French and Italian) as 'official languages' (*Amtssprachen*) and the same three languages together with Romansh as 'national languages' (*Nationalsprachen*). On the other hand, while the situation in Luxembourg might appear similar, in that again three languages[2] coexist and are recognized in the constitution, the position of

---

[2] For the sake of argument, we are considering Luxembourgish as a language here (if perhaps only, in Kloss' terms (1978: 23–30), as an *Ausbausprache*). See also Chapter 8.

German in the two states is in reality very different. And finally, even in those situations where German is clearly a minority language (e.g. eastern Belgium, eastern France, northern Italy) its actual status and functions are by no means uniform.

A sociolinguistic investigation of German, as indeed of any language, must concern itself with variation both in the form of the language and in its status and function in relation to other languages. In considering details of the language itself therefore we should not lose sight of the fact that it is not an autonomous phenomenon existing in a vacuum. This was also one of the reasons why in section 1 of this chapter we asked not only 'What is German?' but also 'Who speaks it?', as the faculty of language is an individual human attribute but the production of language is a form of social behaviour and therefore variation in language use cannot be viewed in isolation from its social setting.

In considering contact between German and other languages, then, we should take note of the fact that just as even monolingual German-speakers habitually vary their production of German according to a complex set of factors that makes up the extralinguistic context, so there are many situations where variation in language use means choosing not a particular variety of German but some form of another language altogether. We can all vary our language use even if in only one language, but many people have a 'linguistic **repertoire**' that includes more than one language. This is what is normally understood by 'individual' as opposed to 'societal' **bilingualism**; the former refers to an individual speaker's linguistic versatility, his or her ability to use two or more languages, if not necessarily equally well; the latter indicates the widespread use of two or more languages throughout a **speech community** or society. In this sense, both Britain and the Federal Republic for example are now characterized by societal bilingualism as languages other than English and German are used widely in these countries, although only a relatively small number of speakers in each case are individually bilingual.

To a large extent, the choice of language for, say, a bilingual Punjabi/English-speaker in England or a bilingual Turkish/German-speaker in the Federal Republic is determined by a very limited range of factors, principally the linguistic ability and/or preference of the ad-dressee. In some bilingual societies, however, the choice of one language or another is determined not at the individual level but according to sometimes quite complex conventions that apply throughout the society. These conventions are usually accepted and observed by most speakers in the society and indeed the ability to select the 'appropriate' variety in any given setting is an important part of 'native speaker competence'. The crucial distinction between these so-called 'diglossic' speech communities and simple bilingual ones is then that in the former the two languages are in 'complementary distribution' with each other (i.e. A is used only for one set of functions, B for another), while in the latter the choice of one language or the other is a purely *ad hoc* decision.[3]

Although most definitions of **diglossia** include a number of criteria, by far the most important one (that is common to all definitions to date) is function. Thus, one language (the 'high' or H variety) is typically said to be used exclusively for major functions in public '**domains**' such as in parliamentary debates, university lectures or news broadcasts, while the other (the 'low' or L variety) is used only in semi-public or private domains such as in conversation with family and friends or in 'light entertainment' (see Ferguson 1972: 236). It may seem at first sight that this is a purely academic distinction but it can have important practical consequences. It has been observed on many occasions (see e.g. Fishman 1972) that in a society characterized by bilingual but not diglossic language use, one language is almost bound to be displaced by the other sooner or later: it is only when each language is ascribed a specific set of functions that both languages stand a good chance of survival in the long run, even if they are in a majority–minority relationship. This is therefore one of the most crucial factors in determining 'language maintenance' (stable bilingualism) and 'language shift' (the transition from bilingualism to monolingualism), and these are processes in which German is constantly involved, both as a majority and as a minority language.

### 1.2.3 Conclusion

We have now considered both the complexity and range of variation in German and its nature and meaning. We have also tried to show why a sociolinguistic study of German can be of interest not just in its own right but also as an illustration of many issues that concern sociolinguists in every part of the world. Our discussion of these issues has provided some possible answers to preliminary questions but in doing so has thrown up further questions, with which much of the rest of the book will be concerned. In the final sections of the present chapter, we shall outline firstly the two main approaches that have been taken to the study of linguistic variation, in particular the development of sociolinguistics in the German-speaking countries, and then the pattern of the following chapters.

---

[3] Diglossia as originally conceived by Ferguson (1972 [1960]) was restricted to two varieties of the same language. The notion has since been extensively discussed and modified and according to the broadest definition (see e.g. Fishman 1972, Fasold 1984) it can apply to any two 'codes'.

## 1.3 Approaches to the study of variation in language

### 1.3.1 Dialectology and sociolinguistics

Neither traditional dialectology nor sociolinguistics is considered by its practitioners to be merely a 'branch of linguistics'. On the other hand, their identity as autonomous disciplines is open to question. The question for dialectologists is whether it is still plausible to maintain a distinction between dialectology and sociolinguistics (see Goossens 1981; Mattheier 1983b: 151–2). For sociolinguists, the question is whether their subject is a discipline in its own right which now subsumes dialectology, or whether it will eventually dissolve itself when its concerns and methodology are incorporated into mainstream linguistics (see Labov 1972a; Löffler 1985).

What then are the differences between these two approaches? Unfortunately, even here it will be difficult to give simple, clear-cut answers. Part of the problem is that there is no consensus amongst practitioners. While, for example, archaeologists and historians have similar and to some extent overlapping interests, each group would normally consider itself distinct from the other, and there is usually no doubt in their minds as to whether they are 'doing' archaeology or 'doing' history; the same cannot necessarily be said of dialectology and sociolinguistics.[4] Much depends then on the views of the individuals concerned; the picture is further complicated by the fact that these disciplines have different traditions in different countries.

As the boundary between dialectology and sociolinguistics is often blurred, it is not unusual to find people who trained in the one doing research more typical of the other. This only serves to reinforce the sense of threat felt by dialectologists, confronted, as they see it, by the irresistible surge of popular and academic interest in the new, modish discipline. Some would say that interest in sociolinguistics peaked in the early 1980s (see e.g. Löffler 1985: 11) but at the time of writing, in the late 1980s, there is no sign that research activity in sociolinguistics is declining, either in the German-speaking countries or elsewhere. Similarly, just as the long-heralded 'decline' in the use and vitality of traditional German dialects has failed to come about (or at least has not led to their demise), so the interest (again both popular and academic) in dialectology has been maintained. What undoubtedly did change in the fifteen years following the emergence of sociolinguistics in the German-speaking countries in the

---

[4] Clear evidence of this is the fact that there are many areas of common interest between two books published simultaneously in the Cambridge Textbooks in Linguistics series: one called *Dialectology* (Chambers and Trudgill 1980), the other *Sociolinguistics* (Hudson 1980).

late 1960s was the nature of its subject matter,[5] and it is this change of direction or broadening of scope that has brought it into competition with dialectology.

The first sociolinguistic work conducted in the United States in the 1960s was prompted by primarily academic, linguistic motives. Depending on your point of view, it could be described as a break with both of the two separate and mutually suspicious disciplines of dialectology and linguistics or as an attempt to bridge the gap between them. On the one hand, dialectologists were interested, if only marginally, in variation, but their methods were increasingly being seen as inadequate and their analysis was considered to be long on description but short on explanation. On the other hand, however, the more rigorous discipline of structural linguistics seemed too remote from the real world, and its central tenets, which William Labov referred to as 'ideological barriers to the study of language in everyday life' (Labov 1972a: xix), were challenged by those who sought to account for patterns of actual language use as opposed to the more abstract linguistic system of an 'ideal speaker-hearer'. So sociolinguistics at this stage might also be called 'social dialectology', in that its main concern was to bring a more scientific approach to the study of dialects, which came to be considered more as social than as merely regional phenomena. Today, this is seen as 'sociolinguistics in the narrow sense' or 'sociolinguistics proper', as the term has since come to cover a wide range of other topics from the ethnography of speaking and anthropological linguistics to the sociology and social psychology of language.

This kind of work remained virtually unknown in the German-speaking countries until the 1970s. Sociolinguistic interest there, especially in the Federal Republic, focussed initially on very different issues and was aroused more by social and political motives than linguistic ones. With the crisis in education and the emergence of the powerful student movement in the late 1960s, a great deal of attention was directed at the work of the British sociologist Basil Bernstein, who attributed the social disadvantage of British working-class children partly to their alleged linguistic deprivation. This was fertile ground for those seeking the origins of class conflict in the Federal Republic and for some years this area was virtually synonymous with sociolinguistics in German-speaking countries. At first, the theory was concerned only with so-called **restricted** and **elaborated codes**: middle-class children were said to have access to both, working-class children only to the former. These codes were not equivalent to dialect and standard but were defined in terms of, for

---

[5] For an idea of how rapidly this occurred, compare the two articles in the journal *Language in Society*: Schröder (1974) and Pfaff (1981).

example, relative syntactic complexity and lexical range. Later, though, attention shifted to the rôle of dialects as possible 'language barriers' (*Sprachbarrieren*).

The language barriers issue remains controversial. However, from about the mid-1970s the scope of German sociolinguistics extended to include many other topics, the most important of which are conversation analysis and pragmatics; sex-specific language use and sexual inequality in the linguistic structure of German; multilingualism both within the German-speaking countries (including the emergence of so-called *Gastarbeiterdeutsch*) and on their borders; and finally what we are calling social or urban dialectology. (See Dittmar 1982 and Löffler 1985 for two, rather differing, accounts of the development of German sociolinguistics.) Dittmar (1982: 22) suggests that sociolinguistics as practised in English-speaking countries especially was slow to catch on in the Federal Republic partly because crucial aspects of the methodology were considered inadequate, but a more significant obstacle may have been the conservative tradition of German dialectology. We shall therefore consider the belated development of German sociolinguistics, in the sense of social dialectology, against the background of this tradition.

### 1.3.2 Sociolinguistics and sociolinguistics

It has been possible here only to sketch some of the issues that unite and divide different approaches to the study of variation in language. The important point for our purposes is to establish firstly that the field of sociolinguistics is potentially vast and secondly that even if we restrict our attention to one area there will be more than one way of tackling it. The theme that we are going to pursue is the notion of variation in German and our investigation will cover two main 'types' of sociolinguistics: variation within German, i.e. 'sociolinguistics proper' or social/urban dialectology; and variation in the status, function and use of German, i.e. the sociology of language or 'language and society'. That is to say, while all of the topics to be discussed are of both social and linguistic interest, in some instances the insights gained tell us more about the structure of the society than about the language and in others the converse is the case. In practice of course the division between these two areas is more a question of emphasis or perspective than a clear-cut distinction.

### 1.4 Outline of following chapters

Our object in this opening chapter was to set the scene for what follows. We have tried to show that while on the one hand apparently simple notions such as 'German' turn out on closer inspection to be highly complex, the complexity and variation in language and language use are not chaotic or random but are capable of analysis, classification and explanation. What we now need to do therefore is to look in more detail at ways of describing and explaining variation in the form and use of German.

Chapter 2 provides a historical background to the general theme by examining the development of German in relation to other Indo-European, and specifically to the Germanic, languages and the emergence of the modern standard variety. The main approaches and findings of traditional dialectology are then outlined in Chapter 3, while Chapter 4 examines the consequences of one of the most important social developments in modern Europe, urbanization, for the form and social meaning of variation in German and the development of new approaches to the study of language in social context. Chapter 5 argues that the traditional focus in German dialectology on the dialect–standard dichotomy gives a false impression of the real linguistic situation and we put the case instead for a continuum of varieties with dialect and standard as the two poles.

In Chapter 6 we consider public and academic attitudes to dialect (or non-standard) speech and the problems of educational policy arising from the widespread persistence of dialects. Various aspects of the contact between German and other languages are investigated in Chapters 7 and 8: firstly, the long-established linguistic pluralism of Switzerland on the one hand and the recently emergent multilingualism of the Federal Republic on the other; then the social and linguistic consequences of contact on the margins of the German-speaking countries, and the influence of English on contemporary German. Finally, in Chapter 9, we shall draw together the various strands of our discussion and offer some conclusions on the present state and future prospects of the study of variation in German.

**Further reading**

There are many introductory textbooks on general sociolinguistics: for example, Trudgill (1983b), Hudson (1980), Wardhaugh (1986). The most detailed survey of issues such as language and nation, ethnicity, multilingualism and diglossia is Fasold (1984). The introduction in Trudgill (1978) gives a concise discussion of the various 'types' of sociolinguistics. For the relationship between sociolinguistics and dialectology, see Chambers and Trudgill (1980) and Trudgill (1983a). Löffler (1985) is an account of the development of German sociolinguistics and Clyne (1984) is a good overview of some topics in the field of language and society in German-speaking countries.

# 2   The historical background

## 2.1 German as an Indo-European language and as a Germanic language

A purely **synchronic** discussion of German can provide only limited answers to the kinds of questions we considered in Chapter 1, and yet they are all of great importance to the present-day sociolinguistic situation. Indeed the current state of affairs seen in isolation may seem quite simply confusing. A historical account, on the other hand, may help to give a more complete picture, and so in this chapter we shall consider the historical development of the language from a sociolinguistic viewpoint.

Historical accounts of German typically state that the group of dialects we call German constitute a single German language, that German is a Germanic language, and that the Germanic languages are themselves part of the larger Indo-European language family. We shall examine the historical evidence for each of these statements, and see what each of them contributes to an understanding of the current sociolinguistic situation.

### 2.1.1 German as an Indo-European language

What does it mean to say that the Germanic languages, including German and English, are members of the Indo-European (IE) language family (German *Indogermanisch* or *Indoeuropäisch*)?

It means that at some time in the past, probably between five and six thousand years ago, the languages in question were a single language or closely related group of dialects, which we label **Proto-Indo-European** (PIE). The family-tree diagram (Fig. 2.1) gives an idea of the major languages of the Indo-European family, and the family's geographical spread. It should be noted that the family-tree diagram considerably over-simplifies the relationships between the languages in question (see 2.1.2 below).

Why do we believe that these languages diverged from a common source? If we view the languages in their present state, the evidence for this

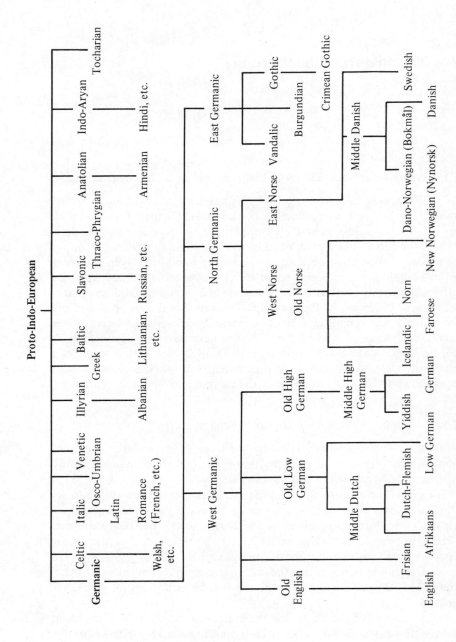

Fig. 2.1 Simplified view of the relationships between Indo-European and between Germanic languages

can be quite substantial, but if we go back to the earliest documents available in the various languages, the evidence becomes more compelling. The evidence is of parallels in the morphological systems of the various languages and, particularly, regular sound correspondences in the basic vocabulary (see Lehmann 1973: Ch. 5). We can give some examples here from English, a Germanic language, and Latin, another Indo-European language (English demonstrates these correspondences rather more obviously than German does): English /f/, /θ/ (written *th*) and /h/ regularly correspond to Latin /p/, /t/ and /k/ (written *c*) respectively, and English /t/ and /k/ (written *c*, *ck* or *k*) regularly correspond to Latin /d/ and /g/ respectively. Hence:

> *for* (preposition), *fish*; Latin *pro*, *piscis*
> *three*, *thin*; Latin *tres*, *tenuis*
> *hundred*, *head*; Latin *centum*, *caput*
> *two*, *ten*; Latin *duo*, *decem*
> *kin*, *acre*; Latin *genus* (tribe), *ager* (field)

German is bounded partly by Indo-European languages of other sub-families, its linguistic relationship to them being clear to scholars, but not immediately obvious to the lay person. The different sub-families represent different developments of Proto-Indo-European in separate areas, there having been at some time separation from Germanic by natural barriers or by intervening languages. The separation of Germanic from the other sub-families may go back three thousand years or more. IE languages in contact with German today belong to the following sub-families: Romance (French, Italian and Rhaeto-Romance, the last-named known as Romansh in Switzerland), Baltic (Lithuanian and Latvian) and Slavonic (Cashubian, Polish, Sorbian, Czech, Slovak, Serbo-Croatian, Slovene) as well as other languages of the Germanic sub-family (Scandinavian, Frisian, Dutch and English).[1]

A further Indo-European sub-family which today is in contact with German is Greek; unlike most of the IE sub-families, this consists of a single language. As a language of immigrant workers modern Greek exerts little influence on German, but there has been a notable influence from classical Greek in the form of numerous learned borrowings.

## 2.1.2 German as a Germanic language

What does it mean to say that German, English and other languages are members of the Germanic sub-family of Indo-European languages? What

[1] For further details of all these languages see Lockwood 1969, 1972; Haarmann 1975.

are the distinctive characteristics of the Germanic sub-family, which mark these languages off from other IE languages? There are a number of such characteristics, but we shall mention only two: **initial stress** and the **first sound shift**.

In the early history of Germanic, stress on words was uniformly shifted to the first (initial) syllable, unless that syllable was a prefix, contrasting with the varying position for stress in different words which is still found in Russian and Greek, for example, and which probably represents the original Indo-European state of affairs.

This shift of stress has continuing sociolinguistic consequences for modern German in that the majority of words of native German origin have preserved the Germanic pattern of initial stress, while words of foreign origin imitate, to an extent, the stress patterns of the language of origin, or at least have an 'exotic' stress pattern, perceived by some as non-German. We can contrast *Atem* (breath), *Heimat* (home area) and *edel* (noble), all of native German origin and with initial stress, with *Atom* (atom, from Greek), *Ornat* (regalia, from Latin) and *fidel* (jolly, from Romance), all with stress on the second syllable. As a result of this many words of foreign origin sound different from native German words (although many others have always had, or have adopted, the same stress-pattern as native German words) and are identifiable. This makes nationalistically inspired attempts to purge the language of foreign words more likely to succeed, though we must add here that the belief that such words are still 'foreign' in the normal sense of the term is somewhat misguided.

A second striking characteristic of Germanic is that it underwent the first, or Germanic, sound shift. This was a radical shift in the consonant system, first described, along with the **second sound shift** (see 2.1.3 below), by Jacob Grimm in 1822, the description often being known as '**Grimm's Law**'. Grimm's Law describes how PIE **voiceless stop consonants**, generally preserved in the other IE languages, became voiceless **fricatives** in Germanic; how PIE **voiced** stops, also generally preserved elsewhere, became voiceless stops in Germanic; and how PIE voiced **aspirate** stops became firstly voiced fricatives, and then usually voiced stops in Germanic. These voiced aspirate stops have also generally undergone changes in the other Indo-European languages. Table 2.1 sets out the major changes involved in the first sound shift. The PIE consonants are exemplified by Latin, where they are quite well preserved. Germanic consonants are exemplified by English, which has preserved them better than German has. For a fuller discussion see Lehmann 1973: Ch. 5.

The modern result of this sound shift for German is to make relationships between words in Germanic and other Indo-European

Table 2.1 *The Germanic sound shift*

<table>
<tr><td colspan="4">a)Proto-Indo-European voiceless stops</td></tr>
<tr><td>PIE</td><td>p</td><td>t</td><td>k</td></tr>
<tr><td>Germanic</td><td>f</td><td>θ</td><td>h/x</td></tr>
</table>

Examples:

| Latin | *pater* | *tres* | *canis* 'dog' |
|---|---|---|---|
| English | *father* | *three* | *hound* originally = 'dog' |

b) Proto-Indo-European voiced stops

| PIE | b | d | g |
|---|---|---|---|
| Germanic | p | t | k |

Examples:

| Latin | — | *duo* | *genus* |
|---|---|---|---|
| English | — | *two* | *kin* |

For b→p no clear examples can be found; /b/ seems to have been very rare in PIE, and there are no clear cases of Germanic words commencing with /p/ of direct Indo-European origin.

c) Proto-Indo-European voiced aspirate stops (these became fricatives in Latin)

| PIE | bh | dh | gh |
|---|---|---|---|
| Latin | f | f (via intermediate θ) | h |
| Germanic | b/v | d/ð | g/γ |

Examples:

| Latin | *ferre* (verb) | *fecit* | *hostis* 'enemy, stranger' |
|---|---|---|---|
| English | *bear* | *did* | *guest* earlier = 'stranger' |

It should be noted that PIE /gh/ has remained as /γ/ or /x/ in Dutch, and has developed into a palatal fricative /j/, or has remained as /γ/, in some German dialects.

languages generally rather obscure, in other words to reinforce the foreignness of the neighbouring IE but non-Germanic languages. Conversely, there are striking and obvious similarities between the basic vocabulary of German and that of the neighbouring Germanic languages. Contrast for example the words for 'dog' in German (*Hund*) and in the neighbouring Germanic languages (Dutch *hond* and Danish *hund*) with those in the Romance languages (French *chien* and Italian *cane*) which nevertheless all derive from the same IE source.

A further factor distancing the vocabularies of Germanic languages from those of other Indo-European languages is that, even in their earliest stages, Germanic languages contain rather more words of non-Indo-European origin than do most other IE languages; for example common Germanic words like *bread* (German *Brot*) and *sea* (German *See*) are not parallelled in other IE languages.

This is a good point at which to make it clear that the family-tree picture of the history of Indo-European languages is in many ways misleading. Firstly, it suggests that 'parent' languages 'died' and were replaced by 'daughter' languages, whereas in reality the 'daughters' are simply the later historical developments of the 'parents'. It also suggests that the division of one 'parent' language into two or more 'daughter' languages was a sudden event, whereas in reality there would be a gradual growing apart of two or more varieties of a single speech form. Another serious defect of the diagram is that it suggests that, having separated, languages are henceforth entirely distinct entities; this is emphatically not so, since there are numerous cases of related languages, and even unrelated languages, exercising influence upon each other.

A quite clear case of influence in the history of Germanic has been the very obvious borrowing of Romance, particularly French, vocabulary into Germanic, occasioned by the greater political and economic power of Romance-speakers for much of the last 1,500 years, and their perceived cultural superiority. There is also a strong Latin influence in the vocabulary of both Romance and Germanic (a factor quite separate from the historical origins of Romance in Latin) caused by the continuing use of Latin as a learned medium in both Romance and Germanic areas and beyond, long after it had ceased to be an everyday spoken language. Both Romance and Germanic have also continued a tradition of borrowing learned vocabulary from classical Greek. These influences mean that, although the basic vocabulary of Germanic is usually quite distinct from that of Romance, there are important similarities in areas where Romance-speakers' cultural or economic influence has been felt, and in scientific and technical areas where lexicon has been borrowed from Latin or Greek (see Keller 1978: 5.8.2, 6.9.2, 7.9.5). Correspondences extend beyond the straightforward borrowing of lexicon; there is also considerable **loan translation**: for example the German *Eindruck* and *Ausdruck* ('impression' and 'expression') are clearly part-for-part translations into Germanic elements of Latin *impressio* and *expressio* respectively. Romance, Latin and Greek influence in the Germanic languages is strongest and most obvious in English, which was replaced as the language of the more influential classes by French for about 250 years after the Norman conquest, but the influence in the other languages is also considerable, and is seen in such common German words as *Hotel, Restaurant, Café, interessant, Chemie* and *Biologie*, all very close to their French equivalents (the isolated Icelandic differs here, having few obvious foreign borrowings, though a considerable amount of the less obvious loan translation).

Although at first sight the Slavonic languages appear to have diverged from Germanic long ago and remained separate, there has actually been considerable contact, the influence here having been mainly of Germanic on Slavonic. The amount of obvious Germanic borrowing in Slavonic is not great, although there is some; yet those languages in closest contact with German, such as Czech, show large numbers of loan translations from German (see Lockwood 1972: 160–1). In addition, although some Slavonic languages were in the Eastern Orthodox cultural orbit (such as Russian, Bulgarian and Serbian) and traditionally took learned vocabulary from **Old Church Slavonic** or Greek, in modern times they have adopted the Western habit of coining learned loans from Latin as well as Greek, and therefore now show strong similarities to Germanic in these areas of vocabulary.

The chief non-Indo-European languages in contact with German are Hungarian, a neighbour, and Turkish, a language of immigrant workers. These languages resemble German even less. The sound correspondences in the basic vocabulary are absent, and the syntactic and morphological structures resemble those of German less than is the case with the neighbouring Indo-European languages. However, German has exercised some influence on Hungarian in the form of borrowed or loan-translated vocabulary and idioms, and there are some **loan words** in German from both Hungarian and Turkish, the latter dating from the period of Turkish political dominance in south-eastern Europe.

### 2.1.3 Relationships between German and other Germanic languages

We have so far examined how, and in what ways, Germanic languages became distinct from other Indo-European languages, and this partly answers the question why some of the languages bordering on German resemble it more than others. We now have to tackle the complex question as to why the other Germanic languages vary in their relationship to German, some – such as Luxembourgish – being arguably dialects of German, others – such as English – being entirely separate languages, while one – Dutch – although separate, is very close to some speech forms which are generally regarded as German, namely the Low German dialects of north Germany.

If we look again at the family-tree diagram (Fig. 2.1) we can see that it divides the Germanic languages into **North Germanic**, East Germanic and **West Germanic** (the last mentioned has occasionally been called *Südgermanisch*, or South Germanic). This division reflects the fact that, in the earliest documents available to us, there are important differences between the languages which are placed in these groups. However, the division is not uncontroversial. For the period when the existence of the Germanic tribes is first clearly recorded by Roman writers, archaeological evidence suggests five tribal groups, with perhaps five incipient distinct Germanic languages, as follows:

(1)   North Germanic tribes (Scandinavians)
(2)   North Sea Germanic tribes (Frisians, Saxons and Angles)
(3)   Weser–Rhine Germanic tribes (Hessen, Franks)
(4)   Elbe Germanic tribes (Langobards, Alemanni, Bavarians)
(5)   Oder–Vistula Germanic tribes (Goths, Vandals, Burgundians)

(For discussion see Moser *et al.* 1981: 24–7.)

These tribal divisions do not correspond at all simply to recorded linguistic divisions, but nevertheless we can link the North Germanic tribes with the North Germanic or Scandinavian languages, the North Sea tribes with the ancestor languages of English, Frisian and Low German–Dutch, the Oder–Vistula tribes with Gothic and related dialects or languages, usually termed 'East Germanic', while the speech of the remaining two groups would give rise to modern (**High**) **German**.

In the following discussion we can leave aside Gothic and the other East Germanic languages, which are all now extinct, and concentrate on the others. Looking at the other languages, one point is quite clear: there are differences between Scandinavian languages and the others (which we shall continue to call 'West Germanic'), which developed quite early, and which mean that, despite similarities, the Scandinavian languages are clearly separate languages from West Germanic. We can hypothesize that these differences arose between the Germanic speech of Scandinavia and that of north Germany because of geographical separation. The differences are to be seen in sounds, in some items of basic vocabulary, and in some grammatical features, most notably in the development in Scandinavian of a suffix definite article (added to the end of a noun) as opposed to the familiar pre-posed definite article of English or German (actually this last-mentioned difference developed long after the assumed separation of North and West Germanic). Examples of the differences can be seen by comparing the following Danish words with their German and English equivalents:

| Danish | *vandet* | *manden* | *skægget* | *barnet* |
|---|---|---|---|---|
| | (the final syllables -*en* and -*et* are articles) | | | |
| German | *das Wasser* | *der Mann* | *der Bart* | *das Kind* |
| English | *the water* | *the man* | *the beard* | *the child* |

This important, and remaining, division within the Germanic languages has nevertheless been considerably obscured by later developments. Firstly, there was a large influence from Scandinavian on English following the Viking raids and settlement (witnessed for example by the

English dialect word 'bairn' **cognate** with Danish *barn* given above). Then from the fourteenth century until the Second World War there was continuous German influence on the Scandinavian languages, through political, cultural and economic dominance. Particularly from the fourteenth until the sixteenth century, when the influence was exercised by the Low German-speaking Hanseatic League, there was large-scale borrowing, even of quite basic vocabulary, and a tradition of copying German words by loan translation was established. This tradition lasted until the present century, as exemplified by the following:

| Danish | *slagord* | *fjernsyn* | *jernbane* |
|---|---|---|---|
| German model | *Schlagwort* | *Fernsehen* | *Eisenbahn* |
| | 'slogan' | 'television' | 'railway' |

Looking now at the West Germanic languages, we can see that the most conspicuous difference between them is represented by the divergent development of English. However, they are separated by other differences, some of which predate the separation of English. As opposed to more southern types of West Germanic, more northern varieties exhibit:

(1)  So-called '**Ingvaeonic palatalization**'
(2)  Loss of **nasal consonants** before fricatives
(3)  Different third person singular pronouns, particularly masculine **nominative** *he*, contrasting with southern *er*
(4)  Absence of the High German sound shift

These differences divide West Germanic speech into northern and southern areas (see 3.9.1), but in each case the dividing line is geographically in a different place.

## (1) 'Ingvaeonic palatalization'

This characteristic today divides English and Frisian on the one hand from the rest of West Germanic on the other. All of the four characteristics are thought by some scholars to have originally divided Ingvaeonic speech, the speech of the Ingvaeones or North Sea Germanic tribes (see above), from the rest of West Germanic, while others consider only the first three or the first two to have been characteristics exclusive to Ingvaeonic, with the third and fourth having been present in some other varieties of West Germanic.

In the basic vocabulary of English and Frisian which has been in Germanic since before about AD 400, **velar stops** adjacent to **front vowels** have become **palatal**, and have also become either fricatives or **affricates** (see e.g. Århammar 1967: 7). Hence English *church*, starting with the affricate /tʃ/, and *yesterday*, starting with the fricative or **approximant** /j/, correspond to Sylt North Frisian *Serk* (where initial [k] is even more radically changed to [s]) and *jüster*, while Dutch has *kerk* and *gesteren* (the latter with a velar fricative [x]), and German has *Kirche* and *gestern*. While this characteristic generally divides English and Frisian from the rest, there are strong traces of the palatalization of voiced velar fricatives or stops in some north and central German dialects, and even in modern colloquial speech (see 5.4.2). It occurs even before **back vowels** in such speech, for example in the Cologne form /juːt/ for standard German *gut*. Conversely, some English dialects have /k/ in some words where standard English has /tʃ/, e.g. in Scots *kirk*. Many such words are considered to be Scandinavian loans (see above).

(2) Loss of nasal consonants before fricatives

This characteristic again separates, on the one hand, Frisian and English from, on the other, the rest of West Germanic; compare English *goose* and *us*, and Sylt North Frisian *Guus* and *üüs*, where an original nasal consonant /n/ has been lost before the fricative /s/, with Dutch *gans* and *ons*, and German *Gans* and *uns* (see Århammar 1967: 7). However, once again this feature does not neatly separate English and Frisian from the rest; many Low German dialects have *us*, and there are actually forms in North Germanic showing loss of /n/, e.g. Danish *gås* and *oss*. Some southern German dialects show loss of nasal consonants too, but this is a feature of more recent origin.

(3) Different third person singular pronouns

The clearest difference to be seen here is between a typically High German masculine nominative pronoun *er*, and northern forms without final /r/, but showing initial /h/, at least in stressed pronunciations, exemplified by Dutch *hij* and English *he*. This feature divides, on the one hand, English, Frisian, Dutch and Low German with /h-/ forms, from, on the other hand, High German dialects with /-r/ forms, exemplified by standard German *er*.

It will be seen (Map 3.6) that the boundary between northern and southern forms for this characteristic is considerably to the south of that for 'Ingvaeonic palatalization', or for the loss of nasal consonants. In fact it is to the south even of the generally accepted dividing line between Low and High German dialects (Map 3.4), since some Middle German dialects of High German have /h-/ pronoun forms.

(4)  Absence of the High German sound shift (see 3.8)

The High German sound shift, also known as the second sound shift, was described by Grimm along with the first or Germanic sound shift as part of Grimm's Law (see above, 2.1.2). It affected High German, and not other parts of West Germanic. The changes, which took place sometime between the fifth and the eighth centuries AD, are summed up in Table 2.2.

The last change ($/\theta/\rightarrow/d/$) is included in Table 2.2 although it is not strictly speaking part of the High German sound shift, since it closely parallels the other changes. It is very important to note that it also affects Low German and Dutch. Frisian (and, incidentally, also mainland Scandinavian, i.e. Danish, Norwegian and Swedish) experienced a change of $/\theta/$ to $/t/$ or sometimes $/d/$; only in English (and, incidentally, Icelandic) was the original dental fricative preserved.

On German dialect maps (such as Map 3.4), there is often a clear line crossing continental West Germanic dividing it into northern dialects (Low German and Dutch), in which the High German sound shift has not operated, and southern dialects (High German), in which it has. This is, however, a rather misleading picture. It is a closer approximation to the truth to say that to the north of the line (known as the **Benrath Line** after the name of the suburb of Düsseldorf where it crosses the Rhine) none of the changes, apart from $/\theta/ \rightarrow /d/$, have taken place, although in the west in the Rhineland the change $/k/ \rightarrow /\varsigma/$ in *ich* is found further north, up to the so-called Ürdingen Line, and isolated forms with shifted consonants are found in Low German dialects. As we move south of the Benrath Line, we gradually find that more and more of the changes have affected local dialects, until when we reach a second line, pursuing a winding course from south of Saarbrücken to the Czech border near Plzen (Pilsen) passing south of Heidelberg and Kassel, we find that, in local dialects, most of the changes have taken place. This second line is sometimes known as the **Germersheim Line**, again from the place where it crosses the Rhine. It is, however, not until we reach the far south that the change $/k/ \rightarrow /kx/$ is found (see above). The Germersheim Line divides **Middle German dialects**, to the north, from **Upper German dialects** to the south (a much fuller account of the complexities of the High German sound shift can be found in Keller 1978: 4.4.3).

It is worth emphasizing here that the High German sound shift operated between 1,200 and 1,500 years ago. It affected only vocabulary items which were present in the dialects in question at that time: words which have entered the language subsequently are unaffected; for example the word for 'pepper', which was borrowed into Germanic in Roman

Table 2.2. *The High German sound shift*

a) Voiceless stop consonants in initial position

| West Germanic | p | t | k |
|---|---|---|---|
| High German | pf | ts | kx, k |

Examples:

| English | *pound* | *ten* | *cow* |
|---|---|---|---|
| German | *Pfund* | *zehn* (/ts-/) | *Kuh* (Swiss German *Chuh* /kx-/) |

The change k→kx is found only in the extreme south of the German-speaking area, in German-speaking Switzerland, southern Austria, and small areas of South Germany.

b) Voiceless stop consonants in **medial** and **final** position

| West Germanic | p | t | k |
|---|---|---|---|
| High German | pf, f | ts, s | x, ç |

Examples:

| English | *hope, hop* (verbs) | *heat, hot* | *book, oak* |
|---|---|---|---|
| German | *hoffen, hüpfen* | *Hitze, heiß* | *Buch, Eiche* |

Whether /p/ and /t/ develop into /pf/ and /ts/ (affricates) or /f/ and /s/ (fricatives) is dependent on the original **phonetic** environment. /k/ develops into /x/ after a back vowel, and /ç/ after a front vowel, though the development is always to /x/ in some regions.

c) Voiced stop or fricative consonants

| West Germanic | b/v | d | g/γ |
|---|---|---|---|
| High German | b, p | t | g, k |

Examples:

| English | *borrow, rib, seven* | *day* | *go, marrow* (Old English *marg* /marγ/) |
|---|---|---|---|
| German | *borgen, Rippe, sieben* | *Tag* | *gehen, Mark* |

The modern results of this change present a very complex picture in High German dialects; they are actually often voiceless **lenis** stops [b̥], [d̥], [g̊] (see 3.11.3, 5.4.2 and 5.4.3). In the earliest West Germanic the stops (b, g) and fricatives (v, γ) were probably **allophones** of single phonemes

d) Voiceless **dental** fricative

| West Germanic | θ |
|---|---|
| German | d |

Examples:

| English | *thing* |
|---|---|
| German | *Ding* |

times, is *peper* or *pepper* in Dutch and Low German, *Pfeffer* in Upper German, while the word for 'paper', not found in Germanic until the late Middle Ages, has a stop consonant [p] or [ḅ] both initially and medially in all West Germanic speech.

It will be seen that the division of West Germanic into more northern and more southern types of speech on the basis of these four characteristics is highly complex; in fact only English and Frisian have all the 'northern' characteristics and only some southern German dialects have all the 'southern' features. It will be seen also that none of the various dividing lines corresponds to the modern boundaries between the different West Germanic languages; in fact most of them correspond to dialectal divisions within one of those languages, German. These complex dialect divisions within West Germanic, which correspond only remotely to the modern language boundaries, arose centuries before the modern standard languages began to develop. We have almost no direct evidence for this, but it seems likely that there arose within West Germanic a difference between northern and southern speech types very early, before the Frankish kingdom was established at the end of the fifth century AD (see 2.2.2). This linguistic divide may have corresponded to an ancient tribal division between, to the north, 'Ingvaeones' and, to the south, other West Germanic-speaking tribes. The division does not seem to have involved a loss of comprehensibility between the two types, i.e. to a true separation between languages. The boundary between the two types of speech probably arose somewhere between the modern Benrath and Germersheim Lines.

The northern speech type would exhibit 'Ingvaeonic palatalization', loss of nasal consonants before fricatives, and third person pronouns of the *he* type. The southern speech type would not show 'Ingvaeonic palatalization' or loss of nasals before fricatives, and would have third person singular pronouns of the *er* type. At this stage, i.e. before the end of the fifth century, the High German sound shift had perhaps not occurred, or had perhaps affected only more southerly dialects; in any case its failure to operate fully in all modern **High German dialects** suggests that it was a later southern feature, and did not in the early period divide northern from southern West Germanic.

Since this early period there has taken place a very slow but persistent rise to prominence of more southern speech types (see below 2.2.2), and their consequent influence on more northern types. As we have seen, English displays all of the 'northern' features to the full; this is explained by the fact that the Anglo-Saxon tribes left their continental homes in north Germany and Jutland and emigrated to England in the late fifth century before this southern influence reached that area. From that time onwards English underwent a separate development, being slowly imposed on the native Celtic-speaking population of the British Isles (a process still not complete, as we see in the survival of Welsh, Scots Gaelic and Irish), undergoing firstly Scandinavian and then French influence, and developing today into a language quite distinct from the rest of West Germanic. The separation has never been total: English has adopted a number of words from German and Dutch (sea-faring and painting terms from the latter are notable, e.g. *skipper* and *easel*), and the present century has seen the large and growing influence of English, more particularly American English, on German in many areas of vocabulary.

If we turn now not to the standard languages but to the traditional dialects of West Germanic, there is some evidence that the 'northern' characteristics extended in the early period to a line crossing central Germany; one of these, the use of *he*-type pronouns, still does extend this far south; the others have, however, generally been pushed further north by the persistent southern influence. 'Ingvaeonic palatalization' of /k/ is now generally confined to Frisian, though as we saw above the change of /ɣ/ or /g/ to /j/ is present in some north German speech. Forms with loss of nasals are now found consistently only in Frisian; elsewhere they are sporadic. The fourth characteristic dividing northern from southern West Germanic, the High German sound shift, operated, as we have seen, between the fifth and eighth centuries, probably starting in the Upper German dialect area (though this is controversial; see Keller 1978: 176–7). It had its full effect only in Upper German dialects; its operation in Middle German dialects is complex and variable, while in Low German dialects it did not operate at all.

So far we have described in outline how the dialectal diversity of continental West Germanic arose; it remains to discuss why there was this persistent spread of forms from south to north. Questions on the causality of linguistic change can scarcely ever be answered to our satisfaction; all that we can say in this case is that, for most of the past 1,500 years, central and south Germany have been economically and culturally more powerful than the north. This has facilitated the influence, but it has not been sufficient to overcome the effects of political fragmentation and to eliminate northern speech forms. Also, a significant exception to it has been the relatively great prosperity and power of the Netherlands for most of the period since the seventeenth century; this has furthered the growth of Dutch as a language independent of German.

## 2.2 The development of a distinct German language

Having seen how diverse an entity West Germanic is, the major question which we have still to answer is 'How did the notion of a single German language arise and persist in an area as linguistically diverse as the German-speaking territory?' The notion of a single language is, of course, in modern Europe, closely bound up with the existence of a single fairly unified standard language, so our question could be rephrased: 'How has a single standard language arisen and persisted in an area of such linguistic and political diversity?'

In discussing this question it is useful to isolate factors which have favoured diversity and political and cultural disintegration of the area, from factors which have favoured unity, and hence the development of the idea of a single language.

The principal factor which has favoured diversity – political, cultural and hence linguistic – has been the sheer size both in geographical area and in population of the German-speaking territory. Existing political and cultural diversity fostered the division of the area at the time of the Reformation in the sixteenth century into Protestant and Catholic regions, and since that time these religious divisions have accentuated political and linguistic fragmentation. If we contrast the German-speaking area with other areas of comparable size in Europe covered by closely related languages, we find that several languages have developed; in the Iberian peninsula there are three standard Romance languages, Castilian Spanish, Portuguese, and Catalan; in the area in which the closely related West Slavonic languages are spoken we find Polish, Czech and Slovak.[2] In each of these areas the diversity of the traditional dialects is arguably less than that found in the area covered by modern German. What is particularly interesting about the German-speaking area is that there has been political fragmentation, and linguistic fragmentation at the level of traditional dialects, but only one standard language has developed.

It is difficult to find factors favouring linguistic unity when we examine the German-speaking area; but this difficulty is greatest if we confine our view to the last five hundred years, a period when the areas of the other major European languages, English, French, Spanish and also Russian, have been politically united (though until 1870 Italy showed a fragment-ation comparable to that of Germany). When we look at the medieval period the fragmentation of Germany is not so striking; from AD 800 until 1815 there was, at least in theory, a single monarchy, the Holy Roman Empire, superimposed on the various German states. In the last few hundred years of its existence it was largely a dead letter, but at times during the Middle Ages it was an effective force. Indeed, for much of the

---

[2]   There are also Upper and Lower Sorbian languages in the small West Slavonic enclave in the modern GDR, but this was separated from the rest of West Slavonic, being long surrounded by German. Since the Second World War it has touched Polish on the new GDR–Polish border.

Middle Ages the German-speaking area was politically more united than either Spain or France, the former being divided between the Moors and various Christian principalities, the latter being divided between the possessions of the French, Burgundian and Angevin–English monarchies. And England was not a united monarchy until the eleventh century, about two hundred years after the establishment of the Holy Roman Empire, and did not effectively control the rest of the British Isles until several centuries after that. Against this must be set the fact that the Holy Roman Empire was never wholly Germanic. In theory it controlled at least the northern part of Italy, but for most of the period this was largely a fiction, though attempts to control Italy were significant in diverting emperors' attention from maintaining the unity of their German possessions. The Empire also controlled Bohemia, always largely Czech-speaking, which was a politically and economically significant area. Despite these reservations, we can say that unity of all kinds in the German-speaking area was favoured by the early establishment of a monarchy which, by medieval standards, was relatively united. The Holy Roman Empire doubtless fostered a nascent sense of German nationality, which was able to survive later fragmentation.

Another factor which has furthered linguistic unity, in a way which is not at all obvious, but which will be explained below, is the great eastward expansion of the German-speaking area in the later Middle Ages, from the late twelfth century onwards.

### 2.2.1 The fragmentation of continental West Germanic

What were, more precisely, the linguistic consequences of the various factors opposing unity? Fifteen hundred years ago communications were of course, by modern standards, very poor; it is therefore not surprising that the differences between more northerly and more southerly types of West Germanic (see above, 2.1.3) were able to arise and persist. Both at that time and since, the sheer size of the continental West Germanic area has favoured the rise and persistence of dialectal differences of all kinds. What is notable about continental West Germanic is that a single modern nation-state did not arise, as it did in, say, France, Britain or Spain in the early modern period, owing in part to the size and diversity of the area. This persistent fragmentation down to the end of the last century has favoured that relatively great dialectal diversity which we have already mentioned, and which we will examine in more detail below (Chapter 3).

Two notable West Germanic areas, German-speaking Switzerland and the Netherlands (in this sense the area of both of the modern states Belgium and the Netherlands), early became separate political units, with important linguistic consequences.

The beginnings of Swiss independence from the Holy Roman Empire go back to the end of the thirteenth century, a period when, in many parts of Europe, the growth of an urban merchant class and of a landed peasantry represented the beginnings of a middle class in the modern sense, which sought to free itself from its economic and political subjugation to the aristocracy within the feudal system. In many parts of the Empire, as elsewhere, towns were granted independence from feudal overlords, and confederations of towns, sometimes including rural communities, arose to protect their common interests.

It is not entirely clear why the Swiss confederation should have developed so far as to become an independent state, but various reasons can be adduced: its peripheral position in the Empire; the fact that its most significant feudal overlords (the Habsburgs) became hereditary Emperors, and hence independence from them tended to imply independence from the Empire; perhaps most significant in resisting attempts at outside domination is simply the Alpine terrain (see Grundmann 1973: Ch. 6; Fuchs 1973: Ch. 4). Despite its full political independence, a reality long before it was formally recognized in 1648, Switzerland did not develop an independent standard language. On purely linguistic grounds this is quite surprising: Swiss German dialects are largely incomprehensible to German-speakers who do not know dialects from areas close to Switzerland. The reasons would seem to lie in the small population and resources of the area at the time when standard German was developing, and in the fact that the confederation which finally emerged contained important non-German areas (French-, Italian- and Romansh-speaking) and a local Swiss German could not therefore serve as an effective symbol of Swiss nationality. However, the fact that the Swiss write standard German (albeit with local features) has not prevented Swiss German speech from diverging very considerably from that of Germany, a point to which we will return later (Chapter 7).

In the Netherlands an emergent local standard language, which we call Middle Dutch, was developing in the late Middle Ages, based chiefly on the dialect of Brussels, at that time a city of Germanic speech. This was a period in which rich trading cities were growing in the Netherlands, as elsewhere, with consequent movements for autonomy from feudal overlords.

When, in the mid-sixteenth century, the Netherlands fell to the Spanish crown, while still being nominally part of the Holy Roman Empire, its citizens were separated from their rulers by language, a separation which was reinforced by a religious difference when the northern part (approximately the modern state of the Netherlands) became, in the course of the Reformation, a largely Protestant area. The conflicts which inevitably arose culminated in the Revolt of the Netherlands (1568–1609), resulting in the independence of the northern provinces (the modern Netherlands). The newly independent state soon became one of the richest and most powerful areas in Europe, and certainly felt no inclination to adopt the emerging standard language of its divided and relatively poor, though much larger, German neighbour. A local standard language arose, which has since developed separately from German.

The area of modern Belgium remained a Spanish possession, passing later to Austria, and not becoming independent until 1830. Both before and after independence French, the language of about half the population, was used as the language of administration and schooling and replaced Germanic speech in the city of Brussels to a considerable extent. When, in this century (1932), Germanic speech – known as either Dutch or Flemish in English, and nowadays representing the speech of over half the population – was accorded official status, the Dutch of the Netherlands was adopted as the standard and official language; there was no question of German, by now a foreign tongue, taking on this rôle. The Dutch of the Netherlands and the Dutch of Belgium are essentially the same language, though of course there are differences between the two countries at the level of traditional dialects, as there are within each country. The use of the term 'Flemish' for the language is misleading: the official name for the language in both the Netherlands and Belgium is *Nederlands*.

### 2.2.2 Factors favouring the unity of German

Let us now return to Germany itself, and examine in more detail the factors which have favoured unity. The Holy Roman Empire, the pan-German political unit of the Middle Ages, achieved in the eleventh century the political form which was to continue for about five hundred years. It represented a partial continuation of the Kingdom of the Franks which had been divided into eastern and western parts, very roughly modern France on the one hand and Germany and Italy on the other, shortly after its apogee, the crowning of its ruler Charlemagne (Karl der Grosse) as Roman Emperor (see Löwe 1973).

The Franks appear to have been not a tribe but a confederation of tribes centred on the middle Rhine; their speech was West Germanic, but was probably quite diverse, encompassing both northern and southern types referred to earlier. The dialects of their home territory range today from Low Franconian – which corresponds roughly to Dutch – to Upper Franconian, the Upper German dialect of the region around Würzburg and Nuremberg.

From the middle Rhine the Franks had invaded northern France and had settled there, giving their name to the country and to the language, but their numbers were insufficient to impose their language, and French, despite its name, is a Romance continuation of Latin, the Franks being assimilated after a few centuries into the Romance-speaking majority. From this central German–northern French area the Franks had, by the time of Charlemagne, extended their political control over much of what is now France, the Netherlands, Germany and northern Italy.

One notable area of West Germanic speech, the area controlled by the Saxons, came under Frankish control very late, in fact not until the end of the eighth century under Charlemagne (see Löwe 1973: Ch. 18). The territory of the Saxons corresponds approximately to the territory covered by Low German dialects, before these expanded eastwards in the later Middle Ages (see below). The late conquest of Saxon territory is therefore held by some to explain the differences between the northern and southern types of West Germanic dialects. There are however problems with this explanation. Firstly, while the southern border of Saxon territory does correspond very roughly to the Benrath Line, i.e. to the northern limit of the operation of the High German sound shift, it does so only east of the Rhine; to the west of the Rhine the southern Netherlands and the northern Rhineland, areas where the sound shift did not operate, had long been under Frankish control – indeed the dialects of these Dutch and German areas have the traditional name *Niederfränkisch* or Low Franconian. A further problem in this explanation is that the Benrath Line is a north–south dividing line for only one set of characteristics, those associated with the sound shift; other characteristics have different dividing lines: the *h-* third person pronouns extend south of the Benrath Line (see 3.9.1), while 'Ingvaeonic palatalization' and loss of nasals before fricatives are found consistently on the Continent only in the Frisian dialects.

However, what does seem likely is that the southern boundary of Saxon speech lost importance as a linguistic boundary after the defeat of the Saxons by the Franks. It seems, in fact, that before this time Saxon speech had more northern characteristics than do the Saxon dialects of the present, or those of the past as preserved in writing. One piece of evidence for this is that the Saxon dialects brought to England by the Anglo-Saxons, and spoken in areas of Saxon settlement such as *Eastseaxe* (Essex), *Middelseaxe* (Middlesex), *Suþseaxe* (Sussex) and *Westseaxe* (Wessex) (the lands of the East, Middle, South and West Saxons respectively), show all the northern characteristics. Not only the name, but also tradition, suggest that the Saxons who invaded England and those who remained in North Germany may originally have comprised a single tribe. Further evidence of loss of northern characteristics is provided by place names on Saxon territory, such as *Celle* [tsɛlə], which show 'Ingvaeonic palatalization' of /k/, not today found in Saxon dialects (see Sanders 1982: 42–6). We should also remember that the palatal pronunciation [j] where High German has [g] in words like *gehen* and *gut* occurs in dialect and colloquial speech in north Germany (see 5.4.2).

We can surmise, then, that with the Frankish conquest of north Germany, some more southern speech characteristics became more fashionable, and gradually moved northwards. Indeed, we can say that from the end of the eighth century onwards there was established a political, economic and hence cultural and linguistic, hegemony of the south in continental West Germanic, in which the more southern areas and their speech forms were generally more **prestigious**. This has led to constant influence upon northern speech of High German forms, so that today, although Low German dialects have a basic vocabulary highly reminiscent of English, their sentence patterns and more technical vocabulary (where more technical matters are discussed in these dialects at all) show a strong common German character. Today Low German dialects have declined considerably and have been replaced in larger towns and among middle-class people generally either by standard High German, or by forms of colloquial speech which have the character of High German with some Low German features.

A decisive break with southern influence was, of course, made by the Netherlands in the seventeenth century (see above); since that period standard Dutch, which arose from the Low Franconian dialects of north and south Holland, with earlier origins in part in medieval Brussels, has itself influenced other West Germanic dialects in the Netherlands, including the Low Saxon (*niedersächsich*) dialects of the eastern Netherlands which are historically very close to Low German. At the level of the most conservative rural dialects Dutch and German still do form a **dialect continuum**, but the influence of the respective standard languages, indeed the replacement of the traditional dialects on both sides of the border by standard or colloquial non-standard, is making this less and less the case.

In the Middle Ages the influence of more southerly speech forms was very much less felt by the speakers of Frisian dialects, isolated in their remote coastal areas and islands. Apart from the originally Frisian areas in what is now the Dutch province of North Holland (west of the Ijsselmeer) the Frisian-speaking areas were able to maintain independence as peasant republics, with some similarities to the Swiss Cantons, in the thirteenth and fourteenth centuries (see Sjölin 1969: 2–3). In the early Middle Ages Frisian was even expansive, invading present-day north Friesland (the western coast of Schleswig-Holstein with the islands off the coast). The development of Frisian relatively free from southern influence, with the preservation of all the northern character-istics of West Germanic, has led to a definite boundary at the edge of the Frisian-speaking area. It is not part of the continental West Germanic dialect continuum (see Heeroma 1962), and its speakers see it as a distinct language. North Frisian actually moved further from German under Danish influence in the period of Danish rule in Schleswig-Holstein. Frisian is now under severe threat from German in north Friesland and from Dutch in west Friesland; at present the influence of the national standard languages on Frisian is strong (see, for example, Århammar 1967: 8). Like many minority languages, lacking the unifying influence of a standard, Frisian shows extreme dialectal diversity, with low mutual comprehensibility between West Frisian (spoken in the Dutch province of Friesland) and North Frisian, separated as they are by the Dutch-speaking area of Groningen and by east Friesland, formerly Frisian-speaking, where standard German and Low German are now spoken. There is an isolated enclave of East Frisian speech in the Saterland near Oldenburg. Within North Frisian there is a sharp difference, with attendant comprehension problems, between the dialects of the islands of Sylt and Amrum, and those of the mainland, probably due to Frisian settlement taking place at very different times in the islands and the coastal area.

So, with the exception of the Frisian dialects, and of Dutch after the early seventeenth century, speakers of continental West Germanic dialects have probably continued, since the days of the Frankish Empire, to consider themselves as speakers of a single language, in some sense or other and, despite the dialectal diversity, influences have passed from one region to another, particularly in a south–north direction.

As we have seen, the political fragmentation of Germany was, in the Middle Ages, not so exceptional; it was only after the Reformation, and the Thirty Years War in its aftermath (1618–48), that the German-speaking area became exceptionally fragmented compared with other language areas. But by this time a crucial development, the establishment of a single standard written language, had taken place. The significance of fragmentation was that the next step, the establishment of this language as a widespread spoken medium, and its gradual replacing of the non-standard dialects, was considerably delayed in comparison with the development of, say, standard French or standard English.

A further factor which was a unifying force in the development of the German language was its eastern expansion between the tenth and thirteenth centuries. In modern Lithuania, Latvia and Estonia this took the form of commercial exploitation by the Hanseatic League, and military expansion by the Teutonic Order of Knights (*der deutsche Orden*) for whom the conversion of the heathen populace was a crusade, along with some settlement, particularly in the form of the foundation of towns. Until the nineteenth century many towns in the Baltic countries were largely German-speaking, the original native languages being confined mainly to the countryside.

In Poland and the Ukraine much of this immigration, settlement and foundation was undertaken by Jews speaking Yiddish, a language derived from medieval German with much Hebrew lexicon, particularly, of course, for religious concepts. Surrounded and influenced by Slav languages, Yiddish developed in these eastern areas into a language independent of German; before the Nazi massacre of the Jews in the Second World War, some Polish towns were over 80 per cent Yiddish-speaking, but now the language, which survives chiefly in Israel and the United States, is in sharp decline.

In the area between the Elbe, which was more or less the eastern frontier of German in the ninth century, and the pre-1939 German–Polish–Lithuanian border, the expansion took the form not only of military control but also, in much of the area, of settlement, both urban and rural; the Slavonic-speaking population (in East Prussia the speakers of the Baltic language Old Prussian) was slowly but surely assimilated to the German-speakers. In Germany only the Sorbian enclave of Slavonic speech remains today.

Over and above this large-scale eastern expansion, throughout the medieval and early modern periods islands of German speech were established throughout eastern Europe, as far as the Volga, where a colony was established in the eighteenth century. There were many such settlements in the non-German parts of the Austro-Hungarian (earlier Austrian) state, which lasted from the fifteenth century until 1918, and which – in addition to Austria and Hungary – included, at its height, most of Czechoslovakia, as well as parts of modern Yugoslavia, Romania and Poland, and in which the German-speakers were the dominant linguistic group.

It was the eastern settlement in the lands between the Elbe and the pre-1937 border which was linguistically most significant, in that settlers migrated to these areas from the entire continental West Germanic area, including the Netherlands. This entailed the consequence that the dialects of these eastern territories had a compromise character: although in the northern part (roughly Brandenburg, Mecklenburg, Pomerania and East and West Prussia) they were Low German, and in the southern part (roughly Saxony, Silesia, and also a small part of East Prussia) they were of the Middle German type of High German, they displayed a local differentiation which was rather less sharp than that of the western dialects, and more easily comprehensible to speakers from different linguistic backgrounds. This meant that when Saxony, centred on Meissen, Dresden and Leipzig, rose to prominence in the sixteenth century, a form of German with origins partly in the Saxon dialect was able to gain acceptance throughout the German-speaking countries (excluding now the Netherlands) as standard German.

It is important to note that the modern province of Saxony referred to here (*Sachsen*), roughly the *Regierungsbezirke* (administrative areas) of Leipzig, Dresden and Karl-Marx-Stadt in the GDR, has no particular linguistic connection with the ancient tribe of the Saxons, whose homeland was approximately the modern Lower Saxony (*Niedersachsen*) in the Federal Republic; the name *Sachsen* was transferred to the more southerly area when the ruling dynasty of the original *Sachsen* (Lower Saxony) gained control of it. The traditional dialects of the modern Saxony (*Sachsen*) are High German of the colonial Middle German type, while those of Lower Saxony (*Niedersachsen*) are Low German.

## 2.3 The rise of standard German

It is important to understand the process by which standard German developed in order to make sense of the highly complex pattern of varieties in modern German. We can distinguish four stages in this process:

(1)  the rise of several standardized written forms distinct from local spoken dialects
(2)  the acceptance of one of these forms as a standard written form for the whole of the German-speaking area
(3)  the development of a standard spoken form as the normal spoken medium of a section of the population
(4)  the acceptance of the standard, or of forms relatively close to the standard, as the normal spoken medium of the majority of the population, and the consequent rise of regional and class varieties within standard and near-standard speech

### 2.3.1 The rise of standard written forms

We can date the emergence of standard written forms distinct from local dialects to the medieval period, the twelfth to fifteenth centuries inclusive. Prior to that the texts, though we group those of central and southern type as **Old High German** and those from the north as **Old Saxon** or **Old Low**

**German**, are local in character, though not without some standardizing tendencies. This does not mean that writers were trying to transcribe their local dialects – there was in fact probably a considerable gulf between speech and writing – but spelling would, for example, reflect, perhaps in rather complex ways, a local pronunciation. The vast majority of people were illiterate in this period, and almost all writing was in Latin, with religious texts predominating alongside administrative documents.

The high Middle Ages, roughly the twelfth and thirteenth centuries, saw the rise of a cultured and leisured nobility and lesser nobility who were not necessarily highly literate in Latin, and to cater for this class a secular literature in the native language arose, represented by such poets as Walther von der Vogelweide and Hartmann von Aue. Some of this literature is not new, but simply represents, like the Niebelungenlied, the first written record of a much older oral literature, suitably adapted to the tastes of the time. The nobility had supra-regional tastes and connections, and it is interesting that, while there is writing in local forms, a reasonably uniform literary standard came into use, closest to the south-western dialects, which we term **Middle High German (Mittelhochdeutsch)**. While most of the writers who used this literary standard came from the High German dialect area, we know that some of them must have been native speakers of Low German (see Sanders 1982: 122–5).

It must be emphasized that, at this period, virtually all speech was still dialectal; although a standard spoken Middle High German would have a limited existence in the recitation of literature, and perhaps for certain other types of occasion, it would certainly be no one's native language. It must also be emphasized that the overwhelming proportion of writing was still in Latin.

In the latter part of the Middle Ages writing in the emergent standard Middle High German declined, as the class which had enjoyed such literature itself declined, but there is a growth from about the middle of the thirteenth century in the use of German for administrative texts, for example in the newly founded or newly important towns, where, we can surmise, there were not the numbers of Latin-educated officials that could be found in noble courts. But princely courts also turned increasingly to German, as the amount of administration increased with growing political complexity. Each major city and each court developed its own written standard style in its chancery (i.e. in its civil service, German *Kanzlei*), which is known as its ***Kanzleisprache***, and which might differ very little as between neighbouring chanceries, a result of the deliberate adoption of a unitary *Kanzleisprache*. The most striking case of this is the development of the emergent standard language **Middle Low German (Mittelniederdeutsch)** which was used in a fairly unitary form by the chanceries of all the cities in the Hanseatic League. This loose confederation of north German cities, of which the principal ones were Hamburg, Bremen and Lübeck, had trading links from England to Russia and beyond, and dominated Scandinavia both economically and politically, having a large linguistic impact there. Middle Low German, which was closest to the dialect of Lübeck, was, like the other *Kanzleisprachen*, not a spoken language, other than perhaps in limited contexts. Despite its great spread and influence, it was ousted by High German in the sixteenth and seventeenth centuries, as the Hanseatic League collapsed, replaced by Holland as the main trading power of northern Europe, and as Sweden and Russia asserted their political and economic independence.

In the seventeenth century Middle Dutch, which had developed some uniformity, was, as we have seen, removed from the German linguistic sphere. There had been some use of Middle Low German in chanceries in the Netherlands, but Middle Dutch now began an independent development into the modern standard language first of the Netherlands and then of Dutch-speaking Belgium (see 2.2.1).

## 2.3.2 The acceptance of a single written standard

In the sixteenth and seventeenth centuries one of the *Kanzleisprachen*, that of the chancery of Saxony, gained general acceptance as a written standard for the whole of the German-speaking area.

The reasons why the need was felt at this time for a single written standard, when such a need had not been felt earlier, are many and complex. We can mention the introduction of printing in the late fifteenth century: printers can work much more efficiently if all the works they print use a standardized form of the language, and if this language is the same as that used in distant areas, sales of books and hence profits are potentially greater. The introduction of printing coincided with and indeed furthered the rise of a literate middle class, many of whom were not readily able to read Latin. Hence, while the proportion of books produced in Latin was still large, an increasing number were produced in German.

The Reformation, which is conventionally seen as a religious movement, can also be seen as a social movement, with a German-using laity demanding a share of responsibility in religious matters from a Latin-using church. The Reformation itself produced an enormous amount of printed material in German, most notably Luther's Bible translation (the New Testament appeared in 1522).

The Reformation can also be seen as a nationalist movement, asserting a German identity against an Italian-dominated Catholic church (see

Fuchs 1973: 79–86). All these factors furthered the cause of a widely understood written German language.

The adoption of the chancery standard of Saxony had a number of causes. In the areas into which German-speakers had moved as part of the eastward expansion (see 2.2.2) – and most of the Principality of Saxony was relatively new colonial territory – the political units were generally larger and more powerful than in the fragmented western territories; the eastern areas hence came to dominate the Holy Roman Empire, Saxony itself ultimately being eclipsed by those other eastern territories, Brandenburg–Prussia and Austria.

At the crucial period, in the sixteenth century, Saxony was wealthy, was a centre of the printing industry, and had long been a centre of learning (see Wells 1985: 139). Also, the language of the Saxon chancery was derived, though not in any simple or direct way, from the dialects of the Saxony region, which, though High German, were of a Middle German rather than an Upper German type, and hence not as different from Low German as, say, Bavarian dialects were (see Von Polenz 1978: 77). They presented comprehension problems for Low German speakers, but not as many as Upper German would. In addition they were colonial dialects (see 2.2.2) and hence more widely comprehensible than many others. It must not be thought that the *Kanzleisprache* ever was identical to Saxon dialects; from the outset it contained elements from other types of German, and in modern times Saxon dialects have been removed from the standard by changes, particularly in the **phonology**, having been subject to **lenition** (see 3.11.3, 5.4.1, 5.4.2) and **unrounding** of front-**rounded** vowels (see 3.11.2, 5.4.3).

The last factor favouring the adoption of the Saxon chancery language was that this was the language which the Protestant reformer Martin Luther chose for his writings: this was his home area, and the Elector of Saxony was his protector.

The adoption of the Saxon chancery language happened considerably earlier in some areas than in others; it was, paradoxically, more rapid in the Low German-speaking north than in the south, and, given its association with Protestantism, more rapid in Protestant than in Catholic areas. It had an important rival in the southern 'Common German' (*gemeines Deutsch*) favoured by the (Austrian) imperial court. The Saxon chancery language and *gemeines Deutsch* exercised significant influences upon each other before the former gradually prevailed (see Von Polenz 1978: 78). By the end of the seventeenth century, the process of adoption of a fairly uniform written standard language for roughly the whole of the modern German-speaking area was virtually complete. This excluded, of course, the Netherlands, but included Switzerland, now politically independent of the Empire, and also the Low German-speaking north, which had had its own emergent standard (see above, 2.3.1), and where the local dialects are sometimes regarded as an independent Low German language.

The adoption of the standard in north Germany is not as surprising as it might seem; speakers of Low German dialects did not and do not generally regard themselves as a separate ethnic group, and it will be remembered from our discussion above (2.1.3) that the division of continental West Germanic into northern and southern types of dialect is in reality much more complex than the conventional separation into Low German and High German at the Benrath Line. Modern standard German originated chiefly in the East Middle German dialect area, not far from the border with Low German, and hence was not as far from Low German speech as most other types of High German. The abandonment of Middle Low German as a standard was hastened by, if not caused by, the collapse of the Hanseatic League, with which it was closely identified, and by the overwhelming adoption of Protestantism in north Germany, with which the new standard was associated. The adoption of the standard was, indeed, often earlier in the north, and in the north a speech form quite close to it more rapidly became the normal spoken medium of the middle class (see 2.3.3).

The adoption of this East Middle German standard in Switzerland is actually more surprising: despite the designation of both the standard and Swiss dialects as 'High German', there is actually a very considerable linguistic gulf between the south-western Upper German dialects of Switzerland, and the north-eastern Middle German dialects which contributed most to the standard. Factors which contributed to its adoption were, no doubt, the small population of Switzerland and the adoption of Protestantism (albeit Calvinist rather than Lutheran) in many areas of Switzerland.

## 2.3.3 The rise of a standard spoken variety

The next stage in the development of the standard language was its adoption by a section of the population as its normal spoken medium. At this point we confront a problem of definitions, since once a variety becomes the spoken medium of a section of the population it is likely to become regionally and socially diverse. In English-speaking countries the standard language is usually taken to mean the fairly standard usage, in terms of grammar and vocabulary, of the educated middle class. In the German-speaking area, with a more defensive and purist attitude to the language, linked to both the weaker position of the standard in a

49

fragmented area and to a greater interest in it as the prime symbol of nationhood, the standard (German: *Standardsprache, Einheitssprache, Literatursprache, Hochsprache*; see Glossary entry for **formal standard language**) has been defined much more narrowly, and has often meant a form of language which is fairly uniform in both grammar and pronunciation, adhering to the norms of the *deutsche Hochlautung* (*DH*) prestige pronunciation (see Chapter 5 for a full discussion of the problem of definitions). If we, for the purposes of this book, take the English notion of a standard language, allowing phonetic diversity, we can say that, by the end of the nineteenth century, standard German had become the normal spoken medium of the middle classes in north and central Germany. The further south one goes, the less this process is complete, but standard German does now seem to be the everyday speech form of younger, educated, urban middle-class people in south Germany and Austria, though not, significantly, in Switzerland.

The reasons for the spread of the standard are many: we can cite, for example, improving communications, the resultant coming together of people from diverse areas, particularly since the Industrial Revolution in the mid-nineteenth century, the spread of education using the standard as a medium of teaching as well as an object of study, the use of a standard as an expression of a growing desire for German unity, and, perhaps most importantly, the rise of a middle class, which wished to distinguish itself in language, as in other areas of behaviour, from the dialect-speaking peasantry and working class.

Apart from the spread of education, the social and political movements mentioned took place more slowly in German-speaking Europe than elsewhere and this, coupled with and indeed partly caused by political fragmentation, meant a slower spread of the standard than in, say, France or Britain; we must also remember that the dialectal diversity to be overcome was greater in German than in English.

The more rapid spread of the standard in the north than in the south led to a certain identification of it with north Germany; indeed the prestige pronunciation *deutsche Hochlautung* of modern standard German is closest to the pronunciation of the educated middle class in north German cities. This has the interesting effect that standard German is High German in its lexicon, grammar and sound *system*, but the *phonetic details* of its prestige pronunciation are strongly influenced by Low German dialects, the original north German speakers of it having introduced into it the phonetic characteristics of their native dialect. It is of course typical on both an individual and a collective level that the pronunciation of a native speech form is by far the most persistent feature of it, being most noticeably transferred into and retained in a second language or second dialect. Hence voiceless stop consonants in the *deutsche Hochlautung* (/p/

/t/ /k/) are aspirated when they occur initially in stressed syllables; this is also generally true of Low German dialects, but is scarcely the case in Middle or Upper German speech.

The identification of standard German with north Germany and with the rising Protestant north German state of Prussia undoubtedly accounts in part for its much slower acceptance in the more Catholic south.

## 2.3.4 The emergence of the modern continuum

In the process of adoption of a standard language there is frequently a period of diglossia, particularly where the linguistic gap between the standard language and the original native dialects is large. In a diglossic situation speakers will make sudden and complete switches from one form of language to another form, or even into a distinct language, as the situation changes (see 1.2.2). In less formal situations a 'low' variety is used, often a traditional dialect, in more formal situations a 'high' variety, a prestige standard, is used. During the period of adoption of standard German, a diglossic situation undoubtedly existed, as it still does in large parts of the German-speaking area; many people who were able to use standard German on formal occasions would habitually use local dialect, switching more or less abruptly to standard German if the occasion demanded it.

Some writers in German (see for instance titles in the *Dialekt–Hochsprache kontrastiv* series; details in the List of References) give the impression that all German-speakers are still today divided sharply into monoglot standard speakers and dialect speakers, with diglossia being normal for the latter, so that speakers who command both varieties switch fairly abruptly from dialect to standard as the situation requires. We believe that this is still true in the Upper German dialect area in rural communities and small towns, particularly among older speakers, in the Low German dialect area in remoter rural areas among older speakers, and in some, mainly rural parts of the Middle German dialect area, but that it is not generally the case elsewhere.

We believe that nowadays virtually every adult in areas where German is an official language has at least a passive command of the standard language, and that an overwhelming majority has at least some active command of it, i.e. is able to use it to some extent in formal situations. We also consider that, except for those groups of speakers for whom the linguistic situation is still diglossic, people's command of the language can be visualized as covering part of a continuum, ranging from **traditional dialect** to standard. Speakers move by small, perhaps sometimes scarcely perceptible, stages along this continuum towards the standard, dependent on formality (for a full discussion see Chapter 5). In this entire exposition our concept of the standard is wider than that found in many German works; it includes forms with standard lexicon and grammar, but regional **accent**. On the continuum between standard and dialect is to be found that very large range of speech forms known in German as *Umgangssprache*, which we have translated as 'colloquial speech' and which we examine more fully in Chapter 5. It ranges from forms close to the traditional dialect, which we term '**colloquial non-standard speech**', to forms which, in an English-speaking context, would be considered to be informal standard, and which we term '**colloquial standard**'.

How did this state of affairs arise? The general competence in the standard language (of course limited for many people) is clearly the result of general education and, in the twentieth century, of the exposure to mass communications; a rural working-class family which formerly might scarcely ever have heard standard German will now hear it daily on television. The rise of colloquial speech has its origins in the learning of the standard language by dialect-speakers. Such dialect-speakers would not follow at all exactly the standard usage of the educated middle class; they would, in a class-divided society, have felt the need to use, particularly for their relaxed conversation, forms more typical of their group or region, given the typical use of language as a mark of group or individual identity. In other words, in what was basically standard German, people would preserve grammatical and lexical forms originating in traditional dialect, or in other forms of group language. This need to identify with one's social group linguistically is still felt even in a society like that of the GDR, in which, it is claimed, traditional class antagonisms are irrelevant (see Schönfeld 1977: 195–6).

Very often, of course, peasants moving to industrial centres in the nineteenth century had no opportunity to learn standard German, but would find their own local dialect incomprehensible to those around them from different linguistic backgrounds. In such circumstances compromise dialects arose (colloquial non-standard speech), which came to merge imperceptibly with less formal forms of standard German on the continuum of colloquial speech. So then the great population movements in the wake of the Industrial Revolution began a process of dialect levelling, which was accelerated by the resettlement of displaced populations in the aftermath of the Second World War. The new colloquial speech represents then the everyday speech of a majority of German-speakers in the twentieth-century, and has become regionally and socially diverse, with forms nearer to and further from standard, and with very noticeable regional variation (see Von Polenz 1978: 131–2). We might assume that modern communications would spread a uniform standard

German, but this is a speech form which many do not learn perfectly, and which even more do not wish to use in their informal conversation.

## 2.4 Currents of change in contemporary German

The various historical processes described in this chapter have not of course simply ceased to operate at the present; they continue. The slow and inexorable change in sounds and grammatical structures, to which any language is subject, and which cannot necessarily be traced to external influences, continues unabated.

Of the types of change which can be clearly related to external social and political factors, and whose operation is clear today, we can cite

(1)   the influence of German on other languages
(2)   the influence of other languages on German
(3)   the influence of standard German on non-standard varieties

### 2.4.1 The influence of German on other languages

Since the German-speaking states of central Europe have lost their dominant position in the aftermath of the two world wars, German no longer exerts the same influence as it did on neighbouring standard languages. However, the status of the Federal Republic as a major economic power is reflected in learned loans into other languages to describe economic and also political phenomena observed in Germany, such as *Wirtschaftswunder* and *Ostpolitik* in English.

Where German remains as a minority language, it may still exert an influence on regional varieties of neighbouring languages, for example on the local Italian variety in South Tyrol or on the local French variety in Alsace.

Where German, or the closely related Yiddish, have been the languages of a large immigrant population, as in the United States, they may have influenced the major language. This is quite noticeable in American English, which has acquired the words 'guidelines', a loan translation of German *Richtlinien*, and 'hopefully' in the sense of 'it is to be hoped that . . .' as a loan-translation of German *hoffentlich* in such sentences as 'Hopefully he'll be here soon.' This type of construction has recently passed from American English into British English where it was unknown twenty-five years ago.

German does, of course, continue to exert a strong influence on the minority languages within the German-speaking countries, all of which are threatened, in varying degrees, with extinction. The most threatened, apart from the virtually extinct East Frisian, is North Frisian, partly because of its extreme internal diversity, partly because it is not the focus of a clearly non-German nationality. Sorbian is perhaps the least threatened, given its very clear distinctness from German, and the strong support which it enjoys in the GDR.

### 2.4.2 German influenced by other languages

The Federal Republic of Germany is firmly in the political, cultural and economic orbit of the United States, which is also economically and culturally very important in the politically neutral Austria and Switzerland, and in these states English, particularly American English, has replaced French as the major foreign language representing power and prestige. Words are still borrowed from French, and learned borrowings are still coined from Latin and Greek roots, but the major source of new vocabulary in modern German is English (see Von Polenz 1978: 139–48). This influence is also carried through broadcasting and personal contacts into the German of the GDR; and of course even in the eastern bloc English is a major language of learning. The influence of English on German is discussed in 8.6.

Not surprisingly, Russian exerts an influence on the German of the GDR, but this influence is noticeably less than that of English in the West; Russian is important in economic, scientific and political thinking in the GDR, but it does not dominate the popular culture as does American English in the West. Some of this Russian influence has percolated through to the West. Specific characteristics of German in the GDR are discussed in 5.7.

### 2.4.3 The influence of standard German on other varieties

Within German the persistent influence of the standard language on other forms of the language results in the modern pattern of variation, which is the subject of Chapter 5, and so need not detain us here. It is not, as might possibly be assumed, levelling the language into an entirely uniform speech form: individuals and groups constantly assert their particular character by retaining local and social peculiarities within what is a generally convergent set of varieties.

### Further reading

Detailed accounts in English of the history of German are Wells (1985) and Keller (1978). Lockwood (1976) has less purely linguistic detail, but takes some account of social and political factors. There are a number of histories of the language in German; a fairly short and readable one, which refers to the social and political background, is Von Polenz (1978).

# 3  The German tradition of dialectology

## 3.1  Definitions and the object of study

We have already seen in Chapter 1 that one of the most fundamental problems in studying any language variety is knowing what to look for: if, for example, we want to study 'German', how do we decide what data or what speech forms are relevant? Perhaps the only sensible conclusion is that there is no right answer to such questions and that the only important thing is for the researchers to identify explicitly what they understand by the object of study. In practice, however, this is often taken for granted and the result may be that two researchers disagree only because, without realizing it, they are talking about different things.

The need for clarity is particularly well illustrated by the use of the concept 'dialect', which has not only varied considerably in the course of time but continues to vary from country to country and from language to language, and even from speaker to speaker (Mattheier 1983b). On the one hand, for example, before the Greek term was adopted by modern European languages from around the mid-sixteenth century, they all had their own terms for designating 'regional speech', such as *lantsprache* in German or *patte* in French. However, the adoption of the term 'dialect' did not mean that it was used as a label for the same phenomenon in each language.

In German, the term **Mundart** is sometimes used to mean the dialect of a small area (typically a village and the surrounding countryside) and **Dialekt** to mean a group of *Mundarten* sharing certain characteristics and covering a wider area; however, this distinction is not clearly maintained in practice and indeed the terms are often synonymous. On the other hand, while both *Dialekt* and *Mundart* refer to spoken varieties,[1] in French the distinction is made between semi-standardized written *dialectes* and spoken *patois*. Furthermore, when used in reference to

---

[1] Although, as Knoop (1982: 2) points out, it is not always clear what distinctions were originally made between these terms, and indeed there are references to *Schreibdialekte* (written dialects).

English, dialect now typically incorporates not only regional but also social connotations and is generally understood to mean 'any non-standard variety'; indeed, some linguists use the term synonymously with 'variety' and talk of both standard and non-standard dialects. In German, *Dialekt* is still understood by most linguists strictly as a spatially defined speech form (see Chapter 5).

On the other hand, of course, names for language varieties are not used exclusively by academics, and the actual speakers of a language may not agree with them on the appropriate choice of label. Dialectologists might call the normal spoken varieties in, say, Schleswig-Holstein, Switzerland, Alsace and Bavaria *Dialekt*, but while speakers in all these areas might accept this, some might prefer another term (for example, **Platt** is the normal colloquial term for Low and Middle German varieties), while others might not consider it dignified enough (the Swiss, for instance, generally consider Swiss German a language in its own right: see Chapter 7).

So in order to avoid confusion and misunderstanding at least in the academic discussion of language varieties, it might seem desirable to find a universally valid definition of the term 'dialect'. However, not only does this turn out to be beset with virtually insurmountable problems (see Hudson 1980: 21–72), but even a definition that will hold in general for varieties of a single language proves to be elusive. For example, starting from the assumption that *Dialekt* cannot be defined in its own terms but only in relation to the standard, Löffler (1980: 3–10) considers a range of criteria that might be applied to distinguish all German dialects on the one hand from standard German on the other; all of them are problematic to some extent.

One possibility, for example, might be to apply strictly linguistic criteria and define dialect as a 'defective version of the standard', but it could then be argued that the grammatical and lexical potential of all varieties is equal, even if in reality more limited demands are made of dialects. Alternatively, we could distinguish between varieties in terms of the domains in which they are used or of the social rôle/status of those who speak them. But while there are some domains in which *Dialekt* would rarely be used, at least in the Federal Republic and the GDR (e.g. in parliamentary debates or court proceedings), there are many domains in which *Dialekt*, standard or some form of colloquial speech (see Chapter 5) are all possible; and in some of the southern parts of German-speaking Europe *Dialekt* is not necessarily associated with any particular social class or grouping. Other criteria include historical development, geographical location and communicative range but although some are more

56

promising than others, none brings us any closer to a watertight definition.

This search for a (quasi-) universal definition is ultimately bound to be fruitless, not only because of a lack of suitable criteria but because the very attempt must fail to take account of the fact that both language itself and our perception of it are subject to change and are rooted in a complex process of socio-historical development (Mattheier 1983b: 138; see also Alinei 1980). It is not possible to abstract a notion such as dialect from this process but rather it must be defined in terms of a particular time and a particular social and political configuration. For this reason, it is more appropriate to specify the object of a particular study rather than attempt to operate with universal categories. In practice, a more pragmatic attitude tends to be taken, which is that 'a dialect is what the researcher wants it to be', and in most studies in German dialectology this has meant the most localized varieties with the most striking distinctions from the standard and that we refer to here as traditional dialects (see Chapter 5).

Studies of any kind are rarely unique but form instead part of a tradition that builds on a set of common assumptions. Our main concern in this book is to see what the modern tradition of sociolinguistics can reveal about the structure and use of contemporary German, but to understand the full significance of these insights we need to set them in the context of the much older tradition of dialectology. In this chapter, therefore, we shall look at the development of this earlier tradition (which has by no means been supplanted by the more recent one) and examine its findings.

## 3.2 Interests in dialect study

### 3.2.1 Attitudes to dialect variation

Interest in dialects in Germany goes back to the Middle Ages, centuries before they were subjected to serious study. In 1300, for example, Hugo von Trimberg characterized the predominant features of various regional speech forms in his poem *Der Renner*:

| | |
|---|---|
| Swâben ir wörter spaltent | Swabians split their words up |
| Die Franken ein teil si valtent | The Franks run them together |
| Die Baire si zerzerrent | The Bavarians tear them to pieces |
| Die Düringe si ûf sperrent | The Thuringians open them out |
| Die Sachsen si bezückent | The Saxons cut them short |
| Die Rînliute si verdrückent | The Rhinelanders suppress them |
| Die Wetereiher si würgent | The Wetterau speakers throttle them |

| Die Misner si wol schürgent | The Meissen speakers emphasize them strongly |
| Egerlant si swenkent | Eger speakers say them with a sing-song voice |
| Oesterrîche si schrenkent | Austrians weave them together |
| Stîrlant sî baz lenkent | Styrians speak them with a rising tone |
| Kernte ein teil si senkent | Carinthians speak them with a falling tone |

Since then, writers as diverse as Luther, Leibniz and Goethe have addressed the question of dialect variation. Then as now, attitudes to this diversity in language varied. Well before the development of a supra-regional standard, an element of social evaluation was attached to language variation: dialect was associated with the peasantry and shared its negative prestige in the eyes of the rest of German society. This negative evaluation was reinforced by the growing search in the eighteenth century for a uniform variety, both for intellectual reasons and for reasons of social status. On the other hand, writers such as Herder and Leibniz saw a more positive value in the rich diversity of German dialects; and for Goethe, who was confronted with a very different variety of German when he moved from Frankfurt to Weimar, dialect made an important contribution to the sense of regional identity in the as yet still not united Germany.

But as these remarks suggest, interest in dialect has not been (and is still not) always of the same type. Later in this chapter (3.3), we shall return to the development of that type of academic interest that led to the emergence of dialectology as a discipline, but first we might briefly consider what other types of interest there are.

## 3.2.2 Types of interest

As Mattheier (1983b: 147–8) points out, the various types of interest in dialects can be subsumed under the headings 'academic' and 'non-academic', although the so-called dialect renaissance of the last twenty years has led to a certain overlap. The formal academic study of dialects was motivated originally by a number of different interests, only some of which lie behind contemporary dialectology. One early, entirely negative interest was touched on above: a principal aim of the Language Societies (*Sprachgesellschaften*) in the seventeenth century was to establish a uniform written and spoken variety at the expense of regional dialects, which were not in themselves considered worthy of study except in order to distinguish them from the emerging standard variety. This 'normative' interest (Löffler 1980: 12) was subsequently countered by surges of more positive interest in the eighteenth and nineteenth centuries, based first on fears of a loss of regional identity and later, especially in the Romantic period, on a positive re-evaluation of rural life and on renewed interest in the tradition of folk culture. This tension between 'normalization' and diversification has not been resolved but has tended to recur periodically and is at the heart of the educational debate discussed in Chapter 6.

As we pointed out earlier (see 2.3.2), the standardized form of High German emerging in the sixteenth century was, for political and commercial reasons, most readily adopted in north Germany both in its written and its spoken forms. Almost inevitably, these varieties began to supplant the corresponding Low German forms and this gave rise to attempts to preserve Low German at least as a museum piece, to maintain the link with the more prestigious days of the Hanseatic League (Knoop 1982: 6). This 'antiquarian' interest (Löffler 1980: 15) is also still alive today, with the continued publication of local dictionaries and grammars. The more strictly linguistic interest in actually studying dialects for their own sake developed after their partial 'rehabilitation' in the nineteenth century, when the first serious attempts were made to collect and record dialect samples. The other main academic motivation at this time lay in the attempt to reconstruct the cultural and ethnic development and the settlement history of the 'German people'. At the same time, as we shall see, the discipline of human geography was to make an important contribution to the methodology of dialect study.

Non-academic interests in dialect are if anything even more varied. Many dialects do have written forms, even if the orthography is not standardized, and the growing use of dialect in various forms of popular culture, from poetry to rock music, has been one of the most striking expressions of the resurgence of the regionalist tendency in public and private life over the last twenty years. We have already mentioned the crucial area of education, where the general public interest is concerned with language policy rather than the academic question of the relationship between dialect and standard. Other sociopolitical issues include the use of dialect in advertising, the social evaluation of individuals on the basis of their speech and the use of language in institutionalized situations such as in court proceedings and in doctor–patient interviews. All of these questions are of course open to, and are indeed frequently the subject of, academic study, but the linguistic insights are secondary to the social and political questions of which they are just one aspect.

## 3.3 Background to the development of German dialectology

It is widely acknowledged that the development of that branch of dialectology known as 'dialect geography' owes much to the pioneering work on German dialects conducted by Georg Wenker and his associates in Marburg in the last quarter of the nineteenth century, and we shall devote the next section to this so-called Marburg School. However, serious interest in the study of dialects had been growing for some considerable time and important work on dialect, without which Wenker would probably not have embarked on his research in the first place, had been published in the earlier years of the century. Indeed, grammars of German dialects had been written as early as the sixteenth century, but the real turning point in terms of academic interest came with the positive re-evaluation of dialects and the rural lifestyle associated with them, and with the increasing mobility and more widespread communications, of the eighteenth and early nineteenth centuries. So despite the gradual emergence and acceptance of a standardized variety, dialects were not suppressed and indeed many writers argued strongly that dialects still had an important contribution to make to the richness and variety of German both in their own right and in their input to the standardized form.

The first publications to result from this new-found interest in dialects were the so-called *Idiotika*, or dictionaries of words and idioms peculiar to specific towns and villages. The real beginning of academic dialectology, however, is marked by the appearance in 1821 of Johann Andreas Schmeller's Bavarian grammar. This work represented a major advance in several respects. Firstly, it incorporated not only lexical but also phonological and morphological factors; secondly, it acknowledged the importance of both historical and social dimensions and the existence of internal variation; and thirdly, much of the material was drawn from Schmeller's first-hand experience rather than from published sources and data supplied indirectly by others.

A further crucial aspect of Schmeller's work in general is his consistent perspective on individual dialects in relation to the 'common' or standard language (*Gesammtsprache*) (Knoop 1982: 14). This is an important theoretical point of view that accords with the 'unitary' conception of language held by perhaps the best-known German linguistic scholars of the time, Wilhelm von Humboldt and Jacob Grimm. For them, language was a single organism, so that there was no theoretical justification for distinguishing in terms of importance or typologically between dialects and standard. According to this view then, variation is an essential element of a linguistic system, although the main interest at that time was in **diachronic**, or historical, variation: thus, Grimm's famous German grammar, published between 1819 and 1837 and itself a milestone in the study of German, was not a synchronic account of the contemporary language but a historical analysis that inevitably drew on dialects as a major source.

Schmeller's work paved the way for many other systematic treatments of local dialects. The development of this proto-dialectology continued through the following decades and culminated, in 1876, in the publication of Jost Winteler's local grammar (*Ortsgrammatik*) of Kerenz in Switzerland, which laid the foundations for dialectology as it has been pursued in Germany ever since. The same year also marked a further significant event: Georg Wenker started work on what was to become the Linguistic Atlas of German (*Deutscher Sprachatlas*), the first attempt to transcend the study of individual dialects and to re-appraise the theoretical basis of dialect study. As the monumental work of Wenker and his followers had the most profound influence on German dialectology, and as dialect geography is for our purposes perhaps the most relevant branch of the discipline, we shall turn next to the development of the Marburg School.

## 3.4 Dialect geography: the Marburg School

Dialect geography is that branch of dialectology which is concerned primarily with the relationship between language and place. Not surprisingly, therefore, many of its techniques are borrowed from human geography, the most obvious of which is the presentation of findings in the form of maps. However, there are other forms of presentation (e.g. local grammars, dialect dictionaries, text samples), as well as a variety of ways of collecting and evaluating or processing raw linguistic data. What distinguishes one 'school' or approach from another, then, is principally a question of methodology, and the methods associated with the Marburg School have acquired a kind of classical status within German dialectology.

Data collection in dialectology presents a series of problems. What kind of data should you collect (phonological, morphological, lexical etc.)? How do you ensure that the data from any one location is genuinely representative of that place? How do you select informants? How do you get informants to produce the data you are interested in? How do you record the data?; and so on. Most of these problems are empirical questions, that is to say, they are concerned with practical issues and fieldwork procedures, rather than with theoretical matters such as providing explanations for the linguistic make-up of a given place. This is an important point because although, as we shall see in the next section, followers of the Marburg School did attempt to explain linguistic patterns, its major contribution to the study of dialects was on the pre-theoretical levels of data collection and presentation. It is also important, however, not to underestimate this contribution, for although this traditional approach is now often dismissed as 'merely taxonomic', the material compiled in Marburg constitutes a vast database for more theoretical research.

This indeed was Wenker's primary motivation in launching his ambitious programme of data collection. It is often maintained that his intention was to gather empirical support for the so-called '**neogrammarian hypothesis**', according to which all sound changes are rule-governed and operate in a uniform and absolute manner (see e.g. Löffler 1980: 27 and Chambers and Trudgill 1980: 37). In fact, there is no evidence for this assertion and indeed Wenker was probably aware before he started his research that the hypothesis was not valid. His real concern was to construct an accurate linguistic map of Germany, as he felt that the existing data were inadequate (Knoop *et al.* 1982: 46–7, 51). In order to achieve this aim, Wenker embarked on a scheme of astonishing proportions, given the limited resources at his disposal: between 1876 and 1895 he sent out questionnaires to places throughout Germany, 48,500 of which were completed and returned. The data contained in these questionnaires were then painstakingly transcribed onto maps, which were ultimately to be published as the *Deutscher Sprachatlas*: in fact, the first map in this series was not published until 1926 and a total of 129 were published between then and 1956.

Although his research was not concerned with the neogrammarian hypothesis, Wenker was primarily interested in phonological (and to some extent morphological) patterns: his survey did produce data on lexical differences but this was initially only a by-product and work on a German Word Atlas did not begin until 1939. His questionnaire was modified several times in the course of the survey, which was first carried out in the Rhineland, then throughout north and central Germany and finally in the south, but the basic pattern remained the same: informants were given a set of about forty sentences in standard German (see Fig. 3.1) and asked to give the equivalent in their dialect; later they were also given a list of individual words. The choice of an 'indirect' method of data collection (as opposed to direct methods such as face-to-face interviews) was clearly imposed by the scale of the survey; however, it is also clear that this method has serious drawbacks.

Firstly, even though it allowed comprehensive coverage of the whole country, it still set out to gather only a single response from each locality; therefore, if the results are to have any validity it must be shown that each response can be considered representative of the speech of the place concerned. Wenker and his associates worked on the assumption that by asking local schoolteachers to fill in the questionnaire, they could obtain a reasonably reliable picture, but even if the language of a given village was indeed largely homogeneous, a considerable burden was placed on these schoolteacher informants-cum-intermediaries. For example, those who were natives of the village would presumably be better equipped to give an

1. Im Winter fliegen die trocknen Blätter in der Luft herum. — 2. Es hört gleich auf zu schneien, dann wird das Wetter wieder besser. — 3. Tu Kohlen in den Ofen, daß die Milch bald an zu kochen fängt. — 4. Der gute alte Mann ist mit dem Pferde durchs Eis gebrochen und in das kalte Wasser gefallen. — 5. Er ist vor vier oder sechs Wochen gestorben. — 6. Das Feuer war zu stark, die Kuchen sind ja unten ganz schwarz gebrannt. — 7. Er ißt die Eier immer ohne Salz und Pfeffer. — 8. Die Füße tun mir sehr weh, ich glaube, ich habe sie durchgelaufen. — 9. Ich bin bei der Frau gewesen und habe es ihr gesagt, und sie sagte, sie wollte es auch ihrer Tochter sagen.—10. Ich will es auch nicht mehr wieder tun! — 11. Ich schlage dich gleich mit dem Kochlöffel um die Ohren, du Affe! — 12. Wo gehst du hin, sollen wir mit dir gehen? — 13. Es sind schlechte Zeiten! — 14. Mein liebes Kind, bleib hier unten stehen, die bösen Gänse beißen dich tot. — 15. Du hast heute am meisten gelernt und bist artig gewesen, du darfst früher nach Hause gehen als die andern. — 16. Du bist noch nicht groß genug, um eine Flasche Wein auszutrinken, du mußt erst noch etwas wachsen und größer werden. — 17. Geh, sei so gut und sag deiner Schwester, sie sollte die Kleider für eure Mutter fertig nähen und mit der Bürste rein machen. — 18. Hättest du ihn gekannt! dann wäre es anders gekommen, und es täte besser um ihn stehen. — 19. Wer hat mir meinen Korb mit Fleisch gestohlen? — 20. Er tat so, als hätten sie ihn zum Dreschen bestellt; sie haben es aber selbst getan. — 21. Wem hat er die neue Geschichte erzählt? — 22. Man muß laut schreien, sonst versteht er uns nicht. — 23. Wir sind müde und haben Durst. — 24. Als wir gestern Abend zurück kamen, da lagen die andern schon zu Bett und waren fest am Schlafen. — 25. Der Schnee ist diese Nacht bei uns liegen geblieben, aber heute Morgen ist er geschmolzen. — 26. Hinter unserem Hause stehen drei schöne Apfelbäumchen mit roten Äpfelchen. — 27. Könnt ihr nicht noch ein Augenblickchen auf uns warten, dann gehen wir mit euch. — 28. Ihr dürft nicht solche Kindereien treiben. — 29. Unsere Berge sind nicht sehr hoch, die euren sind viel höher. — 30. Wieviel Pfund Wurst und wieviel Brot wollt ihr haben? — 31. Ich verstehe euch nicht, ihr müßt ein bißchen lauter sprechen. — 32. Habt ihr kein Stückchen weiße Seife für mich auf meinem Tische gefunden? — 33. Sein Bruder will sich zwei schöne neue Häuser in eurem Garten bauen. — 34. Das Wort kam ihm vom Herzen! — 35. Das war recht von ihnen! — 36. Was sitzen da für Vögelchen oben auf dem Mäuerchen? — 37. Die Bauern hatten fünf Ochsen und neun Kühe und zwölf Schäfchen vor das Dorf gebracht, die wollten sie verkaufen. — 38. Die Leute sind heute alle draußen auf dem Felde und mähen. — 39. Geh nur, der braune Hund tut dir nichts. — 40. Ich bin mit den Leuten da hinten über die Wiese ins Korn gefahren.

Fig. 3.1 Wenker's forty sentences

accurate response than those who had grown up elsewhere. But a more fundamental problem was that in the absence of modern technology, these untrained fieldworkers were obliged to record their responses in writing and they were given only rudimentary advice on transcription. For a survey on vocabulary, this need not present serious obstacles, but there is clearly room for considerable discrepancy when sounds are under investigation.

To return to the question of uniformity, however, two distinct problems were overlooked by the survey. Firstly, even at a time when the population was predominantly distributed through small, stable, rural communities, it is unlikely that there was not at least some degree of linguistic variation associated with social status or identification; and secondly, it is normal even in socially highly homogeneous communities for individual speakers to possess a stylistic repertoire (see 1.1.2) that enables them to vary their speech according to their perception of the context (their relationship with the person they are talking to, the topic under discussion, the specific location, etc.). Wenker was certainly aware of social differences reflected in speech, as notes to his informants show, in which he suggests that they obtain several versions in larger towns, especially from different sections of the population (Knoop *et al*. 1982: 67). However, as his real interest lay in the most extreme forms of what we are calling 'traditional dialects', social variation was not taken into account in the survey. On the other hand, the chosen means of elicitation was by no means best suited to obtain the highest degree of 'dialectality', as there is an essential paradox in the belief that you can elicit the most natural forms of speech by a method that explicitly draws attention to different ways of saying the same thing. Even the objection that it was not the speakers themselves who were consulted but 'inside observers' (the schoolteachers) does not dispel doubts as to the accuracy of the data.

Despite our misgivings about Wenker's methods of data collection, it was not this aspect of his research that was most criticized by his contemporaries but rather the manner in which the findings were processed and presented. From the raw data, in the form of completed questionnaires, information covering a whole range of phonological and morphological features was extracted and transferred, item by item, to maps of Germany. For example, one map would display all the reported instances of /pf/ or /p/ in the middle of a word such as *Apfel/Appel* (apple). The main criticisms levelled at these 'display' maps were that they were excessively detailed and that they failed to distinguish the relative importance of different features (Knoop *et al*. 1982: 63; see also Chambers and Trudgill 1980: 28–33).

In a sense, the project was a victim of its own success, as the sheer volume of data proved virtually unmanageable and the very attempt to conduct research that was unprecedented in its thoroughness and exhaustive coverage threatened to undermine the value of the enterprise. Indeed, Wenker and his team became increasingly modest in their aims as time went on. The original ambition to construct an authoritative dialect map of Germany was eventually superseded by the more limited and realistic objective of producing materials that could serve as the instruments of research rather than purporting to be finished research products. To this extent, the modern tendency to dismiss this pioneering work as mere 'butterfly collecting' is misguided, as any research must be judged in terms of its stated aims (cf. the discussion in Chambers and Trudgill 1980: 17).

It was Wenker's pupil and successor, Ferdinand Wrede, who coined the term 'social-linguistic' (*soziallinguistisch*) in relation to the work of the Marburg team (see Niebaum 1983: 32) and by this he meant the attempt to build on the descriptive foundations laid by the empirical work by interpreting and explaining its results. This is the point at which dialectology can make a contribution to our understanding of language variation and language change, and perhaps of the relationship between language and society. In the next section, we shall look at the emergence of German dialectology as an explanatory discipline and conclude the background part of this chapter with a discussion of why explanations in traditional dialectology are not 'sociolinguistic' as we understand the term.

## 3.5 Explanations in traditional dialectology

### 3.5.1 Interpreting data

In the previous section, we touched on the problem of excessive detail in dialect maps. While it is important to have access to all the available data, it is not essential for each individual item to be displayed, and indeed the clutter of a typical display map is more likely to obscure than to reveal the really significant information. For example, in the survey for the German Word Atlas, three words (or variants of them) were commonly given for 'Saturday': *Samstag, Sonnabend* and *Saterstag*. If each response were to be marked on a map, whether by means of a symbol or the word itself, the result could be confusing, as the use of each word is not strictly confined to a given territory. However, if we broadly mark out those areas in which each word is most commonly used and indicate this just once, as in Map 3.1, a very clear pattern emerges. What this amounts to is an interpretation of the data, which is of course selective and therefore subjective: it is

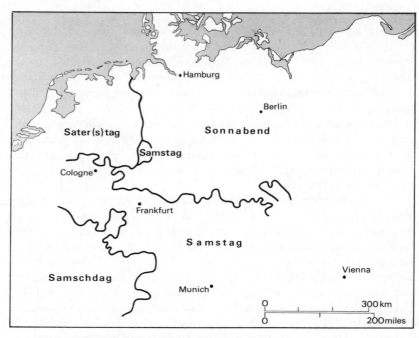

Map 3.1 'Saturday' in traditional German dialects
Source: Adapted from *Atlas zur deutschen Sprache* (König 1978): 186

theoretically possible to draw several quite different interpretive maps based on the same display map. As long as the original, undifferentiated data can be consulted, this does not matter and in fact this interpretation is the first essential step from the specific to the general, and from the descriptive to the explanatory. The data we collect become interesting only if we can make such generalizations, for if every piece of data was unique no patterns would emerge and we would be left with a chaotic picture of language use that would provide no clues to help explain how communication is possible or how language evolves.

In order to represent these generalizations on a map, the standard procedure in dialect geography has been to demarcate those areas in which one variant of a given feature is most typically used by means of lines known as **isoglosses**. These lines are often compared to isobars on a weather map and indeed their function is very similar, but we could also compare them more loosely with the contour lines on a physical map: isoglosses bear no necessary relationship with any physical features of the territory onto which they are plotted (although, as we shall see, they sometimes do), but like contour lines they give shape to a map and it therefore seems quite reasonable to talk of 'linguistic landscapes'. And just as it is true that, although no valley is quite like any other, we can identify certain types of valley, so it is possible to make out certain shapes or patterns in linguistic landscapes that recur again and again.

It is this that dialect geographers seek to explain or, more specifically, they attempt to answer such questions as: why are the boundaries where they are? Do the shapes of linguistic landscapes represent only the pattern of synchronic differences between one area and another or do they also indicate a continuous process of change? If the latter is the case, in which direction are which features moving and why? (Cf. Löffler 1980: 150–4.) Dialectologists have taken two main approaches to these problems, attempting to explain the patterns they find in terms either of extralinguistic influences or of internal structural processes in the language itself, and we shall now take a brief look at each of these approaches in turn.

### 3.5.2 The extralinguistic approach

The extralinguistic approach to the explanation of linguistic landscapes has by no means been abandoned but it dominated this aspect of dialectology only until the mid-twentieth century. One of the main reasons for its popularity in the late nineteenth and early twentieth centuries was that it supported and contributed to a particular view of cultural history, in which the notion of space or territory played a major part. But while the names of traditional British English dialects derive from the geographical area in which they are spoken (e.g. Yorkshire, Devon, Tyneside dialect), many of their German counterparts are named after the tribes who settled in the areas concerned (e.g. Alemannic, Franconian, Saxon dialects). The significance of this in the present context is that language can be seen as one factor among many in the formation of a 'cultural territory' (*Kulturraum*); it is, in other words, a badge or emblem both of geographical location and of cultural or ethnic identity. If it could be shown that dialect boundaries coincide with boundaries historically associated with settlement patterns, so it was argued, this would constitute strong evidence in favour of this theory of cultural development.

However, there is clearly a risk of circularity in this kind of argument, for it would be difficult to establish whether linguistic boundaries were determined by social and political ones or the other way round. This assumption also begs the question as to how we can know where to draw dialect boundaries in the first place. The traditional answer is that it seems reasonable to suppose that one dialect stops and another one starts at a point where a substantial number of isoglosses overlap. The most famous example of such a 'bundle' of isoglosses is the so-called Benrath Line, which is taken to separate Low German dialects, as a group, from High German ones; but even this classic example is no longer considered as significant as it once was (see 2.1.3 and 3.6). As a procedure for determining boundaries between individual dialects, this is an arbitrary and necessarily imprecise approach, and maps such as Map 3.4 are really little more than a convenient fiction. In general it is much more a matter of individual judgement as to what constitutes a sufficiently significant bundle of isoglosses for it to be considered a dialect boundary, and anyway there is never any such thing as a precise boundary between one dialect and another.

There are other drawbacks to this method of interpretation but there is no doubt that many individual isoglosses coincide with both man-made boundaries (marking, for example, administrative districts, principalities or dioceses) and to a lesser extent natural ones (such as rivers or mountain ranges) and there appear to be too many instances of this for it to be dismissed as the result of chance. More substantial support for the extralinguistic approach, however, comes from the recurrent shapes of linguistic landscapes that we referred to in the previous section. The most common patterns are shown in abstract form in Fig. 3.2. What these patterns have in common is that they open up the possibility of interpreting an apparently static picture as a frozen moment in a dynamic process, like a single frame in a movie. In other words, each shape represents one step or stage in the progress of a linguistic innovation.[2] These shapes might then be interpreted in the following way:

(a) Form A is gradually replacing form B but instead of an abrupt change, there is a zone between those areas where only A or B is used in which both coexist. The prediction would then be that the A zone will continue its progress, preceded by a mixed A + B zone, with the B zone gradually diminishing.

(b) Either: forms A and C are simultaneously pushing forward into the territory occupied by form B;
or: form B is expanding into an area where no corresponding form exists (i.e. C = zero).

(c) Either: A is the older form, which has survived as a relic in one place while B has pushed forward around it;

---

[2] It is worth noting that this step or stage could be the final one: i.e. the innovation may go this far and no further.

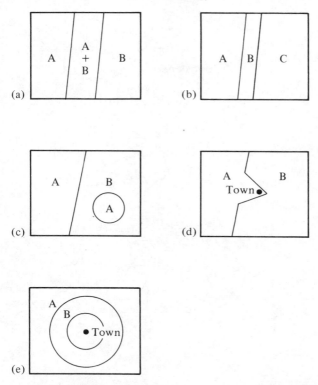

Fig. 3.2 Dialect geography: patterns of linguistic change
Source: Based on Goossens 1977

or: A is the new form, which has already been adopted in one place within 'B territory', ahead of the general advance.

(d) Probably a variant of (c), with again either A making faster progress at one point than elsewhere or B being resisted more strongly at that point.

(e) Both A and B are new forms which are spreading out from a single point in a kind of wave formation; of the two, B is the more recent innovation.

One of the most interesting aspects of this kind of interpretation from our point of view is the central rôle accorded to towns as centres of influence. More often than not it is urban centres that account for patterns (c), (d) and (e) on dialect maps of Germany and traditional

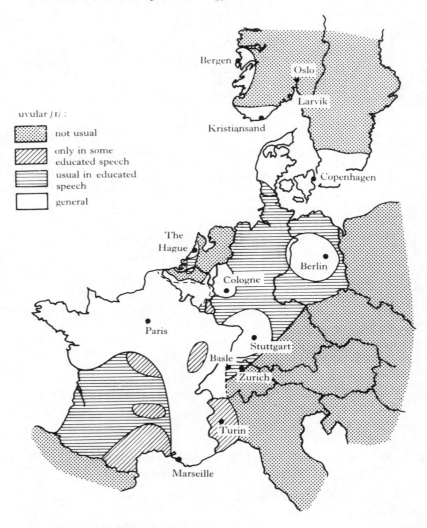

uvular /r/ :

- not usual
- only in some educated speech
- usual in educated speech
- general

Bergen

Oslo

Larvik

Kristiansand

Copenhagen

The Hague

Berlin

Cologne

Paris

Stuttgart

Basle

Zurich

Turin

Marseille

Map 3.2 The spread of uvular /r/
Source: Chambers and Trudgill 1980

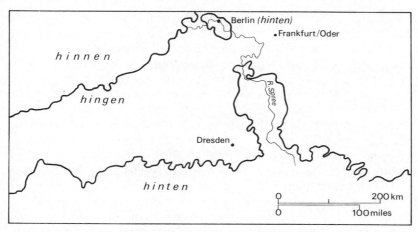

Map 3.3 Variants of *hinten* in East Middle German
Source: Based on Frings 1956

dialectologists clearly recognized their importance: Bach (1969), for example, points out that Cologne has 'attracted' southern forms for centuries and that conversely some northern forms as yet unknown in the surrounding rural areas could be identified in the speech of certain social groups in Stuttgart. If we examine the progress of the **uvular** or throaty /r/, displacing the older tongue-tip pronunciation, we can see that it began in France and spread eastwards and northwards across Switzerland, the Low Countries and Germany to Scandinavia (see Map 3.2). However, the progress of this form has not been a steady, unidirectional advance but rather a combination of patterns (c) and (e) in Fig. 3.2. That is to say, the innovation has tended to jump from town to town, ahead of the general trend, and then to spread outwards into smaller towns and the surrounding countryside. As the map shows, Stuttgart, Cologne and Berlin have been in the vanguard of this change. Berlin in particular is commonly cited as a good example of the crucial rôle of towns and cities in the dissemination of innovations.

Map 3.3 shows the northerly advance of the southern form *hinten* (behind), replacing the northern form *hingen*. In a combination of patterns (c) and (d), the new form is advancing most rapidly up the valley of the river Spree and has indeed already jumped ahead by being adopted in Berlin: the result is a kind of 'push–pull' effect, which is likely to encourage and exaggerate the basic trend. Evidence such as this provides strong support for the extralinguistic approach and it is easy to see why it

71

is still considered revealing. At the same time, this approach has its limitations. Firstly, it is not possible to explain all such phenomena by reference to the extralinguistic context, and even where this method can explain how and why linguistic forms spread, it cannot necessarily account for the emergence of new forms in the first place. Secondly, only those extralinguistic factors which relate to geographical space can be taken into account in this model: there is no room for social or stylistic factors. And thirdly, although the importance of towns is fully acknowledged in terms of their function as agents of change, the very emphasis on the rather vaguely conceived 'intermediary' rôle of towns themselves obscures the relevance and interest of urban speech varieties in their own right. This latter point will form the substance of later chapters (see especially Chapter 4) and we shall return to the second objection in section 3.5.4 below. Firstly, however, we shall turn briefly to the alternative, linguistic, method of explanation in traditional dialectology.

### 3.5.3 The linguistic approach

By contrast with the extralinguistic approach, the linguistic method seeks explanation within the framework of the language itself and it is founded on the assumption that there is an inherent tendency in any language variety to function as efficiently as possible. Efficiency in this context can be measured in terms of how economical the variety is to use, i.e. the extent to which it conforms to the principle of 'least effort'. For example, if the vocabulary of a variety has only one word to designate all domestic animals, it is highly inefficient, for instead of being able to distinguish between dogs and cats by the choice of two single words, we would have to use the generic word for 'domestic animal' for both and then qualify it with a series of distinctive features. The same could be said of a sound system that had, say, eight front vowels and just two back vowels, as the phonetic 'distance' between one front vowel and another would be very slight. This would make it difficult to distinguish between two words that were identical in form except that each had a different front vowel. An efficient sound system would typically have a fairly small number of clearly distinct sounds, so that the risk of confusing two similar-sounding words is minimized.

If this assumption about the nature of linguistic varieties is valid, then it follows that if the structure or economy of the variety (or one of its components) is weakened by the emergence of an anomaly, internal structural pressure will be exerted to correct the balance. Such a system is said to be 'homeopathic', as changes are generated within the system and are explicable in its own terms rather than by means of some external agency or influence. As an illustration, we can consider two lexical examples.

Between two adjacent areas (A and B), with partially different vocabularies, there may be a buffer or contact zone. Under these circumstances, one of two situations could arise:

(1)   If in A the word {a} is used to mean, say, 'bottle' and in B the word {b} is used to mean 'bottle', both {a} and {b} may be used with the same meaning in the contact zone;

(2)   If in A the word {x} is used to mean 'bottle' and in B the same word is used to mean 'jug', then {x} may be used with both meanings in the contact zone.

(1) is an example of **synonymy** (two words, one meaning), (2) is an example of **polysemy** (one word, two meanings). In either situation, the assumption would be that the system would react against any such inefficiency and there are indeed many examples where this has happened. In order to avoid synonymy, as in (1) above, a distinction might be introduced between words {a} and {b} in the contact zone, so that for example {a} means 'coloured bottle' and {b} means 'clear bottle'; to avoid polysemy, as in (2) above, the distinction between 'bottles' and 'jugs' might be dropped so that the word {x} is used with the superordinate meaning 'vessel or container for liquids'.

As we pointed out earlier, the extralinguistic approach owed its early popularity to its compatibility with a particular view of cultural history; the basic method of interpretation is to match up the data on an individual linguistic feature with corresponding non-linguistic features and linguistic change is explained by comparing real linguistic landscapes with a small set of abstract 'templates'. The linguistic approach, on the other hand, is based on assumptions about the system as a whole and individual changes are explained as adjustments to the overall structure. It is therefore essentially one aspect of a structuralist approach to dialectology and its emergence in the mid-twentieth century is not so much a sign that the older method had been superseded as that a new approach evolved in accordance with a prevailing trend in many fields of academic study.[3] As both the linguistic and the extralinguistic approach are capable of supplying satisfactory explanations for many of the phenomena that are revealed by the study of dialect, there is nothing to be gained by trying to demonstrate that one is in an absolute sense 'better' than the other: they both have their advantages and their limitations and it is probably best to say that they complement each other.

[3] For a good, concise account of structuralist and generative approaches to dialectology in general see Chambers and Trudgill (1980: Ch. 3).

**3.5.4** Explanations in dialectology and sociolinguistics

We shall see in the next chapter that recent studies in social dialectology or sociolinguistics differ from those in traditional dialectology on every level: collection, presentation and interpretation of data. However, it is worth pointing out already at this stage the crucial distinctions between these types of study on the level of interpretation, as the different understandings of 'explanation' are rooted in and reflect fundamentally different interests.

Social dialectologists or sociolinguists are interested, not exclusively but principally, in variation in and between speech forms, and their attempts to account for this variation typically incorporate both linguistic and extralinguistic factors. Which extralinguistic factors are taken into account will depend on the purpose of the study and the nature of the speech community under investigation, but they may include attributes of the speaker(s) (such as age, sex, social class, race), the relationship between the speakers and their addressee (not necessarily informant–researcher; it could be e.g. friend–friend, employer–employee or doctor–patient) or aspects of the speech situation (relative formality, public or private exchange, topic and so on). Regardless of whether we are talking about individuals or groups of speakers, these factors can be subsumed in the concept of 'social context', as they all relate to the conception of the speaker as a social being, and so sociolinguistic explanations of linguistic variation should provide insights both into the speech variety and into the speech community. In other words, they should supply answers to questions both on the nature and on the social function and the social meaning of linguistic variation.

Traditional dialectologists, on the other hand, are concerned with trying to establish differences between one speech variety and another and are interested in variation only on the margins of linguistically defined territories (cf. Goossens 1981: 304). For them, variation is not an inherent aspect of speech varieties (at least not of those they choose to study) but rather a peripheral and transitory phenomenon that is a symptom of change in progress. Furthermore, language is seen as an independent organism with a life of its own, so that individual speakers are of interest only as a source of linguistic data for a given location, as human reference books rather than as members of complex social groups or networks (cf. Löffler 1985: 143ff, 161). Therefore, explanations in traditional dialectology do not take account of human behaviour patterns or attribute social meaning to linguistic variation; they are intended as answers to questions on the geographical differentiation between related speech varieties and on the shape of linguistic landscapes.

Against this background on the methods of traditional dialectology, we should now go on to look at some of its findings, for despite the reservations expressed above, there is no doubt that they constitute an enormous fund of linguistic information and at the same time act as a yardstick for contemporary studies.

## 3.6 The contemporary relevance of the findings of traditional dialectology

Before proceeding to variation in colloquial German, that speech type or collection of speech types used by a majority of German-speakers today, we must first give careful consideration to traditional German dialects. It is important to do so for several reasons. Firstly, as we have seen above, the study of traditional dialects forms a very large part of linguistic study in German-speaking countries. Secondly, colloquial speech is in many respects, though not all, a sort of compromise between traditional dialects and the formal standard language; hence, some knowledge of traditional dialects is helpful for an understanding of the characteristics of colloquial speech. Thirdly, traditional dialects and colloquial speech are often not entirely separate entities; particularly in the Middle German dialect area (see Map 3.4), traditional dialects often form, with colloquial speech and formal standard German, a continuum, along a section of which speakers will shift, depending on situational factors. In the Low German and Upper German dialect areas speakers of traditional dialect are more likely to be diglossic, i.e. they will switch abruptly from their traditional dialect to some form of colloquial speech if they find themselves in a more formal situation, or speaking to people from outside their home area.

Given the scope of this book, our study of traditional dialects will not be particularly detailed. Detailed descriptions are listed under 'Further reading' at the end of the chapter.

In order to describe the great diversity of traditional dialect speech, we have to divide the German-speaking area up into different dialects. It might seem at first sight that this is a relatively straightforward matter: Map 3.4 shows the German-speaking area divided into separate dialect areas, some at least of which, for example *Schwäbisch* (Swabian), have names familiar to German-speakers, and linguistic characteristics which many speakers may recognize.

The position is, however, in reality a great deal more complex than this. In the first place, what is popularly recognized as the 'dialect' of a particular area may these days not be traditional dialect at all, but rather some form of colloquial speech, perhaps in some cases nothing more than colloquial standard German with regional accent.

More seriously, the dialect areas delineated on a map like Map 3.4 are

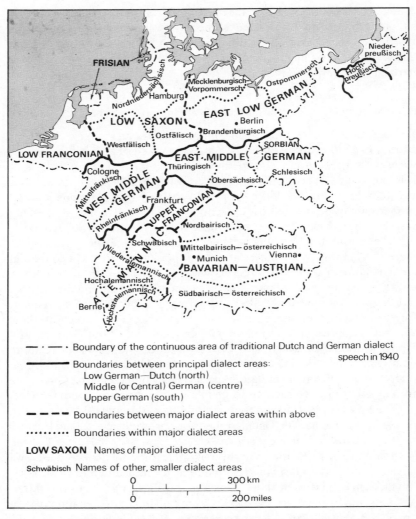

Map 3.4 Conventional divisions of the traditional German and Dutch dialects in the continuous German–Dutch-speaking area at its extent in 1940. (English names for dialects are given, except at the lowest level shown here, where they are not always in current use.)
Source: Adapted from *Atlas zur deutschen Sprache* (König 1978): 138

of highly arbitrary extent. Traditional dialects may vary considerably over very small distances, even from one village to the next. Do we therefore say that each village has a different dialect? This question is generally answered in the negative, but there is no agreement as to how many differences there must be between two speech forms before they are considered to be separate dialects, or roughly what size of area a dialect should cover.

Not only is it not clear how large a dialect area should be, it is also not at all clear how dialect boundaries should be determined. In reality the German-speaking area (like any other area where a related group of dialects has been spoken for several centuries) is criss-crossed by isoglosses (see above, 3.5.1) which proceed in all conceivable directions. Which of these isoglosses are chosen to separate dialect areas is to a considerable extent arbitrary, although it seems reasonable to locate major dialect boundaries where several isoglosses run roughly parallel to each other within a relatively narrow band. However, such bundles of isoglosses are never absolutely parallel, and the isoglosses for different features rarely coincide, so a particular isogloss of a bundle may be arbitrarily selected as the dialect boundary, or alternatively the boundary, while running in a certain general direction, may not be defined precisely. So, while a map such as 3.4 can serve as a basis for describing traditional German dialects, we should not lose sight of the fact that the dialect areas shown are far from homogeneous, and that the boundaries between them cannot usually be located as precisely as the map might suggest.

### 3.7 The dialect boundaries within German

A careful reading of Map 3.4 can show that the German dialects are conventionally divided up on at least three levels. Firstly there is the principal threefold division into (1) Low German dialects, or Low German and Dutch dialects (*Niederdeutsche Dialekte* or *Niederdeutsche und niederländische Dialekte*), (2) Middle (or Central) German dialects (*Mitteldeutsche Dialekte*) and (3) Upper German dialects (*Oberdeutsche Dialekte*), the last two divisions often being grouped together as High German dialects (*Hochdeutsche Dialekte*). High German (*Hochdeutsch*) in this sense is not to be confused with the popular use of the term to mean the (formal) standard language.

In traditional dialectology Dutch and German dialects are often treated together. This joint treatment of Dutch and German is not justified in most other types of linguistic study, the modern reality being the existence of two autonomous languages.

A small group of West Germanic dialects along the North Sea coast of

Schleswig-Holstein and the offshore islands, the North Frisian dialects (*Nordfriesische Dialekte*), is generally considered to represent a separate minority language, as is the tiny enclave of East Frisian speech in the Saterland in Oldenburg, and the larger group of West Frisian dialects in the province of Friesland in the Netherlands (see 2.1.3 and 2.2.2).[4]

At a second level, each of the principal divisions of German dialects is divided into major dialect areas. Within Upper German we find a threefold division into (1) Upper Franconian (*Oberfränkisch*), (2) Alemannic (*Alemannisch*) in the widest sense including Swabian (*Schwäbisch*), and (3) Bavarian or Bavarian–Austrian (*Bairisch* or *Bairisch–Österreichisch*). Within Middle German we find a twofold division into western and eastern dialect areas (*Westmitteldeutsch* and *Ostmitteldeutsch*) and within Low German–Dutch we find a threefold division into (1) Low Franconian (*Niederfränkisch*), (2) Low Saxon (*Niedersächsisch*) in the widest sense including Westphalian (*Westfälisch*) and (3) East Low German (*Ostniederdeutsch*).

At a third level these major dialect areas are often further divided; for example West Middle German can be divided into Middle Franconian (*Mittelfränkisch*) and Rhenish Franconian (*Rheinfränkisch*).

Beyond this, further divisions, not shown on Map 3.4, are of course possible: for example, Rhenish Franconian can be subdivided into *Hessisch* and *Pfälzisch*, and *Hessisch* in turn into *Niederhessisch–Osthessisch, Zentralhessisch* and *Südhessisch*, and so on down to the level of differences between individual villages.

While the principal division into Low, Middle and Upper German is relatively uncontroversial, many of the divisions at the lower levels are subject to differences of opinion between scholars. Even the Low German–Middle German–Upper German distinction is not necessarily as clear as it appears to be in most of the literature (see Wolf 1983: 1116–18).

### 3.8  The north–central–south division based on the High German sound shift

The division into Low, Middle and Upper German dialects is based upon the extent to which the second or High German sound shift operated in the precursors of the modern dialects (see 2.1.3). Map 3.5 shows the principal isoglosses crossing the German-speaking territory from east to west in the traditional dialects, which were produced by the differing

---

[4] Note that the dialects in the German North Sea coastal area known as East Friesland (*Ostfriesland*) are *not* Frisian dialects but Low Saxon dialects of Low German. This area was originally Frisian-speaking and there are traces of Frisian influence in the local Low Saxon dialects.

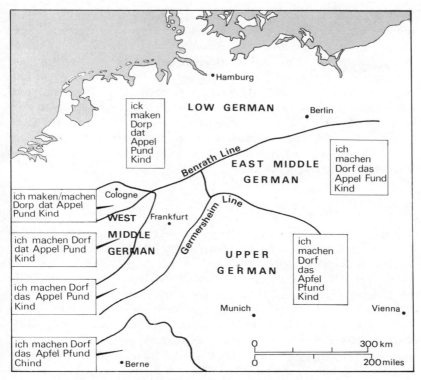

Map 3.5 The operation of the High German sound shift: typical forms of
common vocabulary items in traditional German dialects. Standard German
forms: *ich* (I); *machen* (make, do); *Dorf* (village); *das* (that, the); *Apfel* (apple);
*Pfund* (pound); *Kind* (child)
Source: Adapted from *Atlas zur deutschen Sprache* (König 1978): 64

operation of the sound shift in the West Germanic dialects. For each
principal east–west band of German-speaking territory typical forms of
common words in the inherited vocabulary are given.

### 3.8.1 Low German and Dutch dialects

In dialects north of the Benrath Line, which divides Low German from
Middle German, stop consonants /p/, /t/ and /k/ of those West Germanic
dialects which gave rise to modern German continue to be pronounced
(we believe) much as they were two thousand years ago in words which
have been part of everyday speech since that time. The consonants, /p/, /t/

and /k/ also retain their original pronunciation, at least in many circumstances, in West Germanic languages other than German. Hence English 'pound', 'ten' and 'make' correspond to typical Low German forms *Pund, tein* and *maken*[5] where High German dialects and standard German have forms such as *Pfund, zehn* and *machen*. In a small area around Düsseldorf, just to the north of Cologne, where the traditional dialect is clearly Low German, we nevertheless find the shift of /k/ to /ç/ in a small number of common monosyllabic words, such as *ich* (Low German *ick*). This shift continues north to a line leaving the Benrath Line to the east of Düsseldorf and crossing the Rhine at Ürdingen north of Düsseldorf (the Ürdingen Line).

### 3.8.2 Upper German dialects

Turning now to the south of the German-speaking area, we find that south of the Germersheim Line or the Speyer Line,[6] crossing the territory from east to west south of Frankfurt but north of Würzburg and Nuremberg, all the changes described as the High German sound shift have taken place in the inherited vocabulary derived from the West Germanic dialects, with the exception of the change of /k/ to /kx/ or /x/ in initial position. This /k/ → /kx/ (→ /x/) change took place only in the far south of the German-speaking area (Switzerland, southern Austria, and a very small southern area of Alsace and of Baden and Bavaria in the Federal Republic). The dialects south of the Germersheim Line, including all Swiss and Austrian dialects of German, are described as Upper German dialects. In them we find corresponding to English 'pound', 'ten' and 'make' forms such as *Pfund, zehn* and *machen*, that is forms which, at least in their consonants, are relatively close to the standard variety.

### 3.8.3 Middle German dialects

Between the Benrath and Germersheim Lines we find dialects described as Middle or Central German. What these have in common with each other is the partial operation of the High German sound shift, but there are considerable differences between them in the matter of precisely which

---

[5] In citing forms from traditional dialects we can cite only typical forms; by definition such dialects lack standard forms. We cite forms in conventional orthography (where the letters, unless otherwise stated, have very approximately the values they would have for someone using the *Deutsche Hochlautung* accent). Citations in **phonemic** or phonetic transcriptions are too exact in most cases, having validity only for small areas; the impressionistic, non-standardized orthographic forms used can have greater regional validity.

[6] There is actually a difference of detail between the two lines, which need not detain us here.

changes have taken place. In none of them, however, has the change of West Germanic /p/ to /pf/ taken place medially or finally, so that all have forms such as *Appel* corresponding to English 'apple', to Low German *Appel* and to standard German or Upper German forms such as *Apfel*. In contrast to this, the change of /p/ to /f/ usually has taken place, so that, corresponding to Low German *hopen* and English 'hope' (standard German and Upper German *hoffen*), we find Middle German *hoffen*.

In West Middle German /p/ has not changed to /pf/ word-initially, so here we find forms like *Pund* (English 'pound', Low German *Pund*), corresponding to standard German and Upper German *Pfund*. However, in East Middle German this change has happened word-initially, and indeed has almost always been carried further to /f/, so that the corresponding East Middle German form here is *Fund*. The complex variation in the operation of the sound shift in Middle German dialects will be treated in more detail below (see 3.10.2); for the moment some idea of the position can be obtained from the sample forms of common lexical items given on Map 3.5.

### 3.8.4 The importance of the north–central–south division

Why is there general agreement that these particular isoglosses have a special significance in dividing up the German-speaking territory? Firstly the differences which they refer to are clear and obvious: differences between voiceless stop and fricative consonants are acoustically quite clear and moreover generally represent phonemic differences in European languages. Secondly, differences between the north and south of the German-speaking area are not restricted to language: there are striking social and political differences as well; hence north–south linguistic differences are likely to be seized upon by speakers of the language as reinforcing these other differences. Social and political differences are seen most clearly in the traditional religious divide: the Upper German dialect area is generally Catholic, with important Protestant enclaves, the Low German area is largely Protestant with some Catholic areas, while the Middle German area is a complex patchwork of Protestant and Catholic territories. There are also clear differences of social attitude to non-standard speech between northern and southern areas. In the Upper German dialect area the status of traditional dialects is relatively high, with middle-class speech often close to traditional dialects; in the Low German dialect area the status of traditional dialects is relatively low, and middle-class speech is relatively close to the standard variety. In attitudes to non-standard speech the Middle German dialect area occupies an intermediate position between the other two areas.

### 3.9 Other isoglosses dividing northern from southern dialects

As well as isoglosses arising from the operation of the High German sound shift, German dialects are divided into southern and northern areas by other important isoglosses.

### 3.9.1 Older north–south divisions

Some of these isoglosses are of early origin and form a group of differences which separate southern West Germanic (southern German dialects) from northern West Germanic (northern German dialects, Dutch, Frisian and English) (see 2.1.3). These are the isoglosses separating third person singular masculine pronouns of the *he* type from those of the *er* type, the isogloss separating forms of certain words, including the pronoun *uns* (us) without nasal consonants before fricatives from those with nasal consonants, and the isogloss separating off forms showing shifts of velar consonants, such as /k/, to palatal or alveolar consonants, such as /tʃ/ or /s/ ('Ingvaeonic palatalization'; see again 2.1.3).

The *he*/*er* isogloss, and the isogloss for forms of the first person plural pronoun (standard German *uns*) with and without /n/, are shown on Map 3.6. It will be seen that Upper German dialects have *er* pronouns, that most Low German dialects have *he* pronouns, although some have the *er* type, and that both *he* and *er* types are found in Middle German dialects (see Maak 1983: 1175).

The loss of the nasal consonant /n/ before the fricative /s/ in *uns* can no longer be described as a feature clearly separating northern from southern German dialects; a broad swathe of central and eastern Low German dialects has *uns* forms, while forms without /n/ are now found in the south-west, this being a more recent development in this latter area (see Haas 1983: 1114–15).

The changes in velar consonants likewise no longer clearly divide southern from northern German speech. The palatalization of West Germanic /k/ to /tʃ/, /ʃ/ or /s/ is now found on the Continent only in Frisian (it is also found in English). In Frisian the sound /s/ is usual, so, for example, North Frisian Sylt dialect *Serk* corresponds to German *Kirche* (church). Palatalization of West Germanic /g/ or /ɣ/ to /j/ is more widespread, being found in some Low German dialects, though by no means all, the pattern of its occurrence being rather complex. It also occurs in some Middle German dialects of the Rhineland.

It will be seen that the ancient north–south divisions of West Germanic speech discussed in this section do not correspond at all exactly to that

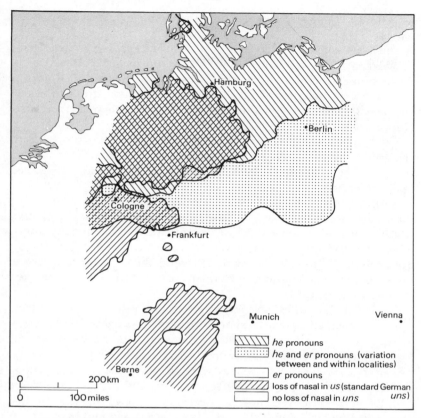

Map 3.6 North–south divisions in traditional German dialects: (1) *he*-type pronouns (north), *er*-type pronouns (south) for standard German *er* (English 'he'); (2) northern (and more recent south-western) loss of nasal consonants before fricatives in certain words, e.g. *uns* (English 'us')
Source: Adapted from *Atlas zur deutschen Sprache* (König 1978): 160, 164

other ancient north–south division based on the High German sound shift, which is conventionally considered to have greater significance.

### 3.9.2 Newer north–south divisions

The north–south divisions discussed so far are ancient but, given the persisting social, political and geographical divisions between north and south, it is not surprising that other isoglosses of more recent origin divide north from south. For example, Upper German dialects, and some Middle German dialects, have no **preterite** tense forms, apart possibly from *war* (preterite of the verb 'to be'), preterites being replaced by perfect tenses.

The isogloss marking the limit of this change again separates a more northern from a more southern area, but does not coincide with any of the north–south dividing lines so far discussed. It is a line of decreasing importance as preterites of all verbs, apart from auxiliaries and **modals** and one or two others, slowly disappear from much colloquial speech (see Hooge 1983: 1214–15, 1217–19).

The loss of preterite tenses represents a morphological and syntactic change in the entire German language-area, carried further in non-standard than in standard speech, and carried further in southern dialects than in northern ones.

A further long-term syntactic and morphological change in German is the loss of **case** distinctions. The case most frequently lost is the genitive, which is replaced by a dative, or by the preposition *von* plus dative, or by other constructions depending on the context. Except for a few set expressions, the genitive is now restricted in the standard language to rather more formal registers; in German dialects it survives only in a few idioms (see Koβ 1983).

German dialects often have further losses of case distinctions, but these losses represent an extremely complex pattern, the isogloss for the loss of a distinction in one item scarcely ever coinciding with the isogloss for the loss of that distinction in another item. As a very sweeping generalization we can say that there is a tendency for the dative/accusative distinction to be lost in the north, the nominative/accusative distinction in the south, with the north, however, showing a generally stronger tendency to lose case distinctions (see Panzer 1983: 1171–3). One representative instance is the loss, in northern dialects, of the dative/accusative distinction in the second person singular pronoun *du*, where southern dialects preserve this distinction. The isogloss in this case does, as it happens, coincide very roughly with the Benrath Line which is, of course, a principal isogloss dividing Low German from Middle German, based on the operation of the High German sound shift.

A further important isogloss dividing north from south is that separating dialects which form **diminutives** of nouns with suffixes containing palatal or velar stop or fricative consonants (either /-kə/ or /-çə/), from those where **lateral** consonants are found (/-lə/, /-li/, /əl/ or /-ərl/). The geographical distribution of the different forms is rather complex, but, as a broad generalization, we can say that Low German dialects have /-kə/, West Middle German dialects have /-çə/, while East Middle German and Upper German dialects have forms with laterals (see Seebold 1983). Again we can see that, while this isogloss separates north from south, it does not coincide with the principal sound shift isoglosses in that East Middle German is similar to Upper German in the matter of diminutives.

## 3.10 Major divisions within the three principal dialect areas

We now move from isoglosses which divide the north of the German-speaking area from the south, and discuss major divisions within the three principal dialect areas of Low German, Middle German and Upper German.

### 3.10.1 Divisions within Low German–Dutch

Although Low German and Dutch dialects show considerable diversity, there is no general consensus as to which isoglosses should be used to divide them up into the smaller dialect areas so necessary for more detailed discussion. However, there is agreement that one isogloss is particularly important, that dividing Low Franconian (*Niederfränkisch*) dialects from Low Saxon (*Niedersächsisch*) dialects, and running from the southern shore of the Ijsselmeer west of Amsterdam to meet the Benrath Line east of Cologne (see Map 3.4). Dialects to the west of this line (Low Franconian) have, in the plurals of present **indicative** tenses of verbs, endings similar to those found in standard German, i.e. *wir mach + en, ihr mach + t, sie mach + en*, while Low Saxon dialects have only one ending throughout the plural, either *-et* (most Low Saxon dialects) or *-en* (some northern dialects), giving verb forms such as *wi maakt* (standard *wir machen*), *ji maakt* (*ihr macht*) and *se maakt* (*sie machen*) (see Schirmunski 1962: 32, and Panzer 1983: 1170–1).

The division between Low Saxon and Low Franconian dialects is sociolinguistically extremely interesting, since it conflicts with the modern political and linguistic boundary between the Netherlands and Belgium on the one hand, and the Federal Republic of Germany on the other; the Low Franconian and the Low Saxon dialects are spoken on both sides of the standard Dutch–standard German boundary which, of course, follows the political boundary. Low Saxon dialects, which are chiefly spoken in Germany, are also spoken in the north-east of the Netherlands (except in the West Frisian enclave) and Low Franconian dialects, which are mainly Dutch dialects, are spoken in the lower Rhineland in Germany. Standard Dutch arose, historically, from the Low Franconian dialects of the coastal area between Rotterdam and Amsterdam, with some surviving features from the medieval emergent standard of Flanders, which had its centre in Brussels (see 2.2.1).

The continuity of dialects across the Dutch–German border has the interesting result that speakers of traditional dialects from the Netherlands side of the border, who would describe their own language as *nederlands* (Dutch), never as *duits* (German), can converse quite easily in traditional dialect with Germans from the other side of the border, who would describe their own language as *Nederdüüts* (Low German). However, as soon as a more formal register is required, almost all of these dialect-speakers would switch to a speech-form closer to the respective standard varieties, and communication would become difficult; in fact these days speakers of Dutch and German usually converse with each other in German or, increasingly, in English. The continuity of the traditional dialects across the political border is being disturbed as these dialects increasingly borrow lexicon from their respective standard varieties to discuss modern developments. For example, in the northern part of the border area Dutch speakers of Low Saxon dialects call a driving licence *rijbewijs*, the standard Dutch term, while German speakers of Low Saxon dialects call it *Föhrerschkien*, a term derived from standard German *Führerschein* (C. Moss, personal communication).

There is general agreement that, to the east, Low Saxon should be divided from East Low German (*Ostniederdeutsch*) approximately, though quite coincidentally, along the modern border between the Federal Republic and the GDR, although there is no general agreement as to precisely where the dialect boundary should lie, or as to which isogloss should be crucial to its delineation. East Low German dialects were taken to their present home relatively recently, i.e. from the twelfth century onwards (see 2.2.2), many centuries after West Germanic speech was established in the Low Saxon area. They developed from the speech of settlers from all over the northern part of the old West Germanic area, who migrated into an originally Slavonic-speaking area (see again 2.2.2). These settlers spoke both Low Saxon and Low Franconian dialects, and the East Low German dialects show a mixture of originally Low Franconian and Low Saxon features, with later innovations of their own.

One isogloss which can be used to divide Low Saxon from East Low German is the line separating plural present tense forms with the ending *-et* for all persons (Low Saxon speech bordering on East Low German) from present indicative forms showing either the pattern of standard German (*-en*, *-et*, *-en*), or *-en* for all persons (East Low German) (see Schirmunski 1962: 32).

The major divisions within Low German–Dutch can all be further subdivided on various criteria; for example Low Saxon can be divided into *Nordniedersächsisch* (North Low Saxon), *Westfälisch* (Westfalian) and *Ostfälisch* (Eastfalian). The Low Saxon dialects are sometimes referred to collectively as West Low German (*Westniederdeutsch*) with 'Low Saxon' being used for those dialects which we have labelled 'North Low Saxon'. East Low German can be divided into *Mecklenburgisch–Vorpommersch, Brandenburgisch, Ostpommersch* (East Pomeranian) and *Niederpreußisch* (Low Prussian). Leaving aside groups of older-generation émigrés in Germany, East Pomeranian and Low Prussian are now spoken only in areas incorporated into Poland or the Soviet Union after the Second World War, areas where the German-speaking population is now small (though no precise figures exist) and where all German speech, dialect and standard, is probably declining rapidly.

### 3.10.2 Divisions within Middle German

The Middle German dialect area is characterized by the differing operation of the High German sound shift, and various dialects can be separated depending on how they have been affected by its operation. In most Middle German dialects the shift of /p/ to /f/ has taken place, with forms like *hoffen* (to hope) occurring, compared with Low German *hopen*, but the shift of /p/ to /pf/ in *medial* and *final* position has not occurred; for example Middle German *Appel* (Low German also *Appel*) contrasts with standard German and Upper German *Apfel*.

However, in East Middle German the shift of /p/ to /pf/, and further to /f/, in *initial* position has occurred, whereas in West Middle German it has not, so West Middle German *Pund* ('pound') contrasts with East Middle German *Fund* and standard German and Upper German *Pfund* (Low German of course has *Pund* also) (see Schirmunski 1962: 28). The *Pund/Fund* isogloss, running to the east of Kassel, can be considered to be the boundary between East and West Middle German; however, other features separate the two, and these features do not necessarily have the same borders as the *Pund/Fund* isogloss, for example diminutives /-çə/ in the west and /-əl/ in the east.

Within East Middle German various characteristics have led to a division into *Thüringisch* (Thuringian), *Obersächsich* (Upper Saxon), *Schlesisch* (Silesian) and *Hochpreußisch* (High Prussian), the last two now being spoken on Polish territory (except by émigrés in Germany) and sharing the fate of the East Pomeranian and Low Prussian dialects of Low German (see above, 3.10.1).

Within West Middle German, isoglosses reflecting the differing operation of the High German sound shift fan out from the main Benrath Line

87

from points between Wuppertal and Kassel, to cross the Rhine at various places (the so-called **Rhenish fan** or *Rheinischer Fächer*); some of these are shown on Map 3.5 (see Schirmunski 1962: 28).

The isogloss of the Rhenish fan which is often given the most importance is the one dividing a north-western part of West Middle German, in which /t/ has not shifted to /s/ in the common monosyllabic pronouns *wat, dat, et, dit* (standard German *was, das, es, dies*) from a south-eastern area where this shift has happened. This isogloss divides West Middle German into Middle Franconian (*Mittelfränkisch*) to the north-west and Rhenish Franconian (*Rheinfränkisch*) to the south-east, the latter roughly centred on Frankfurt-am-Main.

A further isogloss reflects the differing operation of the /p/ → /f/ shift. The shift of /p/ to /f/ generally has occurred in Middle German (as distinct from the /p/ to /pf/ shift, see above), but in the northern part of Middle Franconian /p/ has not been shifted to /f/ after a **liquid** consonant (/l/ or /r/). In the dialects in question we find forms like *hoffen* contrasting with Low German *hopen*, but then we find forms like *Dorp* and *helpen* (Low German also *Dorp* and *helpen*) where standard German and the rest of Middle German has *Dorf* and *helfen*.

The isogloss separating *Dorp, helpen* etc. from *Dorf, helfen* etc. runs through the centre of the Middle Franconian dialect area and subdivides it into the Ripuarian (*Ripuarisch*) dialect area to the north-west, centred on Cologne, and the Moselle Franconian (*Moselfränkisch*) dialect area to the south, roughly centred on Koblenz.

### 3.10.3 Divisions within Upper German

The medieval language Middle High German probably had **diphthongs** pronounced /iə/, /yə/ and /uə/ respectively in words like *lieb, müede* and *guot* (modern standard German *lieb, müde* and *gut*). The modern standard variety has developed the **monophthongs** /iː/, /yː/ and /uː/ in these words, but many Upper German dialects have retained diphthongs, and in fact Upper German dialects can be divided into those with diphthongs and those with monophthongs in such words (Schirmunski 1962: 29). Most, but not all, of the Upper Franconian (*Oberfränkisch*) dialects in the north of the Upper German area have monophthongs, while the other major subdivisions of Upper German, Alemannic (*Alemannisch*) including Swabian (*Schwäbisch*) in the south-west and Bavarian or Bavarian–Austrian (*Bairisch–Österreichisch*) in the south-east, have diphthongs. In Alemannic the diphthongs are /iə/ in *lieb*, either /iə/ or /yə/ in *müde* (depending on the area), and /uə/ in *gut*. In most of

Bavarian–Austrian we find /iə/ in both *lieb* and *müde*, and /uə/ in *gut*, but in North Bavarian (*Nordbairisch*) we find rather different diphthongs: /əi/ in both *lieb* and *müde* and /əu/ in *gut*.

Upper German dialects are also divided according to the development of the Old High German velar fricative sound /x/ in words like *ich* and *Bach*. In Middle German dialects and in the standard variety, a velar fricative has remained after a back vowel in words like *Bach*, but elsewhere a palatal fricative /ç/ has developed, as in *ich*, often developing further in colloquial speech into a **palato-alveolar** fricative /ʃ/, similar to the final sound in *Fisch* (or in English 'fish'). In Upper German dialects /ç/ has not developed in Bavarian–Austrian, nor in the southern part of Alemannic, where /x/ is retained everywhere; in northern Alemannic and in Upper Franconian, there is a /ç/ – /x/ contrast, as in the standard variety.

Upper German dialects also differ from each other in the forms of the diminutive suffixes. Alemannic generally has either /-lə/ or /-li/. Upper Franconian has /-lə/ and Bavarian–Austrian has /-əl/ or /-ərl/ (Schirmunski 1962: 29; Seebold 1983).

A peculiarity of the Bavarian–Austrian dialects lies in the form of the second person plural pronouns, where forms such as *es* are found corresponding to standard German *ihr*, and forms such as *enk* corresponding to standard *euch* (Schirmunski 1962: 29–30; Maak 1983: 1175–7).

On the basis, then, of the development of the diphthongs, the development of the velar fricative sound, of the diminutive forms and of the second person plural pronouns, Upper German dialects are divided into the major dialect areas of Alemannic, Upper Franconian and Bavarian–Austrian. All of these are further divided: Upper Franconian into East Franconian (*Ostfränkisch*) and South Franconian (*Südfränkisch*); Alemannic into Swabian (*Schwäbisch*), Low Alemannic (*Niederalemannisch*), High Alemannic (*Hochalemannisch*) and Highest Alemannic (*Höchstalemannisch*); Bavarian–Austrian into North Bavarian (*Nordbairisch*), Middle Bavarian–Austrian (*Mittelbairisch–Österreichisch*) and South Bavarian–Austrian (*Südbairisch–Österreichisch*).

High Alemannic and Highest Alemannic together correspond roughly to Swiss German, though High Alemannic does extend into southern Alsace and southern Baden, and some eastern Swiss dialects are Low Alemannic. Perhaps the chief difference between High and Highest Alemannic on the one hand and the rest of Alemannic (Low Alemannic and Swabian) on the other is that in the former group of dialects the High

German sound shift has fully operated, in other words /k/ has been shifted to /kx/ or even further to /x/ word initially, so that High Alemannic *Chuh* /xuː/ corresponds to standard German *Kuh* (cow) (Schirmunski 1962: 30).

The full operation of the sound shift also distinguishes South Bavarian–Austrian from the rest of Bavarian–Austrian. The former group of dialects, covering southern Austria (apart from Vorarlberg where the dialects are Alemannic) and a few southern areas of Bavaria, shows the shift of /k/ to /kx/, and hence has *Chu* /kxuː/ for standard *Kuh* (Schirmunski 1962: 30).

Middle Bavarian–Austrian (along with the colloquial speech of both Munich and Vienna) is distinguished from other Bavarian–Austrian dialects by the **vocalization** of /l/ at the end of a word, or before consonants articulated at the front of the mouth. So, for example, /l/ has changed to the vowel sound /i/ in a word like standard German *alt* where it stands before an **alveolar** consonant, a common Middle Bavarian pronunciation being [ɔːi̯d̥] (Schirmunski 1962: 30; Haas 1983: 1112–13).

### 3.11 Other important isoglosses

Traditional German dialects are divided by important isoglosses other than those which have traditionally been used to determine the principal dialect boundaries and other major boundaries. Three of these reflect differences which have a profound effect on the character of the dialects, differences in the diphthongization of vowels and rounding of vowels and distinctions between consonants.

### 3.11.1 Diphthongization

The emergent Middle High German standard language appears to have had **tense** monophthongs, /iː/, /uː/ and /yː/ respectively, in the stressed syllables of the words *zît, hûs* and *hiute*, modern standard German *Zeit, Haus* and *heute* ('time', 'house' and 'today'). In the modern standard these and similar words have diphthongs /ai/, /au/ and /ɔy/ respectively, but many dialects preserve monophthongs, which were also found in the cognate vocabulary items of Middle Low German (Schirmunski 1962: 28, 31, 33). Map 3.7 shows the division of the German dialects into those with diphthongs and those with monophthongs in such words. Many dialects which have monophthongs in the words cited, where the vowels stand before consonants, do have diphthongs in other positions (see Wiesinger 1983a: 1079).

Low German dialects, except some Westfalian speech, have monophthongs. Middle German dialects generally have diphthongs, except for

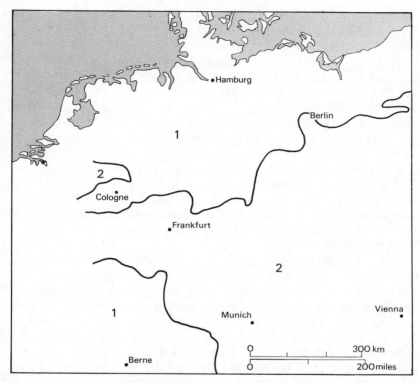

Map 3.7 Monophthongs and diphthongs in words such as *Zeit, Haus, heute* in traditional German dialects: 1, monophthongs; 2, diphthongs
Source: Adapted from *Atlas zur deutschen Sprache* (König 1978): 146

the Ripuarian dialects of Middle Franconian and the Low Hessian (*Niederhessisch*) dialects of Rhenish Franconian. Among the Upper German dialects Alemannic (excluding Swabian) has monophthongs, and Upper Franconian, Bavarian–Austrian and Swabian have diphthongs. Diphthongs in *Zeit, Haus, heute* etc., are one of the main features distinguishing Swabian (a sub-division of Alemannic) from the rest of Alemannic.

### 3.11.2 Unrounding

Modern standard German is relatively unusual among the languages of the world in having front rounded vowels, that is vowels produced with the tongue at the front of the mouth, but with the lips rounded. It is more common in the world's languages for front vowels to be **unrounded**. The front rounded vowels of standard German are /yː/, /ʏ/, /øː/ and /œ/, the stressed vowels of *fühle, Fülle, Söhne* and *Götter* respectively.

In many German dialects these vowels have been replaced by unrounded vowels, usually, but not necessarily, by those unrounded vowels closest in articulation to the rounded vowels: hence /yː/, /ʏ/, /øː/ and /œ/ may be replaced by /iː/, /ɪ/, /eː/ and /ɛ/ respectively. This could mean that the following pairs of words contain the same stressed vowels: *fühle* and *viele, Mütze* and *Sitze, Söhne* and *Szene, Götter* and *Wetter*. Dialects where unrounding has taken place usually also lack the diphthong /ɔy/ or /ɔi/, written *eu* or *äu* in such words as *heute* and *Häuser*. If pronounced /ɔy/ this diphthong has a front rounded vowel as its second element, and it arises either from a front rounded vowel or from a front rounded diphthong of Middle High German. It will usually be replaced by /ai/, meaning that (*ich*) *reite* and *heute* rhyme in many German dialects (Schirmunski 1962: 28, 31, 205–6).

Map 3.8 shows the division of German dialects into those with front rounded vowels, and those without. Front rounded vowels occur in most Low German dialects, but not in some in the south-east of the Low German area. Among Middle German dialects only Ripuarian has front rounded vowels, the rest do not. Most Upper German dialects lack front rounded vowels, but they are present in High Alemannic and Highest Alemannic, and in some Upper Franconian dialects. Upper Franconian dialects can, indeed, be divided on this basis into East Franconian (*Ostfränkisch*) with front rounded vowels, and South Franconian (*Süd-fränkisch*) without.

In some German dialects the Middle High German front rounded vowels have been unrounded, but then new front rounded vowels have arisen as a result of some other sound change. For example in Alsatian dialects Middle High German front rounded vowels have been unrounded, but then the Middle High German back vowel /uː/ has given rise to a front rounded vowel /yː/ in modern Alsatian dialects. For example Alsatian *Fiess* /fiəs/ and *dü* /dyː/ correspond to standard German *Füße* /fyːsə/ and *du* /duː/ (for further details see Wiesinger 1983b: 1103–4).

### 3.11.3 Lenition

In standard German voiced and voiceless **obstruents** (stops and fricatives) are clearly distinct from each other in most positions in words: there are word pairs which are distinguished solely by an opposition between voiced and voiceless obstruents, for example *packen* and *backen, Tier* and *dir, Garten* and *Karten, Leiter* and *leider*. Even in standard German,

Map 3.8 Front rounded vowels /y:/ and /ʏ/, or similar vowels, in words such as *Hüte* and *Mütze* in traditional German dialects: 1, front rounded vowels /y:/ and /ʏ/ or similar; 2, front unrounded vowels /i:/ and /ɪ/ or similar
Source: Adapted from Wiesinger 1983b: 1103

however, this opposition is neutralized in word-final position, or in front of another obstruent; so, for example, despite the difference in spelling, the words *Bund* and *bunt* are pronounced identically, and end in a voiceless stop. In standard German the so-called voiceless obstruents are described not only as voiceless, that is the vocal cords do not vibrate in their production, but also as **fortis**, that is having a relatively energetic articulation. In contrast the voiced obstruents are lenis or relatively weakly articulated. Additionally, the voiceless stop consonants are aspirated when they stand alone at the beginning of a stressed syllable, that is they are followed by a noticeable release of breath, while elsewhere they are unaspirated. Voiced stops are never aspirated.

In Low German dialects the contrast between voiced and voiceless obstruents is much as in the standard variety, although the consonants in question are distributed quite differently through the vocabulary; that is a word which may contain a fricative sound in standard German, like *Wasser*, may have a stop in the corresponding position in the Low German word, for example *Water*.

When we move to Middle and Upper German dialects we find the position is quite different. To start with, in most of them the voiced obstruents have lost their voicing, and are distinguished, at most, from the voiceless obstruents by the lenis–fortis distinction alone. But then the voiceless obstruents have often also undergone changes, frequently losing the aspiration which they have initially in stressed syllables in the standard language; they also often have become lenis, and this change means that they may be indistinguishable from the voiced obstruents. We can summarize these changes as follows:

| *Standard German* | *Many High German dialects* |
|---|---|
| Voiceless fortis obstruents (with initial aspiration) | Voiceless lenis obstruents (without aspiration) |
| CONTRAST WITH voiced lenis obstruents (without aspiration) | NO CONTRAST WITH voiceless lenis obstruents (without aspiration) |
| *Examples* | |
| *Tier, Karten*: [tʰiːɐ̯] [kʰ aːɐ̯tn̩] | [d̥iːr], [g̊ɑːrd̥ə] |
| CONTRAST WITH *dir, Garten*: [diːɐ̯], [gaːɐ̯tn̩] | NO CONTRAST WITH [d̥iːr], [g̊ɑːrd̥ə] |

The symbols [d̥] and [g̊] represent sounds which are lenis like the voiced obstruents, but which are voiceless.

In this group of changes, the one which has been singled out as the most important is the lenition (*Schwächung*) of the voiceless obstruents, and the entire process is usually referred to as the *binnenhochdeutsche Konsonantenschwächung* or central High German lenition (see Schirmunski 1962: 332–6). Its name is explained by the geographical area in which it takes

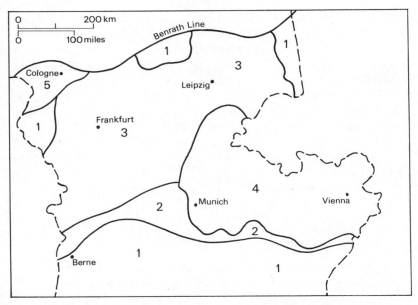

Map 3.9 Lenition in Middle and Upper German dialects: 1, no lenition; 2, initial lenition only; 3, lenition in all positions; 4, Middle Bavarian lenition phenomena (see 3. 11. 3); 5, varying lenition phenomena in different localities (no lenition, initial lenition only, or lenition in all positions)
Source: Adapted from *Atlas zur deutschen Sprache* (König 1978): 148

place: it is central in that it does not generally affect Low German, or the southern part of Upper German, and does not affect some of the eastern and western parts of Middle German (Silesian and Ripuarian respectively) (see Map 3.9).

In some other western Middle German dialects (apart from Ripuarian) some oppositions between aspirated /p/ and /k/ and unaspirated /b̥/ and /g̊/ are maintained in initial position, and in certain Alemannic and Bavarian areas (see Map 3.9) lenition takes place only initially. In some Low German dialects lenition does occur, but only medially (see Schirmunski 1962: 331). In most Middle Bavarian–Austrian dialects, lenition takes place initially (though some /g/–/k/ contrasts are maintained), but not medially, and, rather exceptionally for modern German, a lenis–fortis distinction is possible in final position. However, in these Bavarian dialects, the distribution of lenis and fortis consonants is quite different from that found in the standard variety: for example standard German *Gast* (guest), plural *Gäste* (/gast/ and /gɛstə/), both with a fortis consonant cluster /st/, are, in northern Austria, replaced respectively by

95

[gɔːẓd̥] with a lenis cluster and [gɛst] with a fortis cluster (there have also been complex changes in vowel length).

Medial and final lenition, where it occurs, does not seem to be particularly obvious to German-speakers, that is, it seems to represent an accent difference rather than a dialect difference (see Chapter 5), and it is applied to new words entering the dialects in question. However, initial lenition, though very widespread, does seem to be an obvious dialect difference, and in many areas it is not applied to new words entering the dialect from standard German. Hence, dialects having lenition will often distinguish between /p/, /t/ and /k/ in some new words (pronounced as [pʰ], [tʰ] and [kʰ] with aspiration) and /b/, /d/ and /g/ (pronounced as [b̥], [d̥] and [g̥]) in native words, after the following pattern:

|                       | *Theater* | *Tür*  | *dir*  |
| --------------------- | --------- | ------ | ------ |
| Standard German       | [tʰ-]     | [tʰ-]  | [d-]   |
| Dialect with lenition | [tʰ-]     | [d̥-]   | [d̥-]   |

The pattern of consonant correspondences between standard and dialect can hence become complex, and very confusing to people unfamiliar with the dialects in question.

## 3.12 Dialect vocabulary

The characteristics of German dialects discussed so far have been mainly phonological, with some affecting morphology and syntax. Two characteristics, the Bavarian second person plural pronouns *es*, *enk* (3.10.3) and the North German third person singular pronoun *he* (3.9.1), are lexical. There are many other lexical peculiarities of German dialects, but we will devote little space to them here, since they do not represent at all fundamental characteristics of the dialects. Individuals are capable of learning new vocabulary, and this means that much dialect vocabulary has died out to be replaced by new items, usually from the standard variety, as the speakers of the dialects are subjected to external influences. Indeed it is arguably the loss of distinctive vocabulary which marks the change from a traditional dialect to colloquial non-standard speech. In contrast, the phonological, syntactic and morphological characteristics of German dialects are much more persistent, and are regularly found in colloquial speech (see Chapter 5: passim).

### 3.12.1 Categories of lexical variation

Lexical differences between standard German and German dialects are of at least three kinds. There are cases where the standard language and the dialect have what is clearly the same lexical item, but the pronunciation of the dialect word is different from that of the standard word; an example is south-west German *Samschdag* corresponding to standard *Samstag* (see Map 3.1). In cases like this we believe that we should not be talking about lexical differences at all: the difference between the standard word and the dialect word is not a lexical difference, but a phonological accent difference (see 5.4.1), in this case arising from the fact that in south-western dialects, and also in south-western accents of colloquial and standard German, the cluster /ʃt/ or /ʒd/ replaces *deutsche Hochlautung* /st/ in all positions in a word (see 5.4.1, where we also discuss the related categories of phonetic accent difference and phonological dialect difference).

A further type of lexical difference is also of phonological origin, but results in forms of words in dialects which are so different from those of the standard that speakers feel them to be different words. Words in Low German dialects which, in contrast to the corresponding standard words, have not undergone the second sound shift, fall into this category, such as *Perd, Tid* and *Beke* corresponding to *Pferd, Zeit* and *Bach* ('horse', 'time', 'stream'). Although the dialect words are in some sense the same lexical items as the standard words, they seem to be felt to be dialect lexicon, not just standard words with local accent; in the transition from traditional dialect to colloquial speech, items like *Perd, Tid* and *Beke* have been lost (although the pronouns *dat, wat* and *et* corresponding to standard *das, was* and *es* sometimes have not), while local accent pronunciations like *Samschdag* have been retained.

The third type of lexical difference between the standard and traditional dialects occurs when the two have what are clearly different lexical items. Clear examples are the dialect forms *kallen, praten, küren, schmatzen* and *brachten* (see Map 3.10), corresponding to standard German *sprechen* (speak/talk).

### 3.12.2 Regional lexical variation in both dialect and standard

In the discussion of lexical differences between German dialects, it is important to remember that formal standard German and colloquial German also show considerable lexical variation. For example, two of the synonyms for 'Saturday' shown in Map 3.1 are standard forms in their separate areas: *Samstag* and *Sonnabend* (as we have seen *Samschdag* is simply *Samstag* pronounced with a south-western accent). The three major variants for 'Saturday' hence have quite different status: *Sonnabend* and *Samstag* are both standard and non-standard forms in their respective areas, while *Sater(s)dag* is exclusively a non-standard form;

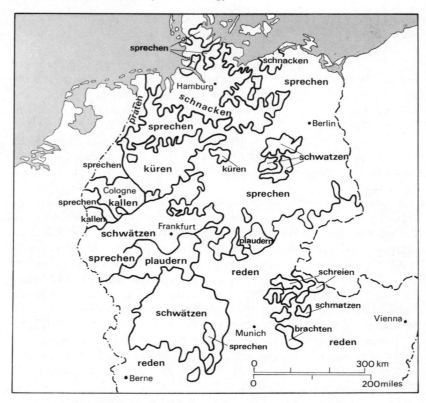

Map 3.10 'Speak' in traditional German dialects. (This is a much simplified presentation of the situation; for further detail see original source.)
Source: Adapted from *Atlas zur deutschen Sprache* (König 1978): 176

standard speech from the *Sater(s)dag* area will use either *Sonnabend* or *Samstag*.

### 3.12.3 Dialect variation and stylistic variation in standard German

Different dialect forms may correspond not only to regional variants in the standard, but also to stylistic variants in the standard. Of the variants given in Map 3.10 for the standard *sprechen* (speak), no fewer than five occur in the standard language as stylistic variants for *sprechen*; *reden* tends in any case to be the southern standard form (with *sprechen* however also used in the south), but in northern standard German it is a somewhat less formal equivalent of *sprechen*. *Schnacken* (north), *schwatzen* (north) and *schwätzen* (south) correspond roughly to English 'chat', while *plaudern*, slightly archaic in the standard, is also 'chat'. Three other dialectal variants also occur in the standard, but not as synonyms of *sprechen*; *schreien* means 'shout' in the standard, *küren* is an archaic word for 'choose' or 'elect' and *schmatzen* means 'to eat noisily'.

## 3.13 Postscript

Discussions of German dialects sometimes imply that the standard variety is a quite distinct entity superimposed upon the dialects. However our remarks in this chapter, particularly in 3.12, will have shown how variation between dialects can be related, often in rather complex ways, to variation in the standard language and in colloquial speech. We shall turn in Chapter 5 to a consideration of the totality of variation in German, which can be seen as a single, highly complex pattern.

## Further reading

Chambers and Trudgill (1980) give a good general account of the methodology of traditional dialectology. The classic works on German dialectology are Bach (1969) and Schirmunski (Zhirmunskij) (1962), but by far the most comprehensive account to date is Besch *et al.* (eds.) (1982–3). More or less accessible introductory texts are Goossens (1977), Löffler (1980), Niebaum (1983) and Keller (1961), but the last-mentioned concentrates on particular localities. A brief general view with, however, a large number of quite detailed maps, can be found in König (1978). A general impression of the dialects of particular regions of the Federal Republic can be gleaned from the series of booklets *Dialekt–Hochsprache kontrastiv*. There are of course numerous detailed individual descriptions of the dialects of particular localities, references to which can be found in the works cited.

# 4 Language and society: urban speech, urbanization and 'new dialectology'

## 4.1 From rural to urban dialectology

The reality of mid- to late-twentieth-century German society is dramatically different from that of the days in which the foundations of dialect study were laid. Mattheier (1980) points out the distinction between long-term gradual social change, such as the reshaping of a whole society by the growth of a bourgeoisie, and sudden radical change, such as the effects of the invention of the printing press or more recently the electronic media. As far as the structure of contemporary German society is concerned, two historical episodes have had the most spectacular and profound effects: the Industrial Revolution, which reached Germany relatively late, and the Second World War. While the most tangible consequence of the resolution of the latter was the physical division of Germany into two states, the war itself led directly to an acceleration in technological development and so also in the process of demographic shift which had started in the late nineteenth century.[1] Although the last few years have seen a slight reversal of this trend, the vast majority of the German population remains concentrated in urban or suburban areas.

In the light of these developments and considering that something like a third of the population of the Federal Republic, for example, live in towns with over 100,000 inhabitants (Dloczik *et al.* 1984: 44), it might seem reasonable to expect that the focus of attention in dialectology would have shifted from the almost exclusive study of rural varieties to the investigation of urban speech. In fact, this has happened only quite recently and still relatively little is known about urban speech in German-speaking countries. Nevertheless, a growing number of studies have addressed this question and so this chapter will focus on the consequences

---

[1] Rosenkranz (1963) gives the following figures for the shift in Germany's population (percentages):

|      | rural | urban |
|------|-------|-------|
| 1875 | 61    | 6     |
| 1925 | 36    | 27    |

of urbanization both directly on language itself and indirectly on the study of language in Germany, and in particular on the gradual emergence of a new brand of dialectology and an understanding of 'sociolinguistics' that has much more in common with the term as used in English-speaking countries than was the case until the mid-1970s.

## 4.2 Social change: 'modernization' and its implications for linguistic study

### 4.2.1 Changing theoretical perspectives

Urbanization can be taken to mean more than the physical concentration of a population in few areas. This primary meaning is nevertheless important here as it helps to establish the preconditions for social and hence linguistic change, especially for the most general linguistic development that has taken place in Germany over the last two hundred years: the growth of the standard variety at the expense of local and regional dialects. While towns have been centres of social, economic, legal and cultural influence since the Middle Ages, the real process of urbanization is associated with the emergence of towns as the focus of industrial development. However, urbanization in this sense and industrialization are themselves just two aspects of the overall process of 'modernization' that has transformed European society. Mattheier (1980: 146–7, following Wehler 1975) outlines the following individual processes that have contributed to the modernization process:

(1)    economic growth through continuing technological expansion;
(2)    increased social differentiation in the division of labour and social functions;
(3)    increased social and geographical mobility;
(4)    expansion of communication and educational systems;
(5)    growing participation in economic and political decision-making;
(6)    the establishment of widely accepted norms and values.

The last of these points leads us to the distinction between the 'literal' sense of urbanization and the 'derived' sense. The ambiguity can be resolved in German by using *Verstädterung* for the former and *Urbanisierung* for the latter, which is taken to imply the establishment of cosmopolitan lifestyles and the adoption of a different system of social values (see Mattheier 1980, 1982, 1985). In the context of a dynamic, largely urban society, then, the static approach of traditional dialectology is clearly inappropriate. But what are the implications of this assertion for the study of language and what theoretical and methodological changes have actually occurred?

The assumption that traditional dialects were homogeneous speech forms (see 3.4) led traditional dialectologists in search of the 'typical speaker', the revered repository of 'pure' dialect, rather irreverently christened NORM – non-mobile, older, rural male – by Chambers and Trudgill (1980: 33). However, by focussing on the full complexity of urban speech varieties American social dialectologists made NORMs redundant. Their work paved the way for urban speech to become the centre of attention in its own right and their view that the absence rather than the presence of variation in any speech form would be 'dysfunctional' (see Weinreich *et al.* 1968: 100) meant that variation could finally shrug off its 'wallflower existence' ('*Mauerblümchen-Dasein*': Senft 1982: 4). Variation is now recognized as an essential feature of any natural language variety and there are theories that claim to be able to account for it in a grammar (such as, for example, the Variety Grammar proposed in Klein 1974 and Klein and Dittmar 1979). It is also a prerequisite for linguistic change: the recognition that variation may represent change in progress has meant that we can shift our attention from the 'laws' for reconstructing 'older' forms from 'newer' ones to the actual processes and mechanisms of change as part of a continuing, open-ended development.

The other major change in the perception of linguistic structure is the result of the now unassailable position of standard German. As it has now achieved widespread acceptance (albeit to varying degrees), dialects are no longer seen simply as regional but also as social varieties and have assumed evaluative connotations: crudely speaking, their speakers see them as an obstacle to social progress in the north (at least in urban areas) and as a badge of identity in the south of German-speaking Europe. However, whether they are perceived by the layman as sub-standard or by the linguist more neutrally as non-standard, the important point is that dialects can now be considered as one type of variety in relation to others in a vertical continuum (see Chapter 5) as well as in a horizontal relationship with other regional varieties. Furthermore, the dichotomy standard–non-standard means that there need be no distinction in principle between urban and rural varieties.

Both the object and the scope of study in dialectology are changing, then. These changes have brought with them greater demands on the purpose of study too: it is no longer considered sufficient to describe varieties; dialectologists now seek to develop models that can account for and explain the variation they find within a variety or a speech community. If dialects are both regional and social varieties, then such a model will have to be at least two-dimensional. However, this would still be unable to account for all variation and the model needs to be extended to include pragmatic factors, generally subsumed under the notion of 'situation' (Mattheier 1980; Schlieben-Lange and Weydt 1978). Even this is not enough, though: as we shall see in later sections of this chapter (cf. also 8.2.1, 8.2.4), it has become increasingly clear that objective social, geographical and pragmatic factors need to be complemented by secondary, subjective factors such as attitudes, prestige, ambition and local loyalty.

### 4.2.2 Changes in methodology

A holistic, multi-dimensional approach to the study of linguistic variation cannot be implemented solely with the tools traditionally available to the dialectologist. It will inevitably involve the borrowing of insights and techniques from other empirical disciplines, especially sociology but also specific areas such as discourse analysis and the ethnography of speaking (see, for example, Saville-Troike 1989 and the introduction to Trudgill 1978), and if its results are to be testable it will need to incorporate the precision of statistical and other mathematical tools into its analytical apparatus.

The main requirement for satisfactory practice in dialectology today is explicitness. In the past it has often not been clear for example on what basis informants were chosen or exactly how the data were collected. By contrast, attention to precisely this kind of detail is the hallmark of more recent studies. We shall discuss specific aspects of methodology when looking at concrete examples in the next section, but it is worth mentioning here five considerations that should always be taken into account. To begin with, there are the two aspects picked out above: informant selection and data collection. With the onset of urban studies, the NORM, virtually the epitome of what modern dialectology does not investigate, has been superseded by the social group. This is a more complex and problematic notion than it may seem and we shall have more to say about it later (see 4.5), but broadly we can say that the emphasis on language as a form of social behaviour led researchers to focus their attention on possible correlations between language use and, for example, socio-economic class, age, sex, race or religion. However, as Hudson (1980: 163–7) shows, while group analysis may be very revealing, it also has a number of major disadvantages. In particular it may give precisely the same false impressions of homogeneity that traditional dialectologists' methods were criticized for and that conceal a vast amount of individual variation. Some studies have therefore chosen to look at both individual and group variation, although the validity of the types of group postulated is still often taken for granted.

There is much to be said about data collection but the crucial point is the need for what Labov (1972a: 209) calls 'good data':

> No matter what other methods may be used to obtain samples of speech (group sessions, anonymous observation), the only way to obtain sufficient good data on the speech of any one person is through an individual, tape-recorded interview: that is through the most obvious kind of systematic observation.

The only exception to this axiom is that good lexical data may still be gathered by the use of questionnaires.

The three other methodological considerations are: the object of analysis, the instrument of analysis and the interpretation and presentation of results. The variety to be studied must be precisely defined and the level to be investigated (phonology, syntax, vocabulary etc.) specified. Most studies still concentrate on phonology as the most distinctive and accessible level of variation, but whereas earlier studies attempted to describe the allegedly homogeneous phonological system of a variety, studies conducted more or less under the influence of American linguists have focussed on variation in the realization of isolated phonological **variables**. Finally, the traditional methods of presenting results (maps, dictionaries) are appropriate only where differences are considered absolute: as the findings of variation studies incorporate statistical information, display devices such as charts, graphs and new types of rule formulations must be devised to show this.

## 4.3 New approaches to dialectology

Studies broadly departing from the traditional approach have been conducted throughout the length and breadth of the German-speaking countries over the last twenty-five years, especially since the early 1970s. Places in which urban research has been carried out range from small towns in Lower Saxony, the Rhineland, Bavaria and Austria to major cities like Berlin, Freiburg, Cologne, Salzburg and Vienna. In this section we shall look at some of the ways in which variation in urban varieties of German has been tackled, before going on in the next two sections to discuss two major recent projects in more detail.

### 4.3.1 Departing from tradition: Nauborn

It is widely acknowledged that the first empirical study concerned with relations between social and linguistic patterns in an urban environment was Else Hofmann's investigation of the influence of the urban speech variety of Wetzlar (about thirty miles north of Frankfurt) on the speech of workers commuting from a neighbouring village, Nauborn (Hofmann 1963). She attempts to account for the observed change in the linguistic make-up of a small suburban community through extralinguistic factors such as age, education and training, sex and social mobility. Constant factors, the significance of which is therefore not investigated, are class (all are industrial workers), place of origin (all were born and bred in the village) and situation (topic, interlocutor etc. are the same in each case).

Although age appears to be a major factor, with the younger generation turning away from the local rural dialect towards the urban variety of Wetzlar, the decisive influence is the extent to which individuals wish to adapt their lifestyle to what they perceive as that of the town. This has to be seen against the background of social changes since the Second World War: while most of the village's inhabitants previously worked on the land, 70 per cent of the working male population in 1963 were industrial workers employed in the town, although many of these were so-called 'hobby farmers' (*Industriebauern*), who cultivated local smallholdings in their spare time (Hofmann 1963: 206–7). This change in the employment structure has been accompanied by the distintegration of the village community and a clearer distinction between work and leisure. Many villagers belong to one or more of the social clubs (mainly sports clubs and choirs), the membership of which reflects social differences in the village.

Those villagers whose spare time was most heavily committed to activities in the village (especially 'hobby farmers' and active club members) also tended to express the strongest attachment to traditional ways and contempt for those with a more 'modern' outlook, and it was these villagers whose speech was most 'conservative' (i.e. with fewest features adapted to the Wetzlar variety). The strongest rejection of village life on the other hand was found among young women, many of whom felt insulted at being interviewed in dialect. The respective views of these two extreme groups are indicated by typical statements such as (for the former) 'We move with the times but don't abandon our customs, and talk [chooses dialect word for talk] the way we're used to talking'; and (for the latter) 'We don't work in the fields and the stables like our mother had to do, we're in the same position as the young women in the town and we want to behave and speak like them too.'[2]

The actual effect on their speech of the young women's willingness to adapt is diminished to some extent by the fact that they work in the town for only a relatively short time and by their relatively intensive contact

[2] 'Wir gehen ja mit der Zeit, vergessen aber unser Herkommen nicht und "schwätze", wie wir es gewohnt sind'; 'Wir gehen ja nicht mehr aud das Feld und in den Stall, wie unsere Mutter es noch tun mußte, wir haben es wie die jungen Frauen in der Stadt und wollen uns auch so benehmen und so sprechen wie die' (Hofmann 1963: 226–7).

with dialect after work within the family. The willingness to adapt is therefore not the only significant factor but it does seem to be the most influential, as the groups linguistically closest to the Wetzlar control group were younger workers (aged 18–44) who were either generally more positively oriented towards urban life or who stressed the importance of 'speaking properly' for social and career reasons. We find therefore within one central German community the conflicting attitudes to traditional dialects that we indicated above (4.2.1) as characteristic of the south–north divide: dialect is a means of preserving local identity or alternatively a hindrance to social mobility.

### 4.3.2 Variation and social groups

One of the most problematic but frequently employed non-linguistic variables used in correlative studies is the concept of socio-economic class: it often produces apparently striking and intuitively satisfying results and yet there is no agreed set of criteria by which to categorize speakers according to class (see e.g. Hudson 1980: 173–4; Milroy 1987a: 29–35, 97–101). Nevertheless, it might seem surprising to linguists in English-speaking countries that many German studies either disregard this factor by keeping it constant (e.g. Hofmann 1963; Senft 1982) or simply ignore it (e.g. Keller 1976; Von Schneidemesser 1984 [1979]).

There are various reasons for this but the main one is probably the fact that the concept of class familiar in the English-speaking countries is less well established in the German-speaking countries. Braverman (1984: 62) confidently, if rather dubiously, speaks of the 'homogeneous populace' of the city of Salzburg, on the grounds that almost the entire population is middle class. She still manages to take social class into account as a variable but concludes that it does not correlate significantly with choice of variety. Wolfensberger (1967) reaches a similar conclusion about linguistic choice in the small community of Stäfa in Switzerland, but Stellmacher (1977) in a small town in Lower Saxony and Günther (1967) in Freiburg find that social class is a major influence.

Günther distinguishes four classes: upper class (UC), upper and lower middle class (UMC, LMC) and lower class (LC). The major distinction seems to be between the UC and the rest: for example, the strongly marked dialect **variant** [gvɪst] for standard [gəvʊst] (=past participle of *wissen*, 'know') was used by only about 50 per cent of UC speakers compared to 80 per cent of all other classes. Broadly speaking, greater dialect use is associated with lower social class, but the picture is complicated by the relatively unsystematic behaviour of the two MC groups. The UMC shows the widest phonological variation and is represented throughout the whole range from deepest local dialect through colloquial speech to standard. This may be a sign of 'linguistic insecurity', as the UMC often show pleasure in using the dialect but also tend to feel inhibited by their consciousness of their social position (Günther 1967: 201).

The speech behaviour of the LMC is irregular in a different way: phonologically they are more 'dialect-oriented' (*mundartlich eingestellt*) than the LC, but as far as syntax is concerned they are closer to the standard than is the UMC. This kind of variation in the middle-ranking group within a social hierarchy is a familiar feature of British and American urban dialect studies (see, for example, Labov 1972a: Chs. 2, 4 and 5; Chambers and Trudgill 1980: 167–71), and is of particular interest for its rôle in linguistic change. The apparently contradictory behaviour of the LMC in Freiburg on the other hand is similar to that of young middle-class Blacks in Detroit as reported by Wolfram (1969). In his discussion of the Detroit study, Hudson (1980: 45) speculates that 'we use pronunci-ation in order to identify our origins (or to imply that we originated from some group, whether we really did or not . . .)' and that 'in contrast, we might use morphology, syntax and vocabulary in order to identify our current status in society'. However, Günther explores neither this question nor linguistic change but rather is largely content with a description of the (then) current situation.

Social groups rather than individuals are the focus of attention in most studies of this period. Apart from the two most important groupings by age and class, a particularly interesting factor in the Freiburg study was the patterns of speech behaviour associated with each of four parts of the town. Each area had its distinctive social composition and Günther (1967: 200) was able to rank them in terms of their 'dialect strength' (*Mun-dartstärke*). While this factor is of marginal importance in this study, though, its significance has recently been stressed by Dittmar and Schlieben-Lange (1982: 64–8) and is the basis of the Berlin project to be discussed in the next section. In the Swiss village of Stäfa, factors such as occupation, education and social class appear to be irrelevant in terms of dialect use and the most significant basis for grouping established by Wolfensberger (1967) was the speaker's origin. It is not surprising that relative newcomers use less local dialect than do the indigenous popu-lation, but there also seems to be a difference in degree of dialect use between those whose families have lived in the town for generations and those who grew up there as the children of newcomers. The situation here seems similar then to that in Hofmann's study, but the explanation of the importance of attachment to a particular place (*Ortsgebundenheit*) as an influential factor in linguistic variation and choice is more likely to depend on subjective questions such as attitudes and local loyalty than on objective matters such as type and place of employment or length of stay in itself (see Mattheier 1980: 72).

Finally, Keller (1976) was able to make significant generalizations about linguistic change on the basis of his analysis of Regensburg speech according to age groups. He established three major phases in the process of change:

(1) Changes in their initial stages – e.g. dialect [ʃ, ʒ̥] being replaced by standard [s] in the consonant cluster -rst-, as in *erst* (first);

(2) Relatively well established changes – e.g. the replacement of one **periphrastic** form by another to represent the genitive: for 'Anna's room', *der Anna ihr Zimmer* becomes *das Zimmer von der Anna*;[3]

(3) Changes in their final stages – e.g. the loss of the distinctive vowel nasalization: Mann becomes /mɔ:/ instead of /mɔ̃:/.

These phases of change correspond to an implicational pattern in terms of age groups: incipient changes are found only in the speech of the younger generation; relatively well established changes in both younger and middle generations; and only the virtually completed changes occur in the speech of the older generation. Most of these changes are towards the regional colloquial speech variety or the standard, although an interesting exception is that there is a greater proportion of dialect forms in some instances amongst the younger generation, so that there is some evidence that dialect has 'covert **prestige**' (see, for example, Chambers and Trudgill 1980: 98–100) for this part of the population.

### 4.3.3 Variation and individuals

As we have already said, group analysis may well be a revealing way of processing information about linguistic usage but it may also conceal important facts of individual variation. In a study of lexical stability and change in Gießen (Von Schneidemesser 1984 [1979]), findings were presented in such a way that both individual responses and group patterns were visible. The informants were selected and grouped according to two criteria, age and 'nativeness', each criterion giving three groups:

*Age*
O = older (50 + )
M = middle (31–50)
Y = younger (15–30)

---

[3] Note that these examples cannot be translated into English, as they are to do with the use of case, and that they are given here in standard written German rather than dialect for ease of comprehension.

*Nativeness*

A = informant and both parents born in Gießen

B = informant born in Gießen but either only father or neither parent born there

C = neither informant nor parents born in Gießen

As Figure 4.1 shows, lexical change is as much subject to an intermediate period of variation as is phonological or syntactic change. The figure appears to show a clear example of change in progress: the traditional term *Kaffee* is still used by most of the older group, the new term *Frühstück* to a large extent by the younger group, and the middle group is fairly evenly divided. We can also see, however, that several speakers claim to use both and that the YA group is less inclined to use the newer form than the YB or YC groups. The number of informants is of course fairly small but it seems reasonable to make at least tentative generalizations; the important point is that these individual findings would get lost if the responses were presented simply as totals for the groups. The methodology of this study, then, makes it possible both to draw general conclusions (for instance, that O is linguistically the most conservative group, Y and to a lesser extent C the main innovators) and to demonstrate individual points explicitly and clearly.

The main object of Senft's study (1982) of the speech of metalworkers in Kaiserslautern is to demonstrate the appropriateness of a particular grammatical model (Variety Grammar: see 4.2.1) for the explicit description and explanation of variation in a linguistic variety and for the definition of the term 'speech community'. In our present context it is of interest mainly in that it is based on interviews with a small number of informants (six women, twelve men) and in that the data are presented in terms of individual realizations of variables.

Q: What do you call the first meal of the day?

| | O 1 | 2 | 3 | 4 | 5 | 6 | 7 | | M 1 | 2 | 3 | 4 | 5 | 6 | 7 | | Y 1 | 2 | 3 | 4 | 5 | 6 | 7 |
|---|---|---|---|---|---|---|---|---|---|---|---|---|---|---|---|---|---|---|---|---|---|---|---|
| A | ●x | ● | ● | ● | ● | ● | ● | | ● | ● | ● | ● | x | x | x | | ●x | x | x | x | ● | ● | ● | x |
| B | x | ● | ● | x | ● | x | ● | | x | ● | x | ● | ● | ● | ● | | ●x | x | x | x | x | x | x | x |
| C | x | x | ● | ● | ● | ● | ● | | ● | x | x | ●x | x | ● | x | | x | x | x | x | ● | x | ● |

● = *Kaffee* (*trinken*) or x = *Frühstück*; see text for explanation of O, M, Y, A, B, C

Fig. 4.1 Lexical variation in Gießen
Source: Von Schneidemesser 1984 [1979]

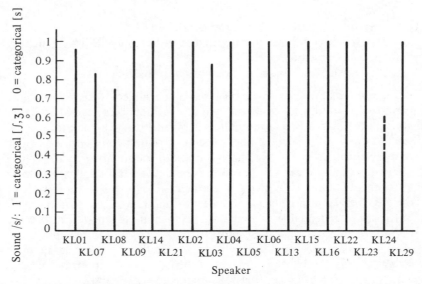

Fig. 4.2 Phonological variation in Kaiserslautern. Standard pattern: /s/→[s] in
V–/t,d/; non-standard pattern: /s/→[ʃ,ʒ̊] in V–/t,d/
Source: Senft 1982

Figure 4.2. for example shows the relative frequency of application of
two phonological rules, which say that the sound /s/ following a vowel
and preceding the sounds /t/ and /d/ may be realized either as standard [s]
or as non-standard [ʃ] or [ʒ̊]. For the majority of speakers, [ʃ] or [ʒ̊] appears
to be (virtually) obligatory in this context. However, it is also clear that
speaker KL24 is a striking exception to this pattern. In an average score
for the whole group this fact would not have emerged but, as it has, an
explanation seems necessary. In the light of other evidence in the study, it
seems likely that this variable operates as a '**sociolinguistic marker**' for this
speaker: that is to say, the speaker is aware that the non-standard variant
is characteristic of 'workers' speech' and as he is strongly socially
ambitious he deliberately avoids this variant as much as possible (Senft
1982: 152–4).

This brings us back to the rôle of subjective extralinguistic factors in
linguistic behaviour. We have already seen how the willingness to adapt to
an urban lifestyle was perhaps the crucial element in the Nauborn study.
Attitudes to language use amongst factory employees were also explicitly
investigated in Kaiserslautern. Five of the workers in the original sample
(one woman, four men) were asked to describe how a particular piece of
machinery worked. A foreman and a departmental head, who were

Q: Is the description given by each speaker clear [= C] or
not so clear [= N]?

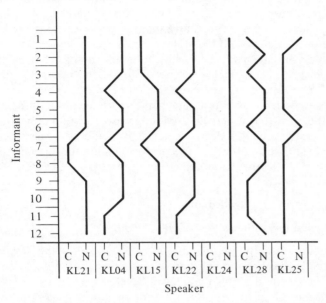

Fig. 4.3 Attitudes to language variation in Kaiserslautern. (Informants: 1,
managing director; 2, head of personnel; 3, senior manager (personnel); 4, head
of department; 5, head of section; 6, foreman; 7, works committee member; 8,
fitter; 9, skilled worker; 10, unskilled worker; 11, trainee; 12, general assistant)
Source: Senft 1982

comparable to the workers in all non-linguistic criteria except for training
and job, were asked to do the same. The recordings were then played to
twelve (male) employees, representing each level of the hierarchy within
the company from auxiliary staff and trainee to senior manager, and they
were asked to judge each description by answering a series of questions.

Figure 4.3 for example shows the responses to the question: 'Is the
description clear or not so clear?' The object of the exercise was to see if
the workers could be distinguished from the foreman (KL28) and the
department head (KL25) and if so, how. The responses to this question
are fairly typical of the test as a whole: the department head was
consistently rated the 'best' and, except for questions concerning
'likeability' and 'natural behaviour', the one woman worker (KL21) was
rated the 'worst', although in this particular instance (Fig. 4.3) it is our
friend KL24 (see above) who comes off worst. The woman's low rating is
probably attributable to the prejudiced view that 'most female industrial

workers are unskilled and therefore incapable of understanding complex machinery'; Senft's own view is that her description was certainly better than that of some of the others. The outstanding 'success' of the department head on the other hand was in part due to accent (his pronunciation was closest to the standard and the responses to certain questions showed that this registered with the informants), but the most important distinguishing factor appeared to be the content and the structure of the descriptions. No clear picture of attitudes to specific varieties emerges from this test, but some of the 'senior' informants expressed the view that it was an advantage for a worker, foreman or department head to be a dialect-speaker as it would be easier to fit in, while all agreed that an ability to use the local colloquial speech variety was essential for effective communication at least from foreman level.

### 4.4 Berlin: portrait of a divided city

#### 4.4.1 The social meaning of *Berlinisch*

Berlin offers a virtually unique opportunity to study the linguistic consequences of the abrupt disruption of a speech community. Although much has been written about the alleged development of two separate languages as a result of the division of Germany into two states after the Second World War (see 5.7 below and Clyne 1984: Ch. 2), there is little evidence to support this thesis, and the basis for comparison (two whole countries) is impossibly large. Berlin, on the other hand, is a single entity that, like London for example, has grown organically through the expansion and amalgamation of several separate settlements, each with its own history and character. The building of the Wall in 1961 not only divided this whole city into two, but isolated from each other some of the oldest and most intimately related parts of the city.

This is the starting point for a project carried out in the early 1980s in an attempt to build up a picture of the 'social meaning' of *Berlinisch*, which in our terms is a form of colloquial non-standard speech (see Chapter 5) and which we shall refer to here as Berlin Urban Vernacular (BUV). The study focusses on three districts: Wedding and Prenzlauer Berg, two old working-class areas which are adjacent but to the west and east of the Wall respectively, and Zehlendorf, an affluent district in the green south-west of the city (see Map 4.1). For practical reasons some aspects of the study were conducted only in the two western districts.

To compose a picture of BUV, four major aspects were considered:

(1)    vocabulary: there are many dictionaries of BUV, but most are based on unidentified sources or derive from the authors' own 'knowledge'

1 Schöneberg
2 Tiergarten
3 Prenzlauer Berg
4 Friedrichshain

Pankow

Reinickendorf

Weißensee

Wedding

Spandau

WEST

Charlotten-burg

Mitte

Lichtenberg

EAST

BERLIN

BERLIN

Kreuzberg

Wilmersdorf

Treptow

Köpenick

Zehlendorf

Steglitz

Tempelhof

Neukölln

Map 4.1 Districts of Berlin
Source: Schlobinski 1987

(Dittmar *et al.* 1986: 85–6). The data for this study were collected by means of a modified, more flexible version of the questionnaire used in traditional dialectology.

(2) phonology: what linguistic and extralinguistic **constraints** apply to a set of phonological variables, considered characteristic of BUV? In particular, is there a correlation between districts and the use of specific variants?

(3) pragmatics: an aspect previously neglected in German urban dialectology (but see, for example, Labov 1972b: Ch. 8, 9 and Cheshire 1982 for studies in English-speaking settings); are there besides regionally defined phonology, vocabulary and grammar also 'manners of speaking' specific to given places or regions (*regionale Sprechweisen*) (Dittmar *et al.* 1986: 9–11)?

(4) attitudes: as speech acts as a form of social identification, attitudes towards speech can reveal a lot about social relations in a speech community and provide a subjective dimension to the analysis of linguistic variation.

### 4.4.2 Vocabulary

Apart from accent, vocabulary is the aspect of people's speech that most readily identifies their geographical origin and, since the early days of

113

dialectology, phonology and lexicon have been the main levels on which dialect studies have been based. However, while word maps may show lexical variation over a whole area (state, province, country), they generally fail to take account of variation within a single place or indeed an individual informant. As Von Schneidemesser's study showed (see 4.3.3), there may be a high degree of lexical variation within a speech community, and furthermore terms listed in dialect dictionaries as typical of a given dialect may well be in the process of being replaced by other terms.

The Berlin questionnaire aimed to tackle these two points by investigating the 'passive' knowledge of informants from Wedding and Zehlendorf: they were shown a list of fifteen words and asked to write down not what word they would use themselves for each item, but which word(s) a 'typical Berliner' would use. The results showed that none of the fifteen standard items had a single, exclusive BUV equivalent, although for ten there was one strongly favoured term (e.g. only six out of 291 responses gave anything other than *Schrippe* for *Brötchen*, 'bread roll'). On the other hand, several supposedly 'typical Berlin' terms were scarcely mentioned (e.g. only ten out of 225 gave *knorke* for *chic*). While the individual findings will be of interest to Germanists and particularly to those specializing in the study of Berlin, the important general point established by this lexical study is that although West Berlin is an 'island', isolated both from the Federal Republic and from the GDR and East Berlin, BUV has not become fossilized as a result but remains a dynamically developing variety (Dittmar *et al.* 1986: 105).

### 4.4.3 Phonology

Just as certain lexical items are traditionally associated with Berlin speech, there are a number of phonological features which, while not exclusive to Berlin, are nonetheless held to be characteristic of it. The variables chosen for analysis here are given in Table 4.1.

The linguistic data consisted of over five hundred route directions (passers-by were asked the way to X) and interviews with thirty-seven informants selected for each district according to sex and age. The informants were chosen following the practice established by Lesley Milroy in Belfast (Milroy 1987b), by first securing the co-operation of a small number of individuals and then asking them to 'nominate' three relatives or friends as further informants, as an interviewer introduced as a 'friend of a friend' has a better chance of eliciting natural speech (Schlobinski 1987: 51–2).

The data were to be analysed with the aim of establishing the social and

Table 4.1. *Berlin: phonological variables*

| Variable | Standard realization | BUV realization |
|---|---|---|
| (g) *gemacht* | [g] | [j] |
| (ai) *einmal* | [ai] | [eː] |
| (au)1 *auch* | [au] | [oː] |
| (au)2 *auf* | [au] | [ʊ] |
| (ç) *ich* | [ç] | [k] |
| (s) *das* | [s] | [t] |

linguistic constraints that operate on each of the phonological variables. The most striking thing to emerge from this aspect of the study is the fact that variation in all variables taken together is strongly stratified according to district. As Fig. 4.4 shows, Prenzlauer Berg in East Berlin has maintained the dialect most strongly, even more than its Western counterpart Wedding, while it is represented very much less in the affluent Zehlendorf. This is an even stronger demonstration than the study of Freiburg speech (see 4.3.2) of the reality of variegated urban linguistic landscapes: there are observable patterns of linguistic usage that correspond to the historical and social development of specific districts.

Individual variables are also subject to other extralinguistic factors. The variables (g), (ai) and (au)1 for instance function as 'sex indicators': in each case the socially marked non-standard variant is used significantly more frequently by men than by women (Schlobinski 1987: 124–6, 132–4). However, while these social factors are clearly important and highly revealing, the rôle played by linguistic constraints is perhaps more interesting, as this analysis provides a more subtle and refined profile of the variables. The actual nature of the linguistic constraints varies. Indeed, it could be argued that some of these features are really examples of lexical differences with a phonological origin. For instance, the non-standard variant of the (au)1 variable is found only in a handful of lexical items and non-standard [k] as a variant of (ç) occurs only in the word *ich* (I). These are well-established and well-known markers of Berlin speech and non-BUV-speakers can and do give their speech a Berlin 'tinge' by incorporating forms like [oːx] for *auch* (also) and [ik] for *ich* but without otherwise adapting their pronunciation in a systematic way.

The (ai) and (s) variables are also lexically restricted but less narrowly. The (g) variable on the other hand is not restricted to certain words but rather varies according to phonological context. It appears that (g) is far more likely to be realized as [j] in initial than in medial position and that in

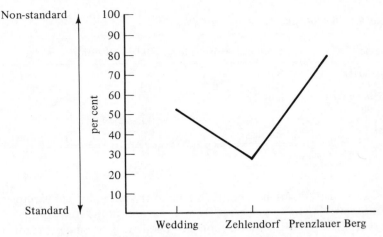

Fig. 4.4 Berlin: overall distribution of the six phonological variables according to district
Source: Schlobinski 1987

both initial and medial positions the likelihood of the non-standard variant being selected depends partly on the preceding and/or following context. Figure 4.5 shows for example that (g) is least likely to be realized as [j] when followed by /r/ and most likely when followed by /ə/; it is particularly common in the past participle prefix *ge-*, especially when in word-initial position.[4]

As we have already remarked, linguistic change presupposes a phase of variation. One interpretation of the variation in the phonological features under investigation here (but not necessarily the only one) is then that they are in the process of changing. There is no adequate earlier phonological analysis on which to base comparisons but on the basis of more or less informal accounts it is at least possible to speculate on changes in progress.[5] For instance, while an earlier study (Lasch 1928: 256) had claimed categorically that (g) was realized as [j] in initial position, Fig. 4.5 shows that this is now the case virtually only when the following sound is a vowel: a few cases of [j] were found before /r/ but once

---

[4] Most German verbs have the prefix *ge-* in the past participle (*machen→gemacht*). Where the verb has a separable prefix, the *ge-* is placed between this and the stem (*aufmachen→ aufgemacht*).

[5] In the absence of historical data it is possible to test hypotheses about linguistic change with an 'apparent time analysis'. This means comparing the speech of different age-groups to see if there is a clear pattern of usage, with older speakers using the 'traditional' form and younger speakers the 'newer' variant. However, the validity of this procedure is controversial (see Chambers and Trudgill 1980: 165–7).

|  | Following context | Significant interactions |
|---|---|---|
| Increasing effect | /r/ | ♯x /ə/ |
|  | /ɣ/ | ♯ x /ɛ/ |
|  | /i/ | + x /ɣ/ |
|  | /uː/ |  |
|  | /u/ |  |
|  | /a/ |  |
|  | /ɛ/ |  |
|  | /aː/ |  |
|  | /eː/ |  |
|  | /ə/ |  |

Fig. 4.5 Berlin: factors influencing the non-standard realization of the (g) variable. (♯, word boundary; +, morpheme boundary; x indicates 'interaction')
Source: Schlobinski: 1987

common forms such as [jryːn] for *grün* (green) or [jloːbn] for *glauben* (think, believe) have now practically disappeared.[6] This suggests that the rule for the realization of (g) in initial position is being simplified, a common process in linguistic change, so that [j] will soon appear only before a vowel. At the same time, the frequency of [j] in the prefix *ge-* suggests that in this context at least the non-standard variant is strongly resistant to change and will therefore probably survive for some time even if the standard form makes inroads in the prevocalic position (Schlobinski 1987: 157–8).

If we accept that variation in these phonological variables is an indication of change in progress, we should not assume that the change is equally advanced in each case. There was no magical historical moment at which all the changes were initiated, and they each proceed at a different pace. However, although change in one variable may be independent of change in others, there appears to be a strong correlation between the use of the non-standard variants and it may be that they are implicationally ordered (Schlobinski 1987: 149–50). That is to say, reading → as 'implies the use of', we can rank the non-standard variants of the six variables like this: variables like this:

[eː] → [ʊ] → [t] → [j] → [k] → [oː]

This means that a speaker who uses [eː] will generally also use the non-standard variant of all the other variables, while one who uses [ʊ] will use

---

[6] It is interesting to note though that such pronunciations are still considered typical: the Berlin transport authority uses the slogan 'Hinaus ins Jrüne!' (literally: 'off into the green!') in its advertising.

all the non-standard variants except perhaps [e:] and so on. If this is the case, it follows that taking all six variables together as part of a general trend away from non-standard towards standard, [e:] will generally be the first variant to be abandoned, while [o:] will be the most resistant to change. This implicational ordering of variants could also enable us to rank speakers in the same way according to their degree of 'dialectality', that is to say, how 'strong' their dialect is.

### 4.4.4 Pragmatics: *Berliner Schnauze*

Dialect studies have always concentrated heavily on phonology and vocabulary, and to a lesser extent on syntax and morphology. More recently, some dialectologists have appealed for other factors to be taken into account, which are more difficult to describe but just as important in the characterization of a speech variety (see Mattheier 1980; Schlieben-Lange and Weydt 1978). For our purposes, we can summarize these factors with the terms situation and style. We shall return to the rôle of situation in section 4.5 and concentrate here on style, which Dittmar *et al.* (1986: 8) understand as 'manner of speaking'.

*Berliner Schnauze* (*Schnauze* is a colloquial term meaning 'muzzle', 'snout') is not simply a popular label for BUV: it is a 'mixture of wit and humour, quick-wittedness, powerful verbal expression, self-assertive aggressiveness and loudmouthed behaviour'.[7] The description of this special 'style' must go beyond those features of phonology and vocabulary that characterize BUV, as BUV is merely a vehicle for *Schnauze*. The goal here is to discover and describe those aspects of a local/regional speech variety which are difficult if not impossible for an outsider to learn: in this case, what is it that distinguishes a Berliner from, say, a Hamburger who has mastered BUV? The importance of this for urban dialectology should be clear if we consider that the kind of social relationships often taken for granted within a small rural community generally have to be established or negotiated in a town, where contact with strangers is potentially much greater. The relative social status of two interlocutors is less likely to be clear in advance and so one of the purposes of verbal interaction is precisely to work out 'where you stand'. This can of course be achieved quite amicably, but it is held to be typical of a (certain type of) Berliner to attempt to establish superiority by means of verbal combat, and by examining this kind of interaction we can provide an analysis of one aspect of the *Schnauze*.

---

[7] 'eine . . . Mischung aus Witz und Humor, Schlagfertigkeit, verbaler Ausdrucksstärke, selbstbehauptender Aggressivität und "Großschnauzigkeit"' (Dittmar *et al.* 1986: 9).

Conflict and the description of conflict can be seen as a type of routine activity and may therefore have an internal structure or pattern in the same way as jokes, stories, requests and commands do. Conflict is a ritual, very similar to the routine insults exchanged by young Blacks in New York (see Labov 1972b: Ch. 8; cf. also Saville-Troike 1989: 250–6), except that its intent is always aggressive. The conflict may be either real or hypothetical, in which case the speakers say 'what they would do if . . .', but the narration of both forms of conflict follows a certain sequence. By way of illustration, we shall deal here only with the first type, real conflict. A typical (description of a) real conflict has three phases: initiation, negotiation and outcome. The first two phases can be analysed with the aid of ten '**speech act** rules', which constitute a kind of discourse grammar (see Dittmar *et al.* 1986: 21–3). In the following example, the square brackets indicate those parts of the narrative corresponding to the original contributions of the two protagonists and the curly brackets indicate those sections covered by a particular speech act rule; the relevant rules themselves are given below.

## Example

### Summary of the **speech event**

N, the caretaker, and O, a neighbour, live in a permanent state of tension. When O threatens to beat up N's children at the next opportunity, the speaker N declares that in that case he will not restrain himself any longer. Although he had been instructed by the landlord to avoid violent arguments while on duty, he would no longer feel bound by this. O should prepare to face a terrible act of retaliation. At this point, the opponent withdraws.

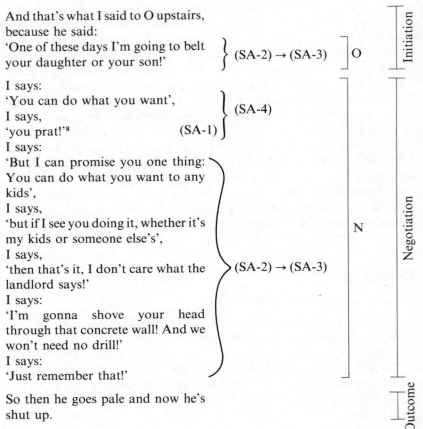

## Language and society

### N's account of the speech event

And that's what I said to O upstairs,
because he said:
'One of these days I'm going to belt
your daughter or your son!'  $(SA-2) \rightarrow (SA-3)$  O  — *Initiation*

I says:
'You can do what you want',
I says,
'you prat!'[8]  (SA-1)  $(SA-4)$

I says:
'But I can promise you one thing:
You can do what you want to any
kids',
I says,
'but if I see you doing it, whether it's
my kids or someone else's',
I says,
'then that's it, I don't care what the  $(SA-2) \rightarrow (SA-3)$  N  — *Negotiation*
landlord says!'
I says:
'I'm gonna shove your head
through that concrete wall! And we
won't need no drill!'
I says:
'Just remember that!'

So then he goes pale and now he's
shut up.  — *Outcome*

### Speech act (SA) rules

#### SA-1: INSULTS

If A and B are in a conflict interaction and A makes a statement about B,
which

> concerns the mental condition of B or
> describes B with an animal metaphor,

then A's statement is considered an insult to B.

---

[8] The speaker's actual words were 'Du Affe!' (literally: 'you ape').

120

### SA-2: THREATS

If A makes a statement to B, which refers to the execution of/failure to carry out an action x by B and announces a consequent action y, and B thinks that A thinks that

he is in a position to carry y out and that
y is undesirable for B,

then A's statement is considered a threat.

### SA-3: STATUS CLAIMS

If A and B are in a conflict interaction and A makes a statement about B in the form of

a threat or
a forceful demand

and B thinks that A has no right to make such a statement on the basis of his status, then B understands A's statement as an attempt to define the relationship between A and B, in which A intends to dominate.

### SA-4: REJECTION OF CLAIM TO DOMINANCE

If A has made a statement to B claiming dominance over him and B replies with a statement, which

rejects the claim or
makes it clear that A's threat has not achieved its **perlocutionary effect**,

then B rejects with his reply the relationship defined by A.

O's threat, which triggers off the conflict, constitutes a claim to a position of dominance over N. N then rejects this claim with an insult and goes on to turn the tables on his opponent with his own, very much more menacing threat. The fact that this threat seems a little unrealistic does not reduce its effect; on the contrary, the effect of a threat lies in its intimidatory power. (For more detailed discussion of this and other examples see Dittmar *et al.* 1986: 14–45 and Dittmar *et al.* 1988: 49–87.)

It would be unfortunate and inaccurate to give the impression that *Berliner Schnauze* manifests itself only in the desire to use one's neighbour as a battering ram, and there are of course other aspects of the style. Berliners are known for their verbal creativity, and anonymous observation in pubs, shops, offices and other public places provides many examples in the form of:

Neologisms
*mohndoof* (extremely stupid)
*rinschmoken* (thump, belt)
*Jedächtniswärmer* ('beret'; literally 'memory warmer')
Semantic extension (the use of words that already exist but with a new meaning)
*Biefies*: normally small salamis but used also to refer to ticket inspectors employed by the Berlin transport department, BVG; it is thus a play on the pronunciation: [beː fau geː].
*Molleküle*: not a molecule but a cold beer – a play on *'eine kühle Molle'*, itself a typical Berlin expression

Idiomatic variation (altering a well-known idiom for surprise effect: the effect is obviously lost in translation)
'Denn fress' ik 'n Nuckel uff!' for: *'ich fresse einen Besen'* ('I'll eat my hat' – literally 'broom', and changed here to 'teat, nipple, baby's dummy').

Berliners also add spice to their speech through a number of rhetorical devices, some of which will be familiar to inhabitants of other cities such as London or New York. Hyperbole is clearly a vital ingredient of many *Schnauze* exchanges but does not necessarily serve an aggressive purpose as in the example above – it may simply be an expression of the 'larger than life' quality of Berliners. Discussing his holiday, for instance, one speaker says: 'Det hat so jeregnet, wir dachten wir kriejn Schwimmhäute' ('It rained so much we thought we were going to get webbed feet'). The Berliners' lively imagination also expresses itself in colourful images, especially to describe personal performance or qualities. One speaker describes for example how he would leave Berlin if he was young again: 'Wat mein Sie, wie ik abhaun würde! Det die Socken qualm!' ('I'd clear off so fast it'd set my socks on fire!'). And a fat woman describes the image she gives cleaning windows as: 'Wie Ballarina auf der Leita!' ('Like a ballerina up a ladder!') (see Dittmar *et al.* 1986: 58–67).

### 4.4.5 Attitudes to variation

The analysis and description of style, as defined above, complements the study of a variety's phonology, vocabulary etc. It enables the linguist to go beyond the description of a speech variety and to attempt to characterize the verbal behaviour of a speech community. So far, this picture consists only of objective information: we know something about the vocabulary and phonology of BUV and about the way Berliners speak, but what do they think of their speech? An attempt to capture the social meaning of a speech variety depends in the end on discovering its speakers' attitudes towards it.

One way of doing this is by the indirect route of testing people's reactions to different speech varieties. You could, for example, record the voices of half a dozen speakers with quite distinct accents and then ask informants to say how interesting, intelligent, trustworthy or entertaining they thought the various speakers are or which of a given set of jobs they would be best suited to. This might seem an unrealistic task and yet it is remarkable how many people appear to find it perfectly reasonable to assess someone's character, personality or job suitability purely on the basis of hearing a sample of their speech.

A particularly revealing version of this technique, devised by the Canadian psychologist Wallace Lambert (see e.g. Lambert *et al.* 1960) and since used in countless studies, is the **matched guise test**. For this test, two of the voices (or in some cases even all of them) belong to the same speaker, so that in theory all factors other than accent may be held constant for each of this speaker's different 'guises'. The advantage of this kind of approach is that it enables us to quantify people's attitudes to different speech varieties or even individual features, and because the data are elicited indirectly (informants are asked what they think about the speakers, not the voices), it is considered to be fairly objective. In practice however it is extremely difficult to design tests in such a way that evaluations really can be attributed to a single factor.

The alternative, qualitative approach involves the interpretation of explicit statements about language and language use. Value judgements made in this way are not quantifiable and the interpretation of them is selective and therefore subjective, but taken in conjunction with the objective data they can provide an interesting and subtle profile of a speech community. Labov (1972a: 248) claims that 'social attitudes towards language are extremely uniform throughout a speech community' and indeed suggests that 'it seems plausible to define a speech community as a group of speakers who share a set of social attitudes towards language'. There seems to be some support for this view here in that West Berliners repeatedly use the same terms in describing BUV: common (*ordinär*), vulgar (*vulgär*), brash (*schnoddrig*), bad grammar (*falsche Grammatik*). There is clearly a widespread awareness of the negative social prestige attached to BUV in West Berlin.

On the other hand, as we have seen, speech is an important aspect of self-image and group identity, so that while they acknowledge the stigma many speakers react strongly against it in defence of their identity. Aesthetic judgements then may combine the acceptance of social norms and the simultaneous rejection of them. Speakers also judged BUV in social/functional terms and these judgements correspond to what we know about its actual use. The non-standard variety is associated in people's minds with particular districts, which are identified as social as well as geographical territories. Equally, BUV is considered more suitable for certain purposes than for others. The fact that speakers claim to shift according to situation, both 'upwards' towards standard and 'downwards' into BUV (see Giles and Smith 1979 for a discussion of the notions 'upward' and 'downward convergence'), seems to confirm that Berliners have a strong awareness of an appropriate functional distribution of BUV and standard according to social contexts (Schlobinski 1987: 196).

A rather different picture emerges in East Berlin. In West Berlin the standard is generally recognized as the 'legitimate language' (*legitime Sprache*), which has prestige and so acts as the target variety for those with social aspirations, while BUV is associated with negative values. In East Berlin however the rôles are effectively reversed, although for different reasons. Here too there is a link between prestigious occupations and language, but as there is widespread resentment amongst native Berliners that Saxon outsiders seem to get the best jobs, the Saxon-influenced standard variety that is the language of public domains is not the prestige variety. On the contrary, it is BUV that enjoys prestige, precisely as the language of everyday speech.

This is particularly so in a district like Prenzlauer Berg. Since 1945 it has remained largely unchanged, both physically and in the composition of its population. This has helped to reinforce the status of BUV as the principal variety of the mainly blue-collar population. Neighbouring Wedding in West Berlin on the other hand has experienced radical changes in the last forty years: the physical structure of the district has changed through large-scale renovation and rebuilding programmes and the previously uniform population has been transformed by the influx of foreigners as well as Germans from the Federal Republic. The result has been the break-up of traditional networks and a tendency towards greater linguistic variation. Wedding now lies somewhere between the two extremes represented by Zehlendorf and Prenzlauer Berg: although local identity and working-class traditions have survived to some extent, they are now increasingly in competition with the prestige norms that dominate West Berlin. For this reason, it can make sense to consider Berlin as a single speech community only if we recognize within it two subordinate 'communication communities', East and West (Schlobinski 1987: 234–6). These two communities share the same speech variety, but its rôle differs both quantitatively and qualitatively, as a result of divergent social and historical developments. It is this combination of differing degrees of use of non-standard variants and differing evaluations of BUV, of objective and subjective factors, that together with the *Schnauze* makes up the distinctive picture of this urban speech community and constitutes the social meaning of BUV.

## 4.5 Erp: suburban dialectology

The account of variation in Berlin speech in the previous section showed that it is possible to develop a framework for investigating urban speech varieties by adopting a more eclectic but at the same time more rigorous approach than was characteristic of traditional dialectology. By turning now to the study of a rural community that, like Nauborn (see 4.3.1), has increasingly come under the influence of a neighbouring city, we can see that an equally sophisticated approach is necessary to give an adequate account of the sociolinguistic consequences of urbanization in a suburban setting. Research into language and language use in this community was carried out in the course of a long-term project in the 1970s and the results are still being assessed (see Forschungsbericht Erp-Projekt: Besch *et al.* 1981; Hufschmidt *et al.* 1983).

### 4.5.1 The speech community

In the course of the last twenty years or so the small town of Erp has effectively become a satellite, if not yet quite a suburb, of Cologne. The formerly stable rural community has been transformed by the decline in the number of agricultural workers and a corresponding growth in the number of commuting 'hobby farmers' and newcomers. It is thus typical of many such communities that have recently experienced the effects of modernization and in particular have undergone a rapid change in their social composition. This in turn has far-reaching consequences for language use, for speech is a form of social behaviour that is influenced and conditioned by prevailing values and social norms and by the communicative needs of the community. So if the social composition of a community becomes more complex and its value system changes, this creates a need for more socially differentiated patterns of speech. For this reason, the analysis of language use in Erp was based not on the individual but the social group, which is defined by both objective and subjective criteria: a social group is composed of those individuals 'who live together as potential communication partners under comparable conditions and who interpret these conditions in a similar way and therefore have acquired and use similar patterns of action in their social actions'.⁹ So individuals are not allocated to pre-established social categories but rather identify themselves in terms of the relationships they establish and the way in which they respond to given situations. Similarly, the notion 'situation' is defined both by objective factors and the individual's perception and interpretation of them. On the basis of these notions, the project (Hufschmidt and Mattheier 1981a: 81) set out to investigate:

(1)   language use – describing the varieties and how they are conditioned by situational factors;
(2)   language variation – describing the varieties used by each social group and the relationship between varieties and groups; and
(3)   language change – looking for current changes in varieties brought about through situational changes and changes in the relationships between varieties.

The realization of these objectives should then contribute to the overall aim of establishing a 'communication profile' of the community. We shall say more about this in the next section.

An ambitious aspect of the programme was the attempt to use not a random sample of inhabitants as informants but the entire working male population aged between 21 and 65. Women were excluded on the grounds that employment was considered a crucial factor: the number of women in employment was too small to form a statistically valid grouping and the category 'housewife' was felt to be too heterogeneous to be useful. Despite this rationale, the exclusion of women from the survey must surely be considered a major weakness of the study and in considering the findings we should bear in mind that any conclusions reached can be applied with any certainty only to the men in the community. In the event, 61 per cent of those contacted were willing to take part and two-thirds of them ( = 144) were finally selected (Klein 1981).

To compose a linguistic picture of a community, a large quantity of natural spoken language is required as data. The method chosen here was to ask the informants to select an acquaintance from the list of participants and then arrange a meeting between these pairs of informants and two researchers. The recording sessions had three phases:

A = 'normal style': informants talked casually about everyday matters, with the researchers present but not participating;

⁹ 'Von allen Individuen, die unter vergleichbaren Bedingungen als potentielle Kommunikationspartner miteinander leben und diese Bedingungen ähnlich interpretieren und deshalb auch ähnliche Handlungsmuster für ihre Sozialhandlungen erlernt haben und verwenden, nehmen wir an, daß sie eine "soziale Gruppe" bilden' (Hufschmidt and Mattheier 1981a: 63).

B = 'careful style': each informant was interviewed about his work;
C = 'very careful style': a third researcher was formally introduced
and gave a short talk on language variation before conducting tests
on linguistic judgement (see 4.5.3).

These sessions were to provide data for both objective linguistic analysis
and the investigation of attitudes to language.

**4.5.2** Composing a communication profile

As in Berlin, the underlying question here is: what is the social meaning of
linguistic variation in Erp? A starting point is to discover the extent to
which the local traditional dialect is still used, and data on dialect use were
gathered by questionnaire from all the inhabitants originally contacted
(Kall-Holland 1981). Unfortunately, however, they were asked whether
they could speak dialect, not whether they actually did, and it was not
even clear whether they all understood the same thing by the notion
'dialect'. Nevertheless, the survey does seem to suggest that the dialect is
far from being obsolescent, as even in the 20–30 age range 62 per cent
claimed an active knowledge of it. Furthermore, there seems to be strong
family pressure exerted on newcomers 'marrying into' established local
families to learn the dialect. The factors most closely related to dialect use,
though, are origin and occupation: dialect knowledge is greatest among
those with the highest degree of integration into the community and the
fewest professional qualifications.

The responses to a questionnaire can only help to describe the current
situation: a different kind of information is required to account for this
situation and to predict what may happen in the future. The decisive
questions here will be the speakers' experience of and attitudes to
variation in language use. Sixty-four per cent of the informants claimed to
be primarily dialect speakers, 23 per cent claimed to speak the developing
local colloquial non-standard speech form and 13 per cent standard. But
how is this pattern reflected in the consciousness of the individual
speakers? How do they experience the tension between the societal norm
(standard) and the main local medium of communication (dialect)? How
do non-dialect speakers, especially newcomers, feel? Questions like these,
posed and explored in great detail here (Hufschmidt 1983), represent a
major innovation in German dialectology, as for virtually the first time
informants are seen as thinking human beings rather than merely
anonymous suppliers of authentic speech.

As with the study of Berliners' attitudes to BUV, the raw material here
consists of personal anecdotes. For the purpose of analysis, however, the
responses may be grouped into four categories:

(1)  'DIALECT IS THE MAIN MEDIUM OF COMMUNICATION HERE.'
Most informants in fact take this for granted but some felt that
newcomers ought to learn the dialect and that it plays an important
rôle in social contact.

(2)  'POSITIVE EXPERIENCE AND EVALUATION OF DIALECT.'
This category includes more assertive statements on the value of
dialect than category (1).

(3)  'STANDARD IS GROWING IN IMPORTANCE,
DIALECT DECLINING.'
Reasons suggested include external causes like the post-war influx
of outsiders and the fact that school-teachers are no longer local
dialect-speakers, as well as feelings that dialect is not essential for
integration, and efforts to speak standard with their children.

(4)  'NEGATIVE EXPERIENCE AND EVALUATION OF DIALECT.'
Many dialect-speakers claim to have suffered at school and others
fear ridicule outside the community (e.g. on holiday) or on public
occasions like parents' meetings at school.

These four types of response then serve as the basis for more refined
analysis according to the key social variables occupation, primary
language use and origin. That is to say, it is possible to construct a crude
'identikit picture' of the attitude of, for instance, the typical worker
( = dialect is no longer the main variety, experience of dialect mixed but
evaluation positive); the typical dialect-speaker ( = dialect is still the main
variety but is losing influence to standard, negative experiences but
positive evaluation); or the typical newcomer ( = does not envisage
standard replacing dialect, no negative experience, positive evaluation).

However unquantifiable this kind of analysis might be, it does at least
provide a relatively subtle account of the interplay between varieties in the
community. It also gives some clues to the likely linguistic development of
the community, but predictions about the future of specific varieties
depend crucially on language use in the family and in school, i.e. in the
raising of the young generation (Mickartz 1983). There is broad
agreement that knowledge of the standard is both necessary and
desirable: views differ only in the degree of importance attached to it and
the relative importance of maintaining the dialect. Here again, occupation of the (potential) parents appears to be decisive, but there are also
differences between generations. The so-called 'new middle class' (NMC:
salaried employees and civil servants) is divided: those with more senior
posts tend to doubt the value of maintaining the dialect, while the rest,
with stronger local ties and perhaps fewer aspirations, believe it has a
place beside the standard. Older members of the 'old middle class' (OMC:

farmers, craftsmen, tradesmen) had spoken dialect with their children, but the younger generation seems to favour a bidialectal upbringing for their children. This social group, together with manual workers, has the strongest local ties and is seen as the most influential in preserving the dialect.

Taking all the findings about attitudes together, we have a complex picture. There is no doubt that the standard is gaining a firm foothold in the community and yet there seems to be little sign of the dialect declining. Attitudes expressed directly by informants are notoriously unreliable and often conflict with actual practice, but it is clear that Erp people are conscious of the importance of language in their lives, both in practical and in symbolic terms. What is not yet clear is the relationship between the statements we have so far considered on the question of linguistic variety and the scope, both actual and perceived, of this variety.

### 4.5.3 Identifying speech varieties

In the final part of the recording sessions each informant was asked to carry out two tests. The object of the first was to find out more about the shape of the linguistic continuum within which the speakers claimed to operate. We know that they have a fairly developed sense of linguistic variation, but it is important to find out just how many individual varieties they think they use and what determines the selection of one rather than another, and it would be interesting to see if there is any correlation between their perceived linguistic range and specific social features (Klein 1983).

In order to avoid circularity, a simple test form was devised on which no linguistic labels appeared except *Hochdeutsch* ('High German' or, in our terms, 'formal standard German': see Chapter 5). This marked one end of a horizontal arrow, representing a linguistic continuum, on which no further points were marked. The informants were then asked to indicate the variety they normally used in conversation with each of thirteen interlocutors by putting the relevant number at the appropriate point on the arrow. Each form could then have any number of varieties marked on it from one to thirteen, and this is indeed what happened. However, as it is scarcely credible that any speaker could use more than perhaps four or five, and in order to make the results more manageable, individual varieties marked as being very close to each other were grouped into 'clusters' (Klein 1983: 133–6). This procedure reduced the spread of varieties to between one and six, which gives a much more plausible image, especially as the repertoire claimed by 70 per cent of the informants would consist of either two or three clusters.

Some tentative conclusions can be drawn in terms of correlations between this self-assessment and objective non-linguistic factors. For instance, younger speakers tend to claim a broad spectrum of linguistic variation, generally recording more than two clusters and covering the full span of the continuum, while older speakers indicate a more limited and clearly divided usage with only one or two clusters. Members of long-established local families claim a highly differentiated pattern with five or more clusters, but newcomers from elsewhere in the Rhineland indicate only two on average. There are various possible explanations for these tendencies, but the conclusions remain rather speculative. What is more significant here is the overall pattern: Fig. 4.6 shows the distribution of linguistic varieties according to interlocutor (the three varieties are derived from a further rationalization of the test results: see Klein 1983: 137, 172).

Professed use of the colloquial speech variety shows little variation: it can apparently be used equally well with anyone. The X-pattern of standard and dialect however indicates that these two varieties have complementary functions: there seems to be a fair consensus about which variety to use with whom. Ranked seventh, 'child' is in the pivotal position in the ranking order, but clearly to the left of the crossover point in Fig. 4.6, i.e. according to the self-evaluation test more standard than dialect is spoken with children (but of course in practice this may not be the case). The interlocutors on either side of 'child' fall neatly into two groups: 1–6 (standard) have a relatively high social status or else are by definition unfamiliar to the informant, 8–13 (dialect) are of relatively low status or personally close to the informant. This suggests that the crucial factor in the choice of variety is the type of interaction: standard is felt to be appropriate in situations where the speakers are engaged in a relatively serious, business-like exchange with the emphasis on the subject matter, while dialect is preferred for exchanges on a more personal level (Klein 1983: 180; this distinction is sometimes referred to in terms of 'transactional' and 'personal' interactions: see Gumperz 1966).

The results of the self-evaluation test were quite revealing but how do they compare with the speakers' ability actually to distinguish between different varieties? After all, one of the factors determining which variety speakers choose will be the variety they think the initiator of the dialogue has chosen and one of the symptoms of 'communicative incompetence' (Hudson 1980) is the inability to pick up a speaker's intention as expressed in his or her choice of linguistic form. In the second test the informants were again asked to locate varieties as points on a continuum but the input this time was not their own perceived linguistic repertoire but six short recordings of speech ranging from standard through

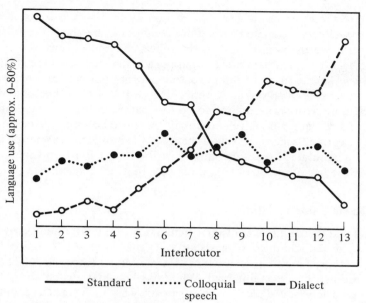

Fig. 4.6 Erp: language use according to interlocutor (1, teacher; 2, stranger; 3, counter clerk; 4, priest; 5, superior; 6, fleeting acquaintance; 7, child; 8, colleague; 9, younger relative; 10, wife; 11, friend; 12, older relative; 13, dialect-speaker
Source: Klein 1983

regional colloquial speech to the traditional dialects of neighbouring villages (Mattheier 1983a).

The results of this test show that while standard and dialect were readily identified, the intermediate forms were not so easily distinguished from each other. This would suggest either that the differences between these varieties are objectively too slight for them to be isolated as discrete varieties or that some speakers at least consider such distinctions insignificant. The first possibility seems less likely, however, as the speech samples were carefully selected and graded in relation to each other in terms of dialectality, that is (in this case) the extent to which they diverged phonologically from the standard. Some support is lent to the second explanation, firstly by the fact that those with most contact with both the regional and the more standard-like colloquial speech variety – the younger newcomers from the Rhineland belonging to the 'new middle class' (NMC) or the commuting working class – were least successful in distinguishing these two varieties, and secondly by the fact that the 'old middle class' (OMC) appeared to be the best judges overall (Mattheier 1983a: 250, 258–9).

Both of these points suggest that the ability to distinguish between varieties is closely associated with, if not conditioned by, the desire to do so. In other words, we are more likely to hear differences if we actually want to hear them. In this context, the important distinction for the NMC is between the intermediate and the extreme forms, not between the two intermediate colloquial speech varieties. The OMC, on the other hand, is perhaps more sensitive as, unlike most other groups, it tends to value both standard and dialect positively and may therefore be more inclined to identify clear and accurate divisions between the intervening varieties, in order to maintain their functional distribution, i.e. the distinction between the use of one variety and another in given contexts.

### 4.5.4 Re-assessing variation

The fact that there is no overall agreement in Erp about how many speech varieties can be identified suggests strongly that linguistic variation in German (at least in this area) is not as clear-cut or as sharply stratified as has traditionally been maintained. While speakers may switch abruptly from one variety (say, dialect) to another (say, what we have been calling standard) according to context, it is increasingly common to make a less marked shift away from one variety towards another. We have already referred to the notion of convergence, as opposed to switching (see 4.4.5), and this implies that the reality of variation in German is better described in terms of a relatively fluid continuum than of discrete varieties. This aspect of variation has had surprisingly little attention paid to it and so the next chapter will attempt to show how it might be tackled and accounted for.

### Further reading

Bausch (1982) contains a number of articles dealing with urban speech and Mattheier (1980) is an excellent discussion of the issues confronting German dialectology and sociolinguistics. The problem of eliciting natural speech is one of the central methodological issues in sociolinguistics and a good survey is given in Hufschmidt and Mattheier (1981b). In addition to the urban studies cited in the text, a major project has also been under way in Vienna for some years: see, for example, Moosmüller (1984). The main publications from the Berlin project in book form are Dittmar *et al.* (1986), Dittmar and Schlobinski (1988), Schlobinski (1984, 1986 and 1987), and Schlobinski and Blank (1985). The results of the Erp project are to be published in four volumes, of which only two have so far appeared: Besch *et al.* (1981) and Hufschmidt *et al.* (1983).

# 5 Sociolinguistic variation and the continuum of colloquial speech

## 5.1 Differing views of variation in German

The study of the German language in German-speaking countries has, more often than not, meant the study of two language types which are markedly different from each other, so different in fact as to be often mutually unintelligible.

### 5.1.1 Standard German

The first of these language types has a number of titles in German, such as *Hochsprache*, **Schriftsprache**, *Literatursprache*, *Einheitssprache* and *Standardsprache*: the favoured term in the GDR is *Literatursprache*; the other terms are variously used in the other German-speaking countries. We label it 'formal standard German'. It is the type of German which German-speaking children were traditionally expected to produce in both speech and writing at school, which is described in most grammar books and dictionaries, and which has usually been taught to foreigners. Its grammar is described in works such as *Duden*, its pronunciation in pronouncing dictionaries such as the *Duden Aussprachewörterbuch* and *Siebs Deutsche Aussprache*. It is very often, but not always, the form of German which carries the highest prestige.

At this point readers with some knowledge of the study of English may imagine that this form of German is closely parallel to the type of English which we call 'standard English', and may wonder why we have included the word 'formal' in the title of the prestige variety of German. The word 'formal' has been added for good reason, and reflects significant sociolinguistic differences between standard English and the German prestige type.

In modern linguistic work 'standard English' designates the written and spoken usage, in virtually all situations, of a considerable section of the population of English-speaking countries; roughly it is the language of the middle class and of a section of the working class. Virtually all native speakers of English can understand it and many who do not habitually speak it are able to do so on occasion. We have termed standard English loosely as a '**type**', but actually it is considerably differentiated; there are different national varieties of it in different English-speaking countries (USA, Britain, Australia, etc.) which differ from each other in pronunciation, to a lesser extent in vocabulary and to a small extent in grammar, and then within each of these countries there is regional and social variation within standard English which affects chiefly pronunciation (see Trudgill and Hannah 1982: 1).

Not only does standard English vary considerably from place to place and person to person, it also encompasses a wide range of registers; that is to say each person's speech differs depending on a whole range of external circumstances such as the topic under discussion, the situation, the person addressed, and so on. Such register variation is highly complex, but we can, for many purposes, group registers into two classes, formal and informal, and talk about formal and informal (or colloquial) language, though for many other purposes this division is too crude. To give examples from standard English, formal standard English tends to use more abstract nouns than does colloquial standard (e.g. formal English 'the consumption of alcohol was high' may correspond to informal English 'people drank a lot') and fewer verbal contractions (e.g. 'he has not seen it' where informal English would have 'he hasn't seen it' or 'he's not seen it'). Formal registers are typically specialized or technical, or are addressed to people whom the speaker does not know well; informal registers are typically everyday relaxed conversation. Formal registers are more often written than are informal registers.

Although the concept of standard English is a very useful one, its limits are not clear. However, certain grammatical forms are clearly stigmatized in English, and may be said to mark speech which contains them as non-standard, for example some past-tense forms of verbs like 'I seen him' or multiple negative constructions such as 'I didn't drink no beer.' While many people may consider such speech 'wrong English', linguists will label it 'non-standard dialect speech' or simply 'dialect speech'. Such non-standard dialect speech represents the informal registers of a very considerable section of the English-speaking population, and is distinct from standard English. The dividing line between standard and non-standard, though indistinct, is highly significant, correlating as it does with important social and educational differences.

It is important to note that standard English is a very broad category, encompassing all the registers of a sizeable proportion of the population. Modern grammars of English usually attempt to describe at least some of the variation in standard English (see, for example, the inclusion of contracted verb forms in Quirk and Greenbaum 1973: 35–8) and modern teaching programmes for English as a second language usually aim to teach some of this range of registers: for example, most learners of English are now taught the relatively informal verbal contractions ('he's, hasn't', etc).

In contrast, grammars of German and teaching materials for foreigners were until recently based on a form of language which represented the everyday informal registers of no German-speaker. Recently there has been rapid change in this respect, with modern grammars – such as Eisenberg (1986) – appearing, and new teaching programmes for foreign learners such as *Deutsch aktiv* (Neuner *et al.* 1979) and *Themen* (Aufderstraße *et al.* 1983). Nevertheless, until the last ten years or so, students who had acquired their knowledge of German purely through learning it at school could well have been surprised on visiting a German-speaking country to discover that people did not speak in the way they imagined they would. The reason for this was that grammars and teaching materials were based not on the speech and writing of educated people in a wide range of registers, that is on an entity comparable to standard English, but rather on the speech and writing, often just on the writing, of educated people in formal registers. For example, while the grammar of English by Quirk and Greenbaum is a fair description of the modern English of educated speakers, one may look in vain even today in German grammars for reference to certain common phenomena in the modern language of educated speakers. For instance, the common use of *der, die, das*, etc., instead of the third person pronouns *er, sie, es*, etc., and particularly of *die* instead of *sie* (plural), even where the pronouns are not emphasized, is not discussed in any reference grammar of German (the use of *der, die, das*, etc., for *er, sie, es*, etc. under conditions of emphasis is, however, a generally recognized feature of standard German). The common replacement of the demonstratives *dieser* and *jener* by *der hier* or *der da* seems to be discussed only in Eisenberg (1986: 191). In other words the basis of the grammars, the *Schriftsprache* or *Standardsprache*, was, and still is to an extent, an entity comparable not to standard English but to formal standard English, and we have therefore labelled it 'formal standard German'.

Despite the scarcity of descriptions of it, a colloquial standard German does exist, analogous to colloquial standard English; there is often less purely social variation in its pronunciation than there is in standard English, but it is more regionally diverse in every respect, in pronunciation, grammar and vocabulary, than is standard English. There are also regional differences in the extent to which it is used, which are generally greater than such differences in English; in areas where English is a first language there are always locally born native speakers of standard English, but in German-speaking Switzerland, for example, none of the native population speaks standard German as a first language, though most learn it to some level of proficiency. Then in south Germany and Austria native speakers of the standard language represent a smaller proportion of the population than do standard English speakers in, for example, any part of England, whereas in north Germany the proportion of speakers of the standard language is probably about the same as the proportion of standard speakers in most parts of England.

If, as we have seen, all Germans speak informally in a type of language that differs from that conventionally described in grammars, we might conclude that there is a standard German which exists in formal registers only, and that the informal speech of all German-speakers is non-standard or dialect; in other words we might conclude that the sociolinguistic situation in German-speaking countries is like that in many minority language communities, where everyone speaks a localized non-standard form, a standard form existing only in writing and perhaps in some very restricted spoken registers. This has indeed been the conclusion of some writers, such as Bodmer (1944/1981:289), but it will not stand up to scrutiny. On the contrary, it is a matter of common experience that, throughout the German-speaking countries, one hears a form of German, different from the formal standard, which, though regionally differentiated, nevertheless shows considerable uniformity in grammar, and sufficient uniformity in pronunciation and vocabulary, for generally easy communication between speakers from different regions. It differs markedly from non-standard German in that it does not contain certain clearly non-standard grammatical constructions, and contains localized vocabulary only to a limited extent.

### 5.1.2 Traditional German dialects

The second type of German which has been extensively studied in German-speaking countries is traditional German dialect, in German *Dialekt* or *Mundart*. This type of German encompasses an enormous range of varieties, differing as it does from village to village. Again, readers familiar with modern linguistic work on English may imagine that we are dealing with an entity closely parallel to English dialect as this is understood by English-speaking linguists, and may wonder why we have given this type of German speech a rather different title, including the word 'traditional'. The answer is that German linguists who use the words *Dialekt* or *Mundart* are not labelling a speech form parallel to English dialect as this is now generally understood. 'Dialect' or 'non-standard dialect' in English cannot be exactly defined, but usually refers nowadays to any form of English which contains grammatical forms or vocabulary not generally found in the speech of educated middle-class people; speech containing stigmatized past-tense forms (e.g. 'I seen him') or multiple negatives (e.g. 'I didn't drink no beer') or clearly localized vocabulary (e.g. 'hoy' = 'throw' on Tyneside) would generally be considered examples of English dialect. Some writers, particularly American, even label all appreciable pronunciation differences as 'dialect differences', but British writing generally reserves the term 'dialect' for speech types which differ from standard English in grammar or vocabulary. Forms of standard English (the majority) which differ only in pronunciation from the most prestigious form – standard English pronounced with '**received pronunciation**' (RP) accent – are described as standard English, but are said to be standard English pronounced with a regional accent (for further discussion see Petyt 1980: 34–5). Regional accents are still socially unacceptable in certain circles (indeed RP is unacceptable in some circles as well), but are generally nothing like so highly stigmatized as non-standard grammatical forms, and do not pose comprehension problems in the way that non-standard vocabulary does.

Note that we use the term 'non-standard dialect' as well as simply 'dialect'. The reason for this is that some writers in English, rather than contrasting the 'standard language' with 'dialects', contrast the 'standard dialect' with 'non-standard dialects'. This usage underlines the fact that linguistically the standard language is in no sense a different type of entity from the non-standard dialects; it merely has different social characteristics. We do not adopt this usage here since it is less common, and is very far from German usage, where the term *Dialekt* is never used to refer to the standard language.

It is most important to note that some departures in pronunciation from the prestige form in some types of English speech do present comprehension difficulties for other speakers, and are generally considered to represent dialect differences. These are (in some sense which it is hard to define precisely) departures in pronunciation which are acoustically large, and which are relatively unsystematic. Speech which contains them would be termed 'English dialect' (see Petyt 1980: 22–4). The difference between such large departures in pronunciation and mere accent differences is best shown by an example: a speaker of English from Tyneside who says the phrase 'A hole in the ground' with the vowel [oː] for RP [əu] in 'hole' and the vowel [au] for RP [au] in 'ground' would be said (other things being equal) to be a speaker of standard English with a Tyneside regional accent. If however he had the vowel [au] in 'hole' and the vowel [ʊ] in 'ground' he would be said to be speaking Tyneside dialect. The substitution of [oː] for [əu] in the standard English speech with regional accent does not present much of a comprehension problem for other speakers; the difference is considered small by English speakers, it is expected by many English-speakers since it occurs in many regional accents, and it is very largely predictable in that the vast majority of words which have [əu] in RP will have [oː] in standard English with Tyneside accent. Similar remarks apply to the substitution of [au] for [ɑu].

The pronunciation differences which represent dialect differences are, however, much more of a problem for other English-speakers. They are considered large by English-speakers, they would not be expected since they will not have occurred in the speech which most people will have heard, and, perhaps most crucially, they are apparently random (at least to someone who has not made a close study of historical English phonology!). Only some words with /əu/ in RP will, like 'hole', have /au/ in Tyneside dialect speech; others with RP /əu/, like 'home' (Tyneside /jɛm/), may have /jɛ/, yet others, like 'know' (Tyneside /naː/), will have /aː/, and so on. A similar unpredictability applies to correspondences to RP /ɑu/. We consider, following Petyt 1980: 2–24, that large or unpredictable sound differences such as these represent dialect differences; speech which shows such differences in appreciable numbers is said to be non-standard dialect.

If we consider non-standard dialect to be a type of speech which differs from the standard language in grammar or vocabulary or in major pronunciation features, we notice that it is quite common in English-speaking countries. However, the type of dialect speech most often heard is not very markedly different from standard English; indeed the dividing line between this type of speech and standard English is not at all clear. In fact, in most English-speaking communities, speech is a continuum, made up of an infinite gradation of varieties stretching from formal standard English with the prestige pronunciation (in Britain RP), at one end of the scale, to non-standard dialect with non-standard grammar and much non-standard vocabulary at the other (though in English-speaking communities outside Britain there may not be such a distinctive prestige accent, and in such communities, as well as in urban communities in Britain, distinctive dialect vocabulary may be relatively little heard). Although certain linguistic features correlate with certain social groups, English speech is a continuum in that there are no very clear dividing lines within it; for example the dividing line between standard English and non-standard dialect, though significant, is impossible to locate precisely. English speech is also a continuum in that individuals typically move along it at will dependent on the formality of the situation and the formal registers of most people are appreciably closer to formal standard English than are their informal registers.

In contrast to English dialects as portrayed above, German traditional dialect (*Dialekt* or *Mundart*), as usually described in the literature, is sharply differentiated from standard German (both formal and collo-quial) in every respect, to the point where the two may not be readily mutually comprehensible. Indeed, to judge from some of the literature (see Chapter 6), the differences are so great that speakers of traditional dialects face problems in learning standard German similar to those faced by speakers of foreign languages, and there may be no continuum; speakers of traditional dialect may make a total switch when they shift to standard German (see Goossens 1977: 20).

We saw earlier how, until recently, foreigners learning German at school might discover that they had not learned German as it is actually spoken. In a similar way, students of German in higher education who have gained some familiarity with linguistic work on German, from works as widely separated in time and orientation as Keller (1961) or Ammon (1986), may be surprised when they examine live German speech to find that it does not match up to expectations; particularly if they visit urban centres in north or central Germany they will in fact notice a continuum much like that described for English-speaking countries. They will hear a little formal standard German, a great deal of colloquial standard German, as described above, but also a great deal of other speech, particularly if they mix informally with working-class people, which contains non-standard grammatical features, and which, incident-ally, may be labelled *Dialekt* by many people, but which will be much closer to standard than is traditional dialect, and which will not usually be labelled *Dialekt* by German linguists. They will hear little of what German scholars call *Dialekt* or *Mundart*, which we have labelled 'traditional dialect'. The speech they hear will, like much English speech, be a continuum; there will be no sharp dividing line between standard and non-standard speech, and, as in English, individual speakers will move along the continuum depending on the formality of the situation.

## 5.1.3 The continuum of colloquial speech

We thus find that in much of the German-speaking world the speech of most people can be placed on a continuum, only the most formal end of which, formal standard German, has been extensively described. Although the rest of the continuum has been noticed by German scholars, there has been little attempt to differentiate within it, and relatively little description of it. It has been labelled *Umgangssprache*, which we translate as 'colloquial speech'. As well as colloquial speech, traditional dialect may or may not form part of the continuum, depending on the region.

We consider it useful to differentiate, within colloquial speech, two types of German, which we shall label 'colloquial standard German' and 'colloquial non-standard German', corresponding roughly to the English phenomena of colloquial standard English (though this is not usually discussed separately from formal standard English) and (non-standard) English dialects respectively. We divide colloquial speech in this way for three major reasons: firstly it corresponds roughly to a division which is generally recognized as significant in English. Secondly, the division is noticed by German speakers, who will often make a division within *Umgangssprache* between *Hochdeutsch* and what they call *Dialekt*, though what they label *Dialekt* will often not be labelled as such by scholars, who will use the term *Dialekt* to refer only to traditional dialect. Thirdly, recent German work, particularly on urban speech, has differentiated within colloquial speech, although no consensus has emerged as to how many significant divisions should be made. Within the urban speech of Frankfurt, Veith (1983) distinguishes five varieties: *Standardsprache*, *Dialekt* and, within *Umgangssprache*, *standardnahe* (close to standard), *mittlere* (intermediate) and *dialektnahe* (close to dialect) varieties. The variety described as *Dialekt* is not spoken in the central areas of the city, only in more remote suburbs, and is close to traditional dialect (1983: 86–90).

Schönfeld, reporting work undertaken in the north of the GDR, again distinguishes five speech levels, but they do not correspond exactly to those postulated for Frankfurt by Veith. Schönfeld distinguished *Literatursprache* (formal standard language), *literatursprachenahe Umgangssprache* (close to standard), *mundartnahe Umgangssprache* (close to dialect), *stärker umgangssprachlich beeinflußte niederdeutsche Mundart* (Low German dialect strongly influenced by colloquial speech) and, finally, *niederdeutsche Mundart* (traditional Low German dialect) (Schönfeld 1977: 170).

Our contention that there is a significant twofold division of colloquial speech is based partly on the informal observation that German-speakers in towns, particularly large towns in north Germany, all of whom would conventionally be described as using *Umgangssprache*, nevertheless divide the speech of their home areas into '*Hochdeutsch*' and '*Dialekt*' (neither term used in the technical linguistic sense) and consider themselves to be speakers of one or the other. It is also based on the findings of the large-scale survey of Berlin speech by Dittmar, Schlobinski and others, who have reported Berliners, all of whom use *Umgangssprache* in the conventional sense, as considering that they speak either

Table 5.1. *A terminology for socially determined varieties of German*

| German terminology | Usual English equivalents | English terms adopted here | |
|---|---|---|---|
| Standardsprache/ Einheitssprache/ Schriftsprache/ Literatursprache | standard language | formal standard | |
| Umgangssprache | | colloquial standard | collo- quial speech |
| | | colloquial non-standard | |
| Dialekt/Mundart | (non-standard) dialect | (traditional) dialect | |

*Hochdeutsch* or *Dialekt* (*Dialekt* here being not traditional dialect, but varieties of Berlin colloquial speech relatively remote from the standard) (see above, 4.4, and also Dittmar *et al.* 1986: 116–20).

Table 5.1 sets out the terminology current in German and contrasts it with the usual English terminology, and with the terminology used in this book. Our terminology owes something to that introduced by Wells (1982: 2–8) for English. Later in this chapter we will examine the ways in which colloquial speech differs from formal standard German, and how, within it, colloquial standard German differs from colloquial non-standard speech.

## 5.2 The nature and study of variation in German

**5.2.1** The relationship between colloquial speech, formal standard German and traditional dialect

As discussed above, formal standard German, colloquial standard and colloquial non-standard form a continuum, with significant differences between these speech types, but no very clear or sharp divisions. In areas where traditional dialects are very far from standard German, such as the Upper German and Low German dialect areas, traditional dialects may be fairly sharply separated from the continuum, with traditional dialect-speakers moving onto the continuum through a conscious code-switch when wishing to use more formal language, or when wishing to converse with people from outside their home area, or for other more complex reasons (see e.g. Stellmacher 1977: 155–70). However, even in these areas, scholars are now recognizing that much urban speech may represent a continuum: see, for example, the work on Austria by Dressler, Wiesinger and Moosmüller, reported in Moosmüller (1987) and elsewhere.

In the Middle German dialect area, whose dialects made the greatest contribution historically to the genesis of standard German, and which are in general not as far linguistically from standard German as others are, traditional dialects may form part of the continuum, and it may be harder to distinguish between traditional dialects and colloquial non-standard speech. This is especially true in the East Middle German dialect area (see in particular Schönfeld and Pape 1981: 159).

It should be noted that, although most contemporary 'English dialects' correspond to German colloquial non-standard speech rather than to traditional German dialects, there are nevertheless some rural British dialects which can be compared with traditional German dialects in their distance from standard. However, except perhaps in some Scots and Ulster cases, English dialects can usually be clearly placed on a continuum along with other types of English speech (see Wells 1982: 2–8).

### 5.2.2 The relative neglect of colloquial speech

Given that colloquial German represents the normal spoken medium of the vast majority of German speakers, why has it been so little investigated? Crucial in this respect are two important historical factors: the late unification of Germany compared to that of Britain and other Western European states, and, connected with this, the late industrialization of Germany.

Although a relatively small educated élite has been able to speak standard German and its precursors for several centuries, political fragmentation meant that such people's normal conversation was undoubtedly in a much more localized form of German, in fact a form of middle-class traditional dialect such as still exists in Switzerland and among older people in other areas, for example the *Honoratioren-schwäbisch* of south-west Germany. This retarded the development of a colloquial standard German in many areas, though such a colloquial standard developed quite early in north German cities where the élite turned away fairly early from sharply localized speech forms. It has developed very rapidly everywhere in Germany since German unification, and with increasing speed since the great mixture of populations in the aftermath of the Second World War.

In the centuries of German political fragmentation the formal standard language, scarcely a spoken standard language, represented German national identity, and hence was fostered and studied in an often purist and prescriptive spirit to the understandable neglect of other forms. Colloquial non-standard speech, on the other hand, is the typical speech form of the urban working class, and the relatively late industrialization of Germany meant, of course, that such speech arose relatively late. We do however have evidence going back several centuries for a form of speech in north German cities known as **Missingsch**; this represented standard German heavily influenced by local traditional dialects, in other words something probably very like modern colloquial non-standard speech. (The term *Missingsch* is today applied mainly to some Hamburg varieties.) Given, however, the late evolution in most places of this speech type, compounded by the low prestige of its speakers, the lack of work on it seems less surprising.

### 5.2.3 The neglect of the continuum

Why has German not often been described as a continuum? Since formal standard German and traditional German dialects differ from each other so markedly, and since the study of colloquial speech was long neglected, we can understand how the continuum of German speech has often not been described as such. It was possible to regard formal standard German and traditional dialects as distinct (though of course related) entities, with colloquial speech (if it was considered at all) as just some sort of random mixture between the two.

Another important factor here has been the popularity of the study of traditional dialects; scholars steeped in the study of these traditional forms have typically regarded users of colloquial non-standard speech as, in some sense, 'really' traditional dialect-speakers whose dialect has nevertheless been 'corrupted' by contact with the standard language. Alternatively they could be seen as traditional dialect-speakers making an unsuccessful attempt to speak the standard language. A similar view of colloquial standard German has also been taken by scholars concerned to defend the formal standard language; colloquial standard could be seen as 'debased' or 'tainted' standard German, containing elements that 'really' belonged elsewhere, usually to traditional dialects.

### 5.2.4 The neglect of divisions within the continuum

Why has the division within colloquial speech into colloquial standard German and colloquial non-standard speech, corresponding roughly to the social division between the middle class and the working class, been relatively little discussed? The answer to this question lies partly in social conditions: before industrialization the most influential classes in most of Germany were the numerically tiny aristocracy and the 'squirearchy' (*Junkertum*), who used formal standard German and colloquial standard relatively close to this and, in certain areas also, types of traditional dialect. By far the largest class numerically was the peasantry using traditional dialect. Social organization was in many respects feudal in character, middle and working classes both being politically 'vassals' (*Untertanen*) with few civil rights. The development of large middle and working classes with different social, political and cultural outlooks and, concomitantly, different speech types has been relatively late and – in comparison with Britain – relatively incomplete and was then, before being complete, overtaken to an extent by the socially levelling developments of post-war Europe. There are, however, undeniably social-class differences within colloquial speech, justifying a rough division into colloquial standard and colloquial non-standard German. These social class differences have, as we have seen, been noticed by more recent writers in German, who have used labels such as *dialektnahe Umgangssprache* and *standardnahe Umgangssprache*.

### 5.2.5 The users of the various types of German

As we have seen, formal standard German is not a native speech-form, but is potentially available to all German-speakers for use in particular circumstances. The main factor determining speakers' facility with it is formal education, which, in its turn, is related in indirect and complex ways to social class. The continuum of colloquial German is the normal spoken medium of most German-speakers, with important exceptions: in German-speaking Switzerland and in Luxembourg everyone uses types of language which can be regarded as traditional dialect, Swiss German (*Schwyzertütsch*) and Luxembourgish (*Letzebuergësch*) respectively, and which have considerable claims to the status of autonomous languages. Another exception is the persistence in south Germany and Austria of forms perhaps best regarded as traditional dialect among some urban working-class speakers, particularly in smaller towns, and even among some, mainly older, middle-class speakers. There are also, throughout the German-speaking area, particularly in the countryside, many self-employed small business people, whose economic status warrants the label 'middle class', who nevertheless use traditional dialect (see, for example, Mickartz 1983: 72–7).

The continuum, then, which includes formal standard German too, represents the speech of most people, its rough division into colloquial standard German and colloquial non-standard speech correlating approximately with the division between manual and non-manual workers. It must be stressed, however, that it is a continuum, and that speakers tend to shift towards the standard end of the continuum with increasing formality. It must also be stressed that other factors influence what type of speech people use, other than their type of occupation. Sex is a factor, but its precise influence on patterns of usage seems very variable, depending on social class and region. The research findings are actually quite contradictory in this regard: women's speech has been observed to be further from standard than men's speech in some studies (see e.g. Ammon 1977: 37), but closer to standard in others (see e.g. Schlobinski 1987: 156, 160, 170). For a good summary of the interaction of sex differences with regional and social factors see Mattheier (1980: 25–39).

Within the continuum of German speech there is, as well as the division into colloquial standard and colloquial non-standard speech, a division within colloquial standard German between those speakers who use the prestige accent *deutsche Hochlautung* (*DH*), and those who use a regional accent of some sort. The group which uses the prestige accent is not closely parallel to the group which uses the prestige accent RP in British English: RP is very much a class accent (though also linked to education), being chiefly used by the upper class, and a small section of the middle class. We have the impression that there is resistance to RP among many educated speakers since it may imply identification with an alien social class. There does not seem to be a parallel resistance to *DH* in German, since it is not so clearly a class accent. On the other hand it is a regional accent in a way that RP is not: RP is not linked to any region, though more common in England and Wales than in Scotland, while *DH* is very clearly a north German accent.

Turning now to traditional dialect we find this used by rural working-class speakers, with, as we have seen, other speakers using it in certain parts of the German-speaking area. There is no doubt that it is on the decline, but this emphatically does not mean that non-standard speech is disappearing: colloquial non-standard speech may even be taking over from traditional dialect as a marker of social and local identity. Indeed, as we have seen, non-specialists will often label it *Dialekt* anyway. The vitality of colloquial non-standard speech is shown by the fact that certain of its features are actually increasing their geographical range: in Lower Saxony Stellmacher (1977: 102) has found non-standard /j/ for standard German /g/ in areas where this is not a feature of the local traditional dialect, and in central German-speaking areas colloquial /ʃ/ for standard German /ç/ is widely found, again also in areas where this is not found in the local traditional dialect (see Herrgen and Schmidt 1985).

In the 1970s there was a considerable revival of interest in dialect, the

'Dialect revival' or *Dialektwelle*, notably among educated middle-class people. This has not meant that such people have become speakers of traditional dialects, but it has meant a change of attitude towards certain elements of dialect speech, particularly local vocabulary, which may now be regarded or even used by such people as positive marks of their local identity, while their speech remains by and large colloquial standard. The dialect revival may have retarded the decline of traditional dialects, though this is not clear, and in any case what has been seen by enthusiasts as *Dialekt* has often been colloquial non-standard speech or *dialektnahe Umgangssprache* in the linguist's terms (see Leippe 1977).

In contrasting the German-speaking with the English-speaking areas we can conclude that the former displays considerably more linguistic differentiation; regional linguistic differences, particularly at the level of traditional dialects, but also within the standard language, are greater than anything found in English, and traditional dialects persist more strongly, particularly in the south. There are, nevertheless, strong similarities between English-speaking and German-speaking areas – more, in fact, than are implied by much of the literature.

### 5.3 The linguistic characteristics of colloquial German

Having outlined the position of the continuum of colloquial speech in the range of varieties of German, we can now proceed to a description of its linguistic characteristics.

### 5.3.1 A social rather than a geographical view of variation in German

In chapter 3 we looked at traditional German dialects, that type of German speech which is maximally different from the formal standard language. Except for this maximal difference from formal standard, perhaps the most marked characteristic of this speech type is its wide variation from one geographical area to another. This wide geographical variation led to Chapter 3 being strongly geographically based, with frequent use of maps.

In moving now to other types of German, we find that geographical variation, though still important and noticeable, is less striking, and in the current chapter the emphasis will be not on geographical variation, but rather on differences between one group in society and another. However, it is most important to recognize that all the types of German discussed here do show geographical variation, particularly those closest to traditional dialects (i.e. colloquial non-standard speech). It has usually been assumed that the colloquial speech of a geographical area contains some of the traditional dialect features of that area, but not all of them, and while this does generally seem to be true, it has nevertheless been pointed out that colloquial speech may contain features not present in the traditional dialect of the area in question (see Stellmacher 1977: 102; Herrgen 1986: 102–11; Schönfeld and Pape 1981: 149). There is inevitably, then, some overlap between the discussion in this chapter and that of traditional dialects in Chapter 3, although the emphases are quite different. In Chapter 3 the focus was on the differences between the various traditional dialects, and there was hence an emphasis on non-standard features of more limited geographical range. In this chapter the focus is on features of non-standard and of standard German which are widespread, and which, over a wide area, tend to distinguish one social group from another.

While never losing sight of geographical variation in the speech types discussed here, we nevertheless believe that it is important to stress certain types of differences which can be found in any geographical area. This chapter is hence non-regional in its basis. This removes it from the primary literature on colloquial speech which is largely regionally based; details of most of the features of colloquial speech mentioned here have to be gleaned from a large number of often isolated references in the primary sources. There is therefore relatively little reference to the primary literature in the body of the text. Much of the material of the chapter is derived from our own informal observation, as well as the studies discussed in Chapter 4. Further details of the phenomena discussed can also be found in the works listed under 'Further reading' at the end of this chapter.

### 5.3.2 The standard of comparison

In our discussion of the linguistic characteristics of colloquial German we shall present them as deviations from formal standard German pronounced with the *deutsche Hochlautung (DH)* accent. We shall term this, simply, 'formal standard German', although this is, to an extent, a convenient fiction, since formal standard German can, in fact, be pronounced with a variety of regional accents; most people are unable to eliminate the finer details of their native accents, assuming they even wish to, and therefore retain them when speaking formal standard German.

Colloquial speech deviates from formal standard on every level, phonetic and phonological, morphological and syntactic, and lexical. In very broad terms we can say that some of these deviations are generally socially acceptable, and hence are characteristics of colloquial standard German. Other deviations have generally less prestige and may, in the eyes of some members of the most influential group in society, the educated middle class, brand the speaker as uneducated or working class; these are characteristics of colloquial non-standard speech. Yet other deviations are of doubtful status, and will be differently judged by different people: speech containing them will be considered acceptable by some educated speakers, unacceptable by others. All this is another way of saying that the boundary between colloquial standard and colloquial non-standard speech is unclear and hazy, though indubitably significant; all generalizations, our own included, must be treated with caution.

## 5.4 Phonetic and phonological variation within German

### 5.4.1 Categories of phonetic and phonological variation

Colloquial speech deviates from formal standard in pronunciation for all those speakers who do not use the *DH* accent, but the deviations are of very different kinds, as are the deviations from RP in British English, discussed above (5.1.2). At one extreme there are differences which, though noticed by German speakers, are considered to be relatively small, and are entirely systematic. These are pure accent differences, or, in more technical terms, purely phonetic differences. The colloquial speech in question has in some sense the 'same' sounds as *DH* – they are just pronounced rather differently. As examples we can cite that much colloquial speech, particularly in the south, has an [ɑ] vowel in words like *fast*, pronounced further back in the mouth than the equivalent sound in *DH*, or has a softer, more lenis [t] sound than *DH* at the end of words like *Bad*. We shall label such deviations from *DH* 'phonetic accent differences'.

At the other extreme, many forms of German speech contain deviations in sounds from formal standard which are considered large by German speakers and which are, to the non-specialist at any rate, unsystematic. For example some north German speech has stop sounds /p/ and /t/ in words where formal standard has fricative sounds /f/ and /s/. Not only is this considered a large and significant difference by German-speakers, but it is also apparently unsystematic, since other words in the speech in question will have /p/ and /t/ where formal standard also has /p/ and /t/, yet other words will have /p/ and /t/ where formal standard has the sound sequences /pf/ and /ts/. To complicate the picture still further, the north German speech in question also has /f/ and /s/ corresponding to formal standard /f/ and /s/, and may even have /f/ corresponding to formal standard /b/. For example, some north German speech has *hopen, het, Pilot, Kante, Peerd, twee, för, Kasse, bleef* corresponding to *hoffen, heiß,*

Table 5.2. *Sound correspondences in certain lexical items between some north German speech (Low German dialects) and standard German with DH pronunciation*

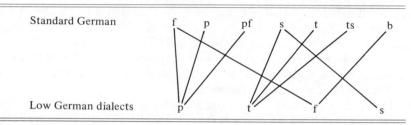

Pilot, Kante, Pferd, zwei, für, Kasse, bleibe respectively. These correspondences are summarized in Table 5.2.

As will be clear from our discussion of English above (5.1.2), divergences on the scale of *hopen* and *twee* for *hoffen* and *zwei* can be said to represent not accent differences but dialect differences. Items containing such sound differences can be seen not as the 'same' word (in some sense) as the standard German word, but as examples of dialect lexicon; they will be treated as lexical or vocabulary deviations from formal standard, and handled along with obvious vocabulary deviations such as north German *lütt* for formal standard *klein* ('little'). In terms of comprehension they can represent difficulties for the outsider almost as great as does obvious dialect lexicon.

Between these two extremes there are pronunciation deviations from formal standard which are, at any rate subjectively, not as great as these north German examples, and not as unsystematic, but which represent the substitution of what are seen as 'different' sounds, or which obliterate sound distinctions which are made in formal standard, or which involve sound distinctions which formal standard does not have; such deviations are systematic to varying degrees, and represent varying degrees of comprehension difficulty for the outsider. As a general rule, comprehension is most impaired where the deviation in question is not particularly widespread, is unsystematic, or obliterates a sound distinction which has a high '**functional load**' in formal standard. For example the distinction between word-initial /k/ and /g/ as in *Karte* and *Garten* carries quite a high functional load in standard German, that is to say it helps to distinguish a considerable number of words. German speech which obliterates this distinction, as does some central and southern German, will present considerable comprehension problems to outsiders; for example in Karlsruhe the *Stadtgarten* (municipal park) is pronounced locally in a way which may sound to the outsider like *Stadtkarte* (town map). (The difficulties presented are not insuperable in this case, since 'town map' is normally *Stadtplan* anyway.) This particular deviation from *DH*, posing problems as it does, will be considered to represent more than a mere accent difference. It will not, however, be considered to represent the occurrence of distinctive dialect vocabulary as does the north German example cited above: the deviation from *DH* is, at least subjectively, less than in the north German case, it is more systematic, and presents fewer comprehension problems. We will label this and similar deviations from *DH* 'phonological dialect differences'.

Less radical deviations from *DH* are those which are not subjectively large, do not obliterate a distinction made in *DH* – or perhaps even create a distinction not made in *DH* – or which obliterate a distinction with low functional load, and which cause at most slight or initial comprehension problems for outsiders. For example the distinction between voiceless stops /p t k/ and voiced stops /b d g/ in medial position (i.e. between vowel sounds) has a relatively low functional load (i.e. it distinguishes few pairs of words), and in some cases it has no functional load at all (i.e. there are no pairs of words kept apart by a difference between the sounds in question). The loss of this distinction therefore poses few comprehension problems for outsiders, and it is, moreover, extremely widespread. For example if *Rappen* (a Swiss coin, 'centime') is pronounced with a voiced medial stop /b/ in place of the voiceless sound /p/ of *DH*, this will present no comprehension problems since there are no words with /b/ in *DH* with which it could be confused. Deviations from *DH* of this kind we will term 'phonological accent differences'.

We therefore distinguish the following four types of phonetic and phonological deviations from *DH* in other types of German speech: phonetic accent differences, phonological accent differences, phonological dialect differences, and lexical differences. It must be strongly emphasized that these are by no means sharply distinct types of differences: the assignment of a departure from *DH* to one of these categories will in many cases be problematical.

Lexical differences will concern us below (5.6). Phonetic accent differences, though they do help listeners to place a speaker regionally, are relatively trivial, and are too numerous to concern us here. We shall therefore devote our attention to phonological accent differences and phonological dialect differences.

It should be noted that speakers of the language do not seem to distinguish consistently between phonetic accent differences and phonological accent differences, both being used to place speakers regionally, with some phonetic differences being in fact more noticeable to speakers than some phonological differences (see Herrgen and Schmidt 1985 for a full discussion). We would maintain that the distinction between phonological accent differences and phonological dialect differences is noticed by speakers, and is used to place speakers socially as well as regionally, phonological dialect differences from standard German being characteristic of colloquial non-standard speech as opposed to colloquial standard.

### 5.4.2 Phonological accent deviations from *DH*

We discuss here just some of the more striking phonological differences between *DH* and the pronunciation of colloquial German.

*DH* final or preconsonantal /k/, written with the letter 'g', corresponding to north and central German /x/ or /ç/.

In words such as *Tag, Teig* and *sagte* the letter 'g' represents the sound /k/ in *DH*; in much north and central German speech it represents the fricative sounds /x/ or /ç/, identical to the sounds usually written 'ch'. South German speech and some central German speech agrees with *DH* here in having /k/ or, with lenition, [g̥] (see below).

Note that in some words *DH* agrees with north German speech in this phenomenon, having /ç/ where south German speech has /k/ or, with lenition, [g̥]. These are words ending in the syllable *-ig* such as *feurig* or *zwanzig*.

The northern and central use of /x/ or /ç/ for *DH* /k/ seems to cause no comprehension problems, is a phonological accent difference, and is part of colloquial standard German as well as colloquial non-standard. There is little or no stigma attached to it, though some speakers do attempt to use the *DH* pronunciations in the most formal registers.

The southern use of /k/ or /g̥/ for *DH* /ç/ in the *-ig* ending is scarcely stigmatized at all.

*DH* initial /ʃp-/, /ʃt-/ corresponding to north German /sp-/, /st-/

In *DH*, written *sp-* and *st-* at the beginnings of words or parts of compound words represent /ʃp-/ and /ʃt-/, with the palato-alveolar fricative (written elsewhere as *sch*). In much colloquial north German speech such sequences are replaced by /sp-/ and /st-/, e.g. in *sprechen* and *Stein*, to which speakers may have some ambivalence of attitude; on the one hand the feature may be stigmatized, and avoided if possible in formal registers, on the other hand it may have prestige as a mark of north

German loyalty, since Moss (personal communication) has observed it in areas where it is not a feature of local traditional dialect. Since it obliterates no distinctions, and causes no comprehension problems, and since it occurs with both colloquial non-standard and standard speech, though not the most prestigious colloquial standard, we have included it with phonological accent features.

## *DH* tense vowels in certain words corresponding to north German lax vowels

In certain common words much north German speech has short, or lax, vowels where *DH* has long, or tense, vowels. The vowel in question is either followed by two consonants, or it is the last vowel in the word and is then followed by a final consonant. Closely related words where the vowel in question is not the last vowel, or is followed by only one consonant, will have a tense vowel as in *DH*. For example *(Ich) sage* (I say) compared with *(er) sagt* (he says) have the pronunciations /zaːgə/ and /zaːkt/ respectively in *DH*, while they are /zaːgə/ and /zaxt/ in this type of north German; *Bad* (bath) and the related verb *baden* are /baːt/ and /baːdn̩/ in *DH*, while they are /bat/ and /baːdn̩/ in the north German speech in question. This departure from *DH* obliterates no distinctions present in *DH*, and can be classed as a phonological accent difference.

## *DH* affricates at the beginnings of words corresponding to north and central German fricatives

The sequences /pf/ and /ts/ of *DH* in words like *Pferd* (horse) and *zwei* (two), often called affricates, are very commonly pronounced without the stop sounds /p/ and /t/ in north and central German speech. This pronunciation is uncommon in the south of the language area, and is less common in the case of /ts/ than in the case of /pf/.

The replacement of /ts/ by /s/ causes no comprehension problem in much of the area in question, since many German speech types do not have /s/ at the beginning of any other words, written 's' being pronounced /z/ in such words as *See* (lake, sea). The replacement of /pf/ by /f/ causes some loss of distinctions, for example *Pferd* (horse) and *fährt* ((he/she) travels, goes) may sound alike (/feːɐ̯t/) for many speakers, but as relatively few words start with /pf/ in German anyway, there is little problem. Stop sounds are lost also in the initial sequences /ps/, /tʃ/ and the rarer /pʃ/, which occur largely in learned words or names, e.g. *Psychologie, Tscheche* (Czech) and *Pschorr* (a name), and are thus relatively uncommon.

The loss of stops before fricatives, though not generally seen as a non-standard or dialect feature, is clearly informal or colloquial, and speakers attempt, not always successfully, to pronounce the stops when speaking formally. It should be noted that the loss of /p/ before /f/ has been recorded as a traditional dialect feature only in the East Middle German dialect area (see 3.10.2). The other cases of loss of stops before fricatives, though very common in colloquial speech, have not been considered significant in traditional dialects.

### Medial lenition (see also 3.11.3)

In the *DH* pronunciation there is a clear contrast between a voiceless series of stop and fricative consonants /p t k f s ʃ ç x/ and a voiced series /b d g v z ʒ j/; the voiced series contains one fewer consonant, /x/ having no voiced counterpart. The difference between the two series is threefold: firstly the vocal cords vibrate in the production of the voiced sounds, not in the voiceless sounds; secondly the voiceless sounds are produced with generally greater energy, i.e. they are 'fortis', while the voiced sounds are 'lenis'; and thirdly the voiceless stop sounds (not the fricatives) are followed by a distinct puff of breath, i.e. they are 'aspirated', when they stand at the beginning of a stressed syllable.

In the vast majority of types of German there is a loss of the voiced–voiceless distinction in some positions in a word. The most common position for this distinction to be lost is at the end of a word or preceding another consonant, particularly if that consonant is itself a stop or fricative sound. In the *DH* the only sounds which can occur in such a position are voiceless and fortis but unaspirated: in other words we can say that in such a position voiced consonants are replaced by voiceless consonants. In some other types of German the consonants in such a position are voiceless and unaspirated, but lenis: in other words are a sort of compromise between the voiced and voiceless series; we can symbolize them thus: [b̥ d̥ g̊ v̥ z̥ ʒ̊ j̊ ɣ̊].

Elsewhere in a word the voiced–voiceless distinction is not generally lost in *DH*, but in many other accents of German it is lost medially, that is between two vowel sounds, or between vowels and syllabic consonants such as /l̩ m̩ n̩/ (the final sounds in most pronunciations of words like *Flügel*, *Atem* and *Boden*). Where the distinction is lost, voiceless lenis sounds occur, corresponding to both the voiceless fortis sounds and the voiced lenis sounds of *DH*: we therefore say that the fortis sounds have undergone medial lenition. The sounds replacing both series medially may even be voiced lenis sounds.

Medial lenition will, then, result in words like *Rippen*, *Ratten*, *hocken*,

*Hafen, Straßen, naschen, sprechen* and *lachen* being pronounced with, in medial position, either voiceless lenis consonants ([b̥ d̥ g̊ v̥ z̥ ʒ̊j̊ ɣ̊]) or voiced lenis consonants ([b d g v z ʒ̊ j ɣ]), the first seven in either case being identical to the consonants found medially in *Robben, baden, lagen, Löwen, Hasen, Pagen* and *Kojen.*

Medial lenition is found in most of the German area except the far south and, though it does obliterate a few distinctions between words, does not much affect comprehension, probably in part because it is so widespread, and it can thus be classed as a phonological accent feature. It is a characteristic of colloquial speech of all types, but it does seem to be more highly stigmatized in the north than in the centre and south. Its lesser stigmatization in the centre and south may be due to the fact that lenition is a much more general feature in these areas, initial lenition often occurring (see below, 5.4.3), a feature which is unknown in the north.

### *DH* medial and final /-sp/, /-st/ corresponding to south German /-ʃp/, /-ʃt/

In *DH* the written sequences *sp* and *st* represent /ʃp/ and /ʃt/ as seen above, but only in initial position, i.e. at the beginning of a word or part of a compound word. Elsewhere they represent /sp/ and /st/, e.g. in *kosten* and *lispeln*. However, in much south-west German speech they represent /ʃp/ and /ʃt/ in all positions, and pronunciations such as /koʃtn̩/, /liʃpln̩/ are heard. This deviation from *DH* obliterates no distinctions, and causes no comprehension problems, and hence represents a phonological accent difference.

### *DH* /ç/ corresponding to south German /x/ (see also 3.10.3)

In most cases where the combination of letters *ch* is written, *DH* has two sounds, a velar fricative /x/ after back vowels (e.g. in *Bach*), a palatal fricative /ç/ elsewhere (e.g. in *ich, durch*). However, much south German speech has only a velar fricative /x/ (or, with lenition, [ɣ̊]); or it may have, instead of the front palatal fricative /ç/, a back palatal fricative acoustically very close to /x/.

The distinction between /ç/ and /x/ in the *DH* has virtually no functional load at all; its obliteration therefore causes no comprehension problems and, perhaps reflecting the prestige and persistence of southern regionalisms, is scarcely stigmatized.

### Reduced forms

Colloquial standard German contains many reductions of unstressed syllables compared to formal standard: in certain unstressed syllables a variety of vowels is replaced by the central vowel /ə/, and certain instances of the vowel /ə/ are deleted.

Replacement of other vowels by /ə/ takes place regularly in pronouns and articles, where this /ə/ then combines with following /ɐ̯/, /n/ or /m/ sounds (written *r*, *n and m*) to produce the vowel /ɐ/ or the syllabic nasal sounds /n̩/ or /m̩/ respectively. For example, when unstressed the following pronouns and articles have the following pronunciations: *er* /ɐ/, *es* /əs/ or even /s/, *der* /dɐ/, *den* /dn̩/, *des* /dəs/, *dem* /dm̩/, das /dəs/. The central vowel /ə/ is deleted most particularly at the end of first person singular and imperative verb forms, e.g. *ich laufe* (I run, am running) becomes *ich lauf'*, and *laufe doch mal* (run!) is usually *lauf' doch mal*. The deletion of /ə/ in these verb forms is normal colloquial German (though considered incorrect by **prescriptive grammarians**), whereas other deletions of /ə/, such as those of noun plural or adjectival suffixes, are a mark of non-standard speech.


### 5.4.3 Phonological dialect differences from standard German

In contrast to the divergences from *DH* discussed above (5.4.2), the following either obliterate distinctions present in *DH*, or cause comprehension problems to speakers from outside the regions where they occur, or are in varying degrees stigmatized, or have a combination of these characteristics. We label them 'phonological dialect differences' and consider them to be characteristics of either colloquial non-standard speech or traditional dialects, as opposed to colloquial or formal standard German. Two points should be reiterated here: firstly, colloquial non-standard speech and traditional dialects differ from *DH* also in those characteristics labelled as phonetic or phonological accent differences; secondly, there is a considerable amount of arbitrariness in the division between phonological accent differences and phonological dialect differences – the classification is certainly open to discussion.

We would also repeat at this point that phonological dialect differences are distinct – though this distinction is not always clear – from lexical dialect differences (such as the difference between North German dialect *Pepper* and standard German *Pfeffer*), even though the latter, as in our example, may arise from phonological divergence. Phonological dialect differences are more obviously systematic than lexical dialect differences, and present fewer comprehension problems for the outsider, though such problems may be considerable, and not relatively trivial as is the case with phonological accent differences.

Standard German initial or medial stop consonant /g/ corresponding to non-standard palatal or palato-alveolar fricative sound /j/ or /ʒ/

This is clearly a non-standard feature, being found little in colloquial standard German. It is found in parts of north and central Germany, and is a well-known feature of Cologne and Berlin colloquial non-standard. An example is non-standard /juːt/ *gut* (good) corresponding to standard /guːt/ (see 4.4.3).

A very interesting characteristic of this non-standard feature is that it is found in colloquial non-standard speech in areas of north Germany where it is not a feature of the local traditional dialect (see Stellmacher 1977: 102; Schönfeld and Pape 1981: 149).

Although this substitution does not obliterate many distinctions, it represents for outsiders the substitution of very different sounds, which do occur in *DH* at the beginning of words like *ja* or words like *Genie*, and it is extremely noticeable; hence it qualifies as a phonological dialect difference.

Standard German /ç/ (written ch) corresponding to colloquial non-standard /ʃ/

The substitution of /ʃ/ (the sound which occurs at the end of words like *Tisch*) for /ç/ in words like *ich* is common in central and north Germany, and is quite highly stigmatized: hence our treatment of it as a non-standard feature; however, it does occur with some speech which could be labelled 'colloquial standard'. It results in some loss of distinctions. Equally stigmatized is the reverse substitution of /ç/ for standard German /ʃ/ (e.g. *Englisch* pronounced as /ɛŋliç/), which may originate from a hypercorrection of the stigmatized substitution of /ʃ/ for /ç/. Quite often both /ç/ and /ʃ/ are replaced by an intermediate sound, which is transcribed [ɕ] (see Herrgen and Schmidt 1985).

Initial **devoicing** and initial lenition (compare with medial lenition discussed above (5.4.2); also see 3.11.3)

In virtually all German speech the voiced stops and fricatives are partially **devoiced** at the beginnings of words, i.e. the vocal cords vibrate only during the latter part of the sound, but in much central and southern German speech they are entirely devoiced. This in itself does not make them identical to the voiceless sounds, since the voiceless sounds may be strongly articulated (fortis), whereas these devoiced variants of the voiced sounds are more weakly articulated (lenis). This initial devoicing is not generally noticed in stop sounds, which are of short duration, but it is noticed in the fricatives. It does not affect the voiced fricatives /v/ and /j/ (as in *Wasser* and *ja*), which, in the accents in question, are actually not generally fricatives, but rather less energetic sounds which we can term 'approximants'.

The fricatives which are affected are /z/ and /ʒ/ (as in *See* and *Genie*), which become [z̥] and [ʒ̊], and can sound very close to /s/ and /ʃ/. If /s/ and /ʃ/ are subject to lenition (see below), as they frequently are in the speech in question, becoming [z̥] and [ʒ̊], then a distinction is potentially lost. Actually, in the case of the /s/–/z/ distinction, it is not lost, since /s/ does not occur initially anyway; the only result is that pronunciation with initial [z̥] is noticed by outsiders and registered as a feature of a southern accent, a case of mere phonological accent difference, or possibly even mere phonetic difference. In the case of the /ʃ/–/ʒ/ distinction, very few comprehension problems arise, since though there are words with initial /ʒ/ in German, they are very few in number (they are mostly of fairly recent French origin). Again, the loss of the /ʃ/–/ʒ/ distinction can be termed a phonological accent difference.

Turning again to stop consonants: if these are devoiced (see above), this devoicing alone is not very noticeable, but problems do arise in speech where /p/, /t/ and /k/ (as in *Peter*, *Tür* and *Karten*) are subject to lenition at the beginning of a word, losing their aspiration and becoming [b̥], [d̥], [g̊], this lenition happening in a number of varieties of German (see 3.11.3). The position here is highly complex. Most south and central German speech has medial lenition (see above, 5.4.2), and much of it has initial lenition, but the distinction between voiced and voiceless consonants is not necessarily lost. The following situations seem to occur in different parts of the area, and in different social groups:

(1) *Distinction not lost*
Voiceless stops are fortis and aspirated
$$p^h \; t^h \; k^h$$
(e.g. in *Peter*, *Tür*, *Karte*)
Voiced stops are lenis and partially devoiced or entirely devoiced
$$b̥ \; d̥ \; g̊$$
(e.g. in *beten*, *dir*, *Garten*)

(2) *Distinction not lost*
Voiceless stops are fortis and unaspirated
$$p \; t \; k$$
Voiced stops are lenis and partially devoiced or entirely devoiced
$$b̥ \; d̥ \; g̊$$

(3) *Distinction not lost but reduced. Distinction may be hard to hear for outsiders*
Voiceless stops are lenis
$$b̥ \; d̥ \; g̊$$

Voiced stops are lenis and fully voiced
b d g

(4) *Distinction lost*
Both series are lenis and devoiced
b̥ d̥ g̊

The first two patterns are typical of colloquial standard in the south and some of the centre, the last two are more likely to be restricted to traditional dialect or colloquial non-standard speech, since important distinctions are lost, and comprehension is difficult for outsiders. Therefore, while we label initial lenition of fricatives a phonological accent difference, we label initial lenition of stops a phonological dialect difference. In some areas it may even be developing into a lexical difference, since the /t/–/d/ distinction has been restored in some dialects, but with the sounds having a different and – from the lay person's point of view – confusingly unpredictable distribution when compared to the standard. For example, in some Alemannic speech corresponding to standard German *dir* [diːɐ̯], *Tier* [tʰiːɐ̯] and *Theater* [tʰeˈaːtɐ], there occur *dir* [d̥iːr], *Tier* again [d̥ːr], but *Theater* [tʰeˈaːd̥ər] with a fortis aspirated consonant (see Besch and Löffler 1977: 45–8).

Standard German front rounded vowels corresponding to non-standard front unrounded vowels (see also 3.11.2)

This feature entails the replacement of the front rounded vowels /yː/ and /ʏ/, both written either *ü* or *y*, and /øː/ and /œ/, both written *ö*, with their unrounded counterparts /iː/, /I/, /eː/ and /ɛ/ respectively. Speakers with this characteristic usually also replace the diphthong /ɔy/, written *eu* or *äu*, with /ai/. The feature is found in various central and southern parts of the German-speaking area. Examples of it are as follows: while standard German *Hüte, Hütte, schön, können, Leute* are pronounced /hyːtə/,/hʏtə/, /ʃøːn/, /kœnən/, /lɔytə/ respectively, their colloquial non-standard counterparts may be /hiːtə/, /hɪtə/, /ʃeːn/, /kɛnən/, /laitə/. The following phonemic distinctions of standard German are thus absent in these forms of colloquial speech: iː–yː, I–ʏ, eː–øː, ɛ–œ, ai–ɔy; and there are therefore comprehension problems for outsiders. It is clearly a phonological dialect difference, and speech exhibiting it can be considered to be colloquial non-standard or traditional dialect.

It is well worth noting at this point that the loss of distinctions frequently referred to in this section poses no problems for speakers of the dialect or colloquial non-standard in question, only for outsiders, and does not mean that the speech form in question has become a less efficient linguistic system; in any case non-standard speech often preserves distinctions, for example the iː–iə distinction in much south German, lost in the standard (see 3.10.3). Where two words become phonetically identical through the loss of a distinction, and where this could be confusing, speakers of the dialect or colloquial non-standard in question will often replace one of them by another item: for example in speech which obliterates the iː–yː distinction *Tier* 'animal' and *Tür* 'door' may be pronounced alike, but then *Tier* is often replaced by *Viech* and *Tür* by *Türe* in such speech anyway.

Standard German final syllable /-ən/ or final syllabic /-ŋ/ corresponding to central and south German /-ə/

This loss of final /n/ is characteristic of virtually all non-standard speech in much of the centre and south of the area. It occurs, for example, in plural verb forms like *wir laufen* (we run/walk), which is replaced by *wir laufe'*. It is quite highly stigmatized and should probably be considered a phonological dialect feature.

## 5.5 Grammatical variation in German

### 5.5.1 Typological differences between varieties of German

There are highly complex grammatical differences between different types of German speech; as a very broad and sweeping generalization we can say that more formal German is more **inflecting** in character, more informal German more **isolating** or analytical. In a typological classification of languages, German lies between the highly inflecting type, exemplified by Latin, classical Greek and Sanskrit, in which grammatical relationships between words are shown by the form of those words (for example by what endings they have), and the analytical type, exemplified by Vietnamese, Chinese and, to a considerably lesser extent by English, in which grammatical relationships are shown by word order. Formal standard German preserves a four-case system (nominative, accusative, genitive and dative), and three genders (masculine, feminine and neuter), in articles, pronouns, adjectives and nouns. Relationships between words in these classes and other elements in the sentence are shown to a considerable extent by the form of the words concerned, particularly the form of articles and pronouns, and hence word order can be relatively free, since it is not the only way of showing such relationships. Formal standard German also has four simple (one-word) finite tense forms of the verb: present indicative, past (or preterite) indicative, present (or first) **subjunctive** and past (or preterite, or second) subjunctive.

*Sociolinguistic variation*

As we move from formal standard German towards more informal and less prestigious speech forms, we find that certain inflectional classes become progressively less common, being replaced by alternatives which may involve the introduction of additional words into a sentence – for example certain case distinctions are lost, or certain cases are replaced by other cases preceded by prepositions – and certain verb tenses are replaced by auxiliary verbs (usually forms of *haben*, *sein* or *werden*) plus infinitives or participles (see Koβ 1983: 1247).

### 5.5.2 The nominal systems of varieties of German

We now treat a sample of the differences between the nominal system (articles, pronouns, adjectives and nouns) of formal standard German, and that found in colloquial German.

#### Alternative forms for third person pronouns

Formal standard German has the following third person pronouns:

|       | *masculine* | *feminine* | *neuter* | *plural* |
|-------|-------------|------------|----------|----------|
| *nom.* | er         | sie        | es       | sie      |
| *acc.* | ihn        | sie        | es       | sie      |
| *dat.* | ihm        | ihr        | ihm      | ihnen    |

When strongly emphasized they are replaced by the following forms:

|       | *masculine* | *feminine* | *neuter* | *plural* |
|-------|-------------|------------|----------|----------|
| *nom.* | der        | die        | das      | die      |
| *acc.* | den        | die        | das      | die      |
| *dat.* | dem        | der        | dem      | denen    |

In colloquial standard German this replacement takes place frequently when there is no particular emphasis: *der*, *die*, *das*, etc. are slowly taking over as the third person pronouns, emphasis being shown in speech simply by greater stress. This development is frowned upon by prescriptivists, but is extremely common, particularly in the case of the forms *sie* (she/her/they/them) and *ihnen* (them), which are identical in speech to *Sie* and *Ihnen* meaning 'you', and which are hence very easily confused with them.

This replacement also occurs in non-standard speech, although more radical developments involving the loss of case distinctions may occur here.

160

## Genitive case

The genitive case is common only in formal standard German, and its presence in a sentence can mark that sentence out as formal and standard. In formal standard German the genitive is used in two types of contexts:

(1) to denote possession or intimate connection, e.g. *der Kopf des Mannes* (the man's head), *am Rand des Waldes* (at the edge of the forest)

(2) after prepositions, e.g. *wegen des Lärms* (on account of the noise), *während des Krieges* (during the war), *trotz des schlechten Wetters* (despite the bad weather), *diesseits des Flusses* (on this side of the river)

Genitives denoting possession or intimate connection are regularly replaced in colloquial German by the preposition *von* plus a dative case, e.g. *der Kopf von dem Mann, am Rand von dem Wald*. It is important to note that this construction is generally accepted as 'correct' German, though some prescriptivists would reject certain instances of it. It even occurs in formal standard German, particularly in situations where a noun is used without an adjective or article, and where that noun cannot itself be marked as genitive. For example *Männer*, genitive plural of *Mann* (man), is – like many noun genitives, particularly of plural or feminine singular nouns – not obviously genitive, and therefore in a phrase such as 'the characteristics of men' has to be replaced by '*von* plus dative' (*die Charakteristika von Männern*); *die Charakteristika Männer* would be quite incorrect, and *die Charakteristika der Männer* with a genitive article is more likely to suggest 'of the (specific) men'.

This construction '*von* plus dative' is current in all types of colloquial German, both colloquial standard and non-standard speech, though the dative is replaced by the **oblique case** in those types of non-standard speech which have no dative–accusative distinction (see below). The other common alternative to the genitive in this type of construction is, however, much less generally acceptable, and is a fairly clear mark of non-standard speech. It is the construction 'dative plus possessive adjective plus noun', e.g. *dem Mann sein Kopf*, 'the man's head', literally '(to) the man his head'; *der Frau ihr Hut*, 'the woman's hat', literally '(to) the woman her hat'. In forms of non-standard which have no dative–accusative distinction the oblique case is used and not the dative: *de(n) Mann sein Kopf, de Frau ihr Hut*. The type of construction described here is possible only where possession is indicated, not for other instances of close association, e.g. *Am Wald sein Rand* is not possible. For further details of the replacement of the genitive by other constructions see Koβ 1983.

Where the genitive occurs after a preposition, colloquial German replaces it in various ways, depending on the preposition involved, though the most common replacement is the dative (or oblique) case. Genitives after the prepositions cited above can be replaced as follows: *wegen dem Lärm* (dative) or *von wegen dem Lärm, während dem Krieg* (dative), *trotz dem schlechten Wetter* (dative), *diesseits vom Fluß* (preposition plus *von* plus dative). In some cases like the last one, colloquial German may use a different expression, e.g. *an dieser Seite vom Fluß*.

While the replacement *von* plus dative for the genitive accompanying another noun is generally acceptable, the various replacements for the genitive after prepositions, though normal in colloquial speech, are widely considered to be incorrect, and therefore certain speakers try to avoid them. This is, however, a clear case where prescriptive grammar is out of step with everyday usage.

## Absence of a dative–accusative distinction in north German speech (see also 3.9.2 and Panzer 1983: 1172–3)

The loss of the genitive case is, as we have seen, typical of colloquial speech as a whole, but the loss of the dative–accusative distinction is clearly a mark of non-standard speech, not of colloquial standard. It is a north German feature, and is shared by traditional dialects. The speech in question has a single case, termed oblique, uniting the functions of dative and accusative. In its function as indirect object the dative may be replaced either by the oblique case, or by *zu* plus the oblique case; indeed *zu* plus dative may be used for the indirect object with some verbs in some colloquial standard German, e.g. formal standard German *ich sagte ihm*, 'I said to him', compared with colloquial standard *ich habe ihm gesagt*, or *ich hab' zu ihm gesagt*.

In articles and possessive and demonstrative pronouns the oblique case tends to resemble the standard German accusative in its form, while in the personal pronouns it may resemble either dative or accusative. Some fairly typical forms for personal pronouns are:

|  | 'I' | 'you' (familiar singular) |  |
| --- | --- | --- | --- |
| *nom.* | ich/ick(e) | du |  |
| *obl.* | mi(r) | di(r) |  |

|  | 'he/it' (masculine) | 'she/it' (feminine) | 'it' (neuter) |
| --- | --- | --- | --- |
| *nom.* | er/de/(r) | sie/die/de | es/et/dat |
| *obl.* | ihm/de(n) | ihr/die/de | es/et/dat |

|  | 'we' | 'you' (familiar plural) | 'you' (polite) | 'they' |
|---|---|---|---|---|
| *nom.* | wi(r) | ih(r) | Sie | die/de |
| *obl.* | u(n)s | euch | Ihnen | die/de |

Note that the forms *et*, *dat* and *ick(e)* are borrowed from Low German dialects; we will return to the matter of lexicon from traditional dialects in colloquial non-standard speech below (5.6.4). Note also that speech with the above system is different from standard German in two ways; not only does it lack a distinction present in standard German (dative–accusative), but in certain instances it possesses a distinction absent in standard: in the 'she/it' and 'you' (polite) forms of standard German nominative and accusative are the same, but in the north German speech we are describing, nominative and oblique (which replaces accusative) are often different: for example standard German *sie ist da, ich hole sie*, 'Sit is there, I'll fetch her', corresponds to some north German non-standard *sie ist da, ich hole ihr*.

Fairly typical forms for the definite article are:

|  | *masculine* | *feminine* | *neuter* | *plural* |
|---|---|---|---|---|
| *nom.* | de | de | dat/det | de |
| *obl.* | de(n) | de | dat/det | de |

A very interesting development here is the increasing obliteration, also found in some traditional Low German dialects, of the masculine–feminine distinction: some speakers could indeed be said to have a two-gender system, similar to that found in spoken standard Dutch, and in Danish and Swedish, with a two-way gender distinction between common gender and neuter.

While the departures from the standard German system described here are highly stigmatized, and avoided by middle-class speakers, the simple borrowing of non-standard or traditional dialect vocabulary items, such as *dat*, is less highly stigmatized, and may on occasion occur in the speech of people who could generally be regarded as speakers of colloquial standard German.

## Overt plural suffixes on nouns

Although there is a tendency for case distinctions to be lost in colloquial German, the singular–plural distinction is as secure as it is in formal standard. In the standard variety, however, the distinction is often carried by an article with masculine and neuter nouns which may lack distinctive plural suffixes, e.g. *der Bäcker* (baker), plural *die Bäcker*. In north German non-standard speech, where masculine singular and plural articles are often identical, the definite article being for instance *de* in both singular and plural, the singular–plural distinction is maintained by the use of the plural suffix -*s*, e.g. *de Bäcker*, plural *de Bäckers*. This suffix is borrowed from Low German dialects, although of course it is also found in standard German with many words, particularly words ending in vowels, and particularly words of recent foreign origin, e.g. *das Auto* (car), plural *die Autos, der Test* (test), plural *die Tests*.

### Loss of a nominative–accusative distinction in articles and adjectives in south German speech

Even in formal standard German nominative and accusative differ in articles and adjectives only in the masculine singular. There is a tendency for this distinction to be lost in south German speech, with, for example, a definite article *de* replacing both the masculine singular nominative (*der*) and the accusative (*den*) forms. This departure from standard German is not as radical as the north German case just discussed, since the distinction is not lost throughout the inflectional system: it is preserved in personal pronouns. Nevertheless, like the other reductions of the case system, it is quite highly stigmatized, and is not usually found in speech which we would wish to label colloquial standard. Incidentally, although south German speech does maintain a distinct dative case, the -*n* suffix of dative plural nouns is lost in most southern speech. This can be seen as a special case of the loss of -*n* in final syllables (see above, 5.4.3), but is less highly stigmatized than other -*n* elisions, and is geographically more widespread.

### 5.5.3 The verb systems of varieties of German

We now move to discussion of the differences in the verb system between formal standard German and other types of German.

### First–second subjunctive distinction

In formal standard German there are six possible tenses of the subjunctive, to which we give the following labels (other writers label them differently): present subjunctive (e.g. *er sage, er komme*); future subjunctive (e.g. *er werde sagen, er werde kommen*); past subjunctive (e.g. *er sagte, er käme*); perfect subjunctive (e.g. *er habe gesagt, er sei gekommen*); pluperfect subjunctive (e.g. *er hätte gesagt, er wäre gekommen*); conditional (e.g. *er würde sagen, er würde kommen*). We consider the entire notion of a future tense, whether indicative or subjunctive, to be a doubtful one in German: the constructions in question are more helpfully regarded as combinations of a modal verb *werden*, expressing various shades of probability, with the infinitive of the verb in question. We will therefore leave the so-called future subjunctive out of the present discussion, and by the same token a possible seventh tense, the future perfect subjunctive.

The subjunctive tenses fall into two groups: the first group consists of the present subjunctive and the perfect subjunctive and is known as the 'first subjunctive', German *erster Konjunktiv*, the second consists of the past and pluperfect subjunctives and the conditional, and is known as the 'second subjunctive', German *zweiter Konjunktiv*.

The subjunctive **mood** is used in three main types of construction: hypothetical or unreal conditional sentences, polite requests, and indirect speech. It is also used in certain idioms, e.g. *das ginge*, 'that would be all right'. In unreal conditional sentences only the second subjunctives are used: the past and conditional are used to refer to present or future time, the pluperfect to refer to past time.

Even in formal standard German, many past subjunctive forms are avoided in certain contexts: these are the past subjunctive forms of regular **weak verbs**, which are identical with the past indicative (i.e. 'normal past') forms of the verbs in question. These forms are avoided in those contexts where their identity with the past indicatives could cause ambiguity, and are replaced by the corresponding conditional forms, or, in certain contexts, by forms combining the past subjunctive of *sollen* (*sollte*) with an infinitive: for example *er sagte* can be replaced by *er würde sagen* or *er sollte sagen*.

In indirect speech, in formal standard, all the tenses of the subjunctive may be used, but there is a preference for first subjunctives.

Foreign learners of German are often puzzled when they discover that German native speakers have had to learn many subjunctive forms, but the reason for this is not too far to seek: in colloquial German most of the subjunctive forms do not occur. In the first place, first subjunctives of all German verbs, including present subjunctives of modal and auxiliary verbs, are formal; their occurrence is a mark of formal standard German and they are absent from relaxed everyday conversation, being replaced by second subjunctives. It must however be stressed that this does not mean that subjunctives as a category are absent from everyday conversation; subjunctives are very much alive in both colloquial standard and colloquial non-standard German. It is just that there are fewer subjunctive forms; the only context where the subjunctive of formal German can be replaced by an indicative in colloquial German is in indirect speech, particularly where this is introduced by a verb of saying or thinking in the present tense.

The identity of form between past subjunctives and past indicatives in regular weak verbs applies, of course, to colloquial standard as much as to formal standard, and so these forms are again avoided where ambiguity could result. In addition to this, however, with the exception of certain idioms such as *das ginge* (see above), past subjunctives of **strong** and irregular verbs are avoided in colloquial German and are normally replaced by conditionals. The position here is complex: some of these past subjunctives are perceived as much more formal than others, but it seems that past subjunctives are particularly avoided where the verbs in question are informal vocabulary items. For example *bliebe* (from *bleiben*, 'stay'), *begänne/begönne* (alternative forms from *beginnen*, 'begin') and *söffe* (from *saufen*, 'booze') are all formal and comparatively uncommon, but whereas *bliebe* could be heard in colloquial speech, *begänne/begönne* are very formal and unlikely in colloquial speech, and *söffe* sounds quite ridiculous, and could probably be used only as a joke.

The only past subjunctive forms which are common in colloquial speech are the past subjunctives of the auxiliary and modal verbs (*hätte, wäre, würde, könnte, sollte, wollte, dürfte, möchte, müßte*) and the compound tenses formed with these such as the pluperfect subjunctive (i.e. *er hätte gesagt, er wäre gelaufen*, etc.) and the conditional (i.e. *er würde sagen*, etc.). As well as being used in the constructions already mentioned, these subjunctive forms are very frequently used in polite requests, e.g. *könnten Sie mir vielleicht sagen . . . ?* ('could you please tell me . . . ?'), *würden Sie vielleicht dort Platz nehmen?* ('would you mind sitting here, please?').

Much non-standard speech and some colloquial standard uses as well as – or instead of – the construction *würde* plus infinitive a construction involving *täte* (past subjunctive of *tun*) plus infinitive, and has conditional constructions such as *er täte sagen*.

It must be stressed that, contrary to the impression of some English-speaking learners, this small group of auxiliary and modal past subjunctive forms is common in all types of colloquial German, including colloquial non-standard speech – even non-standard speech which lacks past (preterite) indicatives. It is impossible to speak adequate colloquial German at any level without them.

## Compound tenses

There is a movement in German towards increasing use of compound tenses, which is most clearly demonstrated by the slow but steady replacement of the preterite by the perfect. The reasons for this are various, but one is that compound tenses allow relatively free movement of the non-finite part of the verb, the infinitive or participle, to various positions in the sentence, while the position of the finite part of the verb, the auxiliary, is fixed: in a main clause which is a statement it must, for instance, be the second element. In contrast, a simple tense, consisting as it does of a finite verb only, is fixed in its position. The mobility of a verbal element in a compound tense is useful, since it can, for example, occur in first position in a sentence to refer back to the previous sentence, or to **given information,** or it can occur in final position in the clause, the normal position for it, in fact. Consider the following piece of German dialogue, where the non-finite parts of compound tenses are italicized:

> **A:** 'Hat er viel *geredet?*' ('Did he talk a lot?')
> [*Geredet* is in final position, where it would be expected.]

> **B:** '*Geredet* hat er schon, aber *gegessen* hat er noch mehr.' ('He certainly talked a lot, but he ate more.')
> [*Geredet* is placed first (not the expected position for the participle) since it refers back to the question and then *gegessen* is placed first in its clause (again not an expected position) since it refers back to and directly contrasts with *geredet*.]

The mobility of verbal elements exemplified here is not possible if simple tenses are used.

It is always possible to use a compound tense or compound verbal expression if reference is to past time, since a perfect or pluperfect tense can be used. However, if reference is to present or future time it is not possible to use a compound form unless there is modal expression involved (as we have seen above, we consider the so-called 'future tense' to be a modal expression); a simple present tense cannot be replaced by a compound tense in formal standard German.

In non-standard speech, however, and in some more informal colloquial standard German a compound tense is common, consisting of *tun* plus infinitive (e.g. *sie tut sehen, sie tut laufen*). This very useful tense, allowing as it does mobility of the infinitive (e.g. *sehen* or *laufen*) to various sentence positions, is gaining ground in colloquial speech, despite being considered incorrect by prescriptive grammarians and purists.

Preterite–perfect tense distinction (see also 3.9.2)

Formal standard German has a distinction between a preterite tense, also called simple past, past or (misleadingly) imperfect (e.g. *ich hatte, ich sagte, ich lief*), and a perfect tense (e.g. *ich habe gehabt, ich habe gesagt, ich bin gelaufen*) for every verb. Prescriptive grammars insist upon a semantic (meaning) difference between these two tenses, but it is highly doubtful whether many German speakers, particularly younger speakers from the south, are now aware of any such difference, except in certain contexts. In modern German a major difference between the tenses is in formality: the preterite is simply more formal, and is often preferred in more literary or technical texts. Quite independently of this, the perfect tense is often preferred, even in the most formal texts, for reasons which we outlined above in our discussion of the whole phenomenon of compound tenses.

When we move from formal standard to colloquial German, we find very few preterites are used at all – in fact the only common ones are the preterites of the auxiliary verbs *haben*, *sein* and *werden* (*hatte*, *war* and *wurde*), of the modal verbs (particularly *konnte*, *wollte*, *sollte*, *durfte*, *mußte*), and of verbs of saying and thinking used to introduce indirect speech (*sagte*, *meinte*, *wußte*). Note that the common occurrence of the preterites of auxiliary and modal verbs does not conflict with the general preference for compound tenses (see above) in modern German since they themselves usually occur as the finite part of compound tenses, or of compound verbal expressions (e.g. *hatte gesagt*, *wollte laufen*, etc.).

Within colloquial German there are important regional differences in the use of preterites: in the south of the area there may be virtually no preterites in speech at all, or perhaps only the preterites of *haben* and *sein*, or of *sein* only, and only in their use as auxiliaries in pluperfect tenses (e.g. *hatte gesehen*, *war gelaufen*). All other preterites are replaced by perfects (e.g. *ich habe gehabt*, *ich habe gekonnt/können*, etc.).

In an intermediate area (e.g. in many parts of Hessen) we find the small common group of preterites (*war*, *wollte*, etc.) occurring, but then the normal perfect forms of most German speech are replaced by the forms which are normally used as pluperfects (*hatte gesagt*, *war gelaufen*, etc.).

When we move from colloquial standard German to non-standard speech, we find, in most of the German-speaking area, a similar pattern of past tense usage, though with even fewer preterites occurring. An important exception here is the Upper German dialect area where much colloquial non-standard speech, in common with Upper German traditional dialects, has no preterite forms at all, not even for the auxiliaries *haben* and *sein*. This means that pluperfects such as the standard German *ich hatte gesagt*, *ich war gelaufen* are replaced by forms in which the perfect tense, itself a compound tense, functions as an auxiliary in the formation of an even more complex compound tense, e.g. *ich habe gesagt gehabt* and *ich bin gelaufen gewesen*.

## 5.6 Lexical variation in German

We now move to a discussion of the lexical differences between different types of German, and discuss, firstly, regional differences which affect all levels of the language, including formal standard. We then discuss differences between formal standard and colloquial speech which affect the German of all regions, and then finally we mention the phenomenon of local peculiarities of vocabulary.

### 5.6.1 Lexical variation in perspective

Lexicon is the level of linguistic structure of which speakers are most consciously aware, and which they most consciously manipulate, and where adults can most easily learn new items, and it is therefore a much less fundamental marker of different language types than are grammatical or phonological differences. The reason for this is that lexical items can very easily spread from one speech type to another, given speakers' ability to innovate. A corollary is that lexical items are much less reliable indicators of speech type than are other items. An exception in this regard is the case of much traditional dialect, which is separated from other speech types by large lexical differences, making it hard to understand for outsiders, often, indeed, marking its speakers off as a marginal group, outside the mainstream of modern industrial society, and communicating little with speakers within that mainstream.

We devote relatively little space to discussion of lexical variation, since it is, for the reasons outlined, such a shifting and changeable matter, since it is something which is in any case fairly accessible to the student without much explanation or introduction, and since lexical differences do not constitute fundamental or complex differences of linguistic structure, unless they are massive, between one variety and another.

### 5.6.2 National varieties of German

Regional differences of lexicon which affect all types of German, including formal standard, have attracted a great deal of interest from linguists, and are fully and well documented elsewhere, particularly in Eichhoff (1977); we shall therefore touch upon them only briefly. An important group of such words are political, legal and economic terms which differ between the various German-speaking states and reflect different political, legal and economic systems. The most striking differences here are between the GDR and the other German-speaking countries. These have led to a great deal of discussion, and have even prompted suggestions that two distinct German languages are developing in east and west. Given the interest shown in this topic, we devote a final section of this chapter (5.7) to 'East' and 'West' German.

There are also similar differences between the German of Switzerland and of other German-speaking countries, and to a lesser extent between

German in Austria and in West Germany, again reflecting differing legal and political systems: *Kanton* (canton) is peculiar to Switzerland; the meaning of *Bundesrat* in Switzerland, '(member of) the federal government', is different from its West German meaning, 'upper house of the federal parliament'; *Matura* '(Austrian and Swiss) school-leaving examination' corresponds to the German *Abitur*, and so on.

Apart from these items which are clearly linked to political divisions, there are a considerable number of vocabulary differences between different parts of the German-speaking area. Many represent a north–south divide with, for example, north German *Sonnabend* (Saturday), *Schlips* (necktie) and *artig* (well-behaved) corresponding to south German (and Swiss and Austrian) *Samstag*, *Krawatte* and *brav*. Some of the non-political differences do follow political boundaries: for example *Spital* (hospital) is now generally confined to Austria and Switzerland where Germany has *Krankenhaus*, and *Obers* (cream) is only Austrian.

### 5.6.3 Formal and informal lexicon

Regional lexical differences within the standard languages are more numerous in German than in languages spoken in smaller and less politically fragmented areas, but our next topic is one with which the investigator of any language is confronted: lexical differences between formal and informal language. Every language which has been investigated has words which are appropriate only to certain types of situation. Since German is not at all peculiar in this respect, there is no particular reason to devote much space to this topic; we will restrict ourselves to some remarks of very wide applicability on verbal prefixes and on new words or words of foreign origin.

### Verb prefixes

Formal standard German has a set of verb prefixes *hinauf, hinaus- hinein-, hinüber-, hinunter-* indicating (roughly speaking) various types of movement away from the speaker, and contrasting with a set *herauf-, heraus-, herein-, herüber-, herunter-* indicating (roughly speaking) corresponding types of movement towards the speaker. This contrast is absent in colloquial German where both sets are usually replaced by *'rauf-, 'raus-, 'rein-, 'rüber-, 'runter-*. The distinction, which foreign learners may find difficult, is thus often also a problem for German native-speakers, since it is not present in everyday conversation.

## Words of foreign origin

The proportion of words of foreign origin is considerably greater in English than in German, but in German they represent (contrary to some impressions) a substantial proportion of the lexicon. In both languages such words may originate from learned contacts either directly with foreign speakers, or simply from the learned custom of coining new technical words based on Latin or Greek roots. Such learned lexicon is usually more formal than native vocabulary of similar meaning, always assuming there is a native word available. For example in German *Geographie* (geography), *Territorium* (territory) and *feminin* (feminine), of Latin or Greek origin, are rather more formal (and slightly different in meaning) from the native German *Erdkunde*, *Gebiet* and *weiblich*, although the boundaries in usage are, for each word pair, at a different level of formality, and in no case do they necessarily coincide at all with the rough division into formal and colloquial German.

Words can also pass into the language from foreign sources through more everyday contacts, and in these cases the word of foreign origin may or may not be more formal than a roughly corresponding native word. In both English and German such words come mostly from Romance languages, particularly French (though Italian is important too, especially for German), whose speakers have, for long periods, been perceived as more civilized and sophisticated than English or German speakers, and the vocabulary in question tends therefore to be rather more formal than equivalents of native origin (assuming there are such equivalents). For example a *Restaurant* is a more 'upmarket' eating-place than a *Gaststätte*; *Allee* (avenue) is a splendid type of *Straße* (street/road); *Dame* (lady) is a more 'refined' word than *Frau* (woman): the first word in each pair cited here is of French origin.

Where English and German differ in the matter of vocabulary of foreign origin is that in German-speaking countries purist movements, often of a strongly nationalistic character, which have tried to eliminate foreign words (*Fremdwörter*) from the language, have been more common than in English-speaking countries (see Von Polenz 1978: 114, 129, 160–2; Wells 1985: 393–401). Such attempts have been largely unsuccessful; in any case their theoretical basis is dubious, since the assumption that words of foreign origin are in some sense still foreign when they are assimilated to German pronunciation and when German-speakers use them every day is a very controversial one (see Von Polenz 1978: 162–3). Moreover, such attempts by academic purists to tinker with the language are very frequently ignored by many speakers of the language.

However, there have been some limited 'successes': what has happened here is that scholars have taken a native German word (in some cases a word which was obsolete or nearly so) and attempted to extend its range of meanings or its stylistic range in order to oust a so-called 'foreign' word. In these cases they have sometimes succeeded in establishing the native word in formal registers, but have only rarely had an effect on everyday speech. We thus find quite a number of pairs of words where the native word is more formal than its near equivalent of foreign origin, a phenomenon which is quite unexpected for English speakers. Examples are the pairs *passieren* and *geschehen* (happen), *extra* and *absichtlich* or *vorsätzlich* (on purpose), *Radio* and *Rundfunk* ('radio', the latter now scarcely used except in the names of radio stations), *Telefon* and *Fernsprecher* ('telephone', the latter being rare). In each pair the first word given is less formal, more common, and of foreign origin. One common purist substitution, *Wagen* for *Auto* (car), has been quite successful, though *Auto* is still more frequent.

In German-speaking countries today purism seems greatly weakened, and a very large number of foreign words are entering the language, particularly from English (for a detailed discussion, see 8.6).

### 5.6.4 Regional variation in lexicon

It is possible that every German-speaker uses at least a small number of distinctly local words, which might not be understood by people from other regions. It seems that the proportion of such words steadily increases as one passes from colloquial standard German through colloquial non-standard speech to traditional dialect. The reason for this increase is not hard to understand: as we move towards traditional dialect we encounter people who are progressively less mobile, socially and geographically. At the extreme, traditional dialect-speakers have the least opportunity and need to converse with people from distant regions, and therefore the least need to avoid markedly local vocabulary.

There is another side to the coin, however, which is that local vocabulary is a strong marker of local identity and local solidarity, and that many speakers of colloquial standard German, who normally use very little local lexicon, will nevertheless, as it were, 'quote' items of local lexicon to show local solidarity on occasion. This 'quotation' of local vocabulary seems to have increased since the dialect revival of the 1960s and 1970s, which was a facet of the resurgent regionalism of the period (see 3.2.2). For example, an educated Berlin speaker has told one of the authors of this book that when he meets other Berliners on holiday in distant parts they will use local Berlin words in conversation but, very interestingly, he said he would never use local non-standard Berlin grammar, such as the oblique case. Furthermore, recent studies of Berlin speech (for example Dittmar *et al.* 1986) have shown convincingly that much of the local lexicon is very well known to middle-class speakers, even though they may not use it very often: indeed the local word for beer, *Molle* (standard German *Bier*), is even used in advertising in Berlin. Standard German speakers, as well as quoting local lexicon, will also quote standard lexicon with local dialect pronunciation (departing more radically from the *DH* norm than standard lexicon with local accent pronunciation). For example in Berlin one hears /juːt/ and /kleːn/ for *DH* /guːt/ and /klain/ (*gut, klein*).

The position, then, seems to be as follows: traditional dialect contains a high proportion (variable and not generally measured) of local lexicon; the proportion is distinctly smaller in colloquial non-standard speech, but still appreciable; in colloquial standard it is smaller still, but speakers of all groups seem to have considerable knowledge of local lexicon and positive attitudes towards it, and even educated middle-class speakers will use it on occasion as a mark of local or regional loyalty.

Well-known items of local lexicon from Berlin (where, remember, traditional dialect is almost by definition virtually absent, since it is a large urban area) are *Molle* (= *Bier*, 'beer'), *Schrippe* (= *Brötchen*, 'bread roll'), and *Göre* (= *Mädchen*, 'girl'). Well-known words from other areas are *veräppeln* (Hessen) (= *verulken, auf den Arm nehmen*, 'make to look foolish'), *Viech* (much of south and centre) (= *Tier*, 'animal'), *Dirndl* (south) (= *Mädchen*, 'girl'), *Pott* (north) (= *Topf*, 'pot'), *Pütt* (Ruhr) (= *Bergwerk*, 'mine'), *lüttge/lütt* (north) (= *klein*, 'small'), *Gaul* (parts of south and centre) (= *Pferd*, 'horse').

We have seen that one of the chief differences between colloquial standard German and colloquial non-standard speech is that the latter shows non-standard grammar; this extends to the occurrence in colloquial non-standard speech of grammatical words (pronouns and articles in particular) which originate in traditional dialects. For example the definite article and demonstrative forms of Low German dialects (see above, 5.5.2) are also common in north German colloquial non-standard speech (*dit* and *det* are the neuter forms heard in Berlin non-standard) – indeed the *dat* neuter article and pronoun which also occurs in some Middle German Rhineland dialects is also common in Rhineland colloquial non-standard. *Dat* and *dit* are also frequently 'quoted' in standard German in north Germany and the Rhineland.

A second example concerns Bavarian and Austrian colloquial non-standard. In traditional Bavarian dialect the second person plural familiar pronoun is often *es* (= *ihr*, 'you') (see 3.10.3). Where verb and subject are inverted, as in questions, contractions usually arise: for example *bleibt es?* ('are you staying?') would become *bleibts?* Forms such as this occur in colloquial non-standard speech where, however, they are interpreted not as verb plus pronoun but, simply, as verb forms, and hence a further pronoun is used. For example in Munich non-standard *bleibts ihr nit?* (= *bleibt ihr nicht?* or *bleiben Sie nicht?*, 'aren't you staying?') may be heard. This example also illustrates the fact that in much traditional dialect and colloquial non-standard speech standard German *Sie* ('you' polite) is replaced by the older *Ihr* (in standard, 'you' plural, familiar).

## 5.7 German in East and West

The political boundaries within German-speaking Europe are, of course, reflected in differences in all types of German. The standard variety, both formal and colloquial, is affected most noticeably in its political, administrative and economic vocabulary, reflecting the varying political, administrative and economic systems (see above, 5.6.2). In addition, all forms of the language are affected by the fact that most people communicate much more frequently with German-speaking citizens of their own state than they do with other German-speakers. This leads to a tendency for all areas of the lexicon to show some differentiation correlating with the political boundaries, and we consider there to be national varieties of standard and colloquial German, which have a common core vocabulary, but which differ from each other in a considerable number of lexical items. The tendency for these national varieties to grow apart is however counterbalanced by the fact that, under modern conditions of trade and communications, German-speakers from the various states do frequently communicate with each other, which means that there is strong pressure for the national varieties not to drift so far apart that communication becomes difficult.

It has usually been considered that traditional dialects are exempt from this tendency to differentiate along national lines, their speakers having a restricted communication radius, and political, economic and administrative matters not being discussed in traditional dialect; it has been assumed that there is a Dutch–German dialect continuum in which the major boundaries do not usually coincide with national boundaries. However, it is very likely that, under modern conditions, traditional dialects are being influenced by the respective national varieties of the standard language, but they have not been investigated from this point of view.

### 5.7.1 Differing views of the East–West linguistic divide

Foreign learners of German who come from the West are most likely to learn the standard variety of German used in the north of the Federal Republic. If they then visit German-speaking countries, they are likely to have fewer comprehension problems in the north of the Federal Republic than in Switzerland and Austria or even than in the south of the Federal Republic. Difficulties will be encountered in these southern areas even where only everyday matters are being discussed, and even where the standard language is being used. These difficulties are likely to be greatest in Switzerland and least within the Federal Republic. In the GDR the difficulties in informal everyday language use will be minimal, in many cases less than in the south of the Federal Republic. The reasons for this lack of difficulty are simple: the boundary between the Federal Republic and the GDR is the newest national boundary in German-speaking Europe, and there has therefore not been time for sharply different everyday spoken standard varieties to develop. Moreover, the standard language in most of what is now the GDR was, before 1945, very close indeed to the north-western standard German used in the north of what is now the Federal Republic.

In view of this lack of difficulty with GDR German, Western students may be surprised to learn that the differences between western and GDR German have been considered by some German-speakers to be most serious and to be threatening to divide the German language into sharply different eastern and western varieties (see Hellmann 1980: 519–20). Why might the students' view differ so sharply from that of some German-speakers? A first answer could be that foreign students are unlikely to share the concerns of some Germans in the West, who feel the East–West boundary to be totally illegitimate, and who react very strongly to emerging East–West differences of any kind. Secondly, they are unlikely to share the concern of some East Germans to stress the separateness of the GDR from the Federal Republic, and hence to welcome any manifestations, linguistic or otherwise, of that separateness. Thirdly, they are unlikely, unless they are very advanced in the language, to have grappled with political or economic texts, where the differences are, indeed, quite marked.

Popular views of the East–West divide in language are varied, but in the academic literature it has not generally been considered since the late 1960s that the language is drifting apart to the extent that all communication is difficult (see Hellmann 1980: 520). It is now generally accepted that the syntax and morphology, the language structure, show no differences worth mentioning; differences are either stylistic, lying in the differing frequency of particular constructions in East and West, or sociolinguistic, lying in the differing prestige of non-standard speech in East and West (see 4.4.5), or lexical. The lexical differences are the most noticeable, and are particularly concentrated in the political and economic spheres. Recent writers from both East and West are virtually unanimous in their view that there still is a single German speech community (see for example Fleischer 1984: 419–20, written in the GDR). We can now see the view of a serious general disruption of communication as a misconception.

Similarly misconceived is the view – once widespread in the West – that it is not in the Federal Republic, but only in the GDR, that there have been innovations, perhaps officially inspired by the ruling Socialist Unity Party (*Sozialistische Einheitspartei Deutschlands* or *SED*) (see Hellmann 1980: 520). It is perfectly clear that western varieties of German also have introduced new forms, the innovations on both sides being largely the result of the growth of two different political and economic systems, and the exposure of the language to differing foreign influences – chiefly English (particularly American English) in the West, and Russian in the East. Although innovations have taken place in both eastern and western German, there is nevertheless a strictly limited sense in which we can regard western German as a norm and GDR German as a deviation from that norm: the innovations which arise in western German are widely understood in the East and may even enter into active usage there, while eastern neologisms are much less well understood in the West. A major factor operating here is the popularity and widespread availability of Western television programmes in the East. Since they are broadcast not only from the Federal Republic but also from West Berlin, in the heart of GDR territory, they can be received by about 80 per cent of the population.

### 5.7.2 The extent of East–West variation

In looking now at examples of innovation in both eastern and western German, we shall concentrate almost exclusively on the lexicon, as this is where most of the noticeable differences occur.

Both German states were founded, in 1949, under the tutelage of the respective occupying powers, and have institutions modelled upon those of the Soviet Union in the East and of the Western Allies in the West. However, in the Federal Republic the names of institutions are frequently modelled on traditional German titles: for example *Bundestag* (lower house of Parliament), *Bundeskanzler* (equivalent to Prime Minister) and *Bundeswehr* (Federal Army) echo the pre-war *Reichstag, Reichskanzler* and *Reichswehr*. At local government level, too, traditional titles are often used.

In contrast, the GDR has developed a new political and administrative vocabulary. Two notable characteristics are the use of *Volks-* (of the people) as a first element in compounds, as in *Volkskammer* (GDR Parliament), *Volkspolizei* (GDR police), *Nationale Volksarmee* (GDR army), and the frequent use of 'noun plus genitive' constructions as in *Palast der Republik* (chief state representative public building), *Rat der Stadt* (town council). Both of these characteristics are also found in western German, but are much less common. The use of the 'noun plus genitive' construction has undoubtedly increased in GDR German under the influence of a similar construction in Russian. This represents a case where there is no fundamental syntactic difference between East and West, but where a particular construction finds more favour in one area than another. The last example given (*Rat der Stadt*) illustrates another facet of Russian influence in GDR German, the loan translation of Russian lexicon: *Rat* (council) is common in both East and West, but its frequency is even greater in the East since it is seen as a translation of the Russian *sov'et* (council, soviet). It is found in compounds which do not occur in the West, such as *Staatsrat* (body carrying out collectively the functions of the head of state, a little like a cabinet) and *Ministerrat* (government, Russian *Sov'et Ministrov*).

Not only have the two German states modelled their political and administrative systems on those of the respective occupying powers, they were also obliged to model their economies on the Soviet or the Western pattern. The Federal Republic retains the inherited vocabulary for capitalist institutions, such as *Börse* (stock exchange), *Aktie* (share), etc., but has gained new vocabulary for modern economic phenomena, much of it borrowed from English, such as *floaten* (to float a currency), or loan-translated from English, such as *Währungskorb* (basket of currencies).

In the GDR, economic vocabulary has generally been created from roots already present in the language, with little obvious Russian borrowing, though often there is ultimately a Russian model for such words. Given the centralized, planned nature of the economy, the element *Plan-* is particularly common, as in *Plansoll* (output target). In the economic as in the political sphere GDR German has a number of neologisms made up of elements of ultimately Latin or Greek origin which copy similar neologisms in Russian, such as *Kombinat* (large-scale socialist industrial enterprise, Russian *kombinat*). Lexicon of native Russian origin borrowed into GDR German is less common, and tends to be rather informal, for example *Subbotnik* (unpaid extra work).

The enormous scientific and technological advances since the war have brought a flood of new vocabulary into both eastern and western German. Many of the western neologisms are well understood in the East through the medium of television. In the physical sciences there is a high correspondence across the border in the new vocabulary; most of it consists of international neologisms, based on Latin and Greek roots, and the German lexicon will in any case be closely parallel to that of English and Russian, and indeed other languages. It is therefore not surprising that terms like *Positron* or *Plasma* are common to East and West. Matters are however different in technology, where western German has received innovations from or through English-speaking countries, and often has names of English origin. GDR German has avoided direct English borrowings, and additionally shows some Russian influence even though many of the items designated may originate in English-speaking countries, or may have reached Eastern Europe through the English-speaking world. Hence West German *Plastik* (the synthetic substances) and *Computer* correspond to eastern *Plast*, *Plaste* or *Plastmasse* (Russian *plastmassa*) and *Rechner*. *Elektronenrechner* or *Rechner* (computer) can be used in both East and West, but in the West are less common than *Computer*. In the East *Computer* is certainly understood and used, but does not normally appear in writing.

In everyday vocabulary of a non-technical nature East–West differences are not numerous, but they are present, sometimes reflecting differences in lifestyle. In a Western restaurant various kinds of *Saft* (fruit juice) are usually available, often concentrated pure fruit juice without added sugar. In GDR restaurants the nearest equivalent often has the name *Juice*, and often contains some sugar, though *Saft* is also used and understood in the East. The GDR example shows an important point: English loans are found in GDR German as well as in the western variety, and, as in the West, may convey an impression of modernity and an international lifestyle. They are however much less common in the East than in the West, and this instance of a loan in eastern German which is not common in the West is an exception.

Even more surprisingly English loans can be found in GDR German which are uncommon in the West, and which have actually entered eastern German through the medium of Russian. An example is *Broiler* (Russian *broiler*) ultimately from the now uncommon English word 'broiler', meaning 'chicken raised for broiling'. In the GDR it means 'mass-produced chicken, often already cooked'; if cooked such a bird would be called *Brathähnchen* in western German. Another instructive example also comes from restaurants and cafés: in the West an order for *eine Tasse Kaffee* (a cup of coffee) will produce a large cup of black coffee with sugar and a pot or jug of milk provided automatically, which may or may not be used, as the customer pleases. In the East the same order will provoke the question *schwarzer Kaffee oder Kaffee komplett?* (black coffee or coffee with milk?). One can speculate that perhaps the GDR does not wish to waste labour and raw materials on lots of little pots of milk which may not be used! The phrase *Kaffee komplett* is not understood in the West.

The differences in everyday vocabulary again show the differing influences of foreign languages. Western German has an enormous number of loans from English (see 8.6), while eastern German has a few Russian loans, which may be little understood in the West. An example is *Datscha* (Russian *dacha*) which means 'house in the country, villa (often quite small)' where western German would have *Wochenendhäuschen* for a small structure, and *Villa* for a larger one, both western terms being understood in the East.

Where formal standard and colloquial standard German had two or more competing terms before the war, the modern division has sometimes favoured one form in one German state, another form in the other. For example, Map 3.1 shows the distribution of words for 'Saturday' in German dialects; what it fails to show is (1) that *Sater(s)tag* is not standard German, and (2) that *Samstag* is the dominant form in the Federal Republic, *Sonnabend* in the GDR. Eichhoff (1977), which is a word atlas of colloquial German speech, clearly shows this; in the Federal Republic, *Samstag* is used in colloquial speech in virtually the whole of the *Sater(s)tag* area, and is making strong inroads into the *Sonnabend* area in the north. It also shows that, in the GDR, *Sonnabend* has ousted *Samstag* in colloquial speech in all areas except the extreme south (Eichhoff 1977: Map 41).

### 5.7.3 East–West variation in context

It will be clear that we view the differences between eastern and western German as special cases within the overall pattern of regional and social differentiation in the continuum of colloquial and standard speech. As they affect largely the lexicon, and not the grammatical structure of the language, we consider them to be relatively superficial; they represent a barrier to communication only when certain limited areas of experience are under discussion.

### Further reading

Accounts of the colloquial speech of major urban centres and of some other areas have appeared in recent years, such as Veith (1983),

Stellmacher (1977), Schlobinski (1987), Herrgen (1986), Dittmar *et al.* (1986) and Dreβler *et al.* (1976); see also Chapter 4 and the references cited there.

Another useful source of information is the series of booklets *Dialekt–Hochsprache kontrastiv*. These booklets tend to suggest that speakers of German use either formal standard German or traditional dialect, i.e. they appear to neglect colloquial speech. However they make frequent references to 'mistakes' made by dialect-speakers in standard German. Such standard German with dialectal mistakes is, of course, implicitly colloquial speech.

Some modern grammars of German describe the grammar of colloquial standard German as well as that of the formal standard language; we can mention here Helbig and Buscha (1977, 1986) and Eisenberg (1986).

The lexicon of colloquial standard and non-standard speech is well covered in an atlas, Eichhoff (1977), and in a dictionary, Küpper (1987). Specific discussion of different lexicon in East and West can be found in many places, such as Fleischer (1984), Hellmann (1980) and Clyne (1984: Ch. 2). A useful short dictionary of GDR lexicon for West Germans is Kinne and Strube-Edelmann (1981).

A brief but useful account of contemporary changes on all levels in colloquial and standard German is Braun (1987).

# 6 Standard and non-standard German: their rôle in society

## 6.1 The political and social correlates of variation in German

We have so far examined in considerable detail how millions of people in central Europe who can be described, and who would describe themselves, as speaking German (*Deutsch*) nevertheless use a very wide range of differing linguistic varieties, which can be described as standard German, or as German dialects, or as colloquial German speech. We have also described in some detail the linguistic characteristics of these varieties of German. However, where a collection of linguistic varieties, such as German, is described as a single language, the differences between the varieties may fulfil a social or political rôle: the speakers of the language may use the linguistic differences to distinguish between one group of speakers and another. We now turn to a closer examination of the consequences of the fact that different speakers of German often speak in remarkably different ways. We turn, in fact, to the more clearly social side of our sociolinguistic study.

We have already dwelt at some length on the relatively simple fact that speakers of German from different geographical regions speak differently; differences within German mark regional differences within each of the German-speaking countries, but they also mark national differences between the various German-speaking countries. Regional differences within a German-speaking country are, not surprisingly, most noticeable within the largest German-speaking state, the Federal Republic, least noticeable within the smallest, Liechtenstein, with the others occupying intermediate positions.

A much more complex pattern of linguistic distinctions is that which correlates not with geographical differences but with differences within each locality between different social groups. We have already mentioned this pattern of distinctions, for example in Chapter 5, where colloquial standard German was repeatedly equated with middle-class speech, colloquial non-standard and traditional dialects with working-class speech. In the current chapter we will progress beyond these relatively simple statements to an examination of the extent to which they are valid, and to the consequences which they have, assuming that they are valid, for the relations between different groups in the societies of German-speaking countries.

As we saw earlier (5.1.1–5.1.3) there are considerable problems in discussing social variation within German. We will, as far as possible, circumvent these problems here, and simply assume that the German speech of most regions where German is both the native language and an official language can be divided into the following speech-types: formal standard German (*Standardsprache*, etc.), colloquial German (*Umgangssprache*), and traditional dialect (*Dialekt* or *Mundart*), with, in most regions, a division within colloquial German into colloquial standard German (*standardnahe Umgangssprache*) and colloquial non-standard German (*dialektnahe Umgangssprache*).

There are great differences between one region and another in the relationships between these various speech types. First of all, in some German-speaking regions one or more of these speech types may be used by very few people: formal standard German is very little used in some regions, such as Alsace, where German is a minority language, and traditional dialect is little used in large urban areas in north Germany. Secondly, even in regions (the majority) where all these speech types are used, the relationships between them may differ markedly both in terms of linguistic distance between the locally occurring varieties, and social distance. In practice linguistic distance as registered subjectively by the speakers of the language is coloured by social attitudes, and is hence to a considerable extent a function of the social distance between them, but nevertheless speakers in some regions do genuinely consider local non-standard forms to be very different linguistically from the standard language, while in other regions the difference is seen to be less great. Speech communities in regions where the difference is very considerable, such as Switzerland, Austria, much of southern Germany, particularly the rural south-west, and the more remote rural areas of north Germany, will be diglossic, in the sense that at some point in the range of local speech forms there will, in the perception of speakers, be a clear break, and they will switch consciously between a markedly local form and a form closer to standard dependent on situational factors.[1] Where the difference is perceived to be less great, for example in most large towns, particularly in the north, there will be no such abrupt switch; speakers will shift more

---

[1] In fact the situation in German-speaking Switzerland is more complex in this respect than traditional accounts suggest, but we shall look at this in more detail in Chapter 7.

gradually from one form to another, and there will be less awareness of a break between different forms (see Mattheier 1980: 162–75 for a sketch of some of the major regional differences in the use of the various speech types, and some further information on the regional differences in movement between speech types).

The social distance between the various forms of German also differs markedly from one region to another, with non-standard forms in rural areas, where they are linguistically further from standard, being generally closer to it in prestige, and with non-standard southern German being generally much more prestigious than northern non-standard varieties.

## 6.2 The social effects of variation in German in the Federal Republic

### 6.2.1 The assumed linguistic disadvantage of the working class

Although there are considerable regional variations in the prestige of non-standard varieties of German, it nevertheless remains true everywhere that for certain types of linguistic activity the standard variety is obligatory; in certain registers only the standard variety can be used.

The extent to which the standard variety is obligatory also varies between regions. In Switzerland and Luxembourg local varieties are used in the vast majority of spoken registers, and indeed certain forms of local dialect in these countries have some of the characteristics of independent standard languages (see Zimmer 1977). In north Germany clearly non-standard forms are restricted to informal conversation, and other areas occupy some sort of intermediate position between the Swiss and north German situations. In all German-speaking areas traditional dialects can on occasion be used in more formal registers, in dialect plays, novels, poems, church services and broadcasting, but in Germany and Austria this is regarded as in some sense unusual, as something for the dialect enthusiast only. In the vast majority of cases in Germany and Austria standard German, usually colloquial standard German with local accent, is the speech form required in official dealings, and from children at school. At least within Germany and Austria the vast majority of conversations on academic topics are conducted in standard German, either formal or colloquial.

Now, as we have seen earlier (5.1.1), standard German, albeit colloquial and not formal standard, is the native speech form of a section of the population, at least in Germany and Austria; in north Germany it is generally the only speech form of the middle class, while elsewhere the middle class make frequent use of it, though in the most intimate sphere they may use forms of more non-standard character. In contrast the working class carry out most of their everyday activities in non-standard German, either colloquial non-standard or traditional dialect, depending on the region, the nature of their home community (urban or rural) and their level of education. Classes are here defined imprecisely, with 'working class' signifying approximately manual workers and their families. Non-standard speech is also frequently used by what German writers refer to as the *alte Mittelschicht* (old middle class) of small farmers, self-employed trades people and small business people (see Mickartz 1983: 69ff and Ammon 1977: 5–19).

Given the social distribution of the various speech forms, it has often been assumed that working-class people are at a social disadvantage because their native speech is not the standard variety which is obligatory in certain situations; conversely middle-class people have been seen as advantaged, since in any situation they can use their native speech form.

The central social consequence, then, of the persistence of standard and non-standard German has been seen to be working-class disadvantage, which is most clearly manifest in differing school performance, particularly in the subject 'German'. This differing school performance is assumed to reflect linguistic differences which will persist throughout life and cause difficulties throughout life.[2] Differing school performance is not restricted to the subject 'German', but is found in all school subjects, since instruction, and pupils' response, in all subjects is expected to take place in standard German (see Mattheier 1980: 114–15). It is most important to note that this linguistic disadvantage has been particularly identified in the Federal Republic of Germany, not in other German-speaking countries, a point to which we return in 6.3. Our remarks in this section apply largely to the Federal Republic.

### 6.2.2 Restricted and elaborated codes

Inferior school performance, and the general social disadvantage which stems partly from it and partly from other factors, has been seen to result not just from the difficulty non-standard speakers experience in switching from their native speech to the obligatory standard language; some writers have attributed it to the very nature of non-standard speech itself, which, they claim, inhibits intellectual development. Non-standard speech could inhibit intellectual development if it were difficult, or perhaps even impossible, to express certain types of ideas in it, if it were, in

---

[2] In West German literature on the subject, the problem is often stated as being the disadvantage of dialect-speakers, rather than the disadvantage of the working class, the two groups not necessarily being identical. However, the problem is perceived by Ulrich Ammon, perhaps the most influential writer on the subject, as one of working-class disadvantage (see Ammon 1972a).

some sense or other, a deficient form of language. Those who have seen non-standard German as a fundamentally deficient variety have labelled it a 'restricted code' (*restringierter Kode*), a term which originates in the work of the British educational sociologist Basil Bernstein (see Bernstein 1971 [1965]).

The use of the term 'restricted code' and its counterpart 'elaborated code' in Bernstein's work is open to varying interpretations and indeed has seemed to mean rather different things at different stages in his work. In his paper (1971 [1965]: 136) restricted code is very clearly equated with working-class speech, whereas middle-class speech consists of both elaborated and restricted codes, and restricted code is described (1971 [1965]: 134) as having 'low-level and limiting syntactic organization . . . and . . . little motivation towards increasing vocabulary'. This view of the social distribution of the codes and of the deficient character of the restricted code can lead to a view of working-class speakers as fundamentally linguistically disadvantaged, but it is in conflict with the interpretation of Bernstein's views given by Halliday in his foreword to the second volume of Bernstein's collected papers (Halliday 1973), which expresses the view that 'Bernstein's work suggests . . . that there may be differences in the relative orientation of different social groups towards the various functions of language in given contexts and towards the different areas of meaning that may be explored within a given function' (1973: xiv), which we would interpret as meaning that speakers of different social groups show merely different attitudes to the use of, or the appropriateness of, various registers in language.

The literature in German on this topic is copious; it ranges from Oevermann (1968), which follows Bernstein (1971 [1965]) fairly closely in its view of the nature and rôle of elaborated and restricted code, through to Dittmar (1973), which adopts a very different position. It includes notably the works of Ammon, for whom restricted code is more or less equivalent to traditional dialect (see 6.2.3). Dittmar (1973) adopts the position of most British and American sociolinguists in rejecting the entire notion of codes in this sense (see, for example, Trudgill 1975). A notion which crops up over and over again in the literature is the *Sprachbarriere* or 'linguistic barrier' separating social classes (see e.g. Löffler 1972). It seems to mean anything from a real barrier to comprehension to, simply, an inhibition about using certain registers.

**6.2.3** Suggested linguistic causes of disadvantage

In this chapter we shall accept that working-class children, at any rate in West Germany, suffer social disadvantage, and seek to examine whether or not this can be traced in part to linguistic differences between these children, on the one hand, and, on the other hand, middle-class children and, crucially, middle-class teachers.[3] We accept this view, however, only because it seems to be supported by most of the literature; by no means is there unanimity here (see Löffler 1985: 184–92 for a summary of the widely different findings in various studies).

Working-class children's speech could, as we have seen above (6.2.1), be a source of disadvantage for quite basic reasons: it could be a restricted code, in the sense of a fundamentally less adequate form of language, compared to the elaborated code of middle-class children and teachers. Its characteristics could, however, cause problems on another level: it could simply be a barrier to communication in school, being difficult to understand for the teacher. Conversely the teacher's standard German could simply be hard to understand for working-class pupils. Or, alternatively, working-class children's language could disadvantage them for a basically non-linguistic reason: it could simply evoke class prejudice on the part of teachers, not necessarily at a conscious level.

The view that working-class speech in West Germany is a restricted code is clearly found in the early writings of Ulrich Ammon, such as Ammon (1972b). This can mean a variety of things: on the one hand it could mean that working-class speech is, in some sense, such an inadequate linguistic system that its speakers' adequate cognitive and social development is not possible. Such is the view held by the proponents of verbal deficit theory, such as Bereiter and Engelmann (see Gordon 1981: 48–65). On the other hand it could merely entail the view, implicit in Halliday (1973) (see above 6.2.2), that working-class children have less confidence in using certain registers. Where working-class speech is described as a restricted code in West German work, then 'restricted code' tends to signify an inadequate linguistic system in some sense or other. This line of thinking is found most clearly in Ammon's own work (1972b: 84). It is difficult to ascertain what writers such as Ammon mean by the inadequate nature of working-class speech, but it seems to boil down chiefly to the fact that non-standard German speech has a restricted vocabulary in areas of experience connected with learning and modern technology (Ammon 1978a: 50). It is however difficult to claim that restricted vocabulary in certain areas marks a linguistic system as fundamentally inadequate. As Mattheier points out (1980: 133) the standard variety has a restricted vocabulary, compared to the traditional dialects, for the description of local flora and fauna. Traditional dialects, and other non-standard speech forms, would indeed be fundamentally

---

[3] The various arguments in this area are developed in somewhat greater detail in Barbour (1987).

inadequate linguistic systems if they were incapable of adding new vocabulary, and Ammon does almost suggest (1978a: 54) that dialects are by definition speech forms with restricted lexicon. This is, however, difficult to maintain; speakers of traditional dialects often employ dialect lexicon which is clearly of non-local, even of foreign origin, and descriptions of dialects can easily be found in which lexicon of obviously foreign origin is discussed. For example Zehetner (1977: 96–8) lists a number of items of Bavarian dialect lexicon such as *Lexikon* (sic), *Radio*, *Email*, *Benzin*, *Terpentin*, *Nikotin*, *Sacharin* and *Schocklad*, which are clearly not of local origin.[4]

What is it, then, in the nature of non-standard speech which places its speakers at a disadvantage? In our opinion it is less likely to be a fundamental characteristic of such speech which has this effect, more likely to be a matter of social convention which dictates that certain areas of experience are discussed exclusively in standard German. This could place a barrier in the way of the working-class child at school who might have to switch to a different linguistic system, say from traditional dialect to the standard variety, in order to discuss academic matters in a generally acceptable way; such a barrier would not be placed in the way of the middle-class child, who is a native speaker of the standard variety. In other words, working-class children may have problems in using certain registers, which middle-class children do not. Even this – in our view more plausible – statement of the problem begs certain questions: it assumes that working-class children speak either traditional dialect or some other speech form which is very clearly distinct from standard German, and it assumes that middle-class children speak the standard variety and need to make no kind of adjustment in order to use learned or formal registers. We shall show below that all these assumptions are open to challenge.

The problems of working-class children, if not caused by the possession of a fundamentally inadequate linguistic system, could, nevertheless, be a result of their language being simply hard to understand for others, including teachers, and, conversely, of the speech of teachers and others being difficult for the working-class child to understand. This explanation of their problem is plausible only if working-class speech is linguistically highly divergent from the standard, that is if it is either traditional dialect or close to traditional dialect, and if the working-class child has little exposure to the standard variety other than at school.

---

[4] We must however remember that Ammon, in the works cited, is not suggesting that traditional dialect as such is a restricted code; restricted code is for him the speech of manual workers which is, in his view, typically traditional dialect, but not necessarily so (see Ammon 1972b: 84). Conversely, he considers that there are speakers of traditional dialect who are not manual workers.

Our remarks so far have perhaps given rise to an assumption that working-class speech is traditional German dialect; the time has now come to challenge this assumption. In the first place, while it is perfectly possible that over wide areas of the Federal Republic children may still arrive at school speaking only a traditional dialect, there is actually little hard evidence that this is now the case in the late 1980s. Secondly, traditional dialect is, it is generally agreed, relatively rare in large cities, where a very high proportion of the population lives. Studies which have been made suggest, albeit on the basis of rather subjective information, that monoglot speakers of traditional dialect are now quite rare among schoolchildren, at least in the centre and north of the country (see for example Macha 1982: 28, 42; Mattheier 1980: 132). It seems in fact fairly safe to assume that a majority of working-class children is able to speak some form of colloquial German, in many cases in addition to a traditional dialect, and that this colloquial speech should not be hard to understand, at least for teachers working near their home locality. Nowadays, in fact, it often seems to be the case that non-standard-speakers actually learn as a first variety a form close to standard, acquiring a clearly non-standard form only from the peer group at school, or even after school in their teens (see Mattheier 1980: 51, 120–1). It seems, then, implausible that indigenous German schoolchildren in the Federal Republic frequently encounter a problem of not being understood at school.

What about the reverse problem, that children from working-class backgrounds fail to understand the standard variety used in school and in official spheres? This seems distinctly implausible; there is very little evidence that colloquial standard German as used in the mass media is not well understood throughout the German-speaking area. Of course the language in use in school or in official institutions, or in some broadcasting, may well contain vocabulary items unfamiliar to many people, but lack of knowledge of specialist vocabulary can affect speakers of the standard variety, and middle-class people, as well as dialect-speakers and working-class people; anyone of any social or linguistic background is capable of learning new vocabulary, unless suffering from certain relatively rare disabilities.

We would, however, not deny that there is a problem here for children from certain social backgrounds; they may well have acquired very little specialist vocabulary from home while other children may have acquired a considerable amount. A further problem arises in that academic and technical matters are conventionally discussed in the standard variety, meaning that, in order to produce socially acceptable language in academic and technical registers, speakers of non-standard German have to make considerable adjustments to their native speech. Conversely, middle-class children may experience that 'continuity of culture between home and school' which Halliday (1973: xiv–xv) remarks upon in his comments upon Bernstein's work in Britain.

However, arguments like these ignore the fact that all speakers of the language need to make adjustments to their spontaneous, relaxed mode of speech in order to perform adequately in formal registers; formal standard German is arguably no one's native speech form. It is nevertheless reasonable to suppose that the problems experienced by the speaker of non-standard German in the learning of the formal standard language are more serious than those of the speaker of colloquial standard German, although not necessarily of an entirely different kind (see Mattheier 1980: 133–4).

### 6.2.4 Linguistic problems facing all social groups

Those who believe that non-standard forms of German are fundamentally inadequate systems (see 6.2.2) may propose with Ammon (1978b: 269–71) that the interests of social equality demand the replacement of non-standard with standard speech. If, on the other hand, one believes that standard and non-standard forms of language are equally viable linguistic systems, then one might propose that both be fostered in society at large and in schools (see Mattheier 1980: 129), producing the type of diglossic or even bilingual situation found in Switzerland (see 7.6).

It is interesting to speculate why this latter type of solution has not been accepted, why non-standard speech in the Federal Republic has a restricted range of registers, being generally considered inappropriate for formal or learned discourse. Part of the answer here must surely lie in attitudes to such speech on the part of teachers, of society at large, and indeed of the users of such speech forms themselves. There seems to be a general consensus in the Federal Republic that the formal standard variety is the only type of language appropriate to formal registers. As we have seen, working-class people are felt to be disadvantaged since this is not their native speech form. However, this is a less than entirely satisfactory explanation for their disadvantage, since often the form of language demanded in schools is not the native speech form of the middle class either. More specifically, there is often a demand that formal or learned registers be expressed in the formal standard language with the prestige pronunciation *Deutsche Hochlautung* (*DH*) (see Mattheier 1980: 116). This demand requires a majority of even middle-class children to make considerable phonetic, phonological and morphological adjustments in their speech, which will present considerable problems for many of them.

Morphological characteristics of formal standard German rare in colloquial standard German include genitive cases (see 5.5.2), first subjunctives and (in the south of the German-speaking area) the preterite tenses of most verbs (see 5.5.3). Moreover the *Deutsche Hochlautung* accent is used by only a minority of middle-class people, a particularly small minority in the south; if it is demanded in school a majority of children will have to make difficult adjustments to the phonology and phonetics of their speech. In fact the goal of a *DH* pronunciation is rarely achieved; even in the most formal registers a majority of speakers of German achieve at most a grammatically fairly standard form of German, but with regional accent. In this situation children from most social backgrounds face problems, but those of working-class children are undoubtedly greater; their everyday pronunciation is in most cases further from the prestige norm than is that of their middle-class counterparts.

The fact that some speakers of German in the Federal Republic use non-standard forms of the language does represent a social barrier, and places working-class children, or speakers of non-standard German, at a disadvantage in school, which they may never overcome successfully. However, disadvantage arises not because non-standard speech is fundamentally inadequate, and not, on the whole, because it represents a barrier to comprehension for either speaker or listener. Disadvantage arises rather because non-standard speech is further from the prestige norm demanded in formal registers than is the colloquial standard of the middle class, and there are therefore linguistic and psychological barriers to the acquisition of acceptable formal standard by non-standard speakers. Non-standard speech, or standard speech with clear traces of non-standard influence, may evoke negative attitudes, or even ridicule, on the part of the dominant middle class.

## 6.3 The social effects of variation in other German-speaking countries

This section will be short, since the social effects of variation have not been considered to be anything like as important outside the Federal Republic, either in public debate or in the academic literature.

In the GDR there is today considerable tolerance of linguistic variety, following a period of great insistence on the standard variety, but the consensus of academic research in this area is that this does not seriously disadvantage any social group (see for example Schönfeld and Pape 1981:

passim, but particularly 181–201). Indeed the existence of elaborated and restricted codes has been seen, perhaps not surprisingly, to be a specific problem of capitalist societies (see Porsch 1983).

It is of course difficult to compare GDR literature with that of the Federal Republic given the different ideological assumptions of the writers, but no such problem exists in comparing accounts of the Swiss and Austrian situations with that in the Federal Republic. It is hence striking that there has been almost no discussion of restricted and elaborated codes or of linguistic barriers, in relation to Switzerland and Austria. The most striking contrast is between the position in Switzerland and that in the Federal Republic. The Swiss case can, perhaps, finally dispose of the notion that German dialects are inadequate linguistic systems: virtually all German-speaking Swiss are native-speakers of Alemannic German dialects, whose structure is very close indeed to that of Alemannic dialects spoken within Germany, and to that of other Upper German dialects, and yet the suggestion that these dialects cause the Swiss to function inadequately in their daily lives is patently absurd. There are linguistic problems within German-speaking Switzerland (see e.g. Ris 1973) but they are not the problems of speakers hampered by being able to use only a restricted code.

## 6.4 Conclusions

The fact that all German-speaking Swiss speak traditional dialect seems to be crucial; as Mattheier (1980: 131) points out, the problem of linguistic barriers and different codes was not noticed in Germany at the time when, in many areas, traditional dialect was more or less universal. It began to be seen as a problem in schools, for instance, only in classes where both dialect-speakers and standard-speakers were present. If, as he suggests, the disadvantage of non-standard-speakers is noticeable only when they are in close contact with standard-speakers, then this strongly suggests that the problem is overwhelmingly one of social attitudes, rather than of the linguistic characteristics of non-standard German.

## Further reading

There is a great deal of literature in this area in German, but much of it is highly technical or polemical. A good general discussion is Mattheier (1980: particularly 107–39).

# 7 Language in multilingual societies: the Federal Republic and Switzerland

## 7.1 Introduction

In our discussion of variation so far we have been concerned chiefly with the form and function of varieties of German as used by native-speakers in the 'German-speaking countries'. Although we have acknowledged that the term 'German-speaking countries' is not much more than a convenient fiction (see Chapter 1), we have paid little attention to the implications of this. In this chapter and the next therefore we shall consider some further dimensions of the notion 'variation', which reinforce the significance of German and its speakers (whether 'native' or otherwise) for sociolinguistic study in general.

Both from a historical and a sociolinguistic perspective the neighbouring states of the Federal Republic and Switzerland are in striking contrast with each other. The Federal Republic is a young state whose physical limits and constitutional status were determined by foreign powers and whose population has had to struggle to come to terms not only with its past but also with the problem of finding a new identity for itself (for a good discussion of the problem of identity in the Federal Republic, see Klönne 1984). Switzerland on the other hand is one of the oldest European states and is renowned both for its internal social and political stability and for its neutrality and fierce independence in relation to international affairs.

Language plays an important rôle here, but again a very different one in each case. A continuous linguistic and cultural tradition provides the most important positive link with the past for the Federal Republic, and the German language is one of the few common bonds that hold the citizens of the new state together. In Switzerland, it is not a single language but rather linguistic pluralism that constitutes one of the most enduring characteristics of the nation. However, massive immigration during the last thirty years of speakers of other languages than German has transformed the Federal Republic too into an embryonic multilingual state.

In this chapter we shall look at issues that span the full range of the sociolinguistic spectrum, all of which however arise as a result of contact between languages or language varieties in these two countries. The social and linguistic problems faced by immigrants in the Federal Republic have raised previously unconsidered questions of educational policy and have given new impetus to the study of how languages develop and how individuals acquire knowledge of a language. Sociolinguistic interest in Switzerland has focussed on two key issues: the supposedly diglossic relationship between Swiss standard German and Swiss German dialects (collectively known, amongst linguists at least, as *Schwyzertütsch* or *Schweizerdeutsch*); and the coexistence in one state of four linguistic communities – German, French, Italian and Romansh. These phenomena are not of course unique to Switzerland but the 'Swiss situation' is often held to be a classic example in each case and both features constitute essential aspects of the country's international 'image'. However, none of these issues is as straightforward as is sometimes assumed and in discussing them we shall consider the extent to which conventional explanations offer a convincing account.

## 7.2 Multilingualism in the Federal Republic

Large-scale immigration of foreign workers into Germany is not a purely modern phenomenon: in the period of rapid industrial expansion between the unification of Germany in 1871 and the outbreak of the First World War many thousands came from neighbouring countries to the south and east in search of work, while in the first years of the Second World War thousands more were forcibly imported as slave labour. The most recent influx began in response to a campaign of recruitment initiated by the government of the Federal Republic in the 1950s and was intended to meet the shortfall in labour that was becoming acute as the 'economic miracle' forged ahead. By the time recruitment was officially stopped in 1973 and tighter immigration restrictions were introduced following the economic decline of the early 1970s, almost 4 million 'new' foreigners were living in the Federal Republic.

However, although the number of foreign workers both in absolute terms and as a proportion of the workforce declined over the following decade, the relatively high birthrate and the continued right of family members to join their relatives in the Federal Republic meant that the overall number of foreigners in the population continued to increase. It reached its peak to date in 1982 at almost 4.7 million (7.6 per cent of the population) and has since declined only slightly. Not surprisingly, the immigrant population is concentrated in the larger towns and industrial conurbations, and in some cities such as Munich, Stuttgart and Frankfurt foreigners represent very substantial proportions of the total population (approximately 17, 18 and 25 per cent respectively).

Many of these supposedly temporary workers and their families have now lived in the Federal Republic for a long time: in 1986 almost 60 per cent had been there longer than ten years. Furthermore, many of their children were born there, and despite the disproportionately high rate of unemployment amongst foreign workers (14 per cent as against 9 per cent overall in 1986) and financial inducements from the government to return to their countries of origin, relatively few show any inclination to leave (statistics from *Datenreport 3*, Statistisches Bundesamt 1987). To a large extent this is due to the fact that employment prospects in the countries concerned are even worse than in the Federal Republic, and in the case of Turkey especially (where a third of the immigrants come from) the political situation discourages many from returning.

So although successive governments have resisted the term *Ein-wanderungsland* (country of immigration), and the immigrants are still denied many fundamental rights of citizenship, the Federal Republic has become a state whose ethnic, cultural and linguistic composition is highly diverse. In this respect, it is not much different from many of its neighbours (e.g. France or England) and it is confronted with most of the social and political issues that are also encountered in these countries. Perhaps the most profound effect in the longer term, if the immigrant populations wish and manage to retain their cultural identity while at the same time achieving a greater measure of legal and political integration into the society of the Federal Republic, could be a radical change in the self-image of that society. However, we have seen how important the association between language and national identity has been in Germany (see Chapters 1 and 2) and we should not underestimate the resistance to the perception of the Federal Republic as a multilingual and multicultural society.

Education policy varies from one *Bundesland* to another but the underlying aims in most cases are still either to assimilate immigrant children as quickly as possible into the 'host' culture or to isolate them from it by running separate classes for German and non-German children. Attempts to integrate foreign children while simultaneously fostering their own culture are the exception rather than the rule, and genuinely multicultural approaches to education for all children are rarer still.

It is admittedly unrealistic to expect that many children might achieve complete bilingualism (sometimes called 'equilingualism'), but there is no reason in principle why most should not be able to achieve native-speaker competence in German while maintaining adequate competence in their first language for most day-to-day needs. What worries many researchers, however (see e.g. Stölting *et al.* 1980), is that in practice the outcome for many children will be *doppelseitige Halbsprachigkeit* (semilingualism). That is to say, there is a real risk that they will never develop complete competence in either language, but will be left in a kind of linguistic limbo that can only lead to further social disadvantage.

### 7.3 *Gastarbeiterdeutsch*

More often than not, adult immigrants have had no tuition in German before arriving in the Federal Republic and rarely have any once they are there. For those who do not intend to stay more than a short time, this does not necessarily pose serious problems as they typically work and live together with speakers of the same language. However, as we pointed out above, most in fact stay for long periods and many settle in the country permanently. Of these long-term residents a large proportion is concentrated in what are effectively immigrant ghettoes, typically the most neglected and run-down areas of large towns. On the one hand, this again means that there is less need for the inhabitants to learn German, but this lack of incentive in turn reinforces their isolation from the rest of the population and inhibits their ability to improve their conditions. The result is a vicious circle.

This situation provided the initial motivation for academic interest in what has come to be known as *Gastarbeiterdeutsch* ('guest-worker German', hereafter *GAD*), a phenomenon first investigated by Clyne (1968). It was argued that in order to provide adult immigrants with an adequate knowledge of German to participate in the normal social processes, more needed to be known about both their actual communicative needs and the process by which they acquired their 'untutored' knowledge of the language. However, although some studies maintained this objective and led to practical attempts to improve the provision of appropriate language teaching programmes for adults (see e.g. Barkowski *et al.* 1979), attention has tended to focus more strongly on *GAD* itself and the light it may throw on the acquisition of any second language than on the social consequences for the speakers of *GAD*.

One of the things that makes *GAD* so interesting from the (socio)linguistic point of view is the fact that there appears to be a remarkable similarity in the way speakers of different first languages speak German. Anyone who has learned German at school or college might anticipate that someone trying to acquire the language without tuition would have considerable difficulty with certain grammatical features in particular. On the other hand, it might also be thought that, for example, speakers of another inflecting language would find it easier than speakers of an isolating or an **agglutinative language** to deal with those aspects and therefore be more successful in reproducing them. However, although there is undoubtedly considerable variation between individual speakers of *GAD*, these differences are less remarkable than the large number of features that seem to be common to most *GAD*-speakers, regardless of their first language.

The fact that speakers of Romance languages (Castilian Spanish, Portuguese, Italian), Slavonic languages (Serbo-Croatian, Slovene, Macedonian) and Turkish independently develop forms of German that have enough in common to justify their inclusion under the single label of *GAD* demands an explanation, and we shall consider this problem in the next section. Firstly, it would be useful to look at some of the features that characterize *GAD*. Consider the following examples:

(1)  *der arbeitet mehr mit Kopf*
     he works more with Ø head

(2)  *ich fahre Espania zwei Wochen*
     I'm going Ø Spain Ø two weeks

(3)  *deine Sohn viel dumm*
     your son Ø much stupid

(4)  *Kind alles in der Türkei geboren*
     child Ø all born in Turkey

Although some of these utterances are deviant in several respects, the Ø symbol in the English glosses indicates that in each case an element that would be obligatory in any other variety of German (whether standard or non-standard) has been omitted: in (1) an article, in (2) two prepositions, in (3) the **copula** (in this case the verb 'be'), and in (4) an auxiliary verb.

Other deviant syntactic patterns include the regular placing of the negator *nicht* (often altered to *nix*) before rather than after the finite verb in a main clause, as in (5); placing the verb at the end of a main clause, as in (6), or failing to do so after a modal verb, as in (7); retaining subject–verb word order instead of inverting in a direct question, as in (8), or when an adverbial occupies initial position, as in (7):

(5)  *aber ich nix verstehe*
     but I not understand

(6)  *ich auch bißchen mehr trinken*
     I also little bit more drink

(7)  *im Momento ich möchte bleiben hier*
     for the moment I'd like to stay here

(8)  *du das verkaufen?*
     you that sell?

As some of these examples show, the complex morphology of German is often simplified too. This may be achieved, for example, by omitting elements (such as articles, as in (1) that would normally be inflected; by reducing the normal three genders to one (typically the feminine) as in (3); by using a single form of a noun regardless of case or whether it is singular or plural, as in (4); or by using a single form of a verb (often the infinitive) regardless of subject or tense, as in (6) and (8). Finally, as many speakers have a limited vocabulary, they often have to extend it by, for example, paraphrasing: *nicht schön* (not beautiful) for *häßlich* (ugly); *tot machen* (make dead) for *töten* (kill).

All of these devices (omission, reduction, paraphrasing, etc.) are aspects of an overall strategy of simplification. The intention is to reduce the complexities of the language to more manageable proportions, although it is worth pointing out that what is simpler for the speaker may be more complex for the hearer. For instance, (6) could be interpreted in a variety of ways, depending on whether you assume a modal or auxiliary verb has been omitted or the infinitive is being used in place of a finite verb form:

(6a)   I must/want(ed) to/would like to drink . . .
(6b)   I drank/am drinking/am going to drink . . .

However, establishing a common purpose does not in itself explain the relatively uniform outcome nor the fact that the *GAD* of some speakers is considerably more simplified than that of others.

### 7.4 Accounting for uniformity and variation in *Gastarbeiterdeutsch*

### 7.4.1 The process of acquisition

One of the most detailed studies of *GAD* (see Clahsen *et al.* 1983) suggests that certain syntactic structures tend to be acquired in a given sequence rather than in an arbitrary manner. Take, for example, the following word order patterns, which, with the exception of (1), are normal in most varieties of German:

(1)   ADV-FRONTING (adverb in initial position but no subject–verb inversion)

   *morgen ich fahre nach Spanien*
   tomorrow I'm going to Spain

(2)   PARTICLE (prefix, participle or infinitive in final position in main clause)

   sie hat mich *eingeladen*
   she has invited me

(3)  INVERSION (subject–verb inversion after adverb in initial position)

gestern *habe ich* nicht gegessen
yesterday I didn't eat

(4)  ADV-VP (adverb placed within verb phrase, between verb and object)

ich kriege *auch jetzt noch* ein Kind
now on top of that I'm going to have a child

(5)  V→END (verb in final position in subordinate clause)

wenn er nach Hause *kommt*
when he comes home

It appears that pattern (1) is typically acquired before pattern (2), (2) before (3) and so on. Therefore if a speaker consistently uses, say, pattern (3) precludes the use of (1)). However, this development is a gradual almost certainly know (1) and (2) (in fact, of course, the consistent use of (3) precludes the use of (1). However, this development is a gradual process and even if all speakers follow this sequence there is still scope for variation along the way. For example, speakers who have not yet acquired pattern (3) may adopt various strategies: they could simply persist with (1); they could omit either the subject or the verb; or they could avoid such contexts altogether.

Furthermore, some speakers may never acquire all five patterns. The extent to which speakers progress through this sequence will depend on many factors, both objective facts such as length of stay in the Federal Republic and degree of contact with native-speakers, and subjective factors like the amount of social or psychological 'distance' speakers perceive between themselves and native-speakers (see Klein and Dittmar 1979; also Schumann 1978). If this applies to all aspects of the language (other syntactic patterns as well as morphology and vocabulary), then we can see that the notion of a continuum, introduced earlier to account for variation in the German of native-speakers, could be appropriate here too. It is possible to identify 'learner-types' according to their relative proximity to native-speaker competence (see e.g. Heidelberger Forschungsprojekt 1975: 76–9), but in principle each individual could occupy a unique position on the continuum.[1]

The kind of evidence we have been discussing here suggests there is some plausibility in the notion of such an entity as *GAD*. However, what it

---

[1] The Heidelberg project in fact attempted to establish a 'syntactic profile' of individual informants by means of a 'syntactic index', which incorporated information about the speakers' knowledge of a set of rules and allowed them to be classified in terms of levels of competence (see Klein and Dittmar 1979).

tells us is how untutored speakers typically develop their knowledge of German; it does not tell us why the forms of *GAD* deviate from other varieties of German in the way they do. Are these deviations to be explained in terms of transfer or interference from the speakers' first language? Is GAD a **'pidgin'**? Is it the result of imitating **'Foreigner Talk'**, the simplified manner of speaking native-speakers sometimes use to foreigners?

### 7.4.2 The transfer hypothesis

At first sight, the transfer hypothesis seems most promising as it is a common strategy adopted at some stage by most language learners. For instance, the grammatical deviance of the following examples is clearly attributable to the fact that the speaker's first language is English:

(1)    *\*Was ist die Zeit?*
      What is the time?

(2)    *\*Diese Entwicklung wird nicht erwartet anzudauern.*
      This development is not expected to continue.

(3)    *\*Die Tür öffnete.*
      The door opened.

This explanation could well apply to some of the deviant features of *GAD* too. However some of these features are open to alternative explanations and even if transfer does account for many aspects of *GAD* it is not clear why some features should be transferred and not others. Some comparative examples given in Keim (1984) may serve to show the limitations of this hypothesis. On the one hand, the subject pronoun was omitted in *GAD* utterances made by speakers of Serbo-Croatian, Italian, Castilian Spanish, Greek and Turkish, as would have been the case in the equivalent utterances in these other languages. It seems plausible therefore that these speakers may have adopted this particular syntactic pattern in their use of German. However, such a degree of correspondence is rare. Consider the following examples, in which the verb in each *GAD* utterance is in final position:

(4)    *GAD*           ich auch bißchen mehr *trinken*
      Serbo-Croatian   (ja) isto malo više pijem
      literally          (I) also little bit more *drink*

(5)    *GAD*           ich nur in Deutschland *gehe*
      Italian           sono andato soltanto in Germania
      literally          *have gone* only to Germany

(6)    *GAD*           deine Sohn Espania wieder *bleibe*
      Castilian Spanish   tu hijo se ha quedado nuevamente en España
      literally          your son *has stayed* again in Spain

(7)     *GAD*          (er) jetzt Wohnung *schaffe*
        Greek       τώρα δουλεύει στό σπίτι
        literally     now *is working* he at home

(8)     *GAD*          ich drei Jahre hier *arbeite*
        Turkish      (ben) üç senedir burada çalışıyorum
        literally     (I) three years here *work*

Under each of the original utterances an equivalent sentence is given in the speaker's first language; this is then translated literally into English. While the Serbo-Croatian and Turkish versions would have the verb in the final position, this is not the case for the other three languages. So even if transfer is an appropriate explanation for two of the utterances, we would have to find an alternative explanation for the others.

### 7.4.3 The pidgin hypothesis

Now, lexical transfer is one of the characteristics of pidgins and indeed *GAD* does have many other features found in most pidgins. However, the circumstances in which it developed are very different from those which gave rise to the 'classic' pidgins in Africa, the Caribbean and elsewhere (see Mühlhäusler 1986; Holm 1988–9). Most obviously, the superstrate language, German, was not exported to other countries but rather, the substrate languages came to the Federal Republic. Perhaps the most important difference then is that, especially for those who intend to stay in the Federal Republic, there is a far greater incentive to learn German than there was for the inhabitants of places visited briefly by European traders to learn, say, English or Portuguese.

Pidgin English varieties typically arose as a form of communication between members of two communities who did not speak the same language but had both developed a rudimentary means of communicating with English traders. This is what Whinnom (1971) refers to as a 'pidgin in the narrow sense'. If *GAD* is a pidgin then it can be so only 'in the broad sense', as it has not developed as a result of communication between, say, Turks and Italians: the various non-indigenous ethnic groups in the Federal Republic tend to have relatively little contact with each other, mixing more with other members of the same group or with Germans. Whether or not we choose to call *GAD* a pidgin, however, it is clear that many of the linguistic processes involved in its development have much in common with pidginization and it is therefore of great interest to students of pidgins and creoles, as it offers a rare opportunity to observe these processes in their early stages.

**7.4.4** Foreigner Talk and the universal simplification hypothesis

Although the analogy with pidgins may not be entirely appropriate, linguistic interaction between Germans and non-Germans is clearly an important factor in the development of *GAD* as untutored learners must have some input on which to base their variety of German. This is directly observable in the fact that *GAD*-speakers typically adopt phonetic and phonological features of the local or regional colloquial speech varieties with which they come into regular contact. It has also been observed that forms of speech have developed amongst Turkish immigrants which are basically Turkish in their syntactic patterns and most of their vocabulary but which incorporate a large number of German words, which are then often adapted to fit the phonological and morphological patterns of Turkish (see Tekinay 1984). This can be illustrated by the following examples:

(1)    Yedinci ayda *urlauba* gittik. Antalya' da *urlaup* yaptık. Benim *famılı* orda, *versteyn*? *Kinderler* gelmedi.
       We went *on holiday* in July. We spent *the holiday* in Antalya. My *family* is there, *you see. The children* didn't come.

(2)    *Avuslantsamt*'a gittim, *anmelduk* yaptırdım. *Arbayserlaupnisim* var, *Gott zay dank.*
       I went *to the foreigners' registration office*, and *registered*. I have *a work permit, thank God.*

In the first example, the German *Familie* has been modified phonetically, and *Urlaub* and *Kinder* have Turkish case and plural suffixes respectively; curiously, *Kinder* is the plural form in German (singular: *Kind*) and so the 'adapted' form is doubly marked for number. In the second example, German *Auslandsamt, Anmeldung* and *Arbeitserlaubnis* have undergone slight phonetic modifications, and the first and last of these words have Turkish case suffixes; in addition, we might note that the fixed expression *Gott sei Dank* is used a great deal by Turks as it is the literal translation of the extremely common Turkish phrase *Allaha şükür*.

**Code-mixing** of this sort is a common phenomenon in language contact situations (see e.g. Wardhaugh 1986: 99–111; also, 8.4.2 and 8.5.2 below). It is essentially a kind of 'reverse transfer'. What it demonstrates is the speaker's ability to adopt and adapt material from another language to produce a kind of mixed or 'compromise' variety. Clearly, the examples above are still predominantly Turkish with a small amount of German lexicon. However, there is no reason in principle why this compromise variety should not develop into one with equal proportions of both languages or even with more German than Turkish.

A further possible explanation for the form of *GAD* is that it is a mixed variety whose particular form is derived partly by transfer from the speakers' first languages but mainly by imitation or attempted reproduction of German Foreigner Talk (FT). According to this argument, the remarkable uniformity of many deviant features in *GAD* is the result not of 'defective' processing of 'normal' input but rather of a fairly close reproduction of defective input. So if we could show that German FT is a fairly uniform and stable variety with features similar to those considered typical of *GAD*, this might provide us with a plausible explanation for the form of *GAD*.

In fact, as Hinnenkamp (1982) has shown, German FT and *GAD* do have many features in common, on all levels. Consider these examples:

(1)  *Komm, Foto machen* (= röntgen).
     Come on, make photo (= x-ray).

(2)  *ich heute viel kaputt.*
     I today much worn out.

(3)  *gestern du immer schnaps trinken, ja?*
     yesterday you always drink schnaps, yes?

(4)  *aber in Deutschland nix Kinder.*
     but in Germany no/not children.

(5)  *vater Kapitalist?*
     father capitalist?

(6)  *naja, Bibel sagt auch: eine Frau genug.*
     yeah, but Bible also says: one wife/woman enough.

The speaker in each case was a German but the structural patterns make the utterances indistinguishable from *GAD*. However, assuming for the moment that there was sufficient evidence of this sort to support the FT hypothesis on linguistic grounds, we would still have to be convinced that FT was the variety of German that foreigners encountered most and that they perceived it as a desirable model. Although there is no conclusive proof either way, it does seem unlikely that FT is the main model, as even relatively non-integrated foreigners come into constant contact with both standard and non-standard varieties of German at the work-place, in pubs, shops and offices, and in the media; and it is at best debatable whether FT is perceived as a well intentioned aid to communication or an expression of contempt (contrast, for example, Heidelberger Forschungsprojekt 1975: 93–8 with Bodemann and Ostow 1975: 145).

Even if we ignore these problems, though, there are linguistic reasons to doubt the validity of the hypothesis. Firstly, to the examples given above could be added many others which reveal important differences between FT and *GAD*. One common example is verb inflection: while *GAD-*

speakers may over-generalize various forms (e.g. infinitive, past participle, third person singular present tense), the infinitive is virtually the only form used in FT. Secondly, and more importantly, a direct causal relationship between these two speech forms would at least be supported if German FT were quite different from any other variety except *GAD*. In fact, it has striking similarities with the FT varieties of other languages such as French, Finnish or Turkish (see Meisel 1980; Hinnenkamp 1982). In other words, speakers of various languages seem to modify their language in much the same way when talking to foreigners.

So if native-speakers of different languages intuitively agree on what constitutes 'simplification', it could be that this is an almost universal aspect of native-speaker competence. Although this is only speculation, it is an interesting possibility as it could provide an alternative explanation for the phenomenon of *GAD*, that would have the added advantage of bypassing questions like the degree of exposure to FT and its desirability as a model. If we all have a built-in device that enables us to simplify our first language in a given way, it might be that we exploit precisely the same strategies in the process of acquiring a second language. That is to say, *GAD* is not the result of imitating German FT but of implementing quasi-universal strategies of linguistic simplification.

Meisel (1980) provides some further support for this hypothesis by distinguishing between restrictive and elaborative simplification. Restrictive simplification means the radical reduction of all linguistic categories (e.g. tense, person and number for verbs; case, gender and number for nouns) and is the basic strategy used in both FT and the most rudimentary forms of *GAD*. Elaborative simplification refers to the expansion or extension of these reduced categories without necessarily introducing greater complexity (e.g. by adding more verbs to your repertoire but still treating them all as weak verbs). This kind of simplification is to be found only in *GAD*, not in FT, and helps to explain the differences between the two speech forms as well as the variation within *GAD* itself.

### 7.4.5 Conclusions

In conclusion, we can say that the various explanations that have been proposed for the form of *GAD* all have something to offer and as none of them appears to be able to account for all aspects of the phenomenon it is probably best to see them as complementary, rather than competing, theories. Although the notion of transfer is clearly inadequate as an explanation in itself, it seems highly likely that it is a strategy used to some extent by all *GAD* speakers, at least in the early stages of acquisition. Foreigner Talk also appears to be an important concept, if not in the way that was first thought. And whether or not we choose to call *GAD* a pidgin may be a trivial terminological issue, but the arguments in favour of universal strategies of second-language acquisition have much in common with some views of pidginization (for example, Bickerton (1977) refers to pidginization as 'second-language learning with restricted input') and in the end it is the processes rather than the labels we attach to them that are of interest to us.

## 7.5 Linguistic pluralism in Switzerland

### 7.5.1 Maintaining social and linguistic stability

Despite its relatively small population (the 1980 census recorded 6.36 million inhabitants), Switzerland is one of the most linguistically diverse countries in Western Europe, more so even than its much larger neighbour to the north, the Federal Republic. In addition to the four indigenous languages, many others are spoken by more or less permanent sub-populations, ranging from English to Scandinavian and Slavonic languages. However, even if we limit our attention to Swiss citizens, the linguistic situation is more complex than is often supposed, as there is considerable diversity within, as well as between, some of the language groups.

For example, although its speakers number only about 50,000 there are several spoken varieties of Romansh and no less than five different written forms, and recent attempts to introduce a single standardized written variety, *Rumantsch Grischun*, have met with only partial success. At the other extreme, the German-speakers, who constitute by far the largest group (73.5 per cent of Swiss citizens: see Map 7.2), do share a common standardized written variety but unlike in the other German-speaking countries there are no native-speakers of formal or colloquial standard German (apart from native Germans or Austrians): the first language of all German-speaking Swiss is one of the many Swiss German dialects, which we refer to here collectively as 'Swiss German'. Furthermore, there are substantial differences between these dialects and, more importantly, between them and Swiss standard German, which is learned only at school (see 7.6). For many German-speaking Swiss, this standard variety is virtually a foreign language and its use is largely confined to written contexts: it is often referred to as *Schriftdeutsch* (written German) and when it is used in speech it tends to sound rather stiff and stilted.

This complex sociolinguistic profile is an essential component of the 'image' of modern Switzerland, and like, for example, Belgium but unlike the Federal Republic or Britain, Switzerland is constitutionally as well as de facto a multilingual state. However, this has not always been so and indeed the much-vaunted linguistic tolerance is very much a feature of the modern federal state (*Bundesstaat*) rather than of the pre-1848 more loosely knit confederation (*Staatenbund*). The 1848 constitution established German, French and Italian as national languages but an important amendment in 1938 acknowledged that the languages of a community have a symbolic function as well as an 'instrumental' one, i.e. they do not only serve the purpose of communication but also bear witness to the identity of their speakers, rather like a flag does to the identity of a nation (McRae 1983: 119–20). This distinction is recognized in the revised Article 116, which now designates French, German and Italian as 'official languages' (*Amtssprachen*), while they and Romansh together constitute the 'national languages' (*Nationalsprachen*) of Switzerland.[2]

The recognition of four national languages reflects the fact that although the principal administrative sub-division of the federal state is the canton, in reality the state is perceived as consisting of four distinct regions. In this respect again, Switzerland resembles Belgium but is in marked contrast with, say, Luxembourg or South Tyrol (see 8.3.1, 8.3.2, 8.3.4). The reason for this lies in the so-called 'territorial principle', according to which each canton has an absolute right to determine which is to be the official language within its boundaries ('une terre, une langue'). Of the twenty-six cantons and half-cantons, twenty-two are officially monolingual and as for historical reasons most speakers of each language are clustered in one area, the German- or French-speaking cantons are not spread discontinuously but form adjacent blocs (see Map 7.1).

One consequence of this language-based division of territory is that speakers of French and German at least, if not of the other two languages, can enjoy considerable mobility within Switzerland without needing to speak a second language. In practice, the speakers of a given language are by no means confined to the cantons in which it is the official language: for example, as Map 7.2 shows, many German-speakers have moved beyond the so-called *Röstigraben* ('*Rösti* trench', *Rösti* being a fried potato dish popular among German-Swiss), which is commonly held to divide the German-speaking area from the rest of the country, especially the French-speaking cantons in the west.[3] Nevertheless, while the state is multilingual, it cannot be assumed that its inhabitants are: a survey carried out in 1973 indeed found that although overall 69 per cent of the population

---

[2] The position of Romansh is complicated by the fact that it does have the status of an official language in one canton (Graubünden/Grisons) but not in the Federation as a whole. However, the language articles of the constitution are currently under review again and it is possible that Romansh will be put on an equal footing with the other three languages, thus eliminating the distinction between official and national languages. A recent step in this direction is that major laws which had previously been published only in the other three languages are now being translated into Romansh.

[3] French terms are *le rideau de rösti* (the *rösti* curtain) or *la barrière de rösti*!

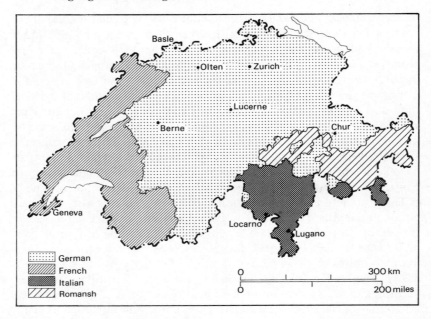

Map 7.1 Switzerland: language areas

had 'some competence' in a second national language, the degree of ability in this other language varied considerably and there was a higher proportion of bilinguals among German- than among French-speakers (Kolde 1981: 61).[4]

Now, while linguistic self-determination as an important democratic principle may be one of the foundation stones of peaceful coexistence in Switzerland, it cannot by itself account for the apparent lack of conflict over the last 140 years, as a glance at Belgium (or even Spain after Franco) would show. Certainly, a strict adherence to the territorial principle reduces the potential for conflict but will not completely eliminate it, for it may guarantee internal control of affairs but it will not prevent a competition of interests between one canton or group of cantons and

---

[4] The limited extent of individual bilingualism is confirmed, as far as French- and German-speakers are concerned at least, by a survey conducted in 1986 by the Institut für Markt- und Meinungsforschung, Zurich. These findings are reinforced by the most detailed analysis undertaken to date, based on the comprehensive survey of twenty-year-olds carried out in 1985 as part of the project *'Sprachen in der Schweiz', Nationales Forschungsprogramm 21: Kulturelle Vielfalt und nationale Identität*, under Prof. Robert Schläpfer (University of Basle).

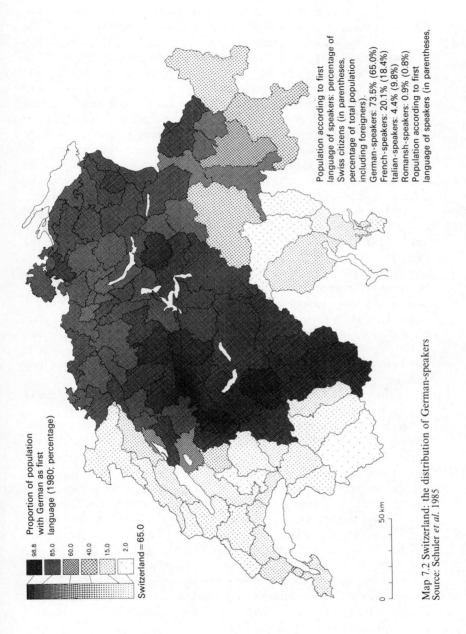

Proportion of population
with German as first
language (1980; percentage)

98.8
85.0
60.0
40.0
15.0
2.0

Switzerland = 65.0

Population according to first
language of speakers: percentage of
Swiss citizens (in parentheses,
percentage of total population
including foreigners).
German-speakers: 73.5% (65.0%)
French-speakers: 20.1% (18.4%)
Italian-speakers: 4.4% (9.8%)
Romansh-speakers: 0.9% (0.8%)
Population according to first
language of speakers (in parentheses,

0      50 km

Map 7.2 Switzerland: the distribution of German-speakers
Source: Schuler *et al.* 1985

another. It is also true that a sense of national cohesion, born out of a long history of defending Swiss identity against external threats, tends in the end to override narrow sectarian interests or parochial attitudes and the importance attached to accepting the principle of consensus and tolerance should not be underestimated. This mutual respect is underpinned at the political level by proportional representation in official federal bodies and by the fact that despite the great differences in the size of the various language groups, there are officially no minority groups (except foreigners, that is!). However, there is some doubt as to whether these laudable principles are effective in practice, and even if they were, the sheer numerical superiority of the German-speakers (see Map 7.2) would impose a considerable burden on them to convince the smaller groups of their good intentions.

In this context, it is interesting to consider the perceptions the different language groups have of each other. Most British people have a mental image of the 'typical' French, German or Spanish person; at the same time, the English, Irish, Welsh and Scots have a good idea of what it means to be English, Irish, Welsh or Scottish. Social psychologists distinguish between these two types of national or ethnic 'identikit' images as 'auto-stereotypes' (how we see ourselves) and 'hetero-stereotypes' (how we see others or how others see us). It is easy to see that a comparison of auto- and hetero-stereotypes for any two or more given groups could be very revealing but the addition of a further factor, 'projective hetero-stereotypes' (or how we think others see us), can help produce a subtle explanation of inter-group relations. In general terms, we might predict that the most harmonious relations would be found where all three stereotypes match.

One specific example in the Swiss context is the finding (in a study by Fischer and Trier (1962) comparing French- and German-Swiss) that the French-Swiss are 'liberal and changeable' according to all three stereo-types, while the German-Swiss are 'conservative and constant' except in the auto-stereotype. In other words, both groups share the same view of the French-speaking population, who are themselves confident of being seen in this way; but the German-speakers rightly suspect that the French-speakers see them in a different light from the way they see themselves. Further findings from this and other studies (see e.g. Kolde 1980: 245 and Ris 1978: 99–102) seem to confirm this impression that French- and German-speakers have different self-images but that both share a favourable stereotype of the French-speaking group. This could help to explain why French rather than German is the most used language of communication between speakers of different languages. For example, according to a survey of army recruits conducted in 1985 (Schläpfer

208

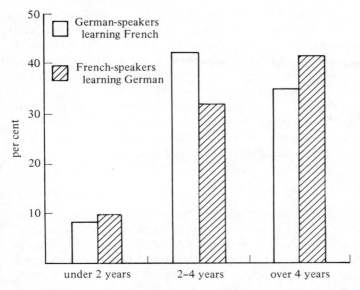

Fig. 7.1 Foreign languages in Swiss schools. Responses to the question: How long did you study French/German at school?
Source: Schläpfer forthcoming

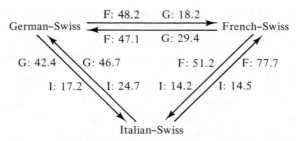

Fig. 7.2 Language use (percentages) between speakers of different languages in Switzerland: G, German (Swiss German and Swiss standard German); F, French; I, Italian
Source: Schläpfer forthcoming

forthcoming) young francophones tended to have studied German longer than their German-speaking counterparts had studied French, but both groups claim to use French much more than German with members of the other group (see Figs. 7.1 and 7.2).

At least as important as the territorial principle, the sense of national identity and the psychology of inter-group relations, however, is the crucial fact that the territorial divisions determined by language do not coincide with any other major division. Maps of Switzerland dividing the country up in terms of religion, demographic structure, geographical terrain, occupations, distribution of income or political affiliation would not look the same as our Map 7.1. In other words, what unites the inhabitants of any one language area is only the language and we can as little predict that, say, a French-speaker will be a Roman Catholic as that a German-speaker will be an urban industrial worker. In this respect, there are in fact much greater differences between cantons than between language areas and this relative overall social balance goes a long way to ensuring the peaceful coexistence of the four language groups.

### 7.5.2 Areas of potential conflict

Nevertheless, it would be misleading to paint too rosy a picture of this *ménage à quatre*. Although the image of harmony is broadly valid in terms of the united front in relation to the outside world in general and to the various cultural relatives across the state borders in particular, it is belied by constant references to internal conflict in the media and put under strain by a growing unrest on a number of counts. It is no coincidence, for example, that we have referred in our discussion so far only to the French- and German-speaking areas, for despite the official policy of equality, it is in these parts of the country that the overwhelming majority of the population lives and where the real economic and political power lies. It is also between these two areas that conflict is most likely to arise, as in the French cantons, relatively recent members of the confederation, there has long been a suspicion that the German-speaking population harbours imperialist intentions.

This potential conflict, starkly reflected in French-Swiss newspaper headlines like 'Le spectre de la germanisation', and book titles such as 'La Romandie dominée' (cited by Kolde 1986: 63), came to a head most explosively in the debate over the so-called Jura Question. The Jura region straddles the division between French- and German-speaking Switzerland and the officially bilingual canton of Berne incorporated two distinct and uneasily coexisting Jura districts, the francophone north and German-speaking south. Years of complex political disputes finally resulted in the establishment in 1979 of a new French-speaking canton of Jura but this did not put an end to the conflict as efforts at reunification have not been abandoned (McRae 1983: 185–212; see also Wardhaugh 1987: 214–16). However, the significance of this affair probably lies less in the importance of the relatively underdeveloped Jura itself than in the fact that it is symptomatic of a more widespread (if not widely supported) separatist tendency in the west of the country.

Although it is still true that economic resources are distributed across both French- and German-speaking areas, there is no doubt that economic power is increasingly concentrated in the latter: it is more highly industrialized, while there is a greater concentration on the service sector in the west, and virtually all important businesses, banks and insurance companies are based in the so-called Golden Triangle formed by Zurich, Basle and Olten (Map 7.1). In addition to this, the Federal Republic is a much more important trading partner for Switzerland than is France (Camartin 1982: 328–9). This economic imbalance is exacerbated by the dominant rôle of German-speakers in the federal administration. In overall numbers of posts each language group may be represented proportionally but it is not clear that this balance is maintained in terms of senior posts (McRae 1983: 133; Kolde 1981: 54–6) and concern at the difficulty in recruiting to the central administration departments from the non-German language groups prompted the *Bundesrat* (Federal Council: the government or administration) to commission an investigation into problems and obstacles faced by these groups. It is perhaps significant that only a fifth of the German-speaking civil servants interviewed acknowledged that there might be problems between them and the other language groups, as opposed to half of the Romansh-speakers and almost three-quarters of the French- and Italian-speakers (Arbeitsgruppe 'Sprachgemeinschaften in der Bundesverwaltung' 1986:4). Furthermore, only the German-speakers considered it to be irrelevant for career purposes to have German as their mother tongue: the other groups not surprisingly saw it as a major advantage.

One of the major potential problems identified by the study was the remarkably high proportion (up to a third) of civil servants other than Italian-speakers who claimed to be monolingual; of those who had learned one or more other languages very few learned either Italian or Romansh. In terms of language use amongst colleagues a rather different picture emerged from that shown in Fig. 7.2: almost all German-speakers use their own language, while this is the case for only 60 per cent of French-speakers and 14 per cent of Italian-speakers (no figure is given for Romansh-speakers, but it is implied that hardly any of them use Romansh in such situations). This and other evidence presented in the report suggests that German-speakers have a distinct advantage over French-speakers and that the Italian and Romansh groups are marginalized. The report therefore made a series of recommendations designed to improve the working conditions of the non-German-speaking groups, including the proposal that German-speakers should in future use standard German rather than dialect in the presence of members of other groups.

Some attempts have been made in recent years to help other Swiss gain at least a passive knowledge of Swiss German (see, for example, the language course *Los emol*: Müller and Wertenschlag 1985) but the widespread antipathy towards dialect (including Swiss French patois) in the francophone area has meant that Swiss standard German continues to be the only variety that francophones are familiar with. Here again the situation is relieved to some extent by the willingness of most German-speakers to use French and by an awareness that French enjoys greater external prestige than Swiss German. But there seems to be no denying a growing cultural divide, with the development amongst francophones of an intermediate level of identification between canton and nation, associated with the name 'Romandie' for 'western Switzerland' (Kolde 1986: 65).

## 7.6 Diglossia and the status of Swiss German

### 7.6.1 The 'classic example' of German-speaking Switzerland

In his original article on diglossia (see 1.2.2), Ferguson chose the relationship between Swiss German and Swiss standard German as one of his four defining examples. As far as some of his criteria are concerned, this seems unproblematic: if, for the moment, we accept Swiss German as the low (L) variety and Swiss standard German as the high (H), then it is true that all children acquire the L as their first language and learn the H through formal education; the H is standardized whereas the L is not; there are extensive grammatical differences between the two varieties, and so on. However, one major problem lies precisely in the designation of these varieties as L and H. According to Ferguson (1972: 237), this distinction is determined by differential prestige: 'In all the defining languages the speakers regard H as superior to L in a number of respects.' Although he goes on to qualify this assertion, the essential notion that the H is felt to be superior remains and it is this that few German-Swiss today would accept.

Standard German enjoyed its heyday in Switzerland around the turn of the century, partly owing to an influx of Germans who occupied influential positions, and this coincided with a decline in the prestige of dialect (Lötscher 1983: 67; Ris 1979: 43; Schwarzenbach 1969: 128). However, since then Swiss German has undergone a resurgence, firstly as a means of 'linguistic patriotism' to protect Swiss integrity in the face of the Nazi threat in the 1920s and 1930s (under the slogans '*sprachlicher Heimatschutz*', '*geistige Landesverteidigung*'),[5] and more recently, since the 1960s, as an expression of democratic and anti-authoritarian values.

---

[5] These terms are difficult to translate but can be glossed as 'linguistic patriotism'.

A further reason is the general increase in the use of spoken as opposed to written forms of communication, telephone and television replacing letters and newspapers (Kolde 1986: 62). Today, it is probably true to say that both varieties have positive prestige but for different reasons and to differing extents: attitudes to Swiss German, as the unifying vernacular that gives the German-Swiss their identity, are positive in every respect, while Swiss standard German enjoys widespread prestige only as a written form that enables them to be part of the international German-speaking community (although even this is considered unimportant by many younger people in particular: see Vogt 1986: 125). It is also probably for this reason that lexical borrowing here is not a one-way street (normally in diglossic situations from H to L) but rather a pattern of mutual exchange. For instance, while the Swiss German word *Färnseer* (television set) derives from *Fernseher*,[6] *Hutte* (tub) and *Beige* (pile) are Swiss German words that are now used also in Swiss standard German (see Haas 1982: 99, 114).

The key feature of Ferguson's definition (as of most others) is 'specialization of function', according to which only H is appropriate in one set of domains and only L in another. In practice, such a strict division is relatively unusual and in many situations that we might still wish to call diglossic there is a certain amount of 'leaking' (Fasold 1984: 54–6), where one of the two varieties begins to encroach on domains previously reserved exclusively for the other. In the case of Switzerland, it has generally been argued that Swiss German as the L variety is the speech-form appropriate for all informal spoken discourse while Swiss standard German as the H variety is the language of writing and formal speech. For the vast majority of German-Swiss, however, Swiss standard German is a variety confined exclusively to writing and indeed it is generally referred to as *Schriftdeutsch* (written German). Many Swiss linguists thus refer now to the relationship between the two varieties as *mediale Diglossie* (diglossia based on medium: see, for example, Vogt 1986: 31; Sieber and Sitta 1986: 20), although even this suggests a more clear-cut distinction than can be observed in reality. What does seem clear is that, uniquely in the German-speaking countries, the importance of the standard variety in relation to dialect has declined in the course of this century as dialect has encroached on more and more domains.

One of the most striking developments of recent years has been the growing perception of Swiss standard German as a foreign language. The German-Swiss have never shown a great warmth for it but the view of the

---

[6] The borrowing of *Fernseher* is an interesting case for another reason too. To a German or Austrian the derivation of the word is relatively transparent (*fern* = far away, *sehen* = see), but it is much less so for a German-speaking Swiss: *fèrn* exists in Swiss German but it means 'last year' and *sehen* does not exist at all (see = *luege*).

standard variety as an alien form has increased, even to the extent that some linguists now feel the pendulum has swung too far in favour of Swiss German and as recently as 1982 a *Verein für die Pflege der deutschen Hochsprache* (Association for the Cultivation of the German Standard Language) was set up in Basle (Sieber and Sitta 1986: 20; and see also the plea on behalf of standard German in Schwarzenbach 1983). Standard is still spoken in certain situations but there are now very few in which it is considered essential or even normal. For example, Schläpfer (1987: 168–9) notes that while Swiss standard German was still used in the 1960s for many of the formal speeches made on the Swiss National Day (1 August), Swiss German is now almost always used. There are other indications too that the formality of the situation is no longer necessarily the factor that determines which variety is used: it is not surprising that Swiss German is the norm in many forms of popular culture and in the recently established local radio network, but it is significant that standard German is now coming under increasing pressure throughout the educational system (Ris 1979: 45; Haas 1982: 106; Schläpfer 1987: 170).

To some extent these developments are political in the narrow, party sense (such as the use of Swiss German by left-wing politicians in those canton parliaments where standard was conventionally used by members of all parties) but this cannot account for the broad general advance of dialect in virtually every sphere of public discourse. Perhaps the most significant indicator for the future is the attitudes expressed by today's younger generation: according to the survey of army recruits referred to in the previous section and a comparable survey of women in the same age-group, the majority favours the use of both dialect and standard in school, but on the levels of popularity and necessity for international communication standard German comes a poor second behind English, or even third behind French (see Bickel 1988; Vogt 1986: 60–4, 95–6).

### 7.6.2 Diglossia reconsidered

So if there was ever a 'classic' diglossic situation in German-speaking Switzerland, in the sense of clear functional distribution of the two varieties used, there no longer is today. As is so often the case, the reality is less neat than many observers would like it to be. It is probably more appropriate to talk of tendencies rather than absolute rules, with one variety more likely to be used than the other in given circumstances (see Fig. 7.3). This implies that there may often be considerable uncertainty as to how to interpret a situation and this in turn may lead to a greater degree of **code-switching**. Indeed, the switch from one variety to the other may define the situation, as in an oral examination when the examiner chats to

SPOKEN

| Context | Speech event | Speaker | Dialect | Standard |
|---|---|---|---|---|
| Casual | Open conversation | all | ///// | |
| Formal meeting | Structured discussion | all | ///// | |
| Public gathering | Plenary discussion | all | ///// | |
| | Paper | expert | ///// | |
| | Speech | public figure | ///// | |
| Parliament | Debate | politicians | ////////// | |
| Court | Questioning | witnesses | ///// | |
| | Summing up | lawyers | ///// | |
| Radio/TV | News | newsreaders | ///// | |
| | Commentary | journalists | ///// | |
| | Interviews | guests | ///// | |
| | Documentary/ discussion | presenters | ///// | |
| School | Classes: | | | |
| | Music, Art, Sport | all | ///// | |
| | German | all | | ///// |
| | Other | all | ///// | |
| | Outside classroom | all | ///// | |
| University | Lecture | lecturer | | ///// |
| | Seminar | all | ///// | |
| | Conversation after seminar etc. | all | ///// | |

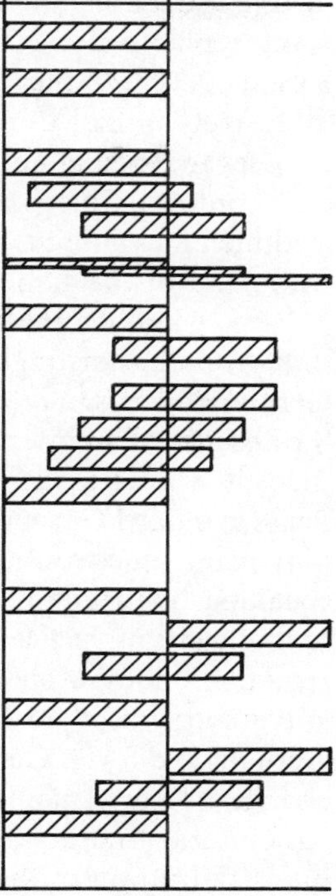

WRITTEN

| Context | Text-type | Writer | Dialect | Standard |
|---|---|---|---|---|
| Private | Letter, note | all | ///// | |
| Business, official | Letter, report etc. | all | | ///// |
| Press | News, sport report | journalists | | ///// |
| | Feature | journalists | ///// | |
| | Advertisement | copy writers | ///// | |
| Academic | Article, book | all | | ///// |
| Fiction | Poem, novel, drama | writers | ///// | |

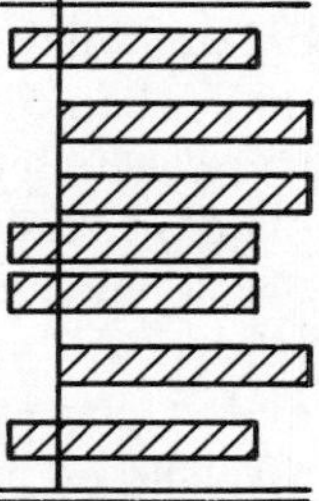

Fig. 7.3 Switzerland: use of Swiss German dialect and Swiss standard German by German-speakers
Source: Based on Schwarzenbach and Sitta 1983

215

students in dialect to put them at their ease and then switches to standard to mark the beginning of the examination proper (Sieber and Sitta 1986: 21). In general terms, what seems to be happening is that the distinction based on medium (speech = dialect, writing = standard) is being replaced by a trend towards 'productive/receptive diglossia' (see Kolde 1986: 63): the 'average German-Swiss' speaks and writes almost exclusively in dialect and reads almost exclusively standard; what (s)he chooses to listen to still depends on medium (television, radio, film, etc.) and content. This in effect means that diglossia is giving way to a 'rudimentary bilingualism', with most speakers having only a receptive command of the standard variety.

Now, whatever the relationship between the two varieties, one of the things that has distinguished it from that between standard German and German dialects in most other parts of the German-speaking countries is the absence of an intermediate form of 'colloquial speech'. That is to say, there is what Ris (1979: 49) calls a 'pragmatic discontinuum' between Swiss standard German and the various dialects. However, this raises an important question about sociolinguistic development in German-speaking Switzerland, for as we have seen (Chapter 4) the process of modernization has led to a growth in the range and importance of regional colloquial speech in the Federal Republic and we might therefore anticipate a need to fill the gap between the poles of Swiss standard German and Swiss German. There has after all been an equally dramatic change in the structure of the Swiss economy from a predominantly agricultural one in the early nineteenth-century via a period of rapid industrialization to the modern nation based increasingly on the service sector.

Is there then a trend towards some kind of 'national dialect' or koine to cover the ground of informal communication between speakers of different dialects? It has certainly been suggested (see e.g. Zimmer 1977) that urban influence has led to a sociolinguistic levelling (*Nivellierung*, *Ausgleich*), but the tension between this tendency and the importance of dialect diversity as a symbol of local identity appears to have arrested the development of a more or less unified form of Swiss German. The present tendency seems to be that many distinctions between individual local dialects have disappeared (except perhaps in the more remote areas) but diversity is maintained at the regional level, so that today it is still generally possible to say whether someone comes from, for instance, the Basle area or the Zurich area, but (s)he can no longer be so readily identified with a particular place. This is complicated by the fact that more mobile members of the population will tend to assimilate features of other dialects into their speech. Nevertheless, it seems unlikely that this levelling process will progress much further, as most speakers still appear to want to maintain an identity with a region rather than with the German-speaking area as a whole. Where the perceived linguistic 'distance' between two dialects does make communication difficult, speakers make *ad hoc* adjustments to their speech by avoiding as far as possible purely local features, but in general the development of larger regional varieties has achieved sufficient mutual comprehensibility for most purposes.

Indeed, the increased use of these modified forms of dialect in German-speaking Switzerland could be considered as functionally equivalent to the growth of colloquial speech in the Federal Republic (see Haas 1982: 108) and as long as we understand 'Swiss German' as an umbrella term covering all Swiss German dialects, it is probably most reasonable to conclude that it is an '*Ausbaudialekt*': collectively, the dialects have developed linguistically and functionally to the point where they are used in domains normally associated with standard varieties, although they may not constitute an '*Ausbausprache*', as they are still scarcely used in, for example, formal prose texts and have no single standardized orthography. In the end, though, the status of Swiss German and its relationship to Swiss standard German is less a linguistic question than a social-psychological or political one and current developments in German-speaking Switzerland suggest that, if anything, the functional range of Swiss German will continue to grow even if there is no corresponding move towards a more standardized form.

**Further reading**

There have been many projects on *Gastarbeiterdeutsch*: apart from the large-scale projects such as those in Heidelberg (see Heidelberger Forschungsprojekt 1975; Klein and Dittmar 1979), Essen (see Stölting *et al.* 1980), Wuppertal (see Clahsen *et al.* 1983) and Saarbrücken (see Antos 1988), other investigations are reported by, for example, Keim (1984), Kutsch and Desgranges (1985), Orlović-Schwarzwald (1978), Sivrikoz-oğlu (1985) and Yakut (1981). Hinnenkamp (1982) is a good study of Foreigner Talk.

The best accounts to date of plurilingualism in Switzerland are McRae (1983), Kolde (1981) and Camartin (1982). Various views worth considering on the situation in German-speaking Switzerland are expressed in Sieber and Sitta (1986), Ris (1979), Haas (1982) and Lötscher (1983). However, the most comprehensive analysis of all major aspects of the sociolinguistic situation in contemporary Switzerland is provided by Schläpfer (forthcoming).

# 8 Contact and conflict

## 8.1 Approaches to the study of language contact

The social and linguistic consequences of contact between languages (i.e. linguistic communities) have been the subject of a vast amount of research, especially since the publication of Uriel Weinreich's *Languages in Contact* in 1953, and the margins of the German-speaking countries have become a kind of laboratory for research in contact linguistics. This development has been fostered both by the dramatic explosion of empirically based sociolinguistic research since the mid-1960s and by the more recent growth of popular and academic interest in ethnic and linguistic minorities. The result has been an increasing awareness that contact situations are highly complex and that while on the surface the linguistic permutations are strictly limited (more or less stable bilingualism or shift to monolingualism) the actual sociolinguistic configurations may vary enormously and can be captured only by means of a holistic approach that takes many different factors into account and employs techniques from several academic disciplines.

Einar Haugen pointed the way in *The Ecology of Language* (1972), concluding with a checklist of 'ecological questions' that we should want to answer for any given language:

(1) What is its classification in relation to other languages?
(2) Who are its users?
(3) What are its domains of use?
(4) What concurrent languages are employed by its users?
(5) What internal varieties does the language show?
(6) What is the nature of its written tradition?
(7) To what degree has its written form been standardized?
(8) What kind of institutional support has it won, either in government, education or private organizations, either to regulate its form or to propagate it?
(9) What are the attitudes of its users towards the language?
(10) What is its status (in terms of a typology of ecological classification) in relation to the other languages of the world?

(adapted from Haugen 1972: 336–7)

218

By tackling questions such as these it may be possible to account for the reciprocal relationship between individual languages (or language communities) and the sociopolitical profile of multilingual countries. At the same time, we may be able to gain a more detailed understanding of how languages in contact interrelate, avoiding the temptation to attribute a given phenomenon (e.g. language shift) to the same cause(s) in each instance.

Not all of Haugen's questions will be of equal importance in each contact area (and note also the limitations of the ecological approach discussed in Nelde 1984, 1986). Nevertheless, any study of languages in contact will have to consider a wide range of factors in order to determine which ones are decisive in the given case, and to enable comparisons between contact areas to be made an analytical apparatus must be devised. Before looking at some concrete examples therefore it will be useful to outline a framework within which language contact may be studied.

## 8.2 Analytical apparatus

Most of the concepts commonly used to analyse varieties of language and language behaviour have already been discussed in earlier chapters. The important distinctions here will be between the use of one language and another (e.g. French and German) and, within any one language, between standard and traditional dialect (which specific dialect is used in any one area is generally less important).

The linguistic configurations in each area may crudely be designated in terms of bilingualism and diglossia although, as will become clear, these terms as traditionally defined are often too discrete to match the rather fuzzy reality. In order to arrive at a characterization of a contact area in these terms without giving a falsely static impression, it will be necessary to see what evidence there is of the extent of individual and group linguistic repertoires, asking such questions as: what is the distribution of the languages concerned in terms of domains and speakers (is there variation according to age, sex, ethnicity etc.)? Which linguistic and extralinguistic factors influence code-switching?

### 8.2.1 Sociological and psychological factors

Status versus solidarity

Social relations between speakers are often reflected in their speech (see, for example, Brown and Gilman 1972, Brown and Levinson 1987, Milroy

1987b and the general discussion in Hudson 1980). In particular, speakers are said to be subject to the competing pressures of status (or power) and solidarity, that is to say, they are confronted with choices between linguistic forms and the choice they make is essentially an expression of their desire to distance themselves from and impose their superiority over others or alternatively to declare their solidarity with the social group to which they feel they belong. The sort of options involved in monolingual situations include the choice of certain speech forms (e.g. forms of address, especially personal pronouns) and in bilingual situations the preference for one language over another in circumstances where either could be used (cf. Ris 1978: 108; 1979: 47).

The principle which is at work here (as far as bilingual societies are concerned) is 'language loyalty', which 'breeds in contact situations just as nationalism breeds on ethnic borders' (Weinreich 1953: 100). If a As we implied above, the 'objective' social status of individual speakers that a linguistic/ethnic minority will adhere to this principle and resist changes in the respective functions of the languages involved that might lead to language shift (the loss of their mother-tongue) and hence loss of identity. As we shall see, this does not always happen, so that the degree of language loyalty shown by a particular social or ethnic group can be taken as one indicator of that group's desire for integration or assimilation into the dominant culture (opting for 'status') or for the retention of a separate identity (opting for 'solidarity').

## Social networks

As we implied above, the 'objective' social status of individual speakers is less significant as an extralinguistic correlate of linguistic behaviour than the speakers' perception of their status. In an attempt to account more precisely for individual variability patterns and the mechanisms of language maintenance and shift, some linguists have adopted the notion of '**social network**', defined by Milroy (1987b: 178) as 'the informal social relationships contracted by an individual'. The usefulness of this construct as an analytic device lies in the fact that, being based on individual patterns of behaviour rather than supposedly objective criteria, it aims to give a more accurate picture of psychological reality. For the study of a bilingual society, the ethnic origins of individuals are less important than the social/ethnic group with which they wish to identify and the personal contacts they maintain. Whenever speakers make conscious choices they make what Le Page and Tabouret-Keller (1985) call an 'act of identity', by locating themselves as individuals in a particular 'social space'. A close-knit network tends to function as a 'norm enforcement mechanism' (Milroy 1987b: 179): the greater the social cohesion, the more likely shared 'communicative preferences' are to persist (with the concomitant resistance to external social pressures to conform to the standard pattern), so that a close-knit network tends to favour language maintenance and conversely the loosening of network ties may encourage language shift.

### 8.2.2 Sociopolitical factors

#### Language planning

Language use is not always simply a matter of personal choice. In many multilingual societies, governments have intervened to determine language use, at least in certain domains, by legislation. Both the reasons for such measures and their consequences vary: for example, one language may be chosen as the sole official language to reinforce the political dominance of one ethnic group or, especially in relatively young states, to forestall or resolve conflict; and the affected populations may accept the loss of status afforded to their language and thus to themselves, or they may launch a rearguard action to preserve their language. Furthermore, the process of shift is not necessarily linear: that is to say, the fate of a language may fluctuate and changes in the sociopolitical climate can arrest or accelerate the process of linguistic decline (cf. Nelde 1984: 221).

The most potent instruments in language planning are standardization, normalization and educational policy. The first of these measures refers to the codification of a language on the basis of one of its varieties and is therefore more applicable to monolingual situations (see 2.3). By normalization we mean the use of legislative processes to establish the status of different languages in a society: for example 'only language X may be used in the courts, in parliament and all public offices'. The most thorough and enduring effects, however, are usually achieved by stipulating which language(s) may be used in which contexts in schools: the status of a language can rapidly be reduced to that of a foreign language by being taught as such, as the pupils are encouraged to see it that way and anyway get insufficient practice in it for it to be anything else.

It may be useful in considering the linguistic and legal/political status of varieties to employ terminology introduced by Auburger and Kloss (see Auburger 1977a, 1977b; Kloss 1976, 1978). They distinguish firstly between official and national languages (*Amtssprachen* and *Nationalsprachen*): an official language is a language of political administration and may be either 'solely dominant' (*alleindominant*), as German is in the Federal Republic, the GDR, Austria and Liechtenstein, or 'co-dominant', as German, French and Italian are in Switzerland; a national language is a language that is 'non-dominant' (*indominant*) but with a legally recognized symbolic function for a specific ethnic group, as German is in Italy or Romansh in Switzerland (see also 7.5.1).

## Centralism and regionalism

The internal political structure of a state may have wide-ranging consequences for social attitudes and organization which in turn influence attitudes to language and hence linguistic behaviour. It could be argued, for example, that the centralism of the French monarchy followed by the centralism of Paris in the Republic led to the evolution of a centralized French culture, and that the consequent decline in importance of the provinces is at least partly responsible for the decline of German dialects in Alsace and Lorraine (cf. Verdoodt 1968: 129). One of the most significant political developments of the last hundred years on the other hand has been the spread throughout Western Europe of a spirit of regionalism in the face of increasingly monolithic and remote centres of power. One manifestation of this trend is the revival of interest in the language and culture of ethnic minorities and, while the effects of this development on the fate of beleaguered linguistic groups should not be over-estimated, there is no doubt that in some cases it has helped to retard the process of decline.

### 8.2.3 Economic and demographic factors

If a stable, close-knit social network favours the maintenance of linguistic behaviour patterns (see 8.2.1), then it follows that we can predict a situation of stable bilingualism in contact areas or communities that are not subject to changes in their economic or demographic structure. This is particularly true of small rural communities such as those discussed in 8.4.2. Not surprisingly, though, industrialization and urbanization on the one hand and migration on the other can have dramatically destabilizing effects on such communities. (Compare also the effects of these processes within a monolingual community as discussed in Chapters 4 and 7.)

The effect on a linguistic community of a change in its ethnic/linguistic composition, whether through the arrival of speakers of another language in a monolingual community or the departure of a substantial proportion of a bilingual one, is often direct and observable (see for example 7.2 and 8.3.4). The influence of industrialization and urbanization, however, tends to be indirect and more subtle. Partly because urbanization is characterized more importantly by a change in lifestyles than by simple demographic shift (see 4.2.1), this kind of development operates primarily on the level of social attitudes (e.g. evaluation of given languages): it is the change in shared social values that may or may not lead to language shift.

### 8.2.4 Sociocultural factors

The extent to which a language plays a significant part in the life of a community will also depend partly on the degree of proficiency with which members of the community speak it. While personal attitudes and individual or group preferences clearly affect proficiency in terms of the amount of practice speakers get, another crucial aspect is the amount of exposure they have to the language. To gain a complete picture, in other words, we need to consider both production and consumption. Each speaker's linguistic environment extends beyond the other speakers with whom (s)he interacts directly and includes the mass media and the various forms of popular culture (music, film, literature) to which speakers have access.

In this context, it may be revealing to view consumption in terms of availability and selection: whether or not, for example, minority-language or bilingual newspapers are available is often interesting in itself, but becomes significant for the 'linguistic ecology' of a speech community only when we know what use the target population chooses to make of the goods on offer. These cultural choices can serve as a rough measure of political/ethnic affiliation and in as much as reading and listening to a language reinforces the 'consumer's' competence in it, cultural habits can help confirm predictions about linguistic trends.

Finally, we can also observe that linguistic behaviour is closely bound up with other aspects of what might be generalized as 'lifestyle': just as the choice of one language rather than another may indicate a desire to be integrated into or remain isolated from the majority culture, so may the use of a minority language serve as a symbol of the rejection of prevailing social norms, a kind of verbal badge declaring membership of a particular sub-culture or association with an anti-authoritarian movement (such as environmentalist or peace groups).

### 8.2.5 Summary

In this section we have drawn up a list of factors that may help to describe and explain patterns of linguistic behaviour in multilingual societies. Not all will be relevant in each case and some factors are clearly more important in certain contact situations than others: to take an extreme example, sociocultural factors are overwhelmingly significant where the linguistic contact does not occur between geographically adjacent communities (e.g. the influence of English on German). We should also bear in mind that although these various factors can be considered separately, they rarely operate in isolation: the linguistic make-up of a community is generally the result of a complex interaction of different factors.

## 8.3 German in competition with other languages

Given the framework outlined in the previous sections, we should now be in a position to look at some concrete examples. As we pointed out in the Introduction (see 1.2.1), German is in contact with many languages both within the German-speaking countries and in neighbouring countries on all sides. We cannot give a comprehensive account of these contact situations here but a selective discussion of several important examples, covering contact with Germanic languages (Danish, Frisian and Luxembourgish), Romance languages (French and Italian), a Slavonic language (Slovene) and Hungarian, should be sufficient to give an idea of the complexity of the subject. We shall also not attempt here to give a complete sociolinguistic profile of the countries concerned but will rather limit our investigation to the contact between German[1] and other languages. In doing so, we shall attempt to answer at least some of Haugen's questions (see 8.1), which we might condense and reformulate as:

(1)  Which languages are used in which way, by whom, when and why?
(2)  In what ways are social patterns reflected in linguistic ones and by what means are social changes translated into linguistic ones?

### 8.3.1 Eastern Belgium

Historical background

The political history of Belgium is extremely complicated and the very fact that the German-speaking area in the east of the country has at various stages belonged to France, Spain, Holland, Austria and Prussia (as well as being occupied by Germany in both world wars) suggests that the linguistic community there has been subject to considerable external pressure. Although largely overshadowed by the frequently violent conflict between the Dutch- and French-speaking populations, the

---

[1] Note that 'German' is used here and throughout this section to cover all relevant varieties of German, as the important thing is to distinguish between (any form of) German and the other languages concerned. Where the distinction between different varieties is relevant, this will be made clear.

fortunes of the German language and its speakers have been in a constant state of fluctuation since the formation of the Belgian state in 1830.

Map 8.1 shows those areas of Belgium in which German is spoken. At first sight a fairly self-contained region (except for Arel in the south), it is in reality anything but homogeneous. The crucial distinction for our purposes is between those areas which have belonged to Belgium since 1830 (collectively referred to as Old Belgium, *Altbelgien*) and those which were ceded to Belgium in 1920 in the Treaty of Versailles (New Belgium, *Neubelgien*). Given these clearly distinct historical profiles, it would be surprising if the sociolinguistic structure of these two areas were identical and in fact the historical division is reinforced by (or reflected in) the constitutional status of German and the attitudes of the respective populations towards the various languages and cultures: as the map shows, the German-speaking territories border variously on the Federal Republic, the Netherlands, Flanders (the Voer area), Wallonia, France and Luxembourg.

Legal and political measures

The revised constitution of 1971 (amended again in 1980) divided Belgium up in three different ways (see Fig. 8.1). There are

(1)     three monolingual Linguistic Regions (Dutch, French and German) and one bilingual one (Brussels);
(2)     three Communities (Flemish-, French- and German-speaking); and
(3)     three Economic Regions (Flanders, Wallonia and Brussels).

As none of these sub-divisions corresponds directly to either of the others, the situation is confusing enough. However, the language laws of 1962–3 show that the full story is more complicated still:

> In Old Belgium North the official language is French but inhabitants have the right to use German or Dutch in administrative matters.
> In New Belgium (Eupen, St Vith and part of Malmédy) German is the official language, while French may also be used; in New Belgium-Malmédy (the rest of Malmédy) the converse applies.
> Old Belgium Central and South are part of French-speaking Wallonia and are not recognized as separate areas by the constitution.

The process of 'Frenchification', initiated after the Second World War, has clearly downgraded the status of German in Old Belgium and despite a certain resistance in the Arel area (cf. Fischer 1979), it looks as if the

Map 8.1 German-speaking areas of eastern Belgium

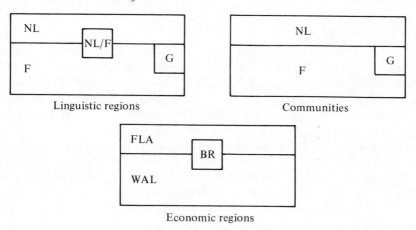

Fig. 8.1 Divisions of Belgium in the 1971/1980 Constitution: NL,
Dutch/Flemish; F, French; G, German; FLA, Flanders; WAL, Wallonia; BR,
Brussels
Source: Clauss 1979: 44

linguistic boundary will shift to the east within the next one or two
generations (Trim 1981, 1983). The situation in Old Belgium North is
rather different and we shall return to this later.

However, even the official recognition of German in New Belgium is no
guarantee of survival, as the reality of political practice puts the German-
speaking community at a considerable disadvantage. Both chambers of
the parliament are divided firstly into party political groupings, but also
into Dutch and French language groups, with German representatives
obliged to join the latter (Clauss 1979: 49). The French and Flemish
Communities both have an elected Council and an Executive, and it is the
task of these bodies to regulate cultural matters within the respective
Community (certain aspects of education, language use, theatre, radio
and television, sport and leisure, etc.). However, while there is also a
Council for the German-speaking Community, this is specified separately
as Article 59c of the Constitution, which states baldly that 'the law
determines its (= the Council's) composition and jurisdiction'. In 1984
New Belgium became a kind of sub-region of Wallonia with its own
Regional Council (*Regionalrat*) with a budget to cover schools, transport,
health, social affairs, family policy and tourism (see Kramer 1984: 125)
but despite its constitutional recognition, the German-speaking population remains politically, culturally and economically subordinate to the
majority groups (Clauss 1979: 49–53; Senelle 1980).

227

Popular attitudes

Reactions to political developments, especially following the two world wars, were quite different in the two parts of German-speaking Belgium. After the border change in 1919, the New Belgians had to come to terms with their change of nationality, and the need to reorientate themselves towards the new host country increased the sense of cultural distance from German influence, while at the same time they were faced with the antagonism of the native Belgians towards the reluctant 'immigrants'.

Not surprisingly, New Belgians have responded in different ways to the opposing pressures of assimilation to the host culture and of preservation of a separate identity through strengthening their internal cohesion. For example, Eisermann and Zeh (1979: 57–63), have identified three distinct sub-groups:

(1)  a stable minority using German in most domains;
(2)  an ambivalent group using both German and French freely, but with some functional distinctions;
(3)  a group with predominant French usage.

These groupings are reinforced by respondents' reported preferences in radio and television usage and by their stated preferences as regards the political status of New Belgium; the growing importance of French suggests a general trend towards bilingualism, this shift being encouraged by the fact that French is still used more than German in secondary schools.

Schooling is another area where actual practice may differ considerably from the provisions made by the law and where public opinion is divided. Since 1963 parents in New Belgium have been entitled to request the use of Dutch or French in addition to German as a language of instruction, while a Royal Decree in 1966 permitted a greater proportion of the curriculum to be given over to the teaching of French. In practice, many schools teach only in French and others are faced with the practical problem of simply not having enough German-speaking teachers qualified in certain subjects. Most, if not all, New Belgians would agree that French should be taught, but how much, and at what stage, depends on whether they see New Belgium as part of Wallonia or as an autonomous cultural area.

Proponents of both views produce political, economic and cultural arguments to support their case. The 'integrationists', for example, argue that the use of German smacks of disloyalty to the state; that as New Belgium is de facto part of the Walloon Economic Region, French is vital for career prospects and for access to positions of prestige and power; and that French opens up a rich cultural world; while their opponents, so they claim, advocate a cultural ghetto. The 'autonomists' counter with the need to preserve the German language and culture in a multilingual state and argue that as there is no natural economic link with Wallonia, New Belgium should build up its own structure and reinforce links with Germany; that a democratic education system demands the provision of teaching in the mother tongue; and that bilingual education as proposed favours only a gifted élite and leads to 'semilingualism' (inadequate competence in both languages) for the majority (Kartheuser 1979: 108–9).

In Old Belgium the situation is also varied and unstable but in a different way. The general trend away from the 'popular' language (*Volkssprache* – German) to the culturally dominant language (*Kultursprache* – French) has made greater progress in some parts of Old Belgium North and Central than others and while the erosion of German has met with some resistance in Old Belgium South, it was actively promoted in other parts in a strong anti-German reaction after both world wars (Pabst 1979: 28; Nelde 1979: 30).

Old Belgium North is a particularly interesting case as the circumstances there seemed to point to language shift but this has not – yet – happened. Quix (1981) suggests that the reason for this lies in what she calls a 'collective neurosis'. Old Belgium North is sandwiched between New Belgium–Eupen in the east, Wallonia in the west and a small Flemish area in the north-west: this latter area was transferred from Wallonia to Flanders under the 1963 Language Law and many of its inhabitants are still French-speakers. Taken together with the general historical and political background, this sensitive sociogeographical situation has led to considerable tension in the population, which is reflected in, among other things, an understandable suspicion towards linguistic investigations! The main fear is that Old Belgium North might be annexed by either Flanders or New Belgium as part of a demographic rationalization process: recent events have shown this fear to be not unfounded (Quix 1981: 231). As far as language use is concerned, this so-called neurosis manifests itself in the adoption of French in many domains as a defence against encroaching 'Germanization'. This language 'disloyalty' is to be seen less as an act of identity with Wallonia than as a demonstration of independence from German-speaking neighbours.

However, this Frenchification process has not operated uniformly throughout Old Belgium North. It appears to be operating on two levels: firstly, it is more advanced in the larger towns, especially Welkenrat, and in small villages directly adjacent to Wallonia, and secondly it is encompassing an increasing number of domains. The first of these processes, the so-called neighbourhood effect, is a familiar and well-documented phenomenon in dialect geography (see Chambers and Trudgill 1980: Ch. 11) and as we shall see when we consider the situations in South Tyrol and Burgenland, language shift typically spreads gradually from domain to domain in a more or less ordered process. In this case, domains may be grouped together to give three spheres of personal life:

public (official business, church, school, etc.)
semi-public (work, pub, media)
private (family)

As we would expect, French is used almost exclusively in all public domains. More surprisingly, perhaps, the use of German in the family varies throughout the whole range from 0–100 per cent, although in most places it is still used more than French. But the crucial area for the future of both languages could well be the semi-public sphere, in which usage varies according to a wide range of extralinguistic factors (e.g. job prospects, availability and quality of media products) and in which French is gaining in importance (see Fig. 8.2). Although it is possible only to speculate at this stage, it seems likely that the trend towards greater use of French in these semi-public domains, which are more exposed to external influences than are private domains and are thus more susceptible to change, will reduce the vitality and ultimately threaten the existence of German in Old Belgium North.

In both parts of German-speaking Belgium, then, the status of German is controversial; and this linguistic dispute is clearly not a peripheral issue but rather one that impinges on virtually every aspect of life. It is equally clear that legislation alone cannot resolve this kind of conflict and if German does disappear in the next two or three generations, it will largely be as a result of shifts in social values and attitudes.

### 8.3.2 Luxembourg

Historical background

Since the Second World War and in particular since the establishment of the European Economic Community, Luxembourg has rapidly grown in international importance. Besides undertaking a major rebuilding programme and large-scale restructuring of industry and agriculture, this small state has also attracted considerable foreign investment and is fast becoming a centre of international finance. It is also the home of several major EEC bodies. At the same time, while it shares borders with France, Belgium and the Federal Republic, in financial, commercial and cultural terms it is increasingly more dependent on the first two than on the latter (Hoffmann 1979: 6–7; Verdoodt 1968: 136).

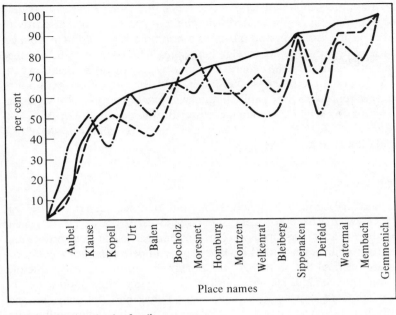

German in the family
German in the pub
German at work

Fig. 8.2 Old Belgium North and Central: language use in private and semi-public domains
Source: Nelde 1979

Historically, Luxembourg has a certain amount in common with Belgium: created by the Congress of Vienna in 1815, it achieved its present shape in 1839 when under the Treaty of London the French-speaking area became part of the Belgian province Luxembourg. All the inhabitants of the new state were then speakers of Luxembourgish but French remained the first official language. Luxembourg, too, was occupied by Germany in 1940 and the subsequent Germanization policy included the establishment of German as the official language.

There, however, the similarity ends, for although there was a strong anti-German reaction after the war, this did not have the same erosive effect on the German language as was the case in eastern Belgium. The reasons for this lie in the ethnic composition of the state and above all in the existence of a unifying national language, Luxembourgish, which can be seen linguistically as a Middle German dialect but sociolinguistically has the characteristics of an independent language. There is no substantial French- or German-speaking minority and all Luxembourgers speak

Luxembourgish. Nevertheless, both French and German are still widely used and a highly sophisticated trilingual pattern has evolved, partly to avoid cultural isolation and partly to maintain a sense of independence: the use of both competing foreign languages helps to keep some distance from both France and the Federal Republic by playing the association with one off against the other (se Verdoodt 1968: 143–4, 169). Luxembourg therefore represents a possibly unique example in Europe of '**exoglossia**' (i.e. a situation in which a language is used that has no population of native-speakers in the community concerned) as a conscious wish of the population (Kramer 1986: 229).

Language use

The basic distinction in linguistic behaviour in terms of language choice is that, between Luxembourgers of all social classes, Luxembourgish is virtually the sole medium of spoken communication in both public and private discourse, while all three languages compete to some extent in the written form. Although there are important exceptions to this principle, the importance of Luxembourgish as a unifying force should not be underestimated, especially as since 1984 it has had the constitutional status of 'national language'. All children are monolingual until they start school: then they are (theoretically) taught in German as well as having 7–8 hours a week of actual German lessons, while French is introduced as a subject in the second year and takes over as the medium of instruction in secondary schools. In practice, however, Luxembourgish continues to be used throughout, especially in explanations, and not surprisingly both teachers and pupils have to become fairly adept at code-switching (Hoffmann 1979: 41–3; Knowles 1980: 356–7). There is no university as such but at the Centre Universitaire de Luxembourg and the Institut Pédagogique teaching is (again theoretically) conducted in French, as the names would suggest. Lecturers at the Institut can choose between French and German and in fact often use Luxembourgish.

In three other important domains there is also an element of choice in speech. Before the Second World War, Latin and German were used in church and although German is still the official language in this domain, it is gradually being replaced by Luxembourgish in many parts of the service (Hoffmann 1979: 49–50; Knowles 1980: 358–9). Parliamentary usage has also changed since the war: German is no longer used at all, but both French and Luxembourgish may be used and the choice tends to be made on party lines, the Conservatives typically choosing the former and the Communists the latter, although it is common for all speakers to switch from one to the other (Knowles 1980: 358). Transcripts of the proceedings are made in the language(s) actually used in the debates, but a summary is distributed free to all households – in German (Hoffmann 1979: 50–1)! As the legal system is similar to the French, French is prescribed as the language of the courtroom, but once again the situation is vastly more complicated in practice. In civil cases, for example, lawyers may address questions to witnesses only through the judge: these exchanges are conducted in French but the judge typically speaks to the witness in Luxembourgish (Hoffmann 1979: 51–2; Knowles 1980: 357–8).

As Luxembourgish has a standardized orthography, it can be used as a written medium – there is indeed a substantial literature; but while it is used in all domains in speech, its use in writing is limited. Although there is no rule, French tends to be preferred to German in public corres-pondence and official documents, partly as it is felt to have an appropriate 'coolness' and partly as it is considered to have the highest social prestige (Hoffmann 1979: 57–65, 124). On the other hand, German is predominant in the press although the four dailies and the weekly *D'Letzeburger Land* contain articles in all three languages, so that reading a paper demands an ability to read in all three languages, regardless of topic.

## Sociolinguistic structure

Is it possible to rationalize this rather confusing situation? As we have seen, all Luxembourgers have in common the fact that they acquire Luxembourgish naturally at home and learn both German and French at school. These two 'foreign' languages are taught with sufficient intensity and are assigned sufficiently important rôles in the life of the community to be considered as something approximating to 'auxiliary mother tongues' (Hoffmann 1979: 115). In other words, Luxembourgers take it for granted that they have access to three languages, one of which is an emblem of national identity; the other two are also indispensable in preventing isolation from neighbouring states while at the same time keeping them at arm's length. Social stability in Luxembourg is at least in part attributable to this sociolinguistic equilibrium.

As each of the various languages is preferred for certain functions and as all Luxembourgers have at least some competence in more than one language, we could characterize the sociolinguistic structure of Luxem-bourg as 'diglossia with bilingualism'. However, the fact that three languages are involved and not simply two complicates the picture. While the distribution of the languages is fairly strictly organized according to specific functions, the actual pattern of usage does not conform to a straightforward High versus Low division, and it is also clear that the degree of trilingualism in individuals varies enormously from bare competence to reasonable fluency. A more accurate, if still greatly simplified, picture can be given using Auburger and Kloss's terminology (see 8.2.2): Luxembourgish is now the sole national language, while French and German are co-dominant official languages, but Luxembourgish also has the somewhat ambivalent status of 'virtually' co-dominant official language, as civil servants are now required ('as far as possible') to use Luxembourgish when writing responses to documents written in that language (see Hoffmann 1979 and Newton 1987 for more detailed accounts).

### 8.3.3 Alsace-Lorraine

Historical background

As we saw in the previous section, eastern Belgium and Luxembourg have a certain amount in common historically but there is no significant German-speaking minority in the latter. In the east of France, historically an even more disputed territory, there is still a German-speaking population accounting for large areas of the *départements* Haut-Rhin, Bas-Rhin and Moselle, which for convenience we shall continue to refer to here as Alsace-Lorraine. As we shall see, however, the situation of German here is far less secure than in either Belgium or Luxembourg.[2]

Alsace-Lorraine has changed hands repeatedly in the course of the last two hundred years and it is important to appreciate the increasing pressure that this constant uncertainty has exerted on the population's sense of identity. After the annexation by Germany in 1871, German was reinstated as the language of instruction in schools until it was replaced by French again when the region was returned to France in 1918. In the period before the First World War, the position of German was bolstered by the immigration of Germans into Alsace and Lorraine and of German-speaking Alsatians into French-speaking areas. Street names and place names were changed as part of a Germanization of official domains and this policy was intensified during the war when, for example, French was banned even in pubs and on the street (Becker-Dombrowski 1981: 150–1).[3] A corresponding Frenchification process undid all these measures in the inter-war years, until history repeated itself when Alsace-

---

[2] We shall refer to Alsatian as a variety of German here, although some Alsatian-speakers would insist on the independence of their 'mother tongue'.

[3] Kramer (1984: 171) refers to a similar attempt at Germanization in Luxembourg after the occupation in 1940, when even some family names were to be changed, e.g. *Brückner* for *Dupont*.

Lorraine was re-occupied by the Germans from 1940 to 1945; then, after the war, German was banned in schools.

The German-speaking population reacted vigorously to the threat posed to their language after each war, but with limited success. Admittedly, parents won the right to a small amount of German teaching as a result of a massive 95 per cent vote in favour in the 1952 referendum (Becker-Dombrowski 1981: 153), but these classes were optional for both pupils and teachers and as often as not did not take place at all. Repeated attempts since then have had little effect. The official reasons given include the fact that the Alsatian dialect is not recognized as a 'regional language' (as, for example, Breton, Basque and Occitan are) and the danger expressed by a former Education Minister 'that the children would end up preferring to speak German rather than French' (Pierre Messmer, quoted in Becker-Dombrowski 1981: 157). The result of these developments is that the dialect has become stigmatized through lack of official recognition and German now has the status of a foreign language through being taught as such.

Language use

'Il est chic de parler français': the post-war slogan intended to persuade tram passengers of the aesthetic superiority of French has now given way to more utilitarian considerations, as the official language is clearly essential for any form of personal social advancement. Recent surveys of language use suggest that while a declining but still substantial proportion of native Alsatians speak the dialect, it is used much more in rural areas than in the towns (see, for examples, Ladin 1982, Hartweg 1981). The dialect is still used in public domains such as shopping and official business but it is above all the language of the family, although even there parents increasingly use French to their children. The situation at the workplace is more complex. A survey of industrial workers, conducted by their union CFDT, found that dialect was frequently used even with middle management, but senior staff were addressed in French and interestingly the pattern within the union was similar: dialect used at union meetings but French with senior officials.

With the decline of the traditional heavy industries, the major growth area has been in the service sector, and this seems to have given considerable indirect support to the promotion of French. Female employment is concentrated in the urban service industries, where French is the dominant language, and the surveys found that more women than men claimed to use French in all domains. The view that women are more sensitive to prestigious linguistic varieties is a controversial one but it is at least possible that women's language preferences are encouraging language shift in Alsace-Lorraine. A survey of schoolchildren in east Lorraine, on the other hand, found that proximity to the German state border correlated more closely than sex with language preferences, while there was also evidence that social class played a major rôle, with working-class speakers adapting to the norm of French usage established by middle-class speakers (see Hoffmeister 1977).

## Attitudes

Although these surveys reveal some potentially interesting developments, statistics regarding language use (especially those drawn from official censuses) should be treated with caution. Nelde (1984: 220) gives striking evidence of this: in three villages in Old Belgium South, where over 85 per cent of the inhabitants had claimed to be German-speakers in 1930, only between 1 per cent and 5 per cent still admitted to speaking German in 1947. In the absence of large-scale population movements or mass amnesia, such figures can surely be interpreted only as an indication of political affiliation, in this case loyalty to the Belgian state. Official figures for Alsace should be seen in the same light. The phrasing of census questions relating to language (e.g. 'Can you speak French/German/dialect/other languages?') was scarcely designed to reveal much about actual use but the response to such questions could be taken as an indicator of public attitudes. The 1962 census (the last time the question was posed) apparently showed that 85 per cent still spoke dialect but 80 per cent could now speak French (1946: 66 per cent). No further detail was given (e.g. How good was their knowledge of French? Could they write it as well as speak it?), but the figures were interpreted as showing that the minority population was managing to retain its traditional speech forms while becoming successfully assimilated into the French state (Hartweg 1981: 97–8).

Regardless of whether the official assimilation policy was directly responsible, the majority of the German-speaking population seems resigned to the loss of their separate identity: after four changes of nationality in seventy-five years and with each generation being educated according to totally different policies, there is a widespread desire to fit in in order to achieve some kind of stability. As far as the younger generation is concerned, a rather confused picture emerges from the surveys by Ladin (1982), Hoffmeister (1977) and Cole (1975). While 88 per cent of Ladin's informants in Alsace considered the dialect an important element of their cultural heritage, only 57 per cent thought it a necessary element of Alsatian identity (against over 80 per cent in Cole's survey). Hoffmeister had similar results in east Lorraine: 44 per cent of the children interviewed would like their own children to learn both German and French at school, 45 per cent only French, but 54 per cent would speak only French to their children.

## Prospects

As in other parts of the German-speaking world, there has been a revival of interest in the dialect in recent years, especially in Alsace and, as elsewhere, this has a lot to do with extralinguistic factors, such as a reaction to changes in traditional lifestyles brought about as a result of industrialization: language maintenance and environmental conservation are closely associated. This trend is reflected in a tough new brand of dialect literature that has rejected pictures of bucolic idylls in favour of a commitment to the cause of Alsatian identity and the struggle to preserve the environment (Hartweg 1981: 110), and political parties of all colours have begun to take a greater interest in the 'language question'.

For all this, the future is not very promising. Despite the continued popular support for German (standard and dialect), most people abdicate the responsibility of maintaining it to the schools and 'the government'. The pressure from French is overwhelming and it is replacing German in more and more domains. Alsatian is perhaps less threatened than other minority language varieties in France, but the official attitude is merely one of tolerance rather than support, and it seems realistic to predict that the shift from the present, highly unstable situation to effective mono-lingualism in French will be completed within the next generation.

### 8.3.4 South Tyrol

## Historical background

In South Tyrol we have a different configuration again: the period of intimate contact between German and Italian here has been relatively short and the current situation is relatively stable. However, this stability has not been achieved without very considerable social upheaval and the trauma of the Fascist period in particular has taken a long time to heal. The southern half of the Austrian province of Tyrol (with two-thirds of the population) was ceded to Italy when international boundaries were redrawn after the First World War. The fact that this was done without a referendum (which would probably have gone against the proposal – see Kramer 1981: 22–4) not surprisingly provoked deep resentment amongst many German-speakers. The policy of the Fascist government, which seized power in Italy in 1922, was to achieve the total assimilation of the German-speaking population, and the principal method was that used repeatedly by both French and German governments in Alsace-Lorraine: the suppression by gradual erosion of (in this case) the German language.

Although German was eventually banned in all public domains, it survived in the family and the church and was obviously reinforced by the German occupation in 1943. By then, however, the position of German as the language of the overwhelming majority in South Tyrol had been undermined by a series of measures that led to a sharp demographic shift in favour of Italian-speakers. The most significant of these measures were the industrialization policy and the so-called '*Option*'. Firstly, the central government pushed through a policy of rapid industrial expansion from 1935 onwards, which was designed to shift the balance of power away from the predominantly agricultural German-speakers and attract Italians from outside the province. Then a far more dramatic development followed the 1939 South Tyrol Treaty between Mussolini's Italy and Hitler's Germany: German-speakers were offered the option of staying in Italy and renouncing any claims to protected minority status or taking German citizenship and leaving. Although over 80 per cent chose the latter course, the outbreak of war prevented the full implementation of the *Option* and indeed after the war many who had left were allowed to return. Nevertheless, the German-speaking population declined by a fifth (50,000) over this period. Taken together with the massive immigration into the area of Italians from other parts of the country during the local 'economic miracle' after the war, these events help to explain how the relative proportions of German- and Italian-speakers changed from 76 per cent and 10.5 per cent of the total population respectively in 1921 to 62 per cent and 33 per cent in 1953 (Kramer 1981: 35–40, 49–51; Egger 1977: 35–7).

After the war, an uneasy peace was established but both parts of the community continued to jostle for position by promoting their own language at the expense of the other; it was only with the passing of the Autonomy Statute in 1972 that a real measure of stability was achieved. Under the Statute, the bilingual status quo was officially recognized and rationalized. Its provisions included the following (Egger 1977: 51–4, 126–8; Kramer 1981: 89–92):

> proportional representation of ethnic groups in the civil service was to be achieved within thirty years (Eisermann (1981: 27) gives the following figures for the civil service in 1971: German-speakers 25.8 per cent, Italian-speakers 72.5 per cent, i.e. virtually the reverse of their proportions of the population as a whole);

all citizens have the right to use their own language in dealings with
public authorities: laws continue to be framed in the national
language, Italian, but the authorities are required to use the
language of the person they are dealing with;

in line with the previous point, all civil servants must now be
competent in German and Italian (although this is emphatically not
yet the case);

while schools are monolingual in terms of the language of instruction (parents have the right to choose whether their children go to
German or Italian schools), the 'other' language is always taught as
a subject and the second-language teachers must have that language
as their mother tongue and must also be competent in the first
language of the pupils. In contrast to Alsace, there is in South Tyrol
a reasonable supply of such teachers, although not many Italian-
teachers can meet the second condition fully.

However, although these measures were intended to placate the German-
speaking population and thereby promote greater harmony in the
province, they have given rise to some less promising developments. A
strict application of the proportional representation rule, for example,
may mean that vacant posts remain unfilled unless a suitable, i.e.
German-speaking, candidate can be found. More seriously, it could mean
that Italian-speakers are virtually excluded from applying for posts until
the year 2000, and this has naturally led to some tension. There are signs,
however, that some Italian-speakers are quite legitimately declaring
themselves officially to be German-speakers, presumably to get round
this problem. In addition, many are sending their children to German
schools, which in turn is seen as a threat by some German-speakers
(Kramer 1981: 57; Lüsebrink 1986: 76; Tyroller 1986: 20).

Language use

As Table 8.1 shows, there have been important shifts in language use in
certain domains over the last fifty years. In particular, the German-
speaking population developed bilingualism towards the end of the
Fascist period and this trend has spread into most public domains since
the war. Meanwhile, however, it has become increasingly apparent to the
Italian-speaking population that an active knowledge of German is
desirable and in some cases indispensable. We shall return to the question
of attitudes to language and specifically to bilingualism shortly, but first it
might be instructive to look briefly at actual language use in bilingual
families.

Table 8.1. *Shifts in language use in South Tyrol 1918–76 by domains*

| Domains | German-speakers | | | Italian-speakers | |
|---|---|---|---|---|---|
| | 1918 | 1938 | 1976 | 1938 | 1976 |
| Family | G | G | G | I | I |
| Neighbours/friends | G | G | G | I | I |
| Church | G | G | G | I | I |
| School | G | I | G | I | I |
| Mass media | G | GI | GI | I | I |
| Workplace: | | | | | |
|   Agriculture | G | G | G | I | I |
|   Industry | | | GI | I | I |
|   Service sector | G | GI | GI | I | GI |
|   Public admin. | G | I | GI | I | GI |
|   Organizations | G | G | GI | I | GI |

G = German, I = Italian, GI = German and Italian
*Source:* based on Egger (1977)

The findings of a study into the speech behaviour of children of mixed marriages included the following:

(1)    50 per cent spoke both German and Italian at home
       34 per cent spoke only Italian at home
       16 per cent spoke only German at home
(2)    Language chosen according to language of parents, in order of preference:
       A. Italian-speaking father, German-speaking mother
         1 German and Italian   2 Italian   3 German

       B. German-speaking father, Italian-speaking mother
         1 Italian   2 German and Italian   3 German

                     (Egger 1977: 69–70)

Bearing in mind that more German-speakers than Italian-speakers are bilingual, we can still cautiously conclude that there is a general preference for Italian (even where both languages are available), especially when the mother is an Italian-speaker: two-thirds of those children who use only one language at home use Italian and half of those with a German-speaking father speak to their father in Italian.

Attitudes

As far as German is concerned, it is worth noting that as in Luxembourg and German-speaking Switzerland the local variety enjoys high prestige as a symbol of group cohesion and identity and is spoken by all members of the German-speaking community. It is nonetheless in a diglossic relationship with Austrian standard German, which is used in formal domains such as church, lectures, school and press. Furthermore, the German-speaking population is keenly aware of the need to maintain close contact with the German cultural world in order to preserve their language and their identity from the phenomenon referred to as the 'Alsace syndrome' (*Verelsässerung*) (Egger 1977: 14–6, 155–7, 161). Historical ties with the German cultural world are constantly stressed and strenuous efforts are made to prevent the contamination of their German by Italian: by far the greatest amount of the literature on language in South Tyrol is concerned with supposed Italian interference (see 8.5).

Despite its fears, the German-speaking population is well aware of the need to know Italian. Until after the war, however, the Italian-speaking population had no incentive to learn German and has only recently appreciated the importance of knowing what is, in this part of Italy, the majority language. As we have shown, the entry to many careers now depends on it. It is true that the vast majority of Italian-speakers live in three towns, and in Bozen/Bolzano, in particular, the two groups tend to live in separate parts of town and have little social contact (Tyroller 1986: 26–7). However, unlike in Switzerland or Belgium, there is no 'territorial principle': linguistic groups are not strictly concentrated in specific areas and so some contact is unavoidable. The most important consequence of this situation is that while each group continues to favour its own language, bilingualism is now more highly valued and in this respect too South Tyrol differs from the situation we discussed earlier. The crucial questions here are (see Egger 1977: 158–60):

(1) for the German-speakers: how far to push bilingualism without putting the future of German at risk?
(2) for the Italian-speakers: as there is no threat to Italian, how to acquire bilingualism most quickly and efficiently?

Prospects

The previous section appears to suggest that linguistic practice in South Tyrol is evolving into stable German–Italian bilingualism but without diglossia. However, this configuration typically arises during periods of rapid social change and rarely persists for long. In South Tyrol there are now virtually no distinctive domains that require the exclusive use of one language or the other: neither language has been assigned any specific function and the basis for the existence of two languages rests purely on the fact that the two groups continue to perceive themselves as distinct. But as Denison (1980: 335) remarks, while there is no necessary causal link between plurilingualism and language shift, the likelihood in such situations is that the transitional phase of non-diglossic bilingualism gives way to monolingualism when the dominant language eventually takes over.

The prospects for stable bilingualism in South Tyrol are therefore not promising, but it is still too early for talk of a 'death march' (*Todesmarsch*) (Egger 1977: 161), as the 'dominant' language is that of the minority social group and the majority shows every sign of putting up stiff resistance to change. In fact, there may be a very real threat to the prospects of a stable bilingualism in the policies of the ruling South Tyrol People's Party (*Südtiroler Volkspartei*), especially since the introduction in 1981 of the compulsory 'declaration of language group membership' (*Sprachgruppenzugehörigkeitserklärung*), in which citizens must register themselves as either German- or Italian-speaking: 'bilingual' is not an accepted category (see Bettelheim 1982: 5). And it is still true that the two ethnic groups merely coexist side by side: this is particularly clear in education, where there is no integration and none in prospect. Compared to the situations in eastern Belgium and Alsace-Lorraine, the German-speakers in this part of Italy are in an enviable position. Indeed, South Tyrol has the potential to become a model of harmonious bilingualism. Whether or not it realizes this potential will depend now less on legislation than on the will to succeed amongst the population as a whole.

## 8.4 Language decline and language shift

While the recent influx of migrant workers and their families especially into the Federal Republic has introduced a number of languages previously unrepresented in the German-speaking countries, other languages which have been in prolonged contact with German in the marginal zone just inside the outer boundaries of these countries are losing their position, so that the long-established multilingualism of these border areas will eventually give way to monolingualism in German. In most cases, the contact varieties are indigenous to neighbouring countries and will therefore simply 'retreat' to these territories. As an example of this process we can consider the shift away from German–Slovene and German–Hungarian bilingualism in south-east Austria. At the other end of the geographical spectrum, however, North Frisian is spoken only in Schleswig, the northernmost part of the Federal Republic, and if its steady decline there is not arrested soon it will cease to exist altogether.

**8.4.1** Schleswig

The southern part of the historical duchy of Schleswig, which has belonged to Germany since 1920 and today forms part of the *Bundesland* of Schleswig-Holstein, is an area of extraordinary linguistic diversity. Various forms of five different language types are used in the relatively small territory between the river Eider and the Danish border on the mainland, and on the islands off the west coast: in addition to standard Danish and colloquial standard and non-standard German, there are still speakers of traditional North Frisian, South Jutlandish and Low German dialects. This mosaic is further complicated by the fact that North Frisian, which is usually accorded the status of an independent language, is a collection of nine highly disparate dialects, some of which are mutually almost unintelligible. However, although this remarkable situation has persisted since at least the mid-nineteenth century, the position of the traditional dialect forms has been declining for a long time, and given continued political stability and social and economic modernization it seems likely that the linguistic make-up of the region will be greatly simplified within the next fifty years.

On the face of it, the juxtaposition of many linguistic varieties seems like a recipe for conflict, especially as they were originally associated with different ethnic groupings: Frisians, Jutes, Saxons amongst others. In fact, although most of these groups have been indigenous to the area for hundreds of years, the only serious conflict arose in the mid-nineteenth century in the course of the territorial struggle between Germans and Danes. In the seventy years up to the end of the First World War similar attempts at linguistic normalization were made to those we have seen in other marginal areas. First the Danes attempted to establish standard Danish as the official language both in those areas where the Danish dialect South Jutlandish was still spoken and further south where it had been supplanted by Low German. Then when all of Schleswig came under Prussian rule in 1864 after the Second Schleswig War the process was reversed (see Søndergaard 1980: 300–2). Since the establishment of the state border in 1920, dividing Schleswig in half, there have been German- and Danish-speaking minorities north and south of the border respectively, both of which are now officially recognized and enjoy considerable security.

Where official language planning measures at the level of standard varieties had little long-term impact, the gradual process of attrition has continued to undermine the existence of the various traditional dialects. South Jutlandish is not threatened with extinction as it is still widespread in southern Denmark, but since the late Middle Ages it has been pushed further north by the advance of Low German and is now spoken in the Federal Republic only in a small pocket of land just south of the border. It will almost certainly be restricted to Denmark by around the turn of the century (see Søndergaard 1980: 298; Walker 1987: 143).

North Frisian was also progressively superseded by Low German and forms of standard German but unlike South Jutlandish it has nowhere else to retreat to if it is finally removed from the western coastal strip of southern Schleswig and the North Frisian islands. In the last hundred years, the estimated number of speakers has declined from over twenty-seven thousand to around eight to nine thousand today (see Schleswig-Holsteinischer Landtag 1987: 26). Many individual factors have contributed to the decline of Frisian but perhaps the most important historically was the fact that the Frisian-speaking population was not a homogeneous group but rather consisted of many relatively isolated communities. It is not surprising then that there are very considerable differences between the various dialects and that there is no single standardized form, either spoken or written. This meant that as mobility eventually began to increase some form of lingua franca was needed for communication with speakers of different Frisian dialects. For a long time this function was fulfilled by dialects of economically and socially dominant Low German, but as the prestige of Low German itself has declined, especially since the Second World War, shift away from Frisian has tended to be more in the direction of colloquial standard or non-standard German.

This global tendency is of course reinforced by the factors that, as we have seen, typically promote language shift: improved communications, a centralized education system, the demands of employment especially in the public sector and the service industries. At the individual level, on the other hand, the intermediate stages of language choice are vastly more complex: while the overall situation resembles a diglossic pattern, individual choice is still often motivated by particular circumstances. Consider, for example, the following account of language use within one family (from Walker 1980a: 23–4):

> The father speaks Frisian (F) with his parents, his brother, his brother's wife and their children. He speaks Low German (LG) with his own wife and High German (HG)[4] with his children. Thus we have the sequence F–LG–HG. The mother on the other hand speaks HG with her parents, LG with her husband and HG with her children. She speaks LG with her mother-in-law and F with her father-in-law; HG with her brother but LG with his wife and children. With her husband's brother and his children she speaks F, but with her husband's brother's wife LG. Their children speak

---

[4]　It is not made clear which variety is meant here but it is reasonable to assume that it refers to what we would call colloquial standard or colloquial non-standard German.

HG together, HG with their maternal and paternal grandmothers but F with the paternal grandfather. With their maternal uncle and all his family they speak HG, they speak F with their paternal uncle and his children but HG with his wife.

Historically, everything speaks against the survival of North Frisian: the number of speakers has never been large, the communities in which it is spoken were slow to develop and the competition from other varieties is overwhelming. Under such circumstances, the prospects for survival depend above all on interventionist measures from official agencies and concerted popular action. Until quite recently, not a great deal was done on either front, and this seems to be partly due to a lack of consensus amongst Frisian-speakers themselves. On the one hand, for example, inhabitants of the popular holiday island Sylt welcome the prosperity brought by tourism but still feel able by virtue of their physical isolation to maintain a separate identity and reinforce this by the use of their traditional Frisian dialect. Some of the economically less developed communities on the mainland, on the other hand, have become increasingly diluted socially by the influx of German-speakers as permanent residents, and the dwindling sense of local identity coupled with a desire to shake off the 'backwoods' image means that in these areas there is relatively little support for Frisian (see Walker 1980b: 456–7).

Nevertheless, popular support for Frisian has increased over the last decade and in 1987 the *Land* parliament commissioned a report on the language and culture of the Frisian population with the intention of increasing general public awareness of the situation and fostering efforts to preserve the Frisian tradition. Positive steps have been taken to provide funds for the teaching of Frisian in schools and financial support for both popular and academic publications about the language, and this has met with a generally favourable response from the public. However, this renewed interest must be seen in the light of the often highly orchestrated enthusiasm for traditional dialects, which itself is just one aspect of the internationally booming 'heritage' industry. The popular interest in Frisian may indeed be genuine but while, for example, many parents welcome some Frisian teaching in schools there is no pressure for this to be compulsory and the same parents will typically speak some form of standard German with their children (Walker 1987: 138). The kind of support that Frisian now enjoys may help to preserve it in rather the same way as traditional crafts are maintained but in the end this is unlikely to do more than postpone its inevitable demise.

### 8.4.2 South-east Austria

Among the minority communities in Austria are Slovene-speakers in Carinthia (bordering on Yugoslavia) and Hungarian-speakers in Burgenland (bordering on Hungary). As appears to be the case with Frisian and South Jutlandish in Schleswig, the minority languages here are declining in use and many of the now familiar factors have contributed to this shift towards monolingualism in German. However, detailed ethnographic studies of these two communities have shown that more subtle processes may also be involved and suggest how patterns of individual choice may determine the progress of language shift. We shall consider the first one relatively briefly and the second in more detail.

### The Gail Valley, Carinthia

In the area straddling what is now the Austrian–Yugoslavian border, German and Slovene have been in contact for centuries. A pattern of diglossia without bilingualism developed under the feudal conditions which separated the dominant German-speakers from the subordinate Slovene-speakers (Gumperz 1977). A further consequence of the social structure was that the villagers developed closed network systems based on complex patterns of mutual support. The process of modernization brought major social changes in the course of the nineteenth century and this in turn led to changes in language use: the formerly monolingual Slovene-speakers were almost all bilingual by the turn of the century but this bilingualism was transitional and most communities are now (at least on their way to being) monolingual in German. However, the remote villages in the Gail Valley have resisted this final shift until now and the best explanation seems to be that the external social changes did not succeed in breaking down the local network system.

Until recently, then, the situation was that these communities had absorbed the effects of social change to the extent of developing a linguistic repertoire incorporating three varieties: Austrian standard German (learned at school), the local traditional German dialect and the local variety of Slovene. As in most bilingual situations, the choice of variety is not entirely arbitrary but rather is determined to some extent by a set of communicative rules. However, it is not merely a question of symbolic function (i.e. signalling identification with either urban or rural values, as in Oberwart – see below), nor of context-specific choice. Both of these factors play a part in language choice, but there is also a third consideration, which Gumperz (1977) refers to as 'complex metaphoric principles' and which give rise to frequent conversational code-switching.

One simple example concerns a mother talking to her small child, who has lost something: she begins in Slovene /muəʃ fain paledatə/ ('you'll have to look hard'), then adds in German /na suəx/ ('go on, look!'). Gumperz' explanation of this switch to German is that it 'can be seen as a metaphoric extension, which builds on the out-group association of the German dialect to lend a tone of seriousness to the repetition' (Gumperz 1977: 92) and this view was supported by villagers.

These shared 'pragmatic conventions' depend for their effect on the stability of the social networks in which they operate and so a change in the nature of the networks should result also in a change in language behaviour. This is what is now beginning to happen. With the growth of local tourism on the one hand and the possibility of commuting to major towns for work on the other, the villagers are no longer dependent economically on each other but rather on urban ties. The short-term linguistic consequence of this change of focus, especially amongst the young, is that the older conventions, based on shifting between German and Slovene, are giving way to the urban norms, which require instead the ability to style-shift in German. In the longer term, it is already clear that German will displace Slovene entirely.

### Oberwart, Burgenland

Like Gumperz, Susan Gal (1979) attempted to find the intervening processes by which major social change leads to changes in language use. A fundamental premiss of her study is that synchronic variation is an indication that change is in progress (Gal 1979: 6): this is an over-generalization, as there is such a thing as inherent variability, but it is a useful working notion. In particular it allows the investigator to make predictions about the progress and direction of change by comparing patterns of variability in speakers of different ages, the underlying assumption being that, while the choices of individuals remain fairly stable throughout their lives (unless there are marked changes in their social networks or status), each generation 'reinterprets the relationship between linguistic forms and social groups and consequently reevaluates the prestige and meaning of linguistic forms' (Gal 1979: 154). In other words, we adopt the dialectologists' adage that older speakers preserve old patterns that were once the norm, and by comparing their linguistic behaviour with that of other age-groups at one point in time, we can interpret this apparently static image in such a way as to give a dynamic picture of the way in which language use and attitudes to language are changing.

In her study, Gal in fact compared the speech of individuals and, following Derek Bickerton's dictum that 'speaking, after all, is not done by . . . the lower middle class of Upper Middletown – it is done by Irma and Ted and Basil and Jerry and Joan' (Bickerton 1971: 483), resisted the temptation to arrange her informants into groups according to 'objective' social criteria. Instead, her interpretation hinges on the fact that the crucial social change in this previously conservative rural area was the shift from agriculture to industry as the principal source of employment. Speakers could then be classified in terms of their self-selected social networks, which Gal designates as either 'peasant' or 'non-peasant'; although social categories here as elsewhere are actually much more fluid and more complex than this dichotomy would suggest, it seems to work at least as a rough measure.

Before the Second World War, German and Hungarian were not rated differently in terms of prestige: Hungarian was simply the local language. German was the language of 'outsiders' and was useful for specific purposes such as trade. It was only with the growth of industrialization after the war, when young peasants were increasingly attracted by the security of employment in neighbouring towns, that the two languages were brought into the same 'conceptual system' and could therefore have values attached to them in respect of each other. For the first time, in other words, German and Hungarian became recognized as markers of status rather than of ethnicity (Gal 1979: 16–17, 161–2) and it was German, the language popularly associated with social progress, that came to enjoy the higher prestige. Not surprisingly, some accepted the new order more readily than others and equally predictably the youngest generation responded most favourably to the change. What is significant for our purposes is that in each generation the use of German is now most widespread among speakers with non-peasant networks and that German is used most of all by the youngest speakers, regardless of their networks (see Figs. 8.3, 8.4).

As we have said, linguistic change is not a sudden event; a community does not shift from language A to language B overnight. We are also now familiar with the fact that in the transitional phase there are a number of domains in which both A and B are used, while others are dominated by either A or B (see, for example, Table 8.1). What has not emerged clearly from the situations we have looked at so far is whether this process of shifting 'domain control' is random or ordered in some way. As the direct observation of change is simply impracticable, however, the investigator must turn to other means to answer this question. Gal's solution rests on the use of the technical device of **implicational scaling** (see Chambers and

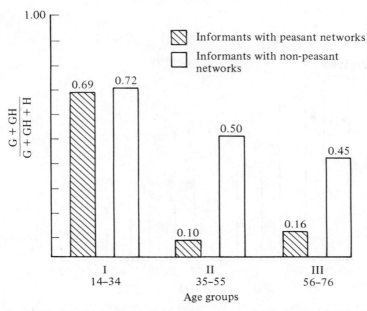

Fig. 8.3 Oberwart: proportion of German used by informants with peasant and non-peasant networks in three age groups. ($n=32$; G, German; H, Hungarian)
Source: Gal 1979: 159

Trudgill 1980: Ch. 9; Hudson 1980: Ch. 5): that is to say, she attempts to account for the actual process of change not so much in the way she collects her data as in the way she presents them. If the process is not random but rather conforms to some underlying sequential pattern, then this may become apparent if the data are arranged as in Fig. 8.5. This idealized display can be glossed as follows: 'Form X (=whatever linguistic feature we are studying: phoneme, word, language etc.) will be used in any one context, if and only if it already appears in all contexts to the left of that context.' In other words, the use of X in one context implies that it is used in a certain specified set of other contexts. However, the typical pattern is more like that in Fig. 8.6. The important modification here is that each change from 'exclusive use of Y' to 'exclusive use of X' is interrupted by a period in which both X and Y are used.

Now we have already seen that language shift passes through a transitional phase in which the two languages compete or at least coexist in certain domains. The technique of implicational scaling and the presentation of data for individual speakers allow us to move a further major step forward. The relevant information from Oberwart is given in

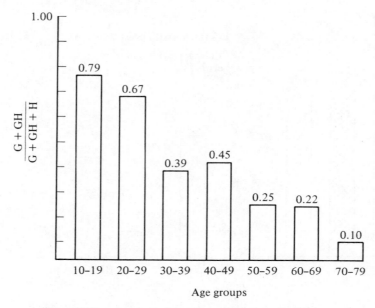

Fig. 8.4 Oberwart: proportion of German used by informants in seven age groups. ($n=32$; G, German; H, Hungarian)
Source: Gal 1979: 158

Table 8.2. This shows that in the absence of externally imposed planning measures language shift may operate by a fairly ordered process, moving simultaneously from domain to domain and from speaker to speaker. As far as the use of German in this peripheral linguistic zone is concerned, we can say that following a period of radical social change German has acquired new connotations in the bilingual community. A growing number of (mainly younger) speakers is using these new connotations as a symbol of identity and adopts the newly prestigious code in more and more domains, so that it seems safe to predict the fairly imminent completion of the shift from Hungarian–German bilingualism to German monolingualism.

## 8.5 Specific linguistic consequences of contact within the German-speaking area

So far in this chapter we have been concerned with large-scale sociolinguistic phenomena, chiefly the maintenance or wholesale loss of languages in certain communities. The effects of language contact may however be

*Contact and conflict*

Speech Varieties        Contexts

|   | 1 | 2 | 3 | 4 | 5 |
|---|---|---|---|---|---|
| a | X | Y | Y | Y | Y |
| b | X | X | Y | Y | Y |
| c | X | X | X | Y | Y |
| d | X | X | X | X | Y |
| e | X | X | X | X | X |

Fig. 8.5 The principle of implicational scaling (1)

Speech varieties        Contexts

|   | 1 | 2 | 3 | 4 | 5 |
|---|---|---|---|---|---|
| a | Y | Y | Y | Y | Y |
| b | X/Y | Y | Y | Y | Y |
| c | X | X/Y | Y | Y | Y |
| d | X | X | X/Y | Y | Y |
| e | X | X | X | X/Y | Y |
| f | X | X | X | X | X/Y |
| g | X | X | X | X | X |

Fig. 8.6 The principle of implicational scaling (2)

manifested in other ways, without necessarily having such drastic consequences. It therefore seems appropriate to conclude our discussion of this topic with a brief look at some of the ways in which individual features of one language may enter another. (Some of the examples in this section are not given in English as some knowledge of German is necessary to understand their relevance.)

## 8.5.1 Lexical transfer

The most common form of transfer is lexical borrowing (especially nouns), as among many reasons for borrowing perhaps the most important besides prestige is the need for labels for new objects and notions acquired through cultural contact (see Weinreich 1953: 37, 56ff). Many words in modern German were derived in this way, most of them now unrecognizable as 'foreign words': e.g. *Pflaume* (plum), *Senf* (mustard), *Münze* (coin), *Küche* (kitchen) (see Masser 1982: 66). As we shall see in the final section of this chapter, modern German continues to draw heavily on English (and to some extent on Russian in the GDR) to fulfil this function and it is therefore not surprising that the German of

Table 8.2 *Oberwart: choice of language*[a]

| Speaker | Age of speaker | Interlocutor[b] | | | | | | | | | | |
|---|---|---|---|---|---|---|---|---|---|---|---|---|
| | | 1 | 2 | 3 | 4 | 5 | 6 | 7 | 8 | 9 | 10 | 11 |
| A | 14 | H | GH | | G | G | G | | | G | | G |
| B | 15 | H | GH | | G | G | G | | | G | | G |
| C | 17 | H | GH | | G | G | G | | | G | | G |
| D | 25 | H | GH | GH | GH | G | G | G | G | G | | G |
| E | 27 | H | H | | GH | G | G | | | G | | G |
| F | 25 | H | H | | GH | G | G | | | G | | G |
| G | 42 | | H | | GH | G | G | G | G | G | | G |
| H | 17 | H | H | | H | GH | G | | | G | | G |
| I | 20 | H | H | H | H | GH | G | G | G | G | | G |
| J | 39 | H | H | | H | GH | GH | | | G | | G |
| K | 22 | H | H | | H | GH | GH | | | G | | G |
| L | 23 | H | H | | H | GH | H | | GH | G | | G |
| M | 40 | H | H | | H | GH | | GH | G | G | | G |
| N | 52 | H | H | H | GH | H | | GH | G | G | G | G |
| O | 62 | H | H | H | H | H | H | GH | GH | GH | G | G |
| P | 40 | H | H | H | H | H | H | GH | GH | GH | | G |
| Q | 63 | H | H | | H | H | H | H | | GH | | G |
| R | 64 | H | H | H | H | H | H | H | GH | GH | | G |
| S | 43 | H | H | | H | H | H | H | G | H | | G |
| T | 35 | H | H | H | H | H | H | H | GH | H | | G |
| U | 41 | H | H | H | H | H | H | H | GH | H | | H |
| V | 61 | H | H | | H | H | H | H | GH | H | | G |
| W | 54 | H | H | | H | H | H | H | H | H | | G |
| X | 50 | H | H | H | H | H | H | H | H | H | | G |
| Y | 63 | H | H | H | H | H | H | H | H | H | GH | G |
| Z | 61 | H | H | | H | H | H | H | H | G | GH | G |
| A1 | 74 | H | H | | H | H | H | H | H | H | GH | H |
| B1 | 54 | H | H | | H | H | H | H | H | H | GH | H |
| C1 | 63 | H | H | H | H | H | H | H | H | H | GH | H |
| D1 | 58 | G | H | | H | H | H | H | H | H | | H |
| E1 | 64 | H | H | | H | H | H | H | H | H | H | H |
| F1 | 59 | H | H | H | H | H | H | H | H | H | H | H |

[a] G = German; H = Hungarian.
[b] Interlocutors: (1) to God; (2) grandparents and their generation; (3) black-market client; (4) parents and their generation; (5) peer group (*kolegák*); (6) brothers and sisters; (7) spouse; (8) children and their generation; (9) government officials; (10) grandchildren and their generation; (11) doctor.
Data are from interviews. Spaces indicate inapplicable questions.
Number of speakers = 32 (both men and women).
*Source:* Gal 1979: 135

South Tyrol should borrow primarily from its most influential 'neighbour language', Italian. This is notably the case where German in the Federal Republic has adopted anglicisms, such as in the field of information technology: English loan words such as *Computer, Operator, Input* and *Output* are used in the Federal Republic, while the corresponding Italian terms *calcolatore, programmatore, entrata* and *uscita* are used in South Tyrol (see Kramer 1981: 126–7). Where there is influence from two foreign languages, as in Luxembourg, there may be 'synonymous neologisms' as a result of a word being borrowed from each contact language: e.g. television in Luxembourgish is either *Färensinn* (< German *Fernsehen*) or *Televisioun* (< French *télévision*). These terms may be interchangeable, but as French generally has higher prestige than German the choice of loans may be sociolinguistically marked. This applies even to pronunciation: for instance, where both French and German have almost identical words – *différence* and *Differenz* – the choice of [diferãs] or [difərɛnts] is sociolinguistically significant (see Kramer 1984).

As we have seen (8.3.4), the peculiar cultural and political circumstances of South Tyrol have made native intellectuals highly sensitive to the undermining of the German language in their community, especially through *Überfremdung*, the infiltration of foreign (i.e. Italian) features. Perhaps because most South Tyroleans are generally aware of the loan forms in their vocabulary, borrowings appear far less in writing than in speech (Moser and Putzer 1980: 168). In an extensive study of four local German-language newspapers, Pernstich (1982) found surprisingly few loan forms; most of these were officialese, such as *Urbanistik* (from *urbanistica* and meaning *Raumordnung, Städtebau*, 'town planning'). It is in this domain too that transfer in speech is most common, even where German equivalents are available, as officials are necessarily confronted with the Italian forms in their daily business. However, there are other reasons, both linguistic and extralinguistic, for the variable use of loan forms. Putzer (1982: 152), for example, proposes the following linguistic reasons for the preference of loans:

(1) economy: *targa* (=car registration number) is shorter than *Kennzeichen*.
(2) simplicity/lack of competition: while *targa* actually has about twelve German equivalents, *Patent* (=driving licence) competes only with *Führerschein*, so that both tend to be used equally.
(3) transparent similarity to the Italian form: South Tyroleans inevitably meet *carta d'identità* very frequently and therefore often choose *Identitätskarte* rather than *Personalausweis*.

There may also be correlations between social factors and the use of loan forms: educated city-dwellers for instance appear to use fewer than their less well educated rural counterparts. Pernstich (1984: 134) also points out the impossibility of translating certain concepts that are peculiar to the contact culture, suggesting for instance that *assenteismo* (absenteeism) is an alien notion to the German-speaker.

Similar types of lexical transfer, mainly from French but also to some extent from Dutch, may be found in the language of Belgium's only German-language paper, the *Grenz-Echo* (see Nelde 1974). Some neologisms are directly translated from French and are preferred, even though there are existing German equivalents, as they designate specifically Belgian institutions: e.g. educational terms like *Normalschule* (< *école normale*, for *Pädagogische Hochschule*, 'teacher training college'). And while some are comprehensible to Germans, e.g. *Parkingplatz*, others are not: e.g. *verbessertes Brot* (< *pain amélioré*, meaning bread with certain added ingredients). Finally, we might note that examples of the same phenomena are to be found in the German-language section of the Strasbourg daily *Le Nouvel Alsacien* (see Becker-Dombrowski 1981).

### 8.5.2 Morphological/syntactic transfer

Some of the examples commonly discussed under this heading may be the result of transfer but could also be explained in terms of generalization or simplification of rules: for example, the reduction in the number of genders and the use of main clause word order in subordinate clauses. Other examples however do seem to be directly attributable to the influence of the second language and it is interesting that the same types of feature are again found in different contact areas.

(1)  Interrogative pronouns – invariable in standard German, variable in French and in Belgian German:
     standard: *Welches*
     Belgian: *Welcher* } *ist der längste Fluß Deutschlands?*

(2)  Position of reflexive and object pronouns:
     *Wir müssen feststellen, daß eine präzise Definition uns fehlt* (standard German would normally have the *uns* immediately after *daß*).

(3)  Prepositions:
     *telefonieren an die Firma* (< 'à la firme') for *mit*
     *Auskünfte auf Verabredungen* (< 'informations sur rendez-vous') for *über*

(4)  Certain participial constructions – much more common in French than in standard German:

*Sie ohrfeigte ihren Gatten ihm seine Untreue vorwerfend* (< 'en lui rapprochant son infidélité') for *Sie ohrfeigte ihren Gatten, indem sie ihm seine Untreue vorwarf.*

(Examples (1) and (2) from Kern 1980; (3) from Nelde 1974; (4) from Becker-Dombrowski 1981.)

In addition to this type of transfer, examples have also been quoted of elaborate code-mixing involving morphological and syntactic accommodation of loan forms: 'Sôt, Monsieur le Vicaire, soll ich d'Ciergen alluméieren?' (Fischer 1979: 90).

## 8.6 German in contact with English

So far in this chapter we have discussed contact between German and other languages arising because areas where those languages are spoken border on and overlap German-speaking territory. Throughout its recorded history, however, German has been in contact with other languages because speakers of those languages occupied powerful positions in German-speaking territories or in territories whose influence was strongly felt in the German-speaking area. Their languages hence had high prestige. This contact has led to large-scale borrowing by German of vocabulary from the languages of high prestige. Certain parallel morphological and syntactic developments in German and these languages may also be due to contact, but this is less certain; borrowed vocabulary is by far the clearest result of contact.

As well as being the recipient of such influence, German has also been a language of prestige in some neighbouring language areas, notably in Scandinavia, and rather less obviously in Hungary and Slavonic-speaking areas (see 2.1.2).

### 8.6.1 English influence in context

At the time of the Roman Empire the precursor of German, the various West Germanic dialects or languages, was in contact with the Latin of the Romans. Long after Latin had ceased to be used as an everyday spoken language, it remained the international language of administration and learning, and was a language of administration even within German-speaking areas. This use of Latin continued until the nineteenth century in German-speaking Europe, and is maintained to this day by the Roman Catholic church. It has led to the position of Latin as an important source of vocabulary, mostly learned, in German, in which Latin words, or Latin roots combined to form new words, are taken into German, following certain conventional patterns. From its revival in the Renaissance, starting in the late fifteenth century, Greek was added to Latin as a source of learned vocabulary. Italian also has influenced German to some extent, particularly since the Renaissance, as an international language, mostly in music and the visual arts.

From the seventeenth century to the early twentieth century, by far the most significant influence from a modern European language was from French, as a language of a powerful neighbouring state, as a fashionable language among the German aristocracy and as an international means of communication. And then, from the eighteenth century, there has been a notable and growing influence of English, traceable first to the political and economic power of Britain, and its advanced science and technology, and then, in the present century, to the world-wide dominance, in many fields, of the United States. British English continues to be influential in the area of sport.

Since 1945 English – as the language of the United States, but also by virtue of its enormous geographical spread and its large number of native-speakers – has become the pre-eminent international language, and hence has great prestige for German-speakers, particularly in the Federal Republic, but also in the GDR, as in other eastern bloc countries. This prestige is reinforced in the Federal Republic by the country's close ties with Britain and the USA in NATO, and by the presence in the country of large numbers of British and American troops. There is a parallel, though smaller, influence of Russian on German in the GDR, some of which is then passed on to western German (see 5.7.2).

It is misleading to think that it is German alone which has been subject to these foreign influences: in the Middle Ages western and central European languages were generally subject to Latin influence, French influence was generally dominant in the seventeenth and eighteenth centuries, and at the present western European languages, including British English, are virtually all heavily influenced by American English. As Braun (1987: 203–4) notes, there is a convergence in these languages in certain areas of vocabulary which arises in two ways: firstly, they have all borrowed from the languages which were particularly prestigious at certain periods, but, secondly, they all have a stock of (chiefly learned) vocabulary composed of roots taken ultimately from Latin and Greek. This learned vocabulary passes freely from one language to another, being modified in certain conventional ways in each language, and it is not always easy, or even particularly important, to determine which modern language first used the term. Hence English 'telegram', French *télé-gramme* and German *Telegramm* are all composed of the same, ultimately Greek, roots. The fact that the word was first coined in English and then passed through French into German cannot be detected from its form; it could equally well have been coined in French or German. In fact such learned coinages from Latin or Greek are more often coined in French or English than in German, these languages having a stronger tradition of such coinage than has German. Nevertheless German does possess such a tradition, and such words are therefore not in any clear sense borrowings from either French or English into German. Such Latin or Greek coinages are often called *Fremdwörter* (foreign words) in modern German, but the term makes little sense; it is true that they often have a stress pattern different from that of native German words, but they have vowel and consonant phonemes identical to those of native German words, unlike some of the loans from English which we shall discuss below (see Von Polenz 1978: 160–4, and also 2.1.2 above).

The modern influence of English on German has clearly increased the use of such Latin- and Greek-based internationalisms in German, but we shall ignore them in the following discussion, and concentrate on lexicon obviously borrowed from English. This includes English lexicon which may ultimately be of Latin or Greek origin, but whose passage through English is clear. *Computer*, from Latin roots, is an excellent example here: in German it has the pronunciation /kɔm'pjuːtɐ/, clearly derived from English, and the suffix *-er*, which German does not normally add to roots of Latin origin. A direct German coinage from the Latin elements found in *Computer* would probably have been *\*Komputator* /kɔmpu'taːtɔɐ/.

The casual observer might possibly imagine that English influence in modern German was restricted to the Federal Republic, Austria and Switzerland, which belong economically to the West, but this would be mistaken; as we have seen, English is a world-wide language of learning and communication, being used in the eastern bloc too, and hence GDR German also has English loans, some even having reached GDR German through Russian (see 5.7.2). English loans also reach the GDR through contacts with West Germans, or through West German television.

### 8.6.2 Examples of English influence on German

We shall divide examples of English influence on the lexicon of modern German into loan words (*Lehnwörter*), loan formations (*Lehnbildungen*) and **semantic loans** (*Lehnbedeutungen*), though more detailed classifications are often used (see Wells 1985: 272–8).

In the case of semantic loans, a meaning has, as it were, been borrowed and added to an already existing German word; or we could say that an existing German word has been extended in meaning under the influence of an English word of similar meaning. For example, German *lieben* (love) used to refer only to strong emotional attachments, and could not mean 'to like/love (to do something)' as can the English 'love', as in 'I love swimming'. Now, however, sentences such as *Schwimmen liebe ich* (I love swimming) are possible in German. In cases like this it is often impossible to prove conclusively that a semantic loan has taken place: the German word might have been extended in meaning, as often happens, independently of any foreign influence. Some semantic loans are however clearly traceable; *feuern*, originally meaning 'to fire (a gun), to heat' or 'to light', would surely not have acquired its additional meaning of 'to sack' or 'to fire (someone from a job)' without the influence of (American) English 'to fire'.

The term 'loan formation' is used in cases where the German word is clearly of native origin, but where it is strongly influenced by a foreign word, or is even an obvious part-for-part translation of a foreign word (loan translation, *Lehnübersetzung*). In practice the process of loan formation is very clear in some cases, but in others it is hard to separate from semantic loans. For example, it seems clear that *Fußball* is a loan translation of 'football', but is *Abseits* (noun) a loan translation of 'offside' (in football) or is it a case of semantic loan where an existing German adverb *abseits* (to one side, remote) has been extended in meaning and has changed word class? As an example of a loan formation which is not a loan translation we can cite *Wolkenkratzer* (skyscraper), literally 'cloudscraper'.

Direct borrowings are usually easier to spot, although they present a wide range of degrees of assimilation to German. There are loans which are relatively unassimilated, which means that German-speakers are clearly aware of their foreignness, and attempt to pronounce them as they would be pronounced in English. Such words retain the English spelling. Often such words are, almost by definition, used only by people with a reasonable knowledge of English, and may have a rather ephemeral existence in German. Examples of these can be found copiously in the press and in advertising, the main channels for English words entering German. A recent copy of the West Berlin magazine *Zitty* (12/1988) revealed, for example, in a few moments' browsing, *Statement, Dinner for two, Stretch, second hand, Window* and many others, none of these being found in a good, quite large, up-to-date German–German dictionary (*Wahrig*).

If English loans gain greater currency, and pass to people with less knowledge of English, then they are certain to be assimilated to some degree to the German sound system. For example *Job*, usually meaning 'job' in the sense of 'employment', and rather informal in style, is pronounced /dʒɔb/, as in English, by those with very good English pronunciation. However, it is now a very common noun, being used by people with a minimal knowledge of English, and is usually pronounced /dʒɔp/, reflecting the absence, in most varieties of German, of the voiced obstruent /b/ at the end of a word. A further change, to /tʃɔp/, replacing the voiced obstruent cluster /dʒ/, not found in German, with the voiceless /tʃ/, is also very common.

Words which are well assimilated into German may acquire a German spelling which reflects their pronunciation better, for example *Streik* meaning 'strike' in the sense of 'industrial action'. Alternatively they may be pronounced using German letter values for the English spelling: for example *Sport* is now usually pronounced /ʃpɔɐt/, where English has /spɔːt/. They may also acquire a stress pattern unlike that of the English word. For example, English 'boycott' is pronounced with stress on the first syllable, while German *Boykott* has stress on the second; this is not the most common stress pattern found in words of native German origin, but is common in Latin and Greek borrowings (see 2.1.2). This word, like some others, is also assimilated to German **derivational morphology**, and can be used to form a corresponding verb *boykottieren*, using the common verb-forming suffix *-ieren* (ultimately partly of Latin origin, but now used to form verbs such as *hausieren*, *gastieren* and *funktionieren* from native German and loan words alike).

It might be assumed that this wealth of words from English in German might make German easier to understand for English-speakers, but this is, sadly, very often not the case. Some of the above examples have shown why this might be so. It is, simply, that English words (or any other foreign words) entering another language, provided they are not utterly ephemeral, become part of that language, and acquire pronunciations, grammatical characteristics and meanings which may distance them from the source word even beyond recognition.

In pronunciation, even words which seem little changed may reveal confusing differences. For example, German-speakers usually fail to differentiate the English phonemes /æ/ and /ɛ/ (as in 'bad' and 'bed'), pronouncing both more or less as /ɛ/, and apply the pronunciation rule 'a' = /ɛ/ in words of English origin. Hence, the German words *Match* and *Test*, both from English, contain the same vowel (/ɛ/), a potential source of confusion for English-speakers. Other common substitutions are /tʃ/ for English /dʒ/, and voiceless for voiced obstruents word finally (e.g. /p/ and /s/ for /b/ and /z/) noted above. These substitutions can make words of English origin totally unrecognizable to English-speakers: for example *Jazz*, pronounced /tʃɛs/, may sound not at all similar to the English /dʒæz/, and will, in fact, sound almost exactly like 'chess', /tʃɛs/.

Even if an English loan in German is close in meaning to its English source, there is likely to be some difference, if only a fairly small stylistic one. This can be explained by examining the motives of German-speakers in borrowing English words. They may take English words to describe new artefacts or concepts, hitherto not known or not clearly designated in German-speaking areas, such as *Software* in computing terminology; such loan words may be close in meaning to the originals. However, many others are taken, not because German lacks a term, but merely because of the prestige of English, reflecting the dominance of English-speakers, particularly Americans, in so many spheres; such loans are borrowed because the words share in the prestige of the language, their first users in German being able to impress others with their knowledge of English. These words add to the objects designated an aura of smartness and modernity. An excellent example is the German word *Shop* which, in contrast to the very general meaning of its English source, means 'a smart, expensive shop, usually small, and often selling clothes', the kind of shop which in English is often called a 'boutique', using, interestingly, a French loan-word.

Once an English loan is assimilated into German, it can acquire new meanings, as can any word of a language, and these may remove it so far in meaning from its English source as to make it quite incomprehensible to an English-speaker. An example is *Splitting* which means, among other things, 'tax system in which husband and wife each pay income tax on half of their total combined income', a meaning quite unknown for the source word in English.

An even greater departure from the English source is seen in '**pseudo-transfers**' (*Scheinentlehnungen*), which are compound words which appear to be of English origin, but which in fact do not exist in English. Examples are *Dreßman* (male model) and *Showmaster* (presenter of a television programme), which are actually German compound nouns composed of elements borrowed from English.

Where words of English origin are used with the same meaning as their English sources, we might imagine that there would be no barriers to their correct use by English-speaking learners of German, but again this would be a mistaken view. A clear majority of new words in German are nouns (80.4 per cent in one sample examined in Braun 1987: 180) and nouns in German must, of course, be assigned a grammatical gender, while gender distinctions in English are very limited. In order to use the English loan correctly in German, the English-speaker has to know and remember its grammatical gender, which is no mean feat: rules of gender assignment in German are so complex as to be virtually unusable by the learner of the language, rote-learning often being the only solution. However, the learner may be comforted to know that this poses problems for German-speakers as well, particularly in words of recent foreign origin (see Carstensen 1980: 74–5).

## Further reading

Weinreich (1953) remains the classic text on languages in contact. Other useful publications include Appel and Muysken (1987), Wardhaugh (1987), and the collections of articles in Nelde (1980), Ureland (1979, 1981) and Hinderling (1986). On the specific contact situations discussed here, see for Belgium Nelde (1979a, 1979b) and McRae (1986); for Luxembourg Hoffmann (1979) and Verdoodt (1968); for Alsace-Lorraine Hoffmeister (1977) and Hartweg (1981); for South Tyrol Egger (1977), Bettelheim and Benedikter (1982) and Kramer (1986); for Schleswig Walker (1987); and for south-east Austria Gumperz (1977, 1982) and Gal (1979).

An interesting historical account of the influence of English on German is Von Polenz (1978: 139–48). The standard work on post-war American influence is Carstensen and Galinski (1975). For the contemporary situation see Braun (1987: 179–83, 190–207), Clyne (1984: Ch. 5) and the articles collected in Viereck (1980).

# 9    Conclusions and prospects

Many books dealing with sociolinguistics draw on data from many languages and paint a broad canvas. This is sometimes necessary where the intention is to give a comprehensive account of all the phenomena one might want to include under the general label sociolinguistics and of course it has the added bonus of offering the reader an insight, or at least a glimpse, into a fascinating range of speech communities throughout the world. Above all this approach helps to transmit a sense of how complex and multi-faceted the subject is, but in doing so it tends to leave the reader feeling rather helpless in the face of a mass of information and ideas gleaned from often unrelated sources. It is difficult to see the wood for the trees. For this reason, we have tried in this book to take things the other way round by investigating just one language and seeing how it might exemplify interesting sociolinguistic issues that are also of relevance to other languages. We hope that this has still allowed us to make the complexity of the subject apparent while at the same time making the discussion of it more focussed.

Our point of departure was our perception of two contrasting approaches to the study of the interaction between language and society. Being schooled in the English-speaking tradition of sociolinguistics, with its strong focus on the study of variation, we were struck by the relative unpopularity of this approach in the German-speaking countries, where traditional dialectology remains firmly entrenched. This book has thus partly been an attempt to bridge what we see as a gap in the study of German language and society by placing German sociolinguistic phenomena within the sociolinguistic framework familiar in English-speaking countries.

In doing this, we may have given the impression that the study of language and society as previously practised in German-speaking countries was in some sense inadequate and that it needed to be informed by the insights of schools of thought current in English-speaking countries. This is probably true in certain respects. For instance, despite the recent

262

growth in the study of urban speech in German-speaking countries, far less is still known about this than in, say, Britain or the United States. Where towns were considered at all in earlier linguistic studies, it was either in the form of non-empirical, informal 'portraits' or as a means of accounting for the development of the standard written variety or for the spread of individual linguistic items (see Besch and Mattheier 1985a: 11; Besch 1981: 241). The existence of urban varieties (*Stadtsprachen*) as such was acknowledged but largely taken for granted and rarely considered either accessible to or worthy of systematic investigation. As we hope to have shown (in Chapters 4 and 5 especially), this is in fact not only possible but important in an increasingly urbanized society.

On the other hand, the more sociologically oriented areas of socio-linguistics, such as language in education or multilingualism and language contact, do not overlap to such an extent with the concerns of traditional dialectology and have generated considerable interest in the German-speaking countries. In some of these areas, investigators working within the relatively new tradition of German sociolinguistics have had more to say than their English-speaking counterparts. For example, although we are critical of some of the work of Ulrich Ammon (see Chapter 6, passim), one cannot read a book like Ammon (1977) without being struck by its breadth of interest; language is related to the economic situation, the ideology and the culture of its speakers in a way which in the work of English-speaking writers is found only quite outside linguistics, typically in the sociology of culture, as in the work of writers like Richard Hoggart and Raymond Williams (see, for example, Williams 1976).

More generally, German-language sociolinguistics has shown detailed interest in topics such as language and politics, language and ideology, and language in institutional settings, areas which, in English-speaking countries, have roused only sporadic interest among linguists, and which have been studied mainly within other academic disciplines, notably sociology.[1] So, while we would welcome more work on language variation from German-speaking linguists, we would equally welcome a greater interest in cultural, political, ideological and institutional contexts of language production from English-speaking linguists.

Although the study of these various aspects of language still tends to be rather rigidly compartmentalized, it is not inconceivable that a more comprehensive approach might develop if linguists working in these various traditions were more receptive to the insights and ideas of others. Indeed, proposals for broadening the scope of language study, albeit falling short of what we have in mind, have been made by both English-

---

[1] See Clyne (1984: Ch. 7) for a discussion of work in German in these areas.

and German-speaking linguists. Jack Chambers and Peter Trudgill conclude their book *Dialectology* (1980) with an appeal to their colleagues to combine the insights and methods of dialect geography, urban dialectology and human geography in the study of spatial and social variation in language. For this merger of disciplines they tentatively proposed the term 'geolinguistics'. More ambitiously, the German linguist Klaus Mattheier has called for a redefinition of dialectology incorporating dialect geography and pragmatic and sociological aspects of dialect study. This, together with the sociology of language and research into language learning and change, might be the basis of a 'new linguistics', for which he proposed the term '*Variationslinguistik*' (Mattheier 1980: 200). The two proposals are by no means identical and neither has, to our knowledge, been widely adopted. Nevertheless, they both constitute an attempt to break down barriers and open up the possibility of a less confined and more profound study of language and society.

In the end, the label we choose to attach to this wide-ranging discipline is of no great consequence. The essential thing is that it enables us to adopt a very open attitude to the study of language, for by extending the boundaries of what is considered relevant and significant we reduce the risk of becoming caught up in demarcation or terminological disputes and increase the likelihood of making a real contribution to our understanding of human societies. Many sociolinguistic questions remain to be asked and answered, about German as about all natural languages, and we should always be prepared to consider new ways of tackling them.

# Appendix: **Phonetic symbols**

Transcriptions in the text are either phonemic, enclosed in slanting lines (/ /), or **sub-phonemic**, allophonic or phonetic, enclosed in square brackets ([ ]) (see Glossary). In the absence of detailed phonological analyses of all of the varieties of German discussed, the precise status of many transcriptions given is not entirely clear.

Examples in the table are taken from the RP accent in English, the *Deutsche Hochlautung* (*DH*) accent in German. Where no examples occur in these accents, examples from other accents are given in brackets. In cases where no sound occurs in English similar to a given German sound, an example from French may be given in brackets.

N.B. RP and *DH* sounds transcribed with the same symbol are in fact rarely identical in pronunciation.

| Symbol | Description of sound | British English examples | German examples |
|---|---|---|---|
| a | **open central** lax short vowel | (northern or western p*a*t) | ʹ K*a*tze |
| aː | open central tense long vowel | (Yorkshire c*a*rt) | V*a*ter |
| ɑ | open back lax short vowel | (some Scots p*a*t) | (some southern K*a*tze) |
| ɑː | open back tense long vowel | f*a*ther | (some southern V*a*ter) |
| æ | **half-open** to open front lax short vowel | p*a*t | |
| ɑ̃ː | open back tense long nasalized vowel | (French ch*a*nce) | some *DH* pronunciations Ch*a*nce |

265

| ai | diphthong rising from open central towards **close** front position | t*i*de | Z*ei*t |
|----|----|----|----|
| au | diphthong rising from open central towards close back position | (some northern h*ou*se); approx. RP h*ou*se | H*au*s |
| ɑu | diphthong rising from open back towards close back position | h*ou*se | (many accents H*au*s); approx. *DH* H*au*s |
| ɐ | half-open central lax short vowel | | Butt*er* |
| ɐ̯ | half-open central non-syllabic vowel | | Pfe*r*d |
| b | voiced lenis bilabial stop | ru*bb*er | Ro*bb*e |
| b̥ | voiceless lenis bilabial stop | | (many central and southern accents Ra*pp*en) |
| ç | voiceless fortis palatal fricative | (some RP pronunciations *h*ue) | i*ch* |
| d | voiced lenis alveolar stop | ru*dd*er | Kla*dd*e |
| d̥ | voiceless lenis alveolar stop | | (many central and southern accents Ra*tt*e) |
| ð | voiced lenis dental fricative | lea*th*er | |
| e | **half-close** front tense short vowel | (French *été*) | l*e*bendig |
| e: | half-close front tense long vowel | (many accents, particularly Northern, Scottish, Welsh b*ay*) | S*ee* |

| ɛ | half-open front lax short vowel | b*e*d | B*e*tt |
| ə | half-open to half-close central lax short vowel | Afric*a*, butt*er* | bitt*e* |
| əi | diphthong rising from half-close central towards close front position | (many accents, particularly Midland b*ee*) | (North Bavarian dialect l*i*eb) |
| əu | diphthong rising from half-close central towards close back position | b*oa*t | (North Bavarian dialect g*u*t) |
| f | voiceless fortis labiodental fricative | *f*oot | *F*uß |
| g | voiced lenis velar stop | la*gg*ing | Ba*gg*er |
| g̥ | voiceless lenis velar stop | | (many central and southern accents ba*ck*en) |
| ɣ | voiced lenis velar fricative | | (some northern Ta*g*e) |
| ɣ̥ | voiceless lenis velar fricative | | (many central and southern accents la*ch*en) |
| h | voiceless glottal fricative | *h*ouse | *H*aus |
| i | close front tense short vowel | (French *i*ci) | *i*deal |
| iː | close front tense long vowel | approx. b*ea*t | b*i*eten |
| ɪ | close front lax short vowel (centralized) | p*i*t | b*i*tte |

| | | | |
|---|---|---|---|
| iə | diphthong falling from close front towards central position | approx. h*ere* | (many southern dialects l*ie*b) |
| j | voiced lenis palatal fricative or approximant | *y*es (approximant) | *j*a (approximant or fricative) |
| j̊ | voiceless lenis palatal fricative | | (many central and southern accents wei*ch*en) |
| k | voiceless fortis velar stop | ba*ck* | ba*ck*en |
| kʰ | voiceless fortis aspirated velar stop | *c*ar | *K*atze |
| l | alveolar lateral | *l*eap | *l*ieb |
| ḷ | syllabic alveolar lateral | bott*le* | Mitt*el* |
| m | bilabial nasal | *m*other | *M*utter |
| m̩ | syllabic bilabial nasal | bott*om* | At*em* |
| n | alveolar nasal | *n*o | *n*ein |
| n̩ | syllabic alveolar nasal | butt*on* | biet*en* |
| oː | half-close back tense long vowel | (many accents, particularly Northern, Scottish, Welsh b*oa*t) | B*oo*t |
| ɔ | half-open back lax short vowel | p*o*t | Sch*o*tte |
| ɔː | half-open back tense long vowel | *caugh*t | (Middle Bavarian dialect G*a*st) |
| ɔ̃ː | half-open back tense nasalized vowel | (French b*on*) | Some *DH* pronunciations B*on* |

*Phonetic symbols*

| | | | |
|---|---|---|---|
| øː | half-close front rounded tense long vowel | (approx. French *jeu*) | sch*ö*n |
| œ | half-open front rounded lax short vowel | (French b*œu*f) | k*ö*nnen |
| ɔi | diphthong rising from half-open back towards close front position | b*oy* | Some *DH* pronunciations n*eu* |
| ɔy | diphthong rising from half-open back towards close front rounded position | approx. b*oy* | n*eu* |
| p | voiceless fortis bilabial stop | li*p* | Li*pp*e |
| pʰ | voiceless fortis aspirated bilabial stop | *p*it | *P*eter |
| r | alveolar trill (in phonemic transcriptions also used for uvular trill [ʀ] | (Scots *r*ed) (uvular trill approx. French *r*ouge) | *r*ot (in *DH* uvular pronunciation dominates) |
| s | voiceless fortis alveolar fricative | *s*ea | ha*ss*en |
| ʃ | voiceless fortis palato-alveolar fricative | fi*sh* | Fi*sch* |
| ç | voiceless alveo-palatal fricative (fortis or lenis) | | (some central accents Fi*sch*, i*ch*) |
| t | voiceless fortis alveolar stop | bi*t* | bi*tt*e |
| tʰ | voiceless fortis aspirated alveolar stop | *t*ea | *T*ee |

| | | | |
|---|---|---|---|
| θ | voiceless fortis dental fricative | *th*in | |
| u | close back tense short vowel | (approx. French c*ou*p) | *U*ran |
| uː | close back tense long vowel | approx. b*oo*t | F*u*ß |
| ʊ | close back lax short vowel (centralized) | approx. p*u*t | B*u*tter |
| uə | diphthong falling from close back towards central position | approx. p*oor* (for older RP speakers, and some northern accents) | (many southern dialects g*u*t) |
| v | voiced lenis labio-dental fricative or approximant | *v*ine (fricative) | *W*ein (fricative or approximant) |
| v̥ | voiceless lenis labio-dental fricative | | (many central and southern accents F*u*ß) |
| x | voiceless fortis velar fricative | (Scots lo*ch*) | Ba*ch* |
| yː | close front rounded tense long vowel | (approx. French d*u*) | H*ü*te |
| Y | close front rounded lax short vowel (centralized) | | H*ü*tte |
| yə | diphthong falling from close front rounded to central position | | (some southern dialects m*ü*de) |
| z | voiced lenis alveolar fricative | buz*z*ing | Ha*s*e |
| z̥ | voiceless lenis alveolar fricative | | (many central and southern accents ha*ss*en) |

ʒ  voiced lenis palato-  meaʒure  Garage
alveolar fricative

ʒ̊  voiceless lenis  (many central and
palato-alveolar  southern accents
fricative  Fiʒche)

# Glossary

**accent**   One of the various pronunciations current in a language. Accents differ from each other in relatively systematic and relatively trivial details of pronunciation. Larger or less systematic pronunciation differences are described, along with grammatical and lexical differences, as dialect differences.

**accusative**   See **cases**.

**affricate**   A sequence of a stop sound followed by a fricative sound, both sounds being articulated in the same area of the mouth (e.g. [tʃ]).

**agglutinative language**   Language in which grammatical relationships are expressed by the forms of words, and where words are formed by the combination of elements (morphemes) in such a way that these individual components remain clearly identifiable.

**allophone** (adj. **allophonic**)   A variant of a **phoneme** in a particular position in a word.

*Althochdeutsch*   See **Old High German**.

*Altniederdeutsch*   See **Old Low German**.

*Altsächsisch*   See **Old Saxon**.

**alveolar sound**   Sound articulated with the tip or blade of the tongue close to or touching the alveoli or tooth-ridge behind the top teeth (e.g. English or German [t]).

**alveo-palatal sound**   See **palato-alveolar sound**.

*Amtssprache*   A language that has official status in a particular country and is used in administration, education and other areas of public life.

**analytic(al) language**   See **isolating language**.

**approximant**   A sound in the production of which articulators do not make contact, i.e. vowels and certain consonants (e.g. English [j]).

**aspirated** or **aspirate consonants**   Consonants followed by a strong release of breath, like an [h] sound (e.g. [pʰ]).

*Ausbaudialekt*   A traditional dialect (or group of dialects) whose range of functions has been extended so that it is spoken in many domains over a wide geographical area.

*Ausbausprache*   A language variety that has developed both spoken and written forms that can be used for most purposes.

**back vowel**   Vowel produced with the tongue towards the back of the mouth (e.g. [uː]).

**Benrath Line**   Line dividing Low German from High German (Middle German) dialects. See Map 3.5.

272

**bilingualism** Many types have been identified but a basic distinction is between individual (one person's ability to speak two or more languages) and societal (the existence in one speech community of two or more languages).

**bundle of isoglosses** A number of **isoglosses** running roughly parallel to each other within a relatively narrow band.

**cases** Different forms of nouns, adjectives, articles and pronouns used to show the grammatical functions of the words concerned. German has nominative, accusative, genitive and dative cases; some non-standard varieties have an oblique case, uniting the functions of accusative and dative (e.g. *der Mann* nominative: subject of clause; *den Mann* accusative: (*inter alia*) direct object of clause; *des Mannes* genitive: (*inter alia*) possession; *dem Mann(e)* dative: (*inter alia*) indirect object of clause). (See 5.5.2.)

**central vowel** Vowel produced with the tongue in the centre of the mouth (e.g. [ə]).

**chancery language** See *Kanzleisprache*.

**close vowel** Vowel produced with the tongue high in the mouth (e.g. [iː]).

**code-mixing** Spontaneous interspersing of forms from one variety into another.

**code-shifting** A move from one variety towards another in the course of an utterance; less abrupt and less categorical than **code-switching**.

**code-switching** Abrupt switch from one variety to another, usually to signal a change in the speech situation (topic, purpose, etc.).

**cognate** (adj.) Referring to a linguistic form which is historically derived from the same source as another linguistic form (e.g. Eng. 'house' and Ger. *Haus* are cognate).

**colloquial non-standard speech/language** (Ger.: *dialektnahe Umgangssprache*) Forms of colloquial speech which are relatively close to traditional dialects. Modern or urban dialects.

**colloquial speech** (Ger.: *Umgangssprache*) Speech which can be described neither as the formal standard variety nor as traditional dialect.

**colloquial standard speech/language** (Ger.: *standardnahe Umgangssprache*) Forms of colloquial speech which are relatively close to the formal standard variety. Informal standard speech.

**constraint** Any factor (linguistic or non-linguistic) that affects or restricts the application of a linguistic rule.

**copula** A verb whose main function is to link two elements of a sentence, especially subject and complement (e.g. be, look: she *is* a writer, you *look* tired).

**creole language** A language which has developed out of a pidgin language by expanding its structural and stylistic range to reach a level of complexity comparable with other languages, and which has become the mother tongue of a speech community. A pidgin language is a language with markedly reduced grammatical structure, lexicon and stylistic range, which is no one's mother tongue.

**dative** See **cases**.

**dental sound** One articulated with the tip of the tongue touching the teeth (e.g. [θ]).

**derivational morphology** Process of formation of one word from another (e.g. the verb *boykottieren* from the noun *Boykott*).

***deutsche Hochlautung (DH)*** The prestige pronunciation (accent) of standard German.

**devoiced sounds**   Sounds similar to voiced sounds, but in which some or all of the vocal cord vibration does not occur.

**devoicing**   Absence, in some varieties, of some or all of the vocal cord vibration in a sound which in other varieties is voiced.

***DH***   See *deutsche Hochlautung*.

**diachronic**   From the point of view of historical development.

**dialect** (the English term)   Any socially or regionally determined variety of a language which differs from other socially or regionally determined varieties in grammar or lexicon, or in phonology, where the phonological differences are apparently unsystematic or subjectively large. We usually refer to the standard dialect as the standard variety, contrary to some other usage.

**dialect continuum**   Area in which the traditional dialect speech of each locality differs slightly from that of the next locality, irrespective of standard language boundaries (e.g. the Dutch–German dialect continuum).

***Dialekt***   Generally the same as *Mundart* and meaning traditional rural dialect, but sometimes used as a label for a group of *Mundarten* (in our terms both are referred to as 'traditional dialect').

***dialektnahe Umgangssprache***   See **colloquial non-standard speech**.

**diglossia**   There are several different definitions but this basically refers to the use in one speech community of two varieties with complementary functions.

**diminutive**   Noun in German ending in a diminutive suffix (standard German *-chen* or *-lein*). The suffix is conventionally described as having the meaning 'small', but it actually can have other functions, such as marking the entire sentence or utterance as informal.

**diphthong**   Vowel sound in which there is a perceptible change in quality during the production of the sound, caused by a movement of the tongue. A diphthong can alternatively be seen as a sequence of two vowel sounds which functions as a single sound in the language in question (e.g. English or German [ai]). Cf. **monophthong**.

**diphthongization**   Change in articulation of a **monophthong** whereby it becomes a diphthong.

**domain**   A specified context of activity: e.g. work, school, home.

***Einheitssprache***   See **formal standard language**.

**elaborated code**   Language varieties not sharing the limitations of **restricted code**.

**exoglossia**   The use of a language in a speech community in which there are no native speakers of that language.

**final** (adj.), **finally** (adv.)   Referring to the end of a word.

**first sound shift**   See **Germanic sound shift**.

**Foreigner Talk (FT)**   A simplified and reduced variety of a language used by native-speakers to people assumed to have incomplete competence in the language or to foreigners in general.

**formal standard language/speech/variety**   The standard variety in formal registers. The German terms which are normally translated into English as 'standard German' (i.e. *Standardsprache, Einheitssprache, Literatursprache, Hochsprache*) usually designate the formal standard variety rather than all the registers of the standard variety.

**fortis** (adj.)   Relatively strongly articulated.

**fricative consonants**   Consonants produced by forcing air through a narrow gap in the vocal tract with audible friction (e.g. [f] [z]).

**front vowel**   Vowel produced with the tongue towards the front of the mouth (e.g. [iː]).

**functional load**   The extent to which a linguistic distinction is used in a language (e.g. a phonological distinction has a high functional load if it is used to contrast a large number of word pairs).

**genitive**   See **cases**.

**Germanic languages**   Languages belonging to the sub-family of Indo-European which includes German, Dutch, English and the Scandinavian languages. (See Fig. 2.1.)

**Germanic sound shift**   Radical shift in the articulation of most of the consonants in the precursor of the Germanic languages. See Table 2.1.

**Germersheim Line**   Line dividing Middle German from Upper German dialects. See Map 3.5.

**given information**   Information which has already been imparted to the listener or reader.

**Grimm's Law**   Description by Jacob Grimm of the **Germanic** and **High German sound shifts**.

**half-close vowel**   Vowel produced with the tongue a little below the close position (e.g. [eː]).

**half-open vowel**   Vowel produced with the tongue a little above the open position (e.g. [ɛ]).

**High German** (Ger.: *Hochdeutsch*)   The non-technical·term for formal standard German.

**High German dialects** (Ger.: *Hochdeutsche Dialekte*)   Central and southern dialects of German, including those spoken in Austria and Switzerland. Usually divided into Middle German and Upper German. The standard variety of German derives largely from High German dialects, and is often known as High German (*Hochdeutsch*).

**High German sound shift**   Radical shift in the pronunciation of many of the consonants in the precursor of the HIgh German dialects. See Table 2.2.

**high vowel**   See **close vowel**.

*Hochdeutsch*   See **High German**.

*Hochdeutsche Dialekte*   See **High German dialects**.

*Hochsprache*   See **formal standard language**.

**implicational scaling**   A technique of arranging data in such a way as to show a logical connection between individual facts, such that e.g. the use of linguistic feature A 'implies' or 'predicts' the use of feature B.

**indicative**   **Mood** of the verb found in most types of sentences. In German indicatives are used in most statements and questions.

**Indo-European (IE) languages**   Languages belonging to the major language family stretching from the Indian subcontinent through to northern Europe, and now to the Americas, southern Africa and Australasia through European colonization. The Indo-European family includes the Indo-Aryan (e.g. Hindustani), Slavonic (e.g. Russian), Greek, Italic (e.g. Latin) and Germanic sub-families. See Fig. 2.1.

**inflecting language**   Language in which grammatical relationships are expressed by the forms of words (inflections), and where the internal structure of words is of a complex nature, with grammatical elements (morphemes) not clearly identifiable.

Glossary

**inflection**  See **inflecting language**.
**inflectional** adj.)  Referring to **inflections**.
**Ingvaeonic** (adj.)  Referring to West Germanic dialects spoken in the North Sea coastal area, and to their speakers.
**initial** (adj.), **initially** (adv.)  Referring to the beginning of a word.
**isogloss**  A line on a map indicating the boundary of the usage of a particular linguistic feature.
**isolating** or **analytic(al) language**  Language in which grammatical relationships are expressed by word order rather than by the forms of words, and where the internal structure of words is simple, with, in the extreme case, all words consisting of indivisible grammatical elements (morphemes).
**jargon**  A variety created by and associated with a sub-culture group usually characterized by an inventive and frequently changing vocabulary.
*Kanzleisprache* (Eng.: chancery language)  Written language of administration in the civil service (*Kanzlei*) of a German city or principality in the medieval or early modern period.
**lateral consonant**  One in which air escapes over the sides of the tongue (e.g. [l]).
*Lehnbedeutung*  See **semantic loan**.
*Lehnbildung*  See **loan formation**.
*Lehnübersetzung*  See **loan translation**.
*Lehnwort*  See **loan word**.
**lenis** (adj.)  Relatively weakly articulated.
**lenition**  Change in the articulation of a sound whereby it becomes less strongly articulated.
*Letzebuergësch*  See **Luxembourgish**.
**lexicon** adj. **lexical**)  Vocabulary.
**lexis** (adj. **lexical**)  (Study of) vocabulary.
**liquid consonants**  Collective term for consonants of the lateral (e.g. [l]) and trill (e.g. [r]) types.
*Literatursprache*  See **formal standard language**.
**loan formation** (Ger.: *Lehnbildung*)  Word in one language which is composed of elements of native origin, but which has been influenced by a word in another language (e.g. German *Wolkenkratzer*, literally 'cloud-scraper', influenced by English 'skyscraper').
**loan translation** (Ger.: *Lehnübersetzung*)  Process whereby words in one language are translated part-for-part into another language (e.g. German *Ausdruck* from Latin *expressio*). Loan translation is a special case of loan formation.
**loan word** (Ger.: *Lehnwort*)  Word in one language which can clearly be seen to have been taken from another language (e.g. German *Computer*).
**Low German dialects** (Ger.: *Niderdeutsche Dialekte*)  Traditional northern German dialects.
**low vowel**  See **open vowel**.
**Luxembourgish** (locally *Letzebuergësch*)  Indigenous Germanic speech of Luxembourg.
**matched guise test**  A technique used in studies of attitudes to language variation. Informants are asked to judge the character or personality of a set of speakers by listening to their voices, two or more of which in fact belong to the same person; responses to these 'guises' can then be compared with each other.
**medial** (adj.)  Referring to any part of a word other than the beginning or the end, but used particularly to refer to a position between vowels.

**Middle German dialects** (Ger.: *Mitteldeutsche Dialekte*)   Subdivision of High German dialects crossing German-speaking territory from east to best in a central band.

**Middle High German** (Ger.: *Mittelhochdeutsch*)   Central and southern German of the high Middle Ages.

**Middle Low German** (Ger.: *Mittelniederdeutsch*)   Northern German of the high Middle Ages and the early modern period.

*Missingsch*   North German colloquial non-standard speech. Today used largely of some Hamburg varieties.

*Mitteldeutsche Dialekte*   See **Middle German dialects**.

*Mittelhochdeutsch*   See **Middle High German**.

*Mittelniederdeutsch*   See **Middle Low German**.

**modal verbs**   Verbs used, generally as auxiliaries, to convey notions of doubt, possibility, volition, duty, desire, permission, ability, obligation, intention, etc. (in German particularly *dürfen, können, mögen, müssen, sollen, wollen*).

**monophthong**   A simple vowel sound with no change in quality during its production (e.g. [iː]). Cf. **diphthong.**

**moods**   Contrasting sets of verb forms expressing, *inter alia*, different attitudes of the speaker towards the information conveyed.

**morphology** (adj. **morphological**)   (Study of) the internal grammatical structure of words.

*Mundart*   Generally the same as *Dialekt* but sometimes used only to refer to highly localized dialects (in our terms both are referred to as 'traditional dialect').

**nasal consonant**   Consonant articulated with air escaping through the nose (e.g. [n]).

*Nationalsprache*   A language that is officially recognized as having symbolic status in a particular country but not (necessarily) used in official domains.

**neogrammarian hypothesis**   The view proposed by followers of a nineteenth-century school of thought in comparative philology that sounds laws admitted no exceptions.

**neologism**   A newly coined word.

*Niederdeutsche Dialekte*   See **Low German dialects**.

**nominative**   See **cases**.

**North Germanic**   Scandinavian.

*Oberdeutsche Dialekte*   See **Upper German dialects**.

**oblique case**   See **cases**.

**obstruent**   Stop or fricative consonant.

**Old Church Slavonic**   Early Slavonic language, probably not very different from the (putative) parent language of the modern Slavonic languages.

**Old High German** (Ger.: *Althochdeutsch*)   Central and southern german of the early medieval period.

**Old Low German** (Ger.: *Altniederdeutsch*)   Northern German of the early medieval period.

**Old Saxon** (Ger.: *Altsächsisch*)   Virtually synonymous with Old Low German.

**open vowel**   Vowel produced with the tongue low in the mouth (e.g. [a]).

**palatal sound**   Sound articulated with the centre of the tongue close to or touching the hard palate (e.g. [ç]).

**palatalization**   Change in the articulation of a sound whereby it acquires a palatal articulation.

**palato-alveolar sound**   Sound articulated with the tip or blade of the tongue close to or touching the alveoli (see **alveolar sound**), and the centre of the tongue raised towards the hard palate (e.g. [ʃ]). **Alveo-palatal sounds** (e.g. the [ɕ] of some Middle German non-standard speech) are articulated slightly further back in the mouth.

**periphrastic**   Refers to the use of separate words rather than inflections to express a grammatical relationship (e.g. 'more pleasant' as opposed to 'pleasanter').

**perlocutionary effect**   An act that is performed when an utterance achieves a particular effect on the listener (e.g. threatening, insulting).

**phoneme** (adj. **phonemic**)   A minimal unit of the sound system of a language. A distinctive sound. Phonemes correspond approximately to the lay person's notion of the sounds of the language.

**phonetics** (adj. **phonetic**)   (Study of) the articulatory and acoustic properties of the sounds of language.

**phonology** (adj. **phonological**)   (Study of) the sound systems of languages.

**pidgin**   A reduced and simplified variety with no native-speakers that is used only for limited purposes of communication.

*Platt*   The common term for traditional dialects in the Low and Middle German areas.

**polysemy**   A term referring to a word that has two or more distinct meanings.

**preconsonantal** (adj.)   In front of a consonant.

**prescriptive grammar**   Grammar based upon what certain authorities prescribe and believe to be correct, rather than upon the observation of actual usage.

**prestige** (adj. **prestigious**)   A language variety may be said to enjoy overt prestige if it is associated with a socially and economically powerful group in a society and acts as a target model for speakers in less powerful groups. A variety is said to enjoy covert prestige if its speakers, although they have little power or status, still choose to identify strongly with it.

**preterite tense**   Simple past tense (the German tense is sometimes called 'imperfect') (e.g. *ich kaufte*, 'I bought'). (See 5.5.3.)

**Proto-Indo-European (PIE)**   Hypothesized Indo-European parent language or group of dialects from which the modern Indo-European languages have developed. May in fact have merely the status of a theoretical construct. See Fig. 2.1.

**pseudo-transfer** (Ger.: *Scheinentlehnung*)   Word in one languages which appears to originate from a second language but which is actually a coinage in the first language (e.g. German *Showmaster* apparently from English, but actually coined in German).

**Received Pronunciation (RP)**   The prestige accent of British (particularly English) English.

**register**   A language variety used in specific social situations or in particular types of text.

**repertoire**   The range of different varieties a speaker is able to use.

**restricted code**   Language varieties characterized by limited syntactic organization, limited vocabulary and small stylistic range.

*Rheinischer fächer*   See **Rhenish fan**.

Rhenish fan (Ger.: *Rheinischer Fächer*)   A group of isoglosses which fan out from the Benrath Line in the Hessen and Rhineland areas, and which reflect a gradual transition from typically High German forms in the south to typically Low German forms in the north. See Map 3.5.

**Romance languages**   Modern languages which have developed from Latin (e.g. French, Italian).

**rounded vowels**   Vowels produced with rounded lips (e.g. [oː]).

**RP**   See **Received Pronunciation**.

*Scheinentlehnung*   See **pseudo-transfer**.

*Schriftsprache*   Literally 'written language' but often designating formal standard spoken language.

*Schwyzertütsch*   Local name for Swiss German dialect speech.

**second sound shift**   See **High German sound shift**.

**semantic loan** (Ger.: *Lehnbedeutung*)   Meaning which is added to a word in one language under the influence of a word in another language (e.g. the meaning of 'fire from a job' added to the German word *feuern*, under the influence of English 'fire').

**semantics** (adj. **semantic**)   (The study of) meaning.

**Slavonic** (or **Slavic**) **languages**   Languages of a large Indo-European sub-family in eastern Europe and the Soviet Union (e.g. Russian, Polish).

**social network**   A means of locating invidual speakers in terms of the social contacts they establish (e.g. workmates, neighbours, friends), rather than allocating them to pre-established groupings such as socio-economic classes.

**sociolinguistic marker**   A linguistic variable that is widely associated with a particular social group and may therefore be consciously adopted or avoided in speech.

**speech act**   A communicative activity defined in terms of the speaker's intentions in speaking and the effects they achieve on their listeners.

**speech community**   There are many definitions, but is is used here in the sense of any group of people who operate and interact according to a set of shared linguistic norms and patterns of usage, that at the same time serves to distinguish this group from others.

**speech event**   The basic unit for the analysis of spoken interation.

**standard variety, standard language** (e.g. standard English, standard German)   That socially determined variety of a language which enjoys the highest prestige, which is (usually) required in schools, which is taught to foreigners, which is (usually) employed in broadcasting, and which bears the closest relationship to the written form of the language.

*standardnahe Umgangssprache*   See **colloquial standard speech**.

*Standardsprache*   See **formal standard language**.

**stop consonants**   Consonants produced by a complete closure in the vocal tract, which is then opened with an audible release of breath (e.g. [p] [d]).

**stress**   Phenomenon whereby one syllable in a word or phrase sounds subjectively louder or more prominent than the other syllables.

**strong verbs**   Verbs whose stem vowel changes in certain forms, such as the preterite or past participle, and whose preterite does not contain a suffix tense marker (e.g. German: *trinken* → *trank*, *getrunken*; English: drink → drank, drunk).

**subjunctive**   Mood of the verb used frequently in requests, conditional sentences and in indirect speech in German. It can express a tentative attitude, or a distancing of the speaker from the information conveyed. (See 5.5.3.)

**sub-phonemic** (adj.)   Referring to the sounds of a language at a level somewhat below the phonemic or distinctive level.

**Swiss German**   Collective term for all Swiss German dialects (see also *Schwy-zertütsch*); not to be confused with Swiss standard German, the standardized variety used only in certain formal contexts.

**synchronic**   Refers to the description of the state of a language at a given point in time.

**synonymy**   A term referring to two or more words that have the same or similar meanings.

**syntax** (adj. **syntactic**)   (Study of) the ways in which words combine to produce higher-level units, such as sentences.

**tense** (adj.)   Articulated with relatively tense mouth muscles.

**traditional dialect** (Ger.: *Dialekt, Mundart*)   Form of dialect in a particular region which differs maximally from the standard variety.

**type**   'Language type' and 'speech type' are used here to denote all the varieties of the language which share the same social (not regional) characteristics (e.g. all traditional dialects).

*Überdachung*   A term used to refer to the 'umbrella' effect of a standard language variety that enables two non-standard varieties to be classified as belonging to the same language.

*Umgangssprache*   See **colloquial speech**.

**unrounded vowels**   Vowels produced with neutral or spread lips.

**unrounding**   Change in the production of a rounded vowel whereby lip rounding is lost.

**Upper German dialects** (Ger.: *Oberdeutsche Dialekte*)   Southern German dialects, including those of Austria and Switzerland. Subdivision of High German dialects.

**uvular sound**   Sound articulated with the back of the tongue touching the uvula at the back of the soft palate (e.g. [ʀ]).

**variable**   A linguistic feature that is subject to social or stylistic variation and thus has two or more possible realizations.

**variant**   One of the possible realizations of a linguistic **variable**.

**variety**   Any form of a language that can, at least for the purposes of analysis, be distinguished from others on a social, regional or situational basis.

**velar sound**   Sound articulated with the back of the tongue close to or touching the velum or soft palate (e.g. [k]).

**vocalic** (adj.)   Of vowels.

**vocalization**   Change in the production of a consonant sound whereby it acquires a vocalic articulation.

**voiced sounds**   Sounds produced with vibration of the vocal cords (e.g. [z], vowel sounds).

**voiceless sounds**   Sounds produced without vibration of the vocal cords (e.g. [p] [s]).

**weak verbs**   Verbs which conform to a particularly regular pattern of conjugation (contrast with **strong verbs**).

**West Germanic languages**   Subdivision of Germanic languages including German, **Dutch and English.**

# References

'Berlin' signifies West Berlin; East Berlin is indicated by '(E)'. *ZDL = Zeitschrift für Dialektologie und Linguistik*

Alinei, M. (1980) 'Dialect: a dialectical approach', in Göschel, *et al.* 1980: 11–37

Amian, W. (1979) 'Die Interdependenz linguistischer und politischer Faktoren im Sprachgrenzbereich', in Nelde, 1979b: 95–100

Ammon, U. (1972a) *Dialekt, soziale Ungleichheit und Schule.* Weinheim: Beltz
(1972b) 'Dialekt, Sozialschicht und dialektbedingte Schulschwierigkeiten', *Linguistische Berichte*, Vol. 22, pp. 80–93
(1977) *Probleme der Soziolinguistik* (Germanistische Arbeitshefte, 15.2). Tübingen: Niemeyer
(1978a) 'Begriffsbestimmung und soziale Verteilung des Dialekts', in Ammon *et al.* 1978: 49–71
(1978b) *Schulschwierigkeiten von Dialektsprechern.* Weinheim, Basle: Beltz
(1986) 'Die Begriffe "Dialekt" und "Soziolekt"', in Von Polenz, P., J. Erben and J. Goossens (eds.), *Kontroversen, alte und neue*, Vol. 4, pp. 223–31. Tübingen: Niemeyer

Ammon, U., U. Knoop and I. Radtke (1978) *Grundlagen einer dialektorientierten Sprachdidaktik.* Weinheim: Beltz

Antos, G. (ed.) (1988) *'Ich kann ja Deutsch!' Studien zum fortgeschrittenen Zweitspracherwerb von Kindern ausländischer Arbeiter.* Tübingen: Niemeyer

Appel, R. and P. Muysken (1987) *Language Contact and Bilingualism.* London: Edward Arnold

Arbeitsgruppe 'Sprachgemeinschaften in der Bundesverwaltung' (1986) *Bericht über die Arbeitsbedingungen der Bundesbediensteten in Bern unter dem Gesichtspunkt der Muttersprache.* Berne: Eidgenössisches Personalamt

Århammar, N. (1967) 'Die Syltringer Sprache', in Hansen, M. and N. Hansen (eds.), *Sylt – Geschichte und Gestalt einer Insel*, pp. 3–21. Itzehoe-Voßkate: Hansen & Hansen

Auburger, L. (1977a) 'Zur Sprache kanadadeutscher Zeitungstexte', in Auburger *et al.* 1977: 149–56
(1977b) 'Bericht der Arbeitsstelle für Mehrsprachigkeit 1976', *Jahrbuch 1976 des Instituts für Deutsche Sprache*, pp. 342–77. Düsseldorf: Schwann

Auburger, L., H. Kloss and H. Rupp (eds.) (1977) *Deutsch als Muttersprache in Kanada.* Wiesbaden: Steiner

Aufderstraße, H., H. Bock, M. Gerder and H. Müller (1983) *Themen.* Munich: Hueber

Bach, A. (1969) *Deutsche Mundartforschung* (3rd edn). Heidelberg: Winter

# References

Barbour, J. S. (1987) 'Dialects and the teaching of a standard language: some West German work', *Language in Society*, Vol. 16, No. 2, pp. 227–44

Barkowski, H., U. Harnisch and S. Kumm (1979) 'Sprachlernen mit Arbeitsmigranten im Wohnbezirk', *Deutsch Lernen*, Vol. 19, No, 1, pp. 5–16

Bausch, K.-H. (ed.) (1982) *Mehrsprachigkeit in der Stadtregion* (Jahrbuch 1981 des Instituts für deutsche Sprache, 56). Düsseldorf: Schwann

Becker-Dombrowski, C. (1981) 'Zur Situation der deutschen Sprache im Elsaß', in Ureland 1981: 149–79

Bernstein, B. (1971 [1965]) 'A socio-linguistic approach to social learning', in Bernstein, B. (ed.), *Class, Codes and Control*, Vol. 1, pp. 118–43. London: Routledge & Kegan Paul

Besch, W. (1981) 'Einige Probleme empirischer Sprachforschung', in Besch *et al.* 1981: 238–60

Besch, W., J. Hufschmidt, A. Kall-Holland, E. Klein and K. J. Mattheier (1981) *Sprachverhalten in ländlichen Gemeinden. Ansätze zur Theorie und Methode* (Forschungsbericht Erp-Projekt, Vol. 1). Berlin: Schmidt

Besch, W., U. Knoop, W. Putschke and H. E. Wiegand (eds.) (1982–3) *Dialektologie: ein Handbuch zur deutschen und allgemeinen Dialektforschung* (2 vols). Berlin, New York: de Gruyter

Besch, W. and H. Löffler (1977) *Alemannisch*. Düsseldorf: Schwann

Besch, W. and K. J. Mattheier (1985a) 'Ortssprachenforschung', in Besch and Mattheier 1985b: 9–23

Besch, W. and K. J. Mattheier (eds.) (1985b) *Ortssprachenforschung: Beiträge zu einem Bonner Kolloquium*. Berlin: Schmidt

Bettelheim, R. (1982) 'Introduction', in Bettelheim and Benedikter 1982: 1–20

Bettelheim, R. and R. Benedikter (eds.) (1982) *Apartheid in Mitteleuropa? Sprache und Sprachpolitik in Südtirol*. Vienna, Munich: Jugend und Volk Verlagsgesellschaft

Bickel, H. (1988) 'Sprachen in der Schweiz'. Unpublished MS, University of Basle

Bickerton, D. (1971) 'Inherent variability and variable rules', *Foundations of Language*, Vol. 7, pp. 457–92

—— (1977) 'Pidginization and creolization: language acquisition and language universals', in Valdman 1977: 49–69

Bodemann, Y. M. and R. Ostow (1975) 'Lingua franca und Pseudo-pidgin in der Bundesrepublik', *Zeitschrift für Literaturwissenschaft und Linguistik*, Vol. 18, No. 5, pp. 122–46

Bodmer, F. (1944/1981) *The Loom of Language*. London: The Merlin Press (page references are to 1981 edn)

Braun, P. (1987) *Tendenzen in der deutschen Gegenwartssprache*. Stuttgart: Kohlhammer

Braverman, S. (1984) *The City Dialect of Salzburg*. Göppingen: Kümmerle

Bright, W. (ed.) (1966) *Sociolinguistics*. The Hague, Paris: Mouton

Brown, P. and S. Levinson (1987) *Politeness: Some Universals in Language Usage*. Cambridge: Cambridge University Press

Brown, R. and A. Gilman (1972) 'The pronouns of power and solidarity', in Giglioli 1972: 252–82

Bynon, T. (1977) *Historical Linguistics*. Cambridge: Cambridge University Press

Camartin, I. (1982) 'Die Beziehungen zwischen den schweizerischen Sprachregionen', in Schläpfer 1982: 301–51

Carstensen, B. (1980) 'Das Genus englischer Fremd- und Lehnwörter im Deutschen', in Viereck 1980: 37–75

# References

Carstensen, B. and H. Galinski (1975) *Amerikanismen der deutschen Gegenwartssprache*. Heidelberg: Winter

Chambers, J. K. and P. Trudgill (1980) *Dialectology*. Cambridge: Cambridge University Press

Cheshire, J. (1982) 'Variation in the use of "ain't" in an urban British English dialect', *Language in Society*, Vol. 10, pp. 365–81

Clahsen, H., J. Meisel and M. Pienemann (1983) *Deutsch als Zweitsprache*. Tübingen: Narr

Clauss, J. U. (1979) 'Die politische und verfassungsrechtliche Problematik des deutschsprachigen Belgiens', in Nelde 1979b: 39–60

Clyne, M. G. (1968) 'Zum Pidgin-Deutsch der Gastarbeiter', *Zeitschrift für Mundartforschung*, vol. 35, pp. 130–9

(1984) *Language and Society in the German-Speaking Countries*. Cambridge: Cambridge University Press

Cole, R. (1975) 'Divergent and convergent attitudes towards the Alsatian Dialect', *Anthropological Linguistics*, vol. 17, pp. 293–304

Coulmas, F. (1985) *Sprache und Staat* (Sammlung Göschen 2501). Berlin, New York: de Gruyter

Denison, N. (1980) 'Sauris: a case study in language shift in progress', in Nelde 1980: 335–42

*Dialekt–Hochsprache kontrastiv. Sprachhefte für den Deutschunterricht*. Düsseldorf: Schwann. Individual booklets:

> Ammon, U. and U. Loewer (1977) *Schwäbisch*
> Besch, W. and H. Löffler (1977) *Alemannisch*
> Hasselberg, J. and K.-P. Wegera (1976) *Hessisch*
> Henn, B. (1980) *Pfälzisch*
> Klein, E., K. J. Mattheier and H. Mickartz (1978) *Rheinisch*
> Niebaum, H. (1977) *Westfälisch*
> Stellmacher, D. (1981) *Niedersächsisch*
> Zehetner, L. G. (1977) *Bairisch*

Dittmar, N. (1973) *Soziolinguistik. Exemplarische und kritische Darstellung ihrer Theorie, Empirie und Anwendung* (for translation see Dittmar 1976). Frankfurt: Athenäum

(1976) *Sociolinguistics: a Critical Survey of Theory and Applications* (translation of Dittmar 1973). London: Edward Arnold

(1982) 'Soziolinguistik in der Bundesrepublik Deutschland', *Studium Linguistik*, Vol. 14, pp. 20–57

Dittmar, N. and B. Schlieben-Lange (1982) 'Stadtsprache. Forschungsrichtungen und -perspektiven einer vernachlässigten soziolinguistischen Disziplin', in Bausch 1982: 9–86

Dittmar, N. and P. Schlobinski (1985) 'Die Bedeutung von sozialen Netzwerken für die Erforschung von Ortssprachen', in Besch and Mattheier 1985b: 158–88

(1988) *Wandlungen einer Stadtsprache*. Berlin: Colloquium Verlag

Dittmar, N., P. Schlobinski and I. Wachs (1986) *Berlinisch. Studien zum Lexikon, zur Spracheinstellung und zum Stilrepertoire*. Berlin: Verlag Arno Spitz

(1988) 'Berlin Urban Vernacular studies: contributions to sociolinguistics', in Dittmar, N. and P. Schlobinski (eds.), *The Sociolinguistics of Urban Vernaculars*, pp. 1–144. Berlin, New York: de Gruyter

Dloczik, M., A. Schüttler and H. Sternagel (1984) *Der Fischer Informationsatlas Bundesrepublik Deutschland*. Frankfurt: Fischer

# References

Dressler, W., R. Leodolter and E. Chromec (1976) 'Phonologische Schnellsprech-regeln in der Wiener Umgangssprache', in Viereck, W. (ed.), *Sprachliches Handeln – soziales Verhalten*, pp. 71–92. Munich: Wilhelm Fink Verlag

*Duden. Grammatik der deutschen Sprache.* Mannheim: Bibliographisches Institut

Durrell, M. (1990) *A Guide to Contemporary German Usage.* Cambridge: Cambridge University Press

Egger, K. (1977) *Zweisprachigkeit in Südtirol.* Bozen/Bolzano: Athesia

Eggerer, W. and H. Rötzer (1978) *Manz Großer Analysenband I.* Munich: Manz

Eichhoff, J. (1977) *Wortatlas der deutschen Umgangssprachen.* Berne, Munich: Francke

Eisenberg, P. (1986) *Grundriß der deutschen Grammatik.* Stuttgart: Metzler

Eisermann, G. (1981) *Die deutsche Sprachgemeinschaft in Südtirol.* Stuttgart: Enke

Eisermann, G. and J. Zeh (1979) *Die deutsche Sprachgemeinschaft in Ostbelgien.* Stuttgart: Enke

Fasold, R. (1984) *The Sociolinguistics of Society.* Oxford: Basil Blackwell

Felix, S. (ed.) (1980) *Second Language Development.* Tübingen: Narr

Ferguson, C. A. (1972) [orig. 1959–60] 'Diglossia', in Giglioli 1972: 232–51

Fischer, G. (1979) 'Untersuchungen zum Sprachgebrauch in der Areler Gegend', in Nelde 1979b: 85–94

Fischer, H. and U. P. Trier (1962) *Das Verhältnis zwischen Deutschschweizer und Westschweizer: eine sozialpsychologische Untersuchung.* Berne, Stuttgart: Huber

Fishman, J. A. (1972) *The Sociology of Language: an Interdisciplinary Social Science Approach to Language in Society.* Rowley, Mass.: Newbury House

Fleischer, W. (1984) 'Zur lexikalischen Charakteristik der deutschen Sprache in der DDR', *Zeitschrift für Phonetik, Sprachwissenschaft und Kommunikationsforschung*, No. 4, pp. 415–24

Frings, T. (1956) *Sprache und Geschichte.* Halle: VEB Max Niemeyer Verlag

Fuchs, W. P. (1973) *Das Zeitalter der Reformation* (Handbuch der deutschen Geschichte, Vol. 8). Munich: DTV

Gabriel, E. and H. Stricker (eds.) (1987) *Probleme der Dialektgeographie.* Bühl, Baden: Konkordia

Gal, S. (1979) *Language Shift.* New York, London: Academic Press

Giglioli, P. P. (ed.) (1972) *Language and Social Context.* Harmondsworth: Penguin

Giles, H. and P. Smith (1979) 'Accommodation theory: optimal levels of convergence', in Giles and St Clair 1979: 45–65

Giles, H. and R. St Clair (eds.) (1979) *Language and Social Psychology.* Oxford: Basil Blackwell

Goossens, J. (1976) 'Was ist Deutsch – und wie verhält es sich zum Niederländischen?', in Göschel *et al.* 1976: 256–82

— (1977) *Deutsche Dialektologie.* Berlin, New York: de Gruyter

— (1981) 'Zum Verhältnis von Dialektologie und Soziolinguistik: der Standpunkt eines Dialektologen', *ZDL*, Vol. 48, No. 3, pp. 299–312

Gordon, J. C. B. (1981) *Verbal Deficit, a Critique.* London: Croom Helm

Göschel, J., P. Ivić and K. Kehr (eds.) (1980) *Dialekt und Dialektologie: Ergebnisse des internationalen Symposiums 'Zur Theorie des Dialekts', Marburg/L, 5–10 September 1977* (ZDL Beiheft NF 26). Wiesbaden: Steiner

# References

Göschel, J., N. Nail and G. Van Der Elst (eds.) (1976) *Zur Theorie des Dialekts* (*ZDL* Beiheft 16). Wiesbaden: Steiner

Grimm, J. (1819–37) *Deutsche Grammatik*. Göttingen

Grundmann, H. (1973) *Wahlkönigtum, Territorialpolitik und Ostbewegung im 13. und 14. Jahrhundert* (Handbuch der deutschen Geschichte, Vol. 5). Munich: DTV

Gumperz, J. (1966) 'On the ethnology of linguistic change', in Bright 1966: 27–49
  (1977) 'Social network and language shift in Kärnten', in Molony *et al.* 1977: 83–103
  (1982) *Discourse Strategies*. Cambridge: Cambridge University Press

Günther, J. (1967) 'Die städtische Umgangssprache von Freiburg im Breisgau'. Dissertation, University of Freiburg

Haarmann, H. (1975) *Soziologie und Politik der Sprachen Europas*. Munich: DTV

Haas, W. (1982) 'Die deutschsprachige Schweiz', in Schläpfer 1982: 71–160
  (1983) 'Vokalisierung in den deutschen Dialekten', in Besch *et al.* 1982–3: 1111–16

Halliday, M. A. K. (1973) 'Foreword', in Bernstein, N. (ed.), *Class, Codes and Control*, Vol. 2. London: Routledge & Kegan Paul

Hard, G. (1966) *Zur Mundartgeographie. Ergebnisse, Methoden, Perspektiven*. Düsseldorf: Schwann

Hartweg, F. (1981) 'Sprachkontakt und Sprachkonflikt im Elsaß', in Meid and Heller 1981: 97–113

Haugen, E. (1972a) 'Dialect, language, nation', in Pride and Holmes 1972: 97–111
  (1972b) *The Ecology of Language*. Stanford: Stanford University Press

Heeroma, K. (1962) 'Die Grenze des Friesischen', in Schröder, W. (ed.), *Festschrift für Ludwig Wolff*, pp. 33–53. Neumünster: Wachholtz

Heidelberger Forschungsprojekt 'Pidgin-Deutsch' (1975) *Sprache und Kommunikation ausländischer Arbeiter*. Kronberg: Scriptor

Heilfurth, G. and L. E. Schmitt (eds.) (1963) *Festgabe K. Winnacker*. Marburg: Elwert

Helbig, G. and J. Buscha (1975) *Deutsche Grammatik*. Leipzig: VEB Verlag Enzyklopädie
  (1986) *Kurze deutsche Grammatik für Ausländer*. Leipzig: VEB Verlag Enzyklopädie

Hellmann, M. W. (1980) 'Deutsche Sprache in der Bundesrepublik Deutschland und in der Deutschen Demokratischen Republik', in Althaus, H. P., H. Henne and H. E. Wiegand (eds.), *Lexikon der germanistischen Linguistik*, pp. 519–27. Tübingen: Niemeyer

Hermanns, F., W. Lenschen and G. Merkt (eds.) (1983) *Lernziele Deutsch. Perspektiven für den Deutschunterricht in der französischen und italienischen Schweiz*. Neuchâtel: Commission Interuniversitaire Suisse de Linguistique Appliquée

Herrgen, J. (1986) *Koronalisierung und Hyperkorrektion*. Wiesbaden: Steiner

Herrgen, J. and J. E. Schmidt (1985) 'Systemkontrast und Hörerurteil. Zwei Dialektalitätsbegriffe und die ihnen entsprechenden Meßverfahren', *ZDL*, Vol. 52, No. 1, pp. 20–42

Hinderling, R. (ed.) (1986) *Europäische Sprachminderheiten im Vergleich*. Stuttgart: Steiner

Hinnenkamp, V. (1982) *Foreigner Talk und Tarzanisch*. Hamburg: Buske

Hoffmann, F. (1979) *Sprachen in Luxemburg: sprachwissenschaftliche und literat-*

# References

*urhistorische Beschreibung einer Triglossie-Situation* (Deutsche Sprache in Europa und Übersee, 6). Wiesbaden: Steiner

Hoffmeister, W. (1977) *Sprachwechsel in Ost-Lothringen*. Wiesbaden: Steiner

Hofmann, E. (1963) 'Sprachsoziologische Untersuchungen über den Einfluß der Stadtsprache auf mundartsprechende Arbeiter', in Heilfurth and Schmitt 1963: 201–81

Holm, J. (1988–9) *Pidgins and Creoles*. Vol. 1: *Theory and Structure*; Vol. 2: *Reference Survey*. Cambridge: Cambridge University Press

Hooge, D. (1983) 'Verwendungstypen der Tempusformen in den deutschen Dialekten', in Besch *et al.* 1982–3: 1209–20

Hudson, R. A. (1980) *Sociolinguistics*. Cambridge: Cambridge University Press

Hufschmidt, J. (1983) 'Erfahrungen, Beobachtungen und Wertungen zum Mundartgebrauch', in Hufschmidt *et al.* 1983: 11–59

Hufschmidt, J., E. Klein, K. J. Mattheier and H. Mickartz (1983) *Sprachverhalten in ländlichen Gemeinden: Dialekt und Standardsprache im Sprecherurteil* (Forschungsbericht Erp-Projekt, Vol. 2). Berlin: Schmidt

Hufschmidt, J. and K. J. Mattheier (1981a) 'Sprache und Gesellschaft', in Besch *et al.* 1981: 43–83

(1981b) 'Sprachdatenerhebung', in Besch *et al.* 1981: 178–205

Hymes, D. (ed.) (1971) *Pidginization and Creolization of Language*. Cambridge: Cambridge University Press

Inglehart, R. F. and Woodward, M. (1972) 'Language conflicts and political community (excerpts)', in Giglioli 1972: 358–77

Jongen, R., S. De Knop, P. H. Nelde and M. Quix (eds.) (1983) *Mehrsprachigkeit und Gesellschaft*. Tübingen: Niemeyer

Kall-Holland, A. (1981) 'Soziale und sprachliche Gliederung in der Ortsgemeinschaft Erp', in Besch *et al.* 1981: 214–37

Kartheuser, B. (1979) 'Die Problematik der Zweisprachigkeit an den Schulen des amtlichen deutschen Sprachgebiets', in Nelde 1979b: 101–22

Keim, I. (1984) *Untersuchungen zum Deutsch türkischer Arbeiter*. Tübingen: Narr

Keller, R. E. (1961) *German Dialects*. Manchester: Manchester University Press

(1978) *The German Language*. London: Faber & Faber

Keller, T. (1976) *The City Dialect of Regensburg*. Hamburg: Buske

Kern, R. (1980) 'Interferenzprobleme bei deutschsprachigen Belfiern', in Nelde 1980: 97–103

(1983) 'Zur Sprachsituation im Areler Land', in Jongen *et al.* 1983: 70–87

Kinne, M. and B. Strube-Edelmann (1981) *Kleines Wörterbuch des DDR-Wortschatzes*. Düsseldorf: Schwann

Klein, E. (1981) 'Sozialdatenerhebung', in Besch *et al.* 1981: 152–77

(1983) 'Situation und Sprachlage', in Hufschmidt *et al.* 1983: 117–99

Klein, W. (1974) *Variation in der Sprache*. Kronberg: Scriptor

Klein, W. and N. Dittmar (1979) *Developing Grammars*. Berlin: Springer

Klönne, A. (1984) *Zurück zur Nation?* Cologne: Diederichs Verlag

Kloss, H. (1976) 'Abstandsprachen und Ausbausprachen', in Göschel *et al.* 1976: 301–22

(1978) *Die Entwicklung neuer germanischer Kultursprachen seit 1800* (2nd edn) (Sprache der Gegenwart, Vol. 37). Düsseldorf: Schwann

Knoop, U. (1982) 'Zur Geschichte der Dialektologie des Deutschen', in Besch *et al.* 1982–3: 1–23

# References

Knoop, U., W. Putschke and H. E. Wiegand (1982) 'Die Marburger Schule: Entstehung und frühe Entwicklung der Dialektgeographie', in Besch *et al.* 1982–3: 38–92

Knowles, J. (1980) 'Multilingualism in Luxembourg', in Nelde 1980: 355–61

Kolde, G. (1980) 'Vergleichende Untersuchungen des Sprachverhaltens und der Spracheinstellungen von Jugendlichen in zwei gemischtsprachigen Schweizer Städten', in Nelde 1980: 243–53

(1981) *Sprachkontakte in gemischtsprachigen Städten.* Wiesbaden: Steiner

(1986) 'Einige aktuelle sprach- und sprachenpolitische Probleme in der viersprachigen Schweiz', *Muttersprache*, No. 1–2, pp. 58–68

König, W. (1978) *Atlas zur deutschen Sprache.* Munich: DTV

Koß, G. (1983) 'Realisierung von Kasusrelationen in den deutschen Dialekten', in Besch *et al.* 1982–3: 1242–50

Kramer, J. (1981) *Deutsch und Italienisch in Südtirol.* Heidelberg: Winter

(1984) *Zweisprachigkeit in den Beneluxländern.* Hamburg: Buske

(1986) 'Gewollte Dreisprachigkeit – Französisch, Deutsch und Letzebuergesch im Großherzogtum Luxemburg', in Hinderling 1986: 229–49

Küpper, H. (1987) *Wörterbuch der deutschen Umgangssprache.* Stuttgart: Klett

Kutsch, S. and I. Desgranges (eds.) (1985) *Zweitsprache Deutsch – ungesteuerter Erwerb.* Tübingen: Niemeyer

Labov, W. (1972a) *Sociolinguistic Patterns.* Oxford: Basil Blackwell

(1972b) *Language in the Inner City.* Oxford: Basil Blackwell

Ladin, W. (1982) 'Mehrsprachigkeit in Straßburg', in Bausch 1982: 303–44

Lambert, W., R. Hodgson, R. Gardner and S. Fillenbaum (1960) 'Evaluative reactions to spoken language', *Journal of Abnormal and Social Psychology*, Vol. 60, pp. 44–51

Lasch, A. (1928) *Berlinisch. Eine Berliner Sprachgeschichte.* Berlin

Le Page, R. and A. Tabouret-Keller (1985) *Acts of Identity.* Cambridge: Cambridge University Press

Lehmann, W. P. (1973) *Historical Linguistics.* New York: Holt, Rinehart & Winston

Lehmann, W. P. and Y. Malkiel (eds.) (1968) *Directions for Historical Linguistics.* Austin: University of Texas Press

Leippe, H. (1977) 'Deutsche Dialekte, I', *Zeit-Magazin*, Vol. 50, No. 2, pp. 30–44

Linguistic Minorities Project (1985) *The Other Languages of England.* London: Routledge & Kegan Paul

Lockwood, W. B. (1969) *Indo-European Philology.* London: Hutchinson

(1972) *A Panorama of Indo-European Languages.* London: Hutchinson

(1976) *An Informal History of the German Language.* Oxford, London: Basil Blackwell, André Deutsch

Löffler, H. (1972) 'Mundart als Sprachbarriere', *Wirkendes Wort*, Vol. 22, No. 1, pp. 23–39

(1980) *Probleme der Dialektologie.* Darmstadt: Wissenschaftliche Buchgesellschaft

(1985) *Germanistische Soziolinguistik* (Grundlagen der Germanistik, 28). Berlin: Schmidt

Lötscher, A. (1983) *Schweizerdeutsch.* Stuttgart: Huber

Löwe, H. (1973) *Deutschland im fränkischen Reich* (Handbuch der deutschen Geschichte, Vol. 3). Munich: DTV

## References

Lüsebrink, C. (1986) 'Möglichkeiten und Grenzen des rechtlichen Schutzes von Sprachminderheiten am Beispiel Südtirol/Burgenland', in Hinderling 1986: 57–79

Maak, H. G. (1983) 'Sonderformen in den Pronominalsystemen deutscher Dialekte', in Besch *et al.* 1982–3: 1174–9

Macha, J. (1982) *Dialekt/Hochsprache in der Grundschule. Ergebnisse einer Lehrerbefragung im südlichen Nordrhein-Westfalen.* Bonn: Röhrscheid

McRae, K. (1983) *Conflict and Compromise in Multilingual Societies.* Vol. 1: *Switzerland.* Ontario: Wilfred Laurier University Press
  (1986) Conflict and Compromise in Multilingual Societies. Vol. 2: *Belgium.* Ontario: Wilfred Laurier University Press

Mangold, M. and P. Grebe *Duden Aussprache-Wörterbuch* (*Der große Duden*, Vol. 6). Mannheim: Bibliographisches Institut

Masser, A. (1982) 'Italienisches Wortgut im Südtiroler Deutsch', in Moser 1982: 63–74

Mattheier, K. J. (1980) *Pragmatik und Soziologie der Dialekte* (Uni.-Taschenbücher, 994). Heidelberg: Quelle und Meyer

Mattheier, K. J. (1981) 'Chronologischer Überblick über Planung und Durchführung der Datenerhebung', in Besch *et al.* 1981: 16–42
  (1982) 'Sprachgebrauch und Urbanisierung', in Bausch 1982: 87–107
  (1983a) 'Sprachlage und sprachliches Kontinuum', in Hufschmidt *et al.* 1983: 226–64
  (1983b) 'Dialekt und Dialektologie', in Mattheier 1983c: 135–54
  (1985) 'Ortsloyalität als Steuerungsfaktor von Sprachgebrauch in örtlichen Sprachgemeinschaften', in Besch and Mattheier 1985: 139–57

Mattheier, K. J. (ed.) (1983c) *Aspekte der Dialekttheorie.* Tübingen: Niemeyer

Meid, W. and Heller, K. (1981) *Sprachkontakt als Ursache von der Veränderung der Sprach- und Bewußtseinsstruktur.* Innsbruck: Institut für Sprachwissenschaft der Universität Innsbruck

Meisel, J. (1980) 'Linguistic simplification', in Felix 1980: 13–46

Mickartz, H. (1983) 'Einstellungsäußerungen zur Verwendung von Hochsprache und Mundart in der Kindererziehung', in Hufschmidt *et al.* 1983: 60–116

Milroy, L. (1987a) *Observing and Analysing Natural Language.* Oxford: Basil Blackwell
  (1987b) *Language and Social Networks* (2nd rev. edn). Oxford: Basil Blackwell

Molony, C., H. Zobl and W. Stölting (1977) *Deutsch im Kontakt mit anderen Sprachen.* Kronberg: Scriptor

Moosmüller, S. (1984) 'Soziale und psychosoziale Sprachvariation: eine quantitative und qualitative Untersuchung zum gegenwärtigen Wiener Deutsch'. Dissertation, University of Vienna
  (1987) 'Soziophonologische Variation bei österreichischen Politikern', *Zeitschrift für Germanistik*, Vol. 87, No. 4, pp. 429–39

Moser, H. (ed.) (1982) *Zur Situation des Deutschen in Südtirol.* Innsbruck: Universität Innsbruck

Moser, H. and O. Putzer (1980) 'Zum umgangssprachlichen Wortschatz in Südtirol: italienische Interferenzen in der Sprache der Städte', in Wiesinger 1980: 139–72

Moser, H., H. Wellmann and N. R. Wolf (1981) *Geschichte der deutschen Sprache.* Vol. 1: *Althochdeutsch–Mittelhochdeutsch* (Uni-Taschenbücher, 1139). Heidelberg: Quelle und Meyer

## References

Mühlhäusler, P. (1986) *Pidgin and Creole Linguistics*. Oxford: Basil Blackwell
Müller, M. and L. Wertenschlag (1985) *Los emol*. Zurich: Langenscheidt
Nelde, P. H. (1974) 'Normabweichungen im Zeitungsdeutsch Ostbelgiens', *Deutsche Sprache*, No. 3, pp. 233–51
   (1979a) *Volkssprache und Kultursprache. Die gegenwärtige Lage des sprachlichen Übergangsgebietes im deutsch–belgisch–luxemburgischen Grenzraum*. Wiesbaden: Steiner
   (1984) 'Aspects of linguistic determination along the Germanic–Romance linguistic boundary', *Journal of Multilingual and Multicultural Development*, Vol. 5, Nos. 3–4, pp. 217–24
   (1986) 'Ecological implications of language contact', in Nelde *et al.* 1986: 111–24
Nelde, P. H. (ed.) (1979b) *Deutsch als Muttersprache in Belgien*. Wiesbaden: Steiner
   (1980) *Languages in Contact and Conflict* (*ZDL* Beiheft 32). Wiesbaden: Steiner
Nelde, P. H., P. S. Ureland and I. Clarkson (1986) *Language Contact in Europe. Proceedings of the Working Groups 12 and 13 at the 13th International Congress of Linguists, 29 August – 4 September 1982, Tokyo*. Tübingen: Niemeyer
Neuner, G., R. Schmidt, H. Wilms and M. Zirkel (1979) *Deutsch aktiv*. Berlin, Munich: Langenscheidt
Newton, G. (1987) 'The German language in Luxembourg', in Russ and Volkmar 1987: 153–79
Niebaum, H. (1983) *Dialektologie*. Tübingen: Niemeyer
Oevermann, U. (1968) 'Schichtenspezifische Formen des Sprachverhaltens und ihr Einfluß auf die kognitiven Prozesse', in Roth, H. (ed.), *Begabung und Lernen*, pp. 297–355. Stuttgart: Klett
Orlović-Schwarzwald, M. (1978) *Zum Gastarbeiterdeutsch jugoslawischer Arbeiter im Rhein–Main-Gebiet*. Wiesbaden: Steiner
Pabst, K. (1979) 'Politische Geschichte des deutschen Sprachgebiets in Ostbelgien bis 1944', in Nelde 1979b: 9–38
Panzer, B. (1983) 'Formenneutralisationen in den Flexionssystemen deutscher Dialekte', in Besch *et al.* 1982–3: 1170–3
Pernstich, K. (1982) 'Deutsch–italienische Interferenzen in der Südtiroler Presse', in Moser 1982: 91–128
   (1984) *Der italienische Einfluß auf die deutsche Schriftsprache in Südtirol*. Vienna: Braumüller
Petyt, K. M. (1980) *The Study of Dialect: an Introduction to Dialectology*. London: André Deutsch
Pfaff, C. (1981) 'Sociolinguistic problems of immigrant workers and their children in Germany', *Language in Society*, Vol. 10, pp. 155–88
Polenz, P. von, (1978) *Geschichte der deutschen Sprache*, Berlin: de Gruyter
Porsch, P. (1983) 'Die Theorie der sprachlichen Kodes und ihr Verhältnis zur Differenziertheit der Sprache', in Hartung, W., H. Schönfeld *et al.* (eds.), *Kommunikation und Sprachvariation*, pp. 259–79. Berlin (E): Akademie-Verlag
Pride, J. B. and J. Holmes (1972) *Sociolinguistics*. Harmondsworth: Penguin
Putzer, O. (1982) 'Italienische Interferenzen in der gesprochenen Sprache Südtirols', in Moser 1982: 141–62
Quirk, R. and S. Greenbaum (1973) *A University Grammar of English*. London: Longman

# References

Quix, M. P. (1981) 'Altbelgien-Nord', in Ureland 1981: 225–35
Ris, R. (1973) 'Dialekte und Sprachbarrieren aus Schweizer Sicht', in Bausinger, H. (ed.), *Dialekt als Sprachbarriere? Ergebnisbericht einer Tagung zur alemannischen Dialektforschung*, pp. 29–62. Tübingen: Tübinger Verein für Volkskunde
   (1978) 'Sozialpsychologie der Dialekte und ihrer Sprecher', in Ammon *et al.* 1978: 93–115
   (1979) 'Dialekte und Einheitssprache in der deutschen Schweiz', *International Journal of the Sociology of Language*, Vol. 21, pp. 41–61
Romaine, S. (1982) *Sociolinguistic Variation in Speech Communities*. London: Edward Arnold
Rosenkranz, H. (1963) 'Der Sprachwandel des Industriezeitalters im Thüringer Sprachraum', in Rosenkranz and Spangenberg 1963: 7–51
Rosenkranz, H. and K. Spangenberg (eds.) (1963) *Sprachsoziologische Studien in Thüringen*. Berlin (E): Akademie-Verlag
Russ, C. and C. Volkmar (eds.) (1987) *Sprache und Gesellschaft in deutschsprachigen Ländern*. Munich: Goethe-Institut
Sanders, W. (1982) *Sachsensprache, Hansesprache, Plattdeutsch: sprachgeschichtliche Grundzüge des Niederdeutschen* (Sammlung Vandenhoek). Göttingen: Vandenhoek & Ruprecht
Saville-Troike, M. (1989) *The Ethnography of Communication* (2nd edn). Oxford: Basil Blackwell
Schirmunski (Zhirmunskij), V. M. (1962) *Deutsche Mundartkunde*. Berlin (E): Akademie-Verlag
Schläpfer, R. (1987) 'Mundart und Standardsprache in der deutschen Schweiz als Problem der Schule und Kulturpolitik in der viersprachigen Schweiz', in Gabriel and Stricker 1987: 166–75
   (forthcoming) 'Sprachen in der Schweiz'. *Nationales Forschungsprojekt 21: Kulturelle Vielfalt und nationale Identität*. University of Basle
Schläpfer, R. (ed.) (1982) *Die viersprachige Schweiz*. Zurich, Cologne: Benziger
Schleswig-Holsteinischer Landtag (1987) *Bericht zur Sprache und Kultur des friesischen Bevölkerungsteils*. Kiel: Schleswig-Holsteinischer Landtag
Schlieben-Lange, B. and H. Weydt (1978) 'Für eine Pragmatisierung der Dialektologie', *Zeitschrift für germanistische Linguistik*, Vol. 6, pp. 257–82
Schlobinski, P. (1984) *Berlinisch für Berliner*. Berlin: arani
   (1986) *Berliner Wörterbuch*. Berlin: Marhold
   (1987) *Stadtsprache Berlin. Eine soziolinguistische Untersuchung*. Berlin, New York: de Gruyter
Schlobinski, P. and U. Blank (1985) *Sprachbetrachtung: Berlinisch* (2 booklets). Berlin: Marhold
Schmeller, J. (1821) *Die Mundarten Bayerns*. Munich
Schneidmesser, L. von (1984 [1979]) *A Study of Lexical Stability and Change in the Urban Spoken Language of Gießen, Germany* (Dissertation), Ann Arbor, Mich.: University Microfilms
Schönfeld, H. (1977) 'Zur Rolle der sprachlichen Existenzformen in der sprachlichen Kommunikation', in Akademie der Wissenschaften der DDR (ed.), *Normen in der sprachlichen Kommunikation*, pp. 163–208. Berlin (E): Akademie-Verlag
Schönfeld, H. and R. Pape (1981) 'Sprachliche Existenzformen', in Akademie der

# References

Wissenschaften der DDR (ed.), *Kommunikation und Sprachvariation*, pp. 130–214. Berlin (E): Akademie-Verlag

Schröder, B. (1974) 'Sociolinguistics in the FRG', *Language in Society*, Vol. 3, pp. 109–23

Schuler, M., M. Bopp, K. Brassel and E. Brugger (eds.) (1985) *Strukturatlas Schweiz*. Zurich: ex libris

Schumann, J. (1978) *The Pidginization Process*. Rowley, Mass.: Newbury House

Schwarzenbach, R. (1969) *Die Stellung der Mundart in der deutschsprachigen Schweiz*. Frauenfeld: Huber
(1983) 'Sorgen mit dem Hochdeutschen', *Schweizer Monatshefte*, Vol. 63, No. 12, pp. 1009–18

Schwarzenbach, R. and H. Sitta (1983) 'Mundart und Standardsprache in der deutschen Schweiz', in Hermanns *et al*. 1983: 62–71

Seebold, E. (1983) 'Diminutivformen in den deutschen Dialekten' in Besch *et al*. 1982–3: 1250–5

Senelle, R. (1980) *The Reform of the Belgian State*. Brussels: Ministry of Foreign Affairs, External Trade and Cooperation in Development

Senft, G. (1982) *Sprachliche Varietät und Variation im Sprachverhalten Kaiserslauterer Metallarbeiter. Untersuchungen zu ihrer Begrenzung und Bewertung* (Arbeiten zur Sprachanalyse, Vol. 2). Berne, Frankfurt: Lang

Sieber, P. and H. Sitta (1986) *Mundart und Standardsprache als Problem der Schule*. Aarau: Sauerländer

Siebs, T. (1969) *Siebs Deutsche Aussprache*, edited by de Boor, H., H. Moser and C. Winkler (19th edn) Berlin: de Gruyter

Sivrikozoğlu, Ç. (1985) *. . . nix unsere Vaterland. Zweitsprache Deutsch und soziale Integration*. Frankfurt, Berne, New York: Lang

Sjölin, B. (1969) *Einführung in das Friesische* (Sammlung Metzler, 86, Abteilung C: *Sprachwissenschaft*). Stuttgart: Metzler

Søndergaard, B. (1980) 'Vom Sprachenkampf zur sprachlichen Koexistenz im deutsch–dänischen Grenzraum', in Nelde 1980: 297–306

Stellmacher, D. (1977) *Studien zur gesprochenen Sprache in Niedersachsen. Eine soziolinguistische Untersuchung* (Deutsche Dialektgeographie, Vol. 82). Marburg: Elwert

Stölting, W., D. Delić, M. Orlović, K. Rausch and E. Sausner (1980) *Die Zweisprachigkeit jugoslawischer Schüler in der BRD*. Wiesbaden: Harrasowitz

Sutton, P. (1984) 'Languages in India', *Incorporated Linguist*, Vol. 23, No. 2, pp. 75–8

Tekinay, A. (1984) 'Wie eine "Mischsprache" entsteht', *Muttersprache*, No. 5–6, pp. 396–403

Trim, R. (1981) 'Central Old Belgium', in Ureland 1981: 237–50
(1983) 'Sprachtod in Altbelgien-Mitte?', in Jongen *et al*. 1983: 157–68

Trudgill, P. (1975) 'Review of B. Bernstein, *Class, Codes and Control*', *Journal of Linguistics*, Vol. 11, No. 7, pp. 147–51
(1983a) *On Dialect*. Oxford: Basil Blackwell
(1983b) *Sociolinguistics* (2nd edn). Harmondsworth: Penguin

Trudgill, P. (ed.) (1978) *Sociolinguistic Patterns in British English*. London: Edward Arnold

Trudgill, P. and J. Hannah (1982) *International English*. London: Edward Arnold

# References

Tyroller, H. (1986) 'Trennung und Integration in Südtirol', in Hinderling 1986: 17–35

Ureland, P. S. (ed.) (1979) *Standardsprache und Dialekte in mehrsprachigen Gebieten Europas. Akten des 2. Symposions über Sprachkontakt in Europa, Mannheim, 1978.* Tübingen: Niemeyer

(1981) *Kulturelle und sprachliche Minderheiten in Europa. Aspekte der europäischen Ethnolinguistik und Ethnopolitik. Akten des 4. Symposions über Sprachkontakt in Europa, Mannheim, 1980.* Tübingen: Niemeyer

Valdman, A. (1977) *Pidgin and Creole Linguistics.* Bloomington: Indiana University Press

Veith, W. H. (1983) 'Die Sprachvariation in der Stadt. Am Beispiel von Frankfurt am Main', *Muttersprache*, Vol. 93, pp. 82–90

Verdoodt, A. (1968) *Zweisprachige Nachbarn. Die deutschen Hochsprach- und Mundartgruppen in Ost-Belgien, dem Elsaß, Ost-Lothringen und Luxemburg.* Vienna, Stuttgart: Braumüller

Viereck, W. (ed.) (1980) *Studien zum Einfluß der englischen Sprache auf das Deutsche.* Tübingen: Narr

Vogt, B. (1986) 'Mundart und Standardsprache in der deutschen Schweiz: das Sprachverhalten junger Schweizer und ihre Einstellung zur Standardsprache'. Dissertation, University of Basle

Wahrig, G. *Deutsches Wörterbuch.* Gütersloh: Mosaik Verlag.

Walker, A. G. H. (1980a) 'North Frisia and linguistics', *Nottingham Linguistic Circular*, Vol. 9, No. 1, pp. 18–31

(1980b) 'Some factors concerning the decline of the North Frisian tongue', in Nelde 1980: 453–60

(1987) 'Language and society in Schleswig', in Russ and Volkmar 1987: 136–52

Wardhaugh, R. (1986) *An Introduction to Sociolinguistics.* Oxford: Basil Blackwell

(1987) *Languages in Competition.* Oxford, London: Basil Blackwell, André Deutsch

Wehler, H. U. (1975) *Modernisierungstheorie und Geschichte.* Göttingen: Vandenhoeck & Ruprecht

Weinreich, U. (1953) *Languages in Contact.* The Hague: Mouton

Weinreich, U., W. Labov and M. Herzog (1968) 'Empirical foundations for a theory of language change', in Lehmann and Malkiel 1968: 95–195

Wells, C. J. (1985) *German: a Linguistic History to 1945.* Oxford: Oxford University Press

Wells, J. C. (1982) *Accents of English* (3 vols.). Cambridge: Cambridge University Press

Whinnom, K. (1971) 'Linguistic hybridization and the "special case" of pidgins and creoles', in Hymes 1971: 91–116

Wiesinger, P. (1983a) 'Diphthongierung und Monophthongierung in den deutschen Dialekten', in Besch *et al.* 1982–3: 1076–83

(1983b) 'Rundung und Entrundung, Palatalisierung und Entpalatalisierung, Velarisierung und Entvelarisierung in den deutschen Dialekten', in Besch *et al.* 1982–3: 1101–5

Wiesinger, P. (ed.) (1980) *Sprache und Name in Österreich.* Vienna: Braumüller

Williams, R. (1976) *Keywords.* London: Fontana/Croom Helm

Winteler, J. (1876) *Kerenzer Mundart des Kantons Glarus.* Leipzig, Heidelberg

Wolf, N. R. (1983) 'Durchführung und Verbreitung der zweiten Lautverschiebung in den deutschen Dialekten', in Besch *et al.* 1982–3: 1116–21

# References

Wolfensberger, H. (1967) *Mundartwandel im 20. Jahrhundert*. Frauenfeld: Huber
Wolfram, W. (1969) *A Sociolinguistic Description of Detroit Negro Speech*. Washington: Center for Applied Linguistics
Yakut, A. (1981) *Sprache der Familie. Eine Untersuchung des Zweitspracherwerbs der türkischen Gastarbeiterfamilien in der BRD*. Tübingen: Narr
Zehetner, L. G. (1977) *Bairisch*. Düsseldorf: Schwann
Zimmer, R. (1977) 'Dialekt–Nationaldialekt–Standardsprache (Vergleichende Betrachtungen zum deutsch–französischen Kontaktbereich in der Schweiz, im Elsaß, und in Luxemburg', *ZDL*, Vol. 44, No. 2, pp. 145–57

# Subject index

accent differences: phonetic, 148; phonological from *DH*, 150, 151–5
accents: prestige, 145; regional, 52, 137–8, 145
acquisition, language: by immigrants to FRG, 193–204; process in *Gastarbeiterdeutsch*, 197–9
administrative factors, in language choice, 211
age factors, in dialectology, 105, 108–9
agglutinative languages, 196
Alemanni, 30
Alemannic (*Alemannisch*), 78, 88, 89, 91, 95, 158, 191: High, 89–90, 92; Highest, 89, 92; Low, 89
Alsace, 53, 182: southern, 89
Alsace syndrome (*Verelsässerung*), 241
Alsace–Lorraine, 14, 234–7: history, 234–5; language use, 235–7
Alsatian, 92, 234n, 235, 237
America, North, 9
American English, 15, 36, 53, 54, 256
Amrum, 43
*Amtssprachen, see* official languages
Angles, 30
Anglo-Saxon tribes, 35, 41–2
Arabic, 9
Arel, 225
aristocracy, 144
attitudes: in dialectology, 103, 106, 108; to non-standard speech, 81, 185–91
*Ausbaudialekt*, 217
*Ausbausprache*, 16n, 217
Australia, 14, 134
Austria, 1, 12, 13, 16, 44, 48, 50, 54, 136, 142, 144, 170, 175, 182, 183, 191, 221: colloquial non-standard, 173–4; language contacts, 15; south-east, 242, 246–50
Austrian standard German, 241, 246–7
Austro–Hungarian Empire, 10, 12, 48

Baden, southern, 89
Baltic countries, 44
Baltic languages, 25
barriers, language (*Sprachbarrieren*), 20–1, 185
Bas-Rhin, 234
Basle, 211, 214
Basque, 235
Bavarian (*Bairisch*), 48, 78, 88, 89, 95, 173, 187: North, 89
Bavarian grammar (Schmeller), 60
Bavarian–Austrian (*Bairisch–Österreichisch*), 78, 88, 89, 91; Middle, 89, 90, 95; South, 89
Bavarians, 30
Belfast, 114
Belgium, 16, 38, 40, 47, 85, 204, 205, 206, 254: Communities, 225; Dutch-speakers, 224, 225; eastern, 224–30:–attitudes to German, 228–30, history, 224–5, legal and political measures, 225–7; Economic Regions, 225; French-speakers, 224, 225, 228, 230; Frenchification process, 225–30; German-speakers, 224, 225, 226–30, 231; history, 40; Linguistic Regions, 225
Bengali, 9
Benrath Line, 33, 41, 49, 68, 79–80, 87–8
Berlin, 71, 112–24, 140–1, 172–3: East, 124; phonology, 114–18; pragmatics, 118–22; speakers' attitudes to variation, 122–4; vocabulary, 113–14; West, 124
Berlin Urban Vernacular (*Berlinisch*) (BUV), 112–24: attitudes, 113, 122–4; functional distribution, 124; phonology, 113, 114–18; pragmatics, 113, 118–22; social meaning of, 112–3; status in East and West Berlin, 123–4; vocabulary, 112–14

# Subject index

*Idiotika*, 60
IE, *see* Indo-European languages
immigration, 14–15: into FRG, 192–204
implicational scaling, 117–18, 248–50, 251
India, 8, 9
individuals, variation and, 108–12
Indo-European languages, 15; German as a member, 23–5
Industrial Revolution, 52, 100
industrialization, 101, 142, 222
informal German, isolating or analytical character, 159
informant selection, 102, 103
Ingvaeones, 30, 31–2
Ingvaeonic palatalization, 31–2, 41
institutional names, East and West German, 176–7
institutional settings, language in, 263
interventionism, 245
Irish, 36
isoglasses: definition, 66–7; in German dialects, 77, 82–96, 90–6; northern–southern dialect divisions, 82–5
Israel, 44
Italian, 14, 25, 171, 196, 199, 211, 224: borrowing from, 256; borrowing in German, 253; in South Tyrol, 237–42
Italy, 13, 37, 38, 222, 238: northern, 16

jargon (*Sondersprache*), 6
Jews, 44
*Junkertum*, 144
Jura Question, 210
Jutland, 35
Jutlandish, South, 243–4

Kaiserslautern, 109–12
*Kanzleisprache*, 46, 47: Saxon in general acceptance 16th and 17th C., 47–9
Karl-Marx-Stadt, 45
Kerenz, 61
Koblenz, 88
koine, 216
*Kulturraum, see* cultural territory

Langobards, 30
language, and society, 100–32; *see also* sociology of language
language groups, perceptions of each other, 208
language laws, Belgium (1962–3), 225, 229
*Languages in Contact* (Weinreich), 218
languages in society, 14–18
lateral consonants, 84
Latin, 28, 29, 41, 46, 54, 159, 171, 177, 178, 232: borrowing from, 255, 256–7

Latvia, 43
Latvian, 25
'learner-types', 198
learning, language and change, 264
legislation on language use, 221–2
Leipzig, 45
lenition, 48, 92–6: central High German (*binnenhochdeutsche Konsonantenschwächung*), 94–5; medial, 153–4
*Letzebuergesch, see* Luxembourgish
lexical features, 5, 7
lexical transfer: in German-speaking area, 251–4; and pidgins, 200
lexical variation, 150: categories of, 96–7, 170–2; in German, 168–74; regional in both dialect and standard, 97–8, 168–70, 172–4
Liechtenstein, 1, 10, 12, 16, 181, 221
lifestyle: differences in East and West German, 178; factors in dialectology, 105–6, 223
Limbourgish, 14
linguistic insecurity, and dialect variants, 106–7
linguistic patriotism, 212
linguistic pluralism, Switzerland, 204–12
linguistic self-determination, 206–8
linguistics, a new, 264
liquid consonants, 88
*Literatursprache, see* formal standard language
Lithuania, 43
Lithuanian, 25
loan formations (*Lehnbildungen*), 15, 257, 258
loan forms, variable use in German, 253–4
loan translation (*Lehnübersetzung*), 28, 258
loan words (*Lehnwörter*), 29, 257: acquisition of new meanings, 260; spelling and reflecting pronunciation, 259
London, Treaty of (1839), 231
Lorraine, east, 236, 237
Low German and Dutch dialects (*Niederdeutsche und niederländische Dialekte*), 13, 33, 36, 41, 42, 44, 49, 68, 77, 78, 79–80, 90–1, 92, 94, 141, 173, 243: correspondence with standard German with *DH* pronunciation, 148–9; divisions within, 85–7
loyalty: language, 14, 219–20; local, 103, 108
Lübeck, 47
Lutheranism, 47, 48, 49

# Subject index

Luxembourg, 12, 16, 144, 183, 205, 253;
diglossia with bilingualism, 232–4;
history, 230–2; language use, 232–3;
sociolinguistic structure, 233–4
Luxembourgish, 11, 16n, 29, 144, 224,
231–2, 233

Macedonian, 196
maintenance, language, 18
Maltese, 9
maps, dialect, 33, 61, 76
Marburg School, 60–5
matched guise test (Lambert), 123
Mecklenburg, 44
*Mecklenburgisch Vorpommersch*, 87
*mediale Diglossie, see* diglossia, based on
medium
Meissen, 45
Middle Ages, 37–8, 40, 43, 46, 57
middle class, 143–4, 146: and colloquial
standard German, 181; continuity of
culture for children, 186, 187, 188–9;
dominant, 190; old (*alte Mittelschicht*),
184; rise of lierate, 47, 48, 49; and
spread of standard German, 50, 52;
standard German usage, 183; teachers,
186
Middle German, divisions within, 87–8
Middle German dialect area, 44, 75, 142
Middle (or Central) German dialects
(*Mitteldeutsche Dialekte*), 33, 36, 77,
80–1, 90–1, 92, 94; eastern
(*Ostmitteldeutsch*), 78, 142; western
(*Westmitteldeutsch*), 78, 95
Middle German Rhineland dialects, 173
Middle High German
(*Mittelhochdeutsch*), 46, 88, 90
Middle Low German
(*Mittelniederdeutsch*), 46–7, 90
Middlesex (*Middelseaxe*), 41
migration, 222
*Missingsch*, 143
modernization, and linguistics, 101–4
monophthongs, 88, 90–1
morphological structure, 15
morphological/syntactic transfer, in
German-speaking area, 254–5
morphology, derivational, 259
Moselle, 234
Moselle Franconian, 88
mother tongues, 'auxiliary', 233
multilingual societies, 16–18, 192–217
multilingualism, 20–1, 263; in FRG, 193–5
*Mundart, see* German dialects,
traditional
Munich, 174, 194

nasal consonants, loss before fricatives,
31, 32, 41
nation-states, monolingual, 10
'national dialect', Swiss, 216
national identity: and formal standard
German, 142–3; and language, FRG,
192, 194; and language boundaries, 12
national languages, 16, 221–2;
Switzerland, 205
nationality, German sense of, 38
*Nationalsprachen, see* national languages
native words, in formal registers, 172
native-speaker competence, 194–5
nativeness, in dialectology, 105, 107–9
NATO, 256
Nauborn, 104–6
Nazism, 44, 212
*Nederdüüts*, 86; *see also* Low German
and Dutch dialects
*Nederlands, see* Dutch
'neo-grammarian hypothesis', 62
neologisms, 15, 177; international, 177–8;
synonymous, 253
Netherlands, 36, 38, 39–40, 47, 78, 85;
history, 39–40, 42; north-east, 13;
Revolt of the (1568–1609), 39–40
New Belgium (*Neubelgien*), 225, 228
New York, blacks in, 119
newspapers, and foreign borrowing, 253,
254
Niebelungenlied, 46
*Niederpreußisch, see* Prussian, Low
nominal systems, of varieties of German,
160–4
nominative–accusative distinctions, 164
non-standard German, rôle in society,
181–91
non-standard speech, and social
conventions, 187
NORM (non-mobile older rural male),
102, 103
norm enforcement mechanisms, 220–1
normalization, in language planning, 221
North Germanic tribes, 30
north Germany, 11, 13, 136, 145, 156,
182, 183: adoption of standard, 49;
cities, 143; spread of standard
German, 50–1
North Sea Germanic tribes, *see*
Ingvaeones
noun plus genitive construction, 177
nouns: diminutives of, 84;
masculine–feminine distinction, 163;
plural suffixes, 163–4
*Nouvel Alsacien, Le*, 254
Nuremberg, 40

# Subject index

'Romandie' (western Switzerland), 212
Romania, 44
Romanian, 14
Romansh, 14, 204, 205 and n, 211, 222
Romantic period, 58, 59
*Romantsch Grischun*, 204
*Röstigraben*, 205
RP, *see* received pronunciation
Russia, 12, 47; *see also* USSR
Russian, 14, 29: influence on German in
  GDR, 54, 176, 177, 179, 251, 256, 257

San Marino, 10
Sanskrit, 159
Saterland, 43, 78
'Saturday', variant forms, 65–6, 97–8,
  170, 179
Saxon, Low (*Niedersächsisch*), 13, 42, 78,
  78n, 85, 86, 87: North
  (*Nordniedersächsisch*), 86
Saxon, Upper (*Obersächsisch*), 87
Saxon dialects, phonology, 48
Saxons, 30, 41–2, 45
Saxony, 44, 45; *Kanzleisprache* in general
  acceptance 16th and 17th C., 47–9;
  Lower (*Niedersachsen*), 45, 145
Scandinavia, 11, 255; *see also* Denmark;
  Sweden
Scandinavian languages, 13, 14, 25, 30–1
Scandinavians, 30
*Scheinentlehnungen* (pseudo-transfers),
  260
Schleswig, 242, 243–5
Schleswig-Holstein, 43, 77–8, 243
school performance, and working-class
  linguistic disadvantage, 184–9
*Schriftdeutsch* (written German in
  Switzerland), 204, 213
*Schriftsprache, see* standard German
*Schwäbisch, see* Swabian
*Schweizerdeutsch, Schwyzertütsch, see*
  Swiss German
Scotland, 145
Scots, 142
Scots Gaelic, 36
semantic features, 7
semantic loans (*Lehnbedeutungen*), 257–8
semilingualism (*doppelseitige
  Halbsprachigkeit*), 195
separatism, 210
Serbian, 29
Serbo-Croatian, 14, 15, 25, 196, 199, 200
sex: and language preferences, 235–6;
  and type of speech used, 20, 145
sex indicators, in dialectology, 115
sexual inequality, in the German
  linguistic structure, 20

shift, language, 18: factors promoting,
  244; language decline and, 242–50;
  process, 248–50
*Siebs Deutsche Aussprache*, 133
Silesia, 44
Silesian (*Schlesisch*), 87
simplification: elaborative, 203; in
  *Gastarbeiterdeutsch*, 196–7; as result of
  transfer, 254; universal hypothesis and
  Foreigner Talk, 201–3
situation factors, in dialectology, 103,
  118–22
Slavonic, Old Church, 29
Slavonic languages, 14, 25, 44, 196, 224:
  contact with Germanic languages,
  28–9; West, 37
Slovak, 12, 25, 37
Slovene, 14, 15, 25, 196, 224: in Austria,
  246–7
social change: and changes in language
  use, 247–50; and linguistics, 101–4
social class, *see* class
social context, 74
social dialectology, 21; *see also*
  sociolinguistics
social effects of variation: in German,
  FRG, 183–90; in other German-
  speaking countries, 190–1
social factors, and variation in language,
  9, 81, 264
social groups, 103: linguistic problems
  facing all, 189–90; variation and,
  106–8
social networks, 220–1
Socialist Unity Party (*Sozialistische
  Einheitspartei Deutschlands*), 176
sociocultural factors, in language use,
  223
sociolinguistic levelling, urban influence
  and, 216
sociolinguistic markers, 110–12
sociolinguistic pattern, in German-
  speaking Europe, 10–11
sociolinguistic variation, and continuum
  of colloquial speech, 133–80
sociolinguistics, 21, 57, 262–4: and
  dialectology, 18–21, 65–75; German,
  263–4
sociological factors, in language use,
  219–21
sociology, 103
sociology of culture, 263
sociology of language, 21, 264; *see also*
  language, and society
sociopolitical factors, and language use,
  221–2

302

# Subject index

Thuringian (*Thüringisch*), 87
towns: as centres of dialect patterns, 69–72, 100; formation of, 44; and language varieties, 182–3
transfer hypothesis, in *Gastarbeiterdeutsch*, 199–200
trilingualism, 232, 234
Turkey, 194
Turkish, 15, 29, 196, 199, 200, 201, 203
Tyneside, 137–8
Tyrol, South, 53, 205, 230, 237–42: Autonomy Statute (1972), 238; history, 237–9; language use, 239–42; the 'Option', 238; stable German–Italian bilingualism without diglossia, 241–2

*Überdachung* (overarching or umbrella effect), 13–14
Ukraine, 44
Ukrainian, 12
Ulster, 142
*Umgangssprache*: *dialektnahe*, 144, 146; *see also* colloquial German: *standardnahe*, 144
unity, linguistic, 36–45
unrounding of front-rounded vowels, 48, 91–2
*Untertanen* (vassals), 144
Upper German dialects (*Oberdeutsche Dialekte*), 33, 36, 77, 78, 80, 92, 94, 141, 168: divisions within, 88–90
urban dialectology, 21, 264
urban speech, 100–32, 143
urban varieties (*Stadtsprachen*), 263
urbanization, 100–32, 222: derived sense (*Urbanisierung*), 101; literal sense (*Verstädterung*), 101; meanings, 101
Ürdingen Line, 33, 80
Urdu, 8, 9
USA, 14, 44, 53, 54, 134, 256: sociolinguistics, 19–20; *see also* American English
USSR, 87, 176; *see also* Russia
uvular /r/, spread of, 70–1

Vandals, 30
variation: and individuals, 108–12; and social group, 106–8; in the status, function and use of German, 21; in urban varieties, 100–32
variation in German: differing views, 133–41; grammatical, 159–68; lexical, 168–74; nature and study of, 141–6; phonetic and phonological, 148–59; political and social correlates of, 181–3; social effects in FRG, 183–90;

social rather than geographical view, 146–7
*Variationslinguistik*, proposed, 264
*Varietät, see* varieties, language
varieties, language (*Varietät* or *Existenzform*), 8
varieties of German, terminology compared with English, 141
Variety Grammar, proposed, 102, 109
verb systems, of varieties of German, 164–8
verbal deficit theory, 186
verbs: modal, 84; prefixes to, 170; strong, subjunctives, 166; weak, subjunctives, 165–6
*Verein für die Pflege der deutschen Hochsprache* (Association for the Cultivation of the German Standard Language), 214
Versailles, Treaty of, 225
*Verstädterung, see* urbanization, literal sense
Vienna, Congress of (1815), 231
Vietnamese, 159
vocabulary, 15: dialect, 96–9; learned, 255–7
vocalization, 90
Voer, 225

Wales, 145
Wallonia, 225, 227, 228, 229
Wedding, 112–24
Welkenrat, 229
Welsh, 36
Wesser–Rhine Germanic tribes, 30
Wessex (*Westseaxe*), 41
West Germany, *see* Federal Republic of Germany
West Low German (*Westniederdeutsch*), 87
West Middle German, 78, 87–8
Westfalian (*Westfälisch*), 13, 14, 78, 86
Wetzlar, 104–6
*Wirtschaftswunder*, 53
women, sensitivity to prestigious linguistic varieties, 235–6
word order, 159, 197–8
working class, 143–4: assumed linguistic disadvantage in FRG, 183–9; colloquial non-standard and traditional dialects, 181; rural, 145; urban, 143
World War I, 193
World War II, 44, 52, 100, 112, 142, 193
written standard German: acceptance of

# Names index

# Names index

Hartmann von Aue, 46
Hartweg, F., 235, 236, 237, 261
Haugen, E., 9, 218–19, 224
Heeroma, K., 43
Helbig, G., 180
Hellmann, M.W., 175, 176, 180
Herder, J.G., 58
Herrgen, J., 145, 147, 151, 156, 180
Hinderling, R., 261
Hinnenkamp, V., 202, 203, 217
Hitler, A., 238
Hoffmann, F., 230, 232–3, 234, 261
Hoffmeister, W., 236, 237, 261
Hofmann, E., 104–6
Hoggart, R., 263
Holm, J., 200
Hooge, D., 84
Hudson, R.A., 8, 19n, 22, 56, 103, 106,
  107, 131, 220, 249
Hufschmidt, J., 125, 126, 127, 132
Hugo von Trimberg, 57–8
Humboldt, von, 60

Inglehart, R.F., 10

Kall-Holland, A., 127
Kartheuser, B., 229
Keim, I., 199, 217
Keller, R.E., 28, 33, 36, 54, 99, 106, 108,
  139
Kern, R., 255
Kinne, M., 180
Klein, E., 126, 129–30
Klein, W., 102, 198, 217
Klönne, A., 192
Kloss, H., 7, 13, 16n, 221, 234
Knoop, U., 55n, 59, 60, 62, 64
Knowles, J., 232
Kohl, H., 4
Kolde, G., 206, 208, 210, 211, 212, 213,
  216, 217
König, W., 66, 76, 79, 83, 91, 95, 98, 99
Koβ, G., 84, 162
Kramer, J., 227, 232, 234n, 237, 238,
  239, 253, 261
Küpper, H., 180
Kutsch, S., 217

Labov, W., 19, 20, 104, 107, 113, 119,
  123
Ladin, W., 235, 236
Lambert, W., 123
Lasch, A., 116
Le Page, R., 220
Lehmann, W.P., 25, 26
Leibniz, G.W., 58
Leippe, H., 146
Levinson, S., 219

Lockwood, W.B., 11, 25n, 29, 54
Löffler, H., 12, 13, 19, 21, 22, 56, 58, 59,
  67, 74, 99, 158, 185, 186
Lötscher, A., 212, 217
Löwe, H., 40, 41
Lüsebrink, C., 239
Luther, M., 47, 48, 58

Maak, H.G., 89
Macha, J., 188
McRae, K., 205, 210, 211, 217, 261
Maser, A., 251
Mattheier, K.J., 19, 55, 57, 58, 100, 101,
  103, 108, 118, 125n, 126, 131, 132,
  145, 183, 184, 186, 188, 189, 191, 263,
  264
Meisel, J., 203
Messmer, P., 235
Mickartz, H., 128, 144, 184
Milroy, L., 106, 114, 219, 220–1
Moosmüller, S., 132, 142
Moser, H., 30, 253
Moss, C., 86, 152
Mühlhäusler, P., 200
Müller, M., 212
Mussolini, B., 238
Muysken, P., 261

Nelde, P.H., 219, 221, 229, 231, 236, 254,
  255, 261
Neuner, G., 135
Newton, G., 234
Niebaum, H., 65, 99

Oevermann, U., 185
Orlović-Schwarzwald, M., 217
Ostow, R., 202

Pabst, K., 229
Panzer, B., 84, 85, 162
Pape, R., 142, 147, 156, 190
Pernstich, K., 253, 254
Petyt, K.M., 137–8
Pfaff, C., 19n
Polenz, P. von, 3, 48, 52, 54, 171, 257,
  261
Porsch, P., 191
Putzer, O., 253

Quirk, R., 135
Quix, M.P., 229

Ris, R., 191, 208, 212, 214, 216, 217, 220
Rosenkranz, H., 100n

Sanders, W., 13, 42, 46
Saville-Troike, M., 103, 119
Schirmunski, V.M., 85, 86, 87, 88, 89,
  90, 92, 94, 99
Schläpfer, R., 206n, 208–9, 214

# Names index

Schlieben-Lange, B., 103, 107, 118
Schlobinski, P., 113, 114–17, 124, 132, 140, 145, 180
Schmeller, J.A., 60
Schmidt, J.E., 145, 151, 156
Schneidermesser, L. von, 106, 108–9, 114
Schönfeld, H., 52, 140, 142, 147, 156, 190
Schröder, B., 19n
Schuler, M., 207
Schumann, J., 198
Schwarzenbach, R., 212, 214, 215
Seebold, E., 89
Senelle, R., 227
Senft, G., 102, 109–12
Sieber, P., 213, 214, 216, 217
Sitta, H., 213, 214, 215, 216, 217
Sivrikozoğlu, Ç., 217
Sjölin, B., 42
Smith, P., 124
Søndergaard, B., 243, 244
Stellmacher, D., 106, 142, 145, 147, 156, 180
Stölting, W., 195, 217
Strube-Edelmann, B., 180
Sutton, P., 9

Tabouret-Keller, A., 220
Tekinay, A., 201
Trier, U.P., 208
Trim, R., 227
Trudgill, P., 14, 19n, 22, 62, 64, 65, 70, 73n, 99, 102, 103, 107, 108, 116n, 134, 185, 230, 249, 264
Tyroller, H., 239, 241

Ureland, P.S., 261

Veith, W.H., 140, 179
Verdoot, A., 222, 230, 232, 261
Viereck, W., 261
Vogt, B., 213, 214
Von Polenz, P., see Polenz, von
Von Schneidemesser, see Schneidemesser, von

Wahrig, G., 258
Walker, A.G.H., 244–5, 261
Walther vonder Vogelweide, 46
Wardhaugh, R., 22, 201, 210, 261
Wehler, H.U., 101
Weinreich, U., 102, 218, 220, 251, 261
Wells, C.J., 48, 54, 171, 257
Wells, J.C., 141, 142
Wenker, G., 59–60, 61–5
Wertenschlag, L., 212
Weydt, H., 103, 118
Whinnom, K., 200
Wiesinger, P., 90, 92, 93, 142
Williams, R., 263
Winteler, J., 61
Wolf, N.R., 78
Wolfensberger, H., 106, 107
Wolfram, W., 107
Woodward, M., 10
Wrede, F., 65

Yakut, A., 217

Zeh, J., 228
Zehetner, L.G., 187
Zhirmunskij, see Schirmunski
Zimmer, R., 183, 216